JOSH McDOWELL
Answers Five Tough Questions

Josh McDowell Answers Five Tough Questions

JOSH McDOWELL

Tyndale House Publishers, Inc.
Wheaton, Illinois

Library of Congress Cataloging-in-Publication Data

McDowell, Josh
   Josh McDowell answers five tough questions / Josh McDowell.
      p.   cm.
   ISBN 0-8423-7909-6
   1. Apologetics—20th century.   2. Evangelicalism.   I. Title.
BT1102.M243   1991
230—dc20   91-23975

Josh McDowell Answers Five Tough Questions, Josh McDowell,
general editor. Great appreciation and acknowledgment to those who
contributed to each section:

Part 1, "The Authority of the Bible," and Part 4, "The Church of Jesus
Christ," edited by Dr. Philip W. Comfort, senior Bible editor, Tyndale
House Publishers, and visiting professor of New Testament, Wheaton
College, Wheaton, Illinois.

Part 2, "Creation and Evolution," reviewed by Dr. Henry M. Morris,
president, Institute for Creation Research, El Cajon, California, and by
Dr. Walter Bradley, professor, Department of Mechanical Engineering,
College Station, Texas; edited by Dave Jackson.

Part 3, "Israel, the Chosen People," edited by Dr. Ted Hildebrandt,
professor and chair of Old Testament, Grace College, Winona Lake,
Indiana.

Parts 1–4 of this book were condensed and adapted from *Family
Handbook of Christian Knowledge,* by Josh McDowell, series editor,
and Don Stewart, author. Published by Here's Life Publishers, Inc.;
copyright © 1983, 1984 by Campus Crusade for Christ, Inc. Used by
permission.

Part 5, "The End Times," written by Dr. Paul R. Fink, professor of
pastoral ministry, Liberty University, Lynchburg, Virginia.

Unless otherwise noted, Scripture quotations are from the *New
American Standard Bible,* copyright © 1960, 1962, 1963, 1968, 1971,
1972, 1973, 1975, 1977 by The Lockman Foundation. Used by
permission. Scripture quotations marked NIV are from the *Holy Bible,
New International Version.* Copyright © 1973, 1978, 1984 International
Bible Society. Used by permission of Zondervan Bible Publishers.
Scripture quotations marked KJV are from *The Holy Bible,* King James
Version.

Front cover photos copyright © 1991, in descending order: Christopher
K. Page, David Welling, H. Armstrong Roberts, Bob Taylor, Willie and
Angie Rumpf.

CONTENTS

PREFACE

Who am I? Where did I come from? Where am I going? Who—or what—can I trust to answer these questions?

People are asking these questions in the 1990s. They were asking them centuries ago. They will ask them as long as human life endures on earth.

There is no shortage of answers. But the various answers conflict. They can't *all* be right, can they?

This book provides some answers. They are what I believe to be the *right* answers to those crucial questions. But I'm not expecting my readers to accept these answers because I believe them. The answers come from a much higher authority than myself or any other individual—the Bible.

That's why this five-part book begins with *The Authority of the Bible.* Authority is a key issue. And the key question is: Is the Bible completely reliable? Is that ancient book, the Bible, a trustworthy guide for life? Is it historically and scientifically correct? Many people say no, but Part 1 of this book is designed to show why I believe the Bible is reliable. The rest of the book is built on this overarching assumption: that the Bible is the inspired and reliable Word of God.

Part 2, *Creation and Evolution,* deals with one of the great issues of today: human origins. What should I believe about evolution? Is it a proven fact, or only a theory? Can the Bible's account of humankind's creation be right? I will share here the findings of solid science, which in no way conflict with the Bible. I will also show that some scientific findings have been downright frauds. Part 2 has a lot of data, but you don't have to be a scientist to understand it. You just have to be willing, as I have been, to find out just how *certain* the scientists are about the origins of the universe.

Is Israel God's chosen people? Is the church necessary today? These questions are at the center of Parts 3 and 4—*Israel, the Chosen*

People and *The Church of Jesus Christ*. These sections change the focus from the human race as a whole to God's special people, the Jews and, later, the Christian church. Parts 3 and 4 look at how God has revealed himself and how he brings redemption to fallen humanity. This is more than a historical survey of the Bible and church history. It is a look at God's dealings with those he loves and watches over. It shows us that we are not just isolated individuals; we are part of a long heritage of divine-human encounters. The history is still being written. You and I are part of it.

Are we living in the End Times? What is our final destiny? Those questions are at the center of Part 5, *The End Times*. The scientists and the politicians offer their speculations about the future of the world, but the best authority, the Bible, offers more reliable guidance. The Bible has proven itself to be the best source of prophecy. Many of its prophecies have already been fulfilled. Many, as Part 5 will show, are yet to be fulfilled.

There is room for diversity among Christians. We differ on some minor points of doctrine. But in my years of teaching and lecturing, I've come to the conclusion that Christians, followers of Christ, do share some key beliefs about who they are, where they came from, where they are going, and who their guide is. These are critical concerns, and this is what I believe about those concerns. Carry an open mind, and walk with me as we deal with them.

JOSH MCDOWELL

PART ONE
The Authority of the Bible

INTRODUCTION

Abraham Lincoln once said, "The Bible is the best gift God has ever given to man. All the good from the Savior of the world is communicated to us through this book."

The Bible is the greatest book ever written. It contains the answers to the most important questions of life: *Who am I? Why am I here? Where am I going? What is life all about?* The Bible has been called the Book of Life, since it gives significance to all people's lives. It proclaims that Jesus Christ is Lord, the ruler and Savior of all creation. Let us look at this "Book of Books," examining its composition, its survival over the centuries, and its inspiration.

This section discusses the making of the Old and New Testaments, how the "canon" of Scripture was compiled, the contents of the Apocrypha, the inspiration of Scripture, the historical reliability of the Old and New Testaments, and the contents of the Old and New Testaments. After reading this section, you should have the information you need to answer the question: Is the Bible completely reliable?

The Bible stands above all other books in the world. In chapter 1 we will discuss ten factors that contribute to its uniqueness as God's Holy Word.

What objective evidence do we have in support of the inspiration and reliability of the Bible? Chapter 2 discusses the trustworthiness of the Old Testament text. It answers the question, Has the text of the Old Testament remained accurate throughout history?

Chapter 3 presents the same issues for the New Testament. Have its words been preserved correctly? Chapters 2 and 3 show that our Bible is a trustworthy representation of the original manuscripts.

Once we have determined that, we will look at the Bible's contents, the biblical canon, that is, those books accepted as the Christian Scriptures. In chapter 4 we will show why the books in our Bible deserve the designation "Holy Scripture," and why other traditionally revered books are not of the caliber of the canonical books.

Chapter 5 is a review of biblical inspiration. Why are these books on a different level from other literature? What do we mean when we say that the Bible is inspired?

Chapter 6 deals with the historical reliability of the Old Testament. We need to see, through additional evidence, that what was accurately transmitted over the centuries is also historically trustworthy. We will look at some archaeological and historical evidence available to confirm the trustworthiness of the Old Testament.

Chapter 7 does the same for the New Testament. We will see through representative examples that we can trust the historical reliability of the New Testament documents.

This section concludes with two chapters describing the contents of the Bible. We will discuss the story of God and his people as revealed in the pages of the Old Testament. We will see God's plan for his people unfolding through the ages. In our review of New Testament contents we will note the exciting events of the incarnation—when the Son of God became a human being to bring us salvation. We will see the dynamic growth of the early church, as the disciples of Jesus Christ proclaimed salvation in the name of their risen Lord throughout the known world.

CHAPTER 1
The Bible—Not Just Another Book

Most of us have heard of the "Wonders of the World," including the pyramids of Egypt, the hanging gardens of Babylon, and so on. There are also "wonders" of the Bible, characteristics that set the Bible apart from all other literature, ancient and modern. Let's look at ten of these "wonders of the Bible."

THE WONDER OF ITS UNITY

One amazing characteristic of the Bible is its unity. The Bible is composed of sixty-six books, thirty-nine in the Old Testament and twenty-seven in the New. Yet those sixty-six books form a cohesive whole, one dynamic message of God's dealings with humankind.

Probably the first books written were what we know as the Books of Moses or the Law (Genesis, Exodus, Leviticus, Numbers, Deuteronomy), composed around 1400 B.C. (This assumes an archaeological dating of 1445 B.C. for the exodus. Others cite 1290 B.C.) The last of the New Testament was written around A.D. 90, and includes the writings of the apostle John (the Gospel of John, 1, 2, and 3 John, and Revelation). Genesis through Revelation involves a time span of around fifteen hundred years.

These sixty-six books were composed by more than forty authors, from a variety of educational and cultural backgrounds. Joshua was a general; Daniel was a prime minister; Nehemiah was a court servant; Amos was a shepherd; Luke, a physician; Paul, a rabbi; and Peter and John were fishermen.

The books of the Bible were composed in a variety of places and cultures. Ezekiel wrote his work while a captive in Babylon. Paul wrote some of his letters from prison in Rome. David wrote some of his psalms while he was a fugitive in the wilderness. Jeremiah wrote while he was in a dungeon. The books were written on three continents: Africa, Asia, and Europe.

The Bible was composed in three languages. The Old Testament was written mostly in Hebrew, with a small part in Aramaic. The New Testament was in the *common* Greek of the day, *Koine.*

The Bible deals consistently with such subjects as the origin of the universe, the existence and nature of God, the nature and purpose of humankind, and the origin and extent of evil.

One would expect that the result of such diversity would be a chaotic text, full of contradictions and distortions. But the Bible is consistent, coherent, and trustworthy. None of the authors or books is either internally, of themselves, or externally contradictory.

The unity of the teachings of the Bible is consistent from the beginning to the end. These teachings include the following:

- man—his origin, fall, redemption, earthly and eternal destiny
- sin—its beginning, consequences, punishment in this world and the next
- Satan—the instigator of evil, the liar and murderer from the beginning, his war against God and against believers, his final judgment
- Israel—her social and political development, idolatry, preservation, and final destiny
- the church—her history, from her establishment to her glorification
- salvation—its provision, according to the divine plan
- repentance, faith, the life of the believer, prayer, the service of God, etc.—subjects for infinitely rewarding study, carrying us through the entire Bible
- the Holy Spirit—present at creation, pronouncing the last prayer of the Bible (Genesis 1:2; Revelation 22:17)
- God—forever the same, in his sovereignty, his eternality, his spirituality, his omnipotence, his uniqueness, his omniscience, his omnipresence, his holiness, his righteousness, and his love
- Jesus Christ—the person par excellence of all the written revelation

THE WONDER OF ITS HISTORICAL ACCURACY

Another feature that separates the Bible from other ancient literature is its fidelity to historical accuracy. Within the pages of the Bible are countless references to events, people, and places. The science of archaeology and secular historical records have repeatedly confirmed the precision of the references in the various biblical books. The minute attention to detail observed by the biblical writers is unparalleled in any other ancient literature. Nelson Glueck, a famous Jewish archaeologist, observed, "It may be stated categorically that no archaeological discovery has ever controverted a biblical reference."[1]

THE WONDER OF ITS INDESTRUCTIBILITY

The fact that the text of the Bible has survived throughout history is a wonderful testimony to the preserving power of God. The Scriptures have survived time, persecution, and criticism.

The first book of the Bible was composed some thirty-five hundred years ago; the last was completed nearly two thousand years ago. The original manuscripts were all written on perishable materials and have long since disappeared. The thousands of copies we possess, however, accurately represent the originals. Through the science of textual criticism, we can arrive at a very close reproduction of the originals. We will develop this point further in our chapter on the reliability of the Old and New Testaments.

The Bible has also survived the persecution of its adherents. Consider the following examples of the tenacity of the followers of the Bible in preserving its text in the midst of persecution.

Voltaire, the noted French infidel who died in 1778, said that in one hundred years from his time Christianity would be swept from existence and passed into history. But what has happened? Voltaire has passed into history, while the

---

[1] Nelson Glueck, *Rivers in the Desert: History of Negev* (Philadelphia: Jewish Publication Society, 1969), p. 84. Because the historical evidence in support of the Bible is so great, chapters 6 and 7 are devoted to exploring some of that evidence.

circulation of the Bible continues to increase in almost all parts of the world, carrying blessing wherever it goes. For example, the English Cathedral in Zanzibar is built on the site of the Old Slave Market, and the Communion Table stands on the very spot where the whipping-post once stood! The world abounds with such instances.[2]

There is a historical irony about the Voltaire matter. Fifty years after his death, the Geneva Bible Society used Voltaire's house and printing press to print hundreds of Bibles. Further, two hundred years after Voltaire's death, Christianity is still not extinct.

In A.D. 303 the Roman emperor Diocletian wrote an imperial letter ordering the destruction of all churches, the burning of all Scriptures, and the loss of civil liberties by all professing Christians. That did not stop the spread of Christianity or the proclamation of God's revelation in the Bible. Constantine, the Roman emperor who succeeded Diocletian, converted to Christianity and eventually ordered Eusebius to make fifty copies of the Scriptures, to be produced by the best scribes at government expense.

Time passes, but the Bible remains a dramatic testimony to the keeping power of God for his revelation. Rulers come and go. The Bible remains. Critics come and go. The Bible remains.

THE WONDERS OF ITS SCIENTIFIC ACCURACY

One of the wonders of the Bible is its scientific accuracy, even though the Bible is not primarily a scientific book. Whenever the biblical writers touch on scientific matters, their observation about nature, man, history, and society are generally accurate and free of the ancient and unsophisticated scientific inaccuracies of their contemporaries. The mythologies in ancient cultures are missing from the Old and New Testaments. Charles Woodrull Shields observed, "Although scientifically the Hebrews did not make the advances that the Assyrians or Egyptians or Greeks did, nevertheless, the Hebrews were free from the

---

[2] Sidney Collett, *All about the Bible* (Old Tappan, N.J.: Revell, n.d.), p. 63.

grotesque absurdity that disfigures the astronomy or geology of their contemporaries as found in the sacred books of the east or even in the more artistic mythology of the Greeks."[3]

There are vast differences between the historically sound accounts of creation found in the Bible and the unscientific, absurd accounts of creation popular at the same time in other cultures.

The Babylonian mythological account of creation is a good example of the views current in the ancient world. The account below is quoted from a commentary by religions expert John B. Noss:

> The present world order was formed after a primeval conflict between the dragons of darkness and chaos, led by the bird-god Zu (or in other accounts by Tiamat) and the gods of light and order, headed by Ninurta, the war-god. But the Babylonian priests rewrote whatever materials they inherited, and they made Marduk both the hero of the struggle against chaos and the creator of the world and of man. Their story began with Apsu, the god of fresh water, and Tiamat, the dragon of the unbounded salt water (chaos). By their intermingling, this pair over a period of years produced the gods, but the youthful gods were so lively and boisterous that Apsu could not rest and resolved to destroy them, against the wish of Tiamat. . . .
>
> But before Apsu could execute his plan, he was destroyed by Ea, who got wind of it, whereupon Tiamat resolved on avenging him. She created monsters to be her allies, and both Anu and Ea fled before her. Not until Marduk, assured by the gods that he would be their chief, came forth to meet her in combat was she halted. . . .
>
> After next subduing the monsters she had arrayed against him, Marduk turned back to Tiamat and split her open like a shellfish into halves. With one half he made the canopy which holds back the waters that are above the heavens; with the other half he formed the covering which lies above the waters under the earth. He constructed stations for the

---

[3] Charles Woodruff Shields, *The Scientific Evidences of Revealed Religion* (New York: Scribner's, 1900), p. 27.

gods in the heavens. With Ea's help he made man from the blood of the god Kingsu, Tiamat's ally and second husband. Seeing what he had done, the delighted gods bestowed on him many titles as their undisputed leader.[4]

This account contrasts sharply with both the scientific evidence regarding creation and with the biblical account, which tells of an all-powerful, eternal Creator who created the heavens and the earth from nothing. The Genesis account of creation, while not a scientific narrative in itself, is harmonious with scientific evidence. Theologian James Orr observed:

No stronger proof could be afforded of the truth and sublimity of the biblical account of the origin of things than is given by the comparison of the narrative of creation in Genesis 1–2:4, with the mythological cosmogonies and theogonies found in other religions.[5]

As another example of the harmony between science and Scripture, we turn to Noah's ark. The dimensions of Noah's ark as revealed in the Bible are completely credible when compared to barges and large ocean-going vessels in use in this present century. But the Babylonian account of the flood describes an ark that would be completely unseaworthy and scientifically impossible.

Whenever the Bible touches on areas of science (for example, in discussing creation, the flood, etc.), it does it accurately. No scientific observation in the Bible contradicts known scientific evidence. Understand, however, that the Bible is not written in scientific vocabulary. It is primarily a book about God's relationship with humankind. The language of Scripture is neither scientific nor unscientific, but *nonscientific*. It is the language of everyday communication.

A pitfall should be avoided concerning the Bible and science. The tendency is to accuse the Bible of being unscientific for using nonscientific language. An example often pointed to by critics is

---

[4]John B. Noss, *Man's Religions* (New York: Macmillan, 1969), pp. 50-51.

[5]James Orr, *The International Standard Bible Encyclopedia*, s.v. "World: Cosmological." (Grand Rapids: Eerdmans, 1939, 1956).

the biblical account of the sun "standing still" in the sky during Joshua's long day. The critics failed to take common language conventions into consideration. How many critics hear their local television weather report state, "The rotation of the earth on its axis will move our area out of the path of direct sunlight at 5:45 this evening"? None. The common report is, "Sunset this evening will be at 5:45." The critic places greater restrictions on the language of the Bible than he does on himself and those around him. To do so is untenable and, ultimately, unscientific.

Though the Bible is not a scientific textbook and is not written in scientific language, it is wonderful that in all of its particular observations concerning science, it is accurate, faithful to scientific evidence, and in dramatic contrast to other primitive and mythological religious writings.

THE WONDER OF ITS FRANKNESS

An amazing feature of the Bible is the frankness with which it deals with the frailties of people and even with the shortcomings of its own authors. The Bible paints a realistic portrait of its characters, resisting the temptation to mythologize or perfect them. For example, the book of Genesis reveals that Noah, a great man of God who saved the remnant of humanity from the Great Flood, was once found in a drunken stupor: "Then Noah began farming and planted a vineyard. And he drank of the wine and became drunk, and uncovered himself inside his tent" (Genesis 9:20-21).

We see in 2 Samuel 11 that David, a man who loved God, was an adulterer and murderer. Verses 3-4, 14-15 tell us:

> So David sent and inquired about the woman. And one said, "Is this not Bathsheba, the daughter of Eliam, the wife of Uriah the Hittite?" And David sent messengers and took her, and when she came to him, he lay with her; and when she had purified herself from her uncleanness, she returned to her house. . . . Now it came about in the morning that David wrote a letter to Joab, and sent it by the hand of Uriah. And he had written in the letter, saying, "Place Uriah in the front line of the fiercest battle and withdraw from him, so that he may be struck down and die."

The Bible does not hide the fact that the apostle Paul argued with his companion, Barnabas:

> And after some days Paul said to Barnabas, "Let us return and visit the brethren in every city in which we proclaimed the word of the Lord, and see how they are." And Barnabas was desirous of taking John, called Mark, along with them also. But Paul kept insisting that they should not take him along who had deserted them in Pamphylia and had not gone with them to the work. And there arose such a sharp disagreement that they separated from one another, and Barnabas took Mark with him and sailed away to Cyprus. (Acts 15:36-39)

The fact that the personalities in the Bible are flawed does not detract from the biblical message: it is the holiness of the Lord God that the Bible proclaims, not the perfection of his followers and prophets. Yet Jesus, the greatest personality revealed in the Bible, the one of whom in some sense the whole Bible speaks, is described as being without sin.

THE WONDER OF ITS PREDICTIVE PROPHECY

One of the most incredible features of the Bible is its prophecies. In no other book do we find the wealth of prophecies, clearly made years before their fulfillment, and all accurately fulfilled in history.

The biblical prophet was a spokesman for God to the people. He not only predicted future events in God's plan, he also exhorted the people according to the directives of the Lord. His task of exhortation, in fact, occupied more of his time and words than did his prophesying of future events. It is with predictive prophecy, however, that we are here concerned.

There are dozens of examples of fulfilled prophecy to which we could point in both the Old Testament and the New. The most important prophecies, some fulfilled and some yet to be fulfilled, concern Jesus Christ, the most important person in the Bible.

One set of Old Testament prophecies about the Messiah has to do with his family line. Those prophecies, given long before Jesus was born, indicate that his lineage would be through the royal house of Israel. That is something over which Jesus himself could have no control: he could not manipulate the fulfillment of such prophecies in himself. The one coming would come from the line of Abraham: "The Lord appeared to Abraham and said 'To your seed I will give this land'" (Genesis 12:7). According to the apostle Paul, this "seed" was Christ (Galatians 3:16).

Out of Jacob's twelve sons the Messiah was to descend from the line of Judah: "The scepter shall not depart from Judah, nor the ruler's staff from between his feet, until Shiloh comes, and to him shall be the obedience of the peoples" (Genesis 49:10).

Jesse, of the tribe of Judah, had eight sons; the Bible predicts that the Messiah would come from his son David: "And your house and your kingdom shall endure before Me forever; your throne shall be established forever" (2 Samuel 7:16); "'Behold, the days are coming,' declares the Lord, 'when I shall raise up for David a righteous Branch; and he will reign as king and act wisely and do justice and righteousness in the land. In his days Judah will be saved, and Israel will dwell securely; and this is his name by which he will be called, 'The Lord our righteousness'" (Jeremiah 23:5-6).

Thirty times in the New Testament Jesus Christ is said to be descended from David. Three of those statements are: "The book of the genealogy of Jesus Christ, the son of David, the son of Abraham" (Matthew 1:1); "And when he began His ministry, Jesus himself was about thirty years of age, being supposedly the son of Joseph, the son of Eli . . . the son of Melea, the son of Menna, the son of Mattatha, the son of Nathan, the son of David" (Luke 3:23, 31); and "concerning his Son, who was born of the seed of David according to the flesh" (Romans 1:3).

There are several other Old Testament prophecies that were fulfilled in the life of Jesus, prophecies that could not have been manipulated by any human being. For example, it was predicted that he would be born of a virgin (Isaiah 7:14; Matthew 1:22-23), born in Bethlehem (Micah 5:2; Matthew 2:5-6), be filled with the Spirit to begin his ministry (Isaiah 11:2; 61:1-2; Luke 4:18-19), be rejected by his own people (Isaiah 53:3; Psalm 69:8; John 1:11), be betrayed by his companion (Judas) for thirty pieces of silver (Psalms 41:9; 55:12-14; Matthew 26:14-16, 21-25), be forsaken by his disciples (Zechariah 13:7; Matthew 26:31, 56), be crucified with malefactors (Isaiah 53:12; Matthew 27:38), be pierced (Psalms 22:16; Zechariah 12:10; Mark 15:25; John 19:34, 37; 20:25-27), be buried with the rich (Isaiah 53:9; Matthew 27:57-60), and be raised from the dead (Psalm 16:10; Matthew 28:2-8). This abundance of predictive detail was beyond the control of any human being and shows the inspiration of the Scriptures and the Messiahship of Jesus of Nazareth.

THE WONDER OF ITS CHRIST-CENTEREDNESS

Another unique and wonderful feature of the Bible is its Christ-centeredness. The Bible, from beginning to end, in both Old and New Testaments, is a testimony to Jesus Christ, the "Son of Man" and the Lord of glory. After the resurrection, Jesus Christ himself explained how the Old Testament Scriptures pointed to him:

> "O foolish men and slow of heart to believe in all that the prophets have spoken! Was it not necessary for the Christ to suffer these things and to enter into His glory?" And beginning with Moses and with all the prophets, He explained to them the things concerning Himself in all the Scriptures. (Luke 24:25-27)

Even before his death, Jesus Christ pointed out the Christ-centeredness of the Scriptures. When the Jews who continually harassed Jesus challenged his authority, he responded:

> You search the Scriptures, because you think that in them you have eternal life; and it is these that bear witness of Me; and you are unwilling to come to Me, that you may have life. (John 5:39-40)

The Old Testament records the preparation for the coming of Christ: "A voice is calling, 'Clear the way for the Lord in the wilderness; make smooth in the desert a highway for our God'" (Isaiah 40:3). The theme toward which the Old Testament is pointing is the establishment of the kingdom of God through the reign of the Messiah (the Christ). The Old Testament looks forward to his coming and tells us what it will be like.

Genesis
- Adam is the type of him "who was yet to come" (Romans 5:14)
- the posterity of the woman was to be Christ, who would bruise and crush the head of the serpent (Genesis 3:15)
- the blood of Abel, the righteous man, is compared to the blood shed on the cross (Hebrews 12:24)
- Melchizedek is said to be like unto the Son of God (Genesis 14:18-20; Hebrews 7:1-10)
- Isaac, the son loved of his father, was offered as a sacrifice (Genesis 22)
- Shiloh is the Sovereign from the tribe of Judah (Genesis 49:10)

Exodus
- the Passover Lamb (Exodus 12; John 1:29; 1 Corinthians 5:7)
- the manna, miraculous bread sent down from heaven (Exodus 16; John 6:31-33)
- the smitten rock, which "was Christ" (Exodus 17:1-7; 1 Corinthians 10:4)

Leviticus
- the bleeding sacrifices, picture of Christ's sacrifice on the cross (Hebrews 9:12-14; 10:1-4, 11-14)
- the sacrifice of atonement (Leviticus 16:1-35; Hebrews 9:24-25)

Numbers
- Aaron's rod, picture of the resurrection of the Lord (Numbers 17:1-11)
- the red heifer, another prefiguration of the purifying sacrifice (Numbers 19: Hebrews 9:13)
- the brazen serpent, representing Christ on the cross (Numbers 21:4-9; John 3:14-16), etc.

Going over to the Psalms, we see further details in the portrayal of the coming Messiah:

2: the Anointed One
8: the Son of Man and his humiliation
16: the Beloved delivered to the place of the dead
22: the sufferings on the cross
69: the insults and the gall and vinegar

72: the King of Peace
110: the Lord glorified

Among the prophets, Isaiah has been called the evangelist of the Old Testament because he presents a full picture of the coming Messiah. Isaiah speaks of the Messiah as:

7:14: Immanuel, born of a virgin
9:6: the Son, the Mighty God, the Prince of Peace
11:1-10: the shoot out of the stock of Jesse, the One clothed with the Spirit who "will rest" upon him
40:1-10: the God who was to come
40:11: the Shepherd of the sheep
42:1-4; 49:1-7: the Servant of Jehovah (Yahweh)
53: the man of sorrows
61:1-2: the Anointed of God, the Emancipator
63:1-6: the Judge

The New Testament tells of his first coming and anticipates his second coming. Before his death Jesus Christ described to his disciples the necessity for his death, burial, and resurrection in order to accomplish redemption for the world. But he did not stop there. He also described to them his second coming, with glory, power, and judgment at the end of the age:

For just as the lightning comes from the east, and flashes even to the west, so shall the coming of the Son of Man be. . . . And then the sign of the Son of Man will appear in the sky, and then all the tribes of the earth will mourn, and they will see the Son of Man coming on the clouds of the sky with power and great glory. And He will send forth His angels with a great trumpet and they will gather together His elect from the four winds, from one end of the sky to the other. (Matthew 24:27, 30-31)

The Old Testament records the preparation for the coming of the Messiah. The Gospels record the coming of the Messiah, Jesus Christ our Lord. The book of Acts records the propagation of the gospel (the good news) concerning Jesus Christ. The Epistles (letters) explain the gospel and its implications for our lives. The book of Revelation anticipates and describes the second coming of Jesus Christ and the establishment of his eternal kingdom. From beginning to end, the Bible glorifies Jesus Christ and centers on him. Its Christ-centeredness is one of its wonderful features.

THE WONDER OF ITS INTELLECTUAL INTEGRITY

One of the Bible's most wonderful features is the intellectual integrity it inspires in its readers. Although it was composed between two and four thousand years ago, it still has the power to challenge intelligent men and women to develop their full intellectual capabilities in studying its rich teachings and history. It can stand the test of the most rigorous intellectual assault. Those who have dedicated their lives to understanding and appreciating the Scriptures have not been disappointed.

A contemporary example of a person whose intellectual pursuits were spurred on by his devotion to the Scriptures is the noted Christian scholar E. M. Blaiklock. He writes:

Here are the alternatives. Either four men, only one of them with any education in the liberal sense of the word, invented the Character who altered the whole course of history, or they wrote of One they knew or had heard about from those who knew him, a Person so extraordinary that he could claim deity, sinlessness, all authority, and rouse no revulsion among those who long knew him intimately and experimentally. The religious leaders, collaborators with the occupying power, so feared him that they betrayed and murdered him, and in so doing, like the doomed actors in an Aristotelian tragedy, loosed forces which swept the world.[6]

The Bible tells us we are to love the Lord our God with all our mind (Matthew 22:37). Twentieth-century men and women can use their minds, taking the Bible and evaluating it with full intellectual

---

[6]E. M. Blaiklock, ed., *Why I Am Still a Christian* (Grand Rapids: Zondervan, 1971), p. 16.

scrutiny. The Bible will prevail and continue to satisfy and stimulate the intellect of any who fairly investigate its claims.

THE WONDER OF ITS TEACHINGS

Another wonderful aspect of the Bible separates it from all other religious books and is a testimony to its divine origin. This is the wonder of its unique teachings. The teachings in the Bible cannot be explained as a product of the religious environment of its authors, since many of its teachings were contrary to contemporary religious thought and were hard for the Jews themselves to accept. Of many such examples we will discuss a few representative ones.

Much of the unique teaching in the Bible centers around the personal God it reveals. Israel was surrounded by polytheistic cultures (cultures that believed in more than one God). Israel often slipped into idolatry itself. Yet its holy Scriptures, the Old Testament, betray not a word in favor of idolatry. The Old Testament, in fact, is filled with warnings against idolatry. In addition, the Bible repeatedly emphasizes monotheism (belief in one God). Here are two scriptural examples:

> Hear, O Israel! The Lord is our God, the Lord is one! And you shall love the Lord your God with all your heart and with all your soul and with all your might. (Deuteronomy 6:4-5)
> "You are my witnesses," declares the Lord, "and My servant whom I have chosen, in order that you may know and believe Me, and understand that I am He. Before Me there was no God formed, and there will be none after Me. I, even I, am the Lord; and there is no savior besides Me." (Isaiah 43:10-11)

The New Testament continues the absolute monotheism of the Old Testament:

> We know that there is no such thing as an idol in the world, and that there is no God but one. For even if there are so-called gods whether in heaven or on earth, as indeed there are many gods and many lords, yet for us there is but one

God, the Father, from whom are all things, and we exist for Him; and one Lord, Jesus Christ, through whom are all things, and we exist through Him. (1 Corinthians 8:4-6)

The nature and attributes of the God of the Bible are also different from the concepts of God in cultures surrounding the Jews. The Bible reveals a God who is infinite and personal, who cares for human beings as a Father and who personifies love, respect, justice, and mercy. This is in contrast to other gods of the ancient world who were to be obeyed and served out of fear rather than from loving respect. An idea of the fatherly attitude of the God of the Bible was revealed by Jesus Christ:

And I say to you, ask, and it shall be given to you; seek, and you shall find; knock, and it shall be opened to you. For everyone who asks receives; and he who seeks, finds; and to him who knocks, it shall be opened. Now suppose one of you fathers is asked by his son for a fish; he will not give him a snake instead of a fish, will he? Or if he is asked for an egg, he will not give him a scorpion, will he? If you then, being evil, know how to give good gifts to your children, how much more shall your heavenly Father give the Holy Spirit to those who ask Him? (Luke 11:9-13)

In many other religious settings God is to be obeyed in order for the faithful to receive rewards. In the Bible we are taught to obey God out of love: "If you love Me, you will keep My commandments" (John 14:15).

A final unique teaching from the Bible is the resurrection of the founder of Christianity, Jesus Christ. This teaching is a wonder, since in no other religious literature do we have a resurrection that was *bodily* and that can be *tested* by the most rigorous historical methods. While many other religious traditions have ideas of spiritual or spirit resurrections (untestable hypotheses), only the Bible proclaims a bodily resurrection that passes all tests of historical reliability.

We conclude that the Bible, in both Old and New Testaments, contains teachings that are unique and wonderful in comparison to the best teachings offered in any other religious or nonreligious writings.

THE WONDER OF ITS
LIFE-TRANSFORMING POWER

We now come to the last of the ten wonders of the Bible considered here. This wonder is the Bible's effect on individuals. If the Bible is indeed the Word of God, it should demonstrate its ability to transform lives.

We must first note that the Bible claims that Jesus Christ can fill the spiritual void within all people.

> Blessed are those who hunger and thirst for righteousness, for they shall be satisfied. (Matthew 5:6)

> Come to Me, all who are weary and heavy laden, and I will give you rest. Take My yoke upon you, and learn from Me, for I am gentle and humble in heart; and you shall find rest for your souls. For My yoke is easy, and My load is light. (Matthew 11:28-30)

> Whoever drinks of the water that I shall give him shall never thirst; but the water that I shall give him shall become in him a well of water springing up to eternal life. (John 4:14)

> I came that they might have life, and might have it abundantly. I am the good shepherd; the good shepherd lays down His life for the sheep. (John 10:10)

Christian scholar Harold Lindsell gives this perspective on the life-transforming importance of Christianity as revealed in the Scriptures:

> We can trust the Bible [because] it does what it claims it will do: it transforms lives. Millions of people have testified that they have been forgiven and have received the gift of eternal life. Their prayers have been answered; their deepest needs satisfied. Lives have been radically changed. Thieves steal no more, liars become honest, adulterers live holy lives, and covetous people lose their greed. Churches, schools, and hospitals have risen as proof of the salutory effect the gospel of Jesus Christ has had on multitudes.[7]

---

[7]Harold Lindsell, "The Bible: God's Inspired Word" in *KJV Study Bible* (Wheaton, Ill.: Tyndale, 1986), p. 2001.

Psychiatrist J. T. Fisher put it this way:

> If you were to take the total of all authoritative articles ever written by the most qualified of psychologists and psychiatrists on the subject of mental hygiene—if you were to combine them and refine them and cleave out the excess verbiage—if you were to take the whole of the meat and none of the parsley, and if you were to have these unadulterated bits of pure scientific knowledge concisely expressed by the most capable of living poets, you have an awkward and incomplete summation of the Sermon on the Mount. And it would suffer immeasurably through comparison. For nearly two thousand years the Christian world has been holding in its hands the complete answer to its restless and fruitless yearnings.[8]

The wonderful, life-transforming power of the Bible is a fact.

CONCLUSION

The remarkable credentials of the Bible do not mean that it is true, but they do mean that it deserves serious consideration. Any sincere seeker after truth should look into this book for answers to the ultimate questions of existence.

Now that we have seen that the Bible is not just another book, but a wonderful record of God's voice to humankind, we will go on to review the making of the Old and New Testaments. We will first delve into questions concerning the reliability of the Hebrew Scriptures. Can we really trust our Old Testament? Is the text we have today truly representative of the original? We will cover these and other interesting features about the making of the Old Testament in the next chapter.

---

[8] J. T. Fisher and L. S. Hawley, *A Few Buttons Missing* (Philadelphia: Lippincott, 1951), p. 273.

CHAPTER 2
The Making of the Old Testament

Originally, the Hebrew Scriptures consisted of twenty-four books composed between 1400 and 400 B.C. They are placed into three major divisions: the Law (*Torah*), the Prophets (*Nebhiim*), and the Writings (*Kethubim*). They include:

THE LAW (or Pentateuch)
    Genesis
    Exodus
    Leviticus
    Numbers
    Deuteronomy

THE PROPHETS
    The Former Prophets
        Joshua
        Judges
        1 and 2 Samuel
        1 and 2 Kings
    The Latter Prophets
        Isaiah
        Jeremiah
        Ezekiel
        The Twelve (Hosea—Malachi)

THE WRITINGS
    The Poetical Books
        Job
        Psalms
        Proverbs

The Five Rolls
Ruth
Esther
Ecclesiastes
Song of Songs
Lamentations
The Historical Books
Daniel
Ezra
Nehemiah
1 and 2 Chronicles

These twenty-four books are divided further into a total of thirty-nine books—those that form the Old Testament as we know it. To understand how these books reached their present grouping and authority in the Old Testament, we need to look at the history of the text, observing how the various books were preserved and transmitted over the centuries.

HISTORY OF THE TEXT

The books of the Old Testament were considered special by the Jews. They were not ordinary literature or ordinary history. They were God's Word communicated to his people. Because of the high regard for these books, great care was taken to preserve their texts precisely as they were written.

The Pentateuch identifies the priests in Israel as the ones responsible for the preservation of the law. They were to store it beside or in the ark of the covenant, which was placed in the Holy of Holies in the tabernacle and, later, in the temple. The Old Testament records this command: "Take this book of the law and place it beside the ark of the covenant of the Lord your God, that it may remain there as a witness against you" (Deuteronomy 31:26).

The kings of Israel were required to have the law before them as a guide in their administration of the kingdom:

Now it shall come about when he sits on the throne of his kingdom, he shall write for himself a copy of this law on a scroll in the presence of the Levitical priests. And it shall be with him, and he shall read it all the days of his life, that he may learn to fear the Lord his God. (Deuteronomy 17:18-19)

Since the Pentateuch and other writings that make up the Old Testament were considered holy, they were preserved with great care. There is adequate evidence from history that this preservation was consistent and precise.

The *Mishnah* (a codification of the traditional Jewish oral law, committed to writing around A.D. 200) supplies us with an unbroken historical tradition about the people responsible for the preservation of the text from the time of Moses until the Council of Jamnia (first century A.D.).

The Council of Jamnia was very important. It solidified the Jewish canon of inspired books into the form we know as the Old Testament today. Biblical scholar F. F. Bruce commented:

The books which they decided to acknowledge as canonical were already generally accepted, although questions had been raised about them. Those which they refused to admit had never been included. They did not expel from the canon any book which had previously been admitted. "The Council of Jamnia," as J. S. Wright puts it, "was the confirming of public opinion, not the forming of it."[1]

From the Mishnah and the tradition since the Council of Jamnia we have documented accounts of the history of the preservation of the Old Testament.

THE SOPHERIM
From the completion of the Old Testament (400 B.C.) in the time of Ezra until the time of the Jewish scholars known as *Masoretes* (A.D. 500), the transmission and care of the Old Testament text was in the hands of a group of scribes. This group was called the *Sopherim* (meaning "counters"). The scribes got this name because of the manner in which they checked the accuracy

---

[1] F. F. Bruce, *The Books and the Parchments* (Westwood, N.J.: Revell, 1963), p. 98.

of their copying of the texts. The Sopherim counted the number of letters and words in each copy and compared them to the texts from which they copied. This minute accounting was described by biblical and literary scholar Sir Frederic Kenyon:

> Besides recording varieties of reading, tradition, or conjecture, the Masoretes undertook a number of calculations which do not enter into the ordinary sphere of textual criticism. They numbered the verses, words, and letters of every book. They calculated the middle word and middle letter of each. They enumerated verses which contained all the letters of the alphabet, or a certain number of them; and so on. These trivialities . . . had yet the effect of securing minute attention to the precise transmission of the text. . . . The Masoretes were anxious that not one jot nor tittle, not one smallest letter nor one tiny part of a letter, of the Law should pass away or be lost.[2]

THE MASORETES

The scribes called the Sopherim were entrusted with the preservation and interpretation of the Scriptures. They were specialists in preserving the sacred writings, laws, history and tradition of the Jewish people. A group of such specialists emerged around A.D. 500. They were known as the *Masoretes*, deriving their name from the Hebrew word *Masorah*, meaning "tradition." The Masoretes did their work in both Palestine and Babylon from approximately A.D. 500 to A.D. 900. They contributed to Old Testament textual preservation in several significant ways.

The Masoretes collected all the textual-critical remarks of the rabbis (Jewish teachers), all the additional marks added to the margins of the sacred texts (including memory devices, pronunciation aids, etc.), and entered these in the side margins of the copies they made. Another contribution of the Masoretes was

---

[2]Sir Frederic G. Kenyon, *Our Bible and the Ancient Manuscripts* (New York: Harper and Row, 1941), p. 38.

their invention of a complete Hebrew vowel system as an aid in pronunciation. Hebrew is traditionally a language only of consonants, without vowels. Because the same combinations of Hebrew consonants could sound different with different vowel sounds, when Hebrew ceased to be predominantly a spoken language, word pronunciation was forgotten. The Masoretes remedied this problem by inventing a system of symbols that were placed near the consonants and yet did not interfere with the consonant text at all. These "vowel points" are still used in printed editions of the Hebrew Old Testament.

The Masoretes also added a system of accent indicators that aided in the public reading of the text and are still a great help in determining where a sentence or clause begins or ends.

The contributions of the Masoretes to the textual preservation of the Old Testament cannot be minimized. Not only did they carefully enhance understanding of the texts by their marginal contributions, they also carefully preserved all of the alternate readings of the texts, a service invaluable to today's textual critics in their work to determine the original text.

HEBREW MANUSCRIPTS

Why are there so few extant (existing) ancient copies of the Old Testament? The reason we do not possess many older copies of the Hebrew Scriptures is because of the reverence with which the Jews protected the purity of God's Word. The Jews considered the text so sacred that they ceremoniously disposed of worn copies. The worn copies were first stored in a special room in the synagogue, called a *Genizah*. After a number of copies accumulated, they were all buried together (usually in the grave of some Jewish scholar). The Jews believed that this would protect readers from misreading God's Word because of worn spots in older manuscripts. That practice accounts for our having very few early manuscripts of the Old Testament.

Accuracy was not lost by destroying the worn copies because of the meticulous care with which the Jews copied the manuscripts. The new copy was identical to the worn-out copy in every detail. Because the Jews considered the text so sacred, they refused to change it in any way.

FURTHER TESTIMONY TO THE
TEXT OF THE OLD TESTAMENT

Besides the Hebrew manuscripts already mentioned, we possess further testimonies to the accuracy of our Old Testament text. Textual critics also consult the Aramaic *Targums*, the Greek *Septuagint*, the *Samaritan Pentateuch*, and the *Dead Sea Scrolls*. Let us now look at the evidence from each of these sources.

THE TARGUMS

The Targums were Jewish paraphrases of the Old Testament, written mostly in the Aramaic language. The first recorded instance of a Targum is found in the Old Testament itself. When Judah returned from its seventy-year exile in Babylon, many of the people had forgotten Hebrew and now spoke Aramaic. That change made the Hebrew Scriptures incomprehensible to them. Those learned Jews who understood both languages read aloud to the citizens in Hebrew and then gave a paraphrase of the passage in Aramaic. This practice is recorded in Nehemiah 8:8 ("And they read from the book, from the law of God, translating to give the sense so that they understood the reading").

That practice continued until the entire Old Testament, except for the passages already in Aramaic in Daniel and Ezra, were given Aramaic paraphrases. The Targums, no matter how practical, were never given the holy authority accorded to the Hebrew originals.

To textual critics, the Targums are helpful in establishing the correct text of the Old Testament. Some Targums date back centuries before the standard Masoretic text. The Targums had a long oral history before they were first recorded. They thus become a very ancient witness to the true text of the Old Testament.

THE SEPTUAGINT

The Septuagint, the standard Greek translation of the Old Testament, was composed to meet the needs of Greek-speaking Jews in Egypt during the Hellenistic period (c. 250 B.C.). This large Jewish community was concentrated in the city of Alexandria. The Jewish leaders there began to translate the Old Testament into Greek around 250 B.C. The standardized Greek text of the whole Old Testament became known as the Septuagint (Greek for "seventy"). The Septuagint is often abbreviated as LXX, the Roman-numeral notation for seventy. According to tradition, the Septuagint was prepared by seventy learned Jews during a seventy-day period, each working separately. The Lord so honored their effort, tradition goes, that when the scholars met, their translations were identical in every respect. However, in reality, the LXX took several centuries to complete, and as a translation it varies in quality. Some parts are faithful renderings of the Hebrew, other parts are less so. In places it seems to diverge from the Masoretic text.

The importance of the LXX is that it is an ancient witness to the text of the Old Testament. Even in those places where the text differs from the Masoretic text, the percentage of difference is not great, and the differences do not represent significant changes in meaning.

THE SAMARITAN PENTATEUCH

Another source used by textual critics for the text of the Old Testament is the Samaritan Pentateuch. The people who lived in Samaria were a result of interbreeding of Jews and Assyrians. After the Babylonian captivity they cut themselves off entirely from the Jews (about 586 B.C.), and their development was independent from that point on. They possessed their own text of the Bible (only the Pentateuch) and their own temple on Mount Gerizim. The Gospel of John reminds us that Jews had no dealings with Samaritans (John 4:9).

The Samaritans believed that only the Pentateuch (first five books of the Old Testament) was the inspired Word of God. They rejected both the Prophets and the Writings. The oldest manuscripts of the Samaritan Pentateuch still in existence date from the tenth century A.D. The Samaritan Pentateuch, written in a unique script with no vowel signs, differs little from the Masoretic text. What is remarkable is that their close similarity was maintained over a fifteen hundred-year independence from each other.

THE DEAD SEA SCROLLS

Until 1947 the oldest complete manuscript of the Old Testament in our possession dated from around A.D. 1000, a full fourteen hundred years after the completion of the Old Testament. Many speculated that during that long span of years significant changes could have crept into the text.

In 1947, however, a dramatic event took place, which laid to rest doubts about the reliability of the Old Testament text. In that year a young Bedouin goatherd was looking for a lost goat in the caves in the cliffs above Wadi Qumran, near the Dead Sea. In one cave he found several clay jars over two feet high and approximately ten inches wide. Those jars contained leather scrolls wrapped in linen cloth.

One of the first scholars to examine the scrolls was E. L. Sukenik of the Hebrew University of Jerusalem, who immediately recognized their antiquity and value. The amazing find was confirmed by W. F. Albright, one of this century's eminent archaeologists. Confirming that the scrolls were of the Old Testament, Albright labeled the find "the most important Old Testament manuscript discovery ever made."

Recovery of more scrolls was halted by Arab-Israeli conflicts, so it was not possible to investigate further until the peace of 1948. Investigation then revealed hundreds of scrolls or fragments of scrolls in different caves. The scrolls had been placed there by a Jewish sect called the Essenes, who had established a fortress nearby, which they occupied from about 100 B.C. to A.D. 68, when they fled the advancing Roman armies. Before they abandoned their community they carefully hid their library in the nearby caves of Wadi Qumran. There they lay undisturbed for almost nineteen hundred years.

Analysis showed that the scrolls were composed mostly during those years between 100 B.C. and A.D. 68. They contain portions of every book of the Old Testament (except Esther) and numerous documents relating to the doctrines and practices of the Essenes. Particularly significant is the complete scroll of Isaiah, found in Cave 1 and dating to one hundred years before Christ. An important fragment of Samuel, dating four hundred years before Christ, was found in Cave 4. These and other finds revolutionized Old Testament textual criticism.

The Dead Sea Scrolls provide clear evidence of the complete faithfulness of the Old Testament text to the originals in spite of transmission through long centuries.

After comparing the entire Isaiah manuscript from Qumran with the present Hebrew text of Isaiah, Old Testament scholar Gleason L. Archer concluded that the Dead Sea Scroll "proved to be word for word identical with our standard Hebrew Bible in more than 95 percent of the text. The 5 percent of variation consisted chiefly of obvious slips of the pen and variations in spelling."[3]

CONCLUSION

The evidence in support of the trustworthiness of the Old Testament text is overwhelming. It accurately represents the original. One of the great Old Testament scholars of our century, Robert Dick Wilson, affirmed that the evidence favors the veracity of the Old Testament text. He declared:

In 144 cases of transliteration from Egyptian, Assyrian, Babylonian and Moabite into Hebrew and in 40 cases of the opposite, or 184 in all, the evidence shows that for 2,300 to 3,900 years the text of the proper names in the Hebrew Bible has been transmitted with the most minute accuracy. That the original scribes should have written them with such close conformity to correct philological principles is a wonderful proof of their thorough care and scholarship; further, that the Hebrew text should have been transmitted by copyists through so many centuries is a phenomenon unequaled in the history of literature.[4]

So, though the oldest parts of the Old Testament are probably thirty-four hundred years old, we can be confident that the text we possess today accurately represents what was originally written.

---

[3]Gleason L. Archer, *A Survey of Old Testament Introduction* (Chicago: Moody, 1964), p. 19.

[4]Robert Dick Wilson, *A Scientific Investigation of the Old Testament* (Chicago: Moody, 1959), pp. 70-71, 85.

CHAPTER 3
The Making of the New Testament

The books of the New Testament were written in *Koine* Greek, the most widely spoken language in the first century. As with the Old Testament, we do not possess the originals, or autographs, because of age. That makes us dependent on copies—copies of copies—to construct the text. How good are the copies? Can we be sure the text has not been tampered with?

The discipline that deals with reconstructing texts is known as *textual criticism*. The reason for using textual criticism in New Testament study is twofold: (1) We do not possess the original manuscripts, and (2) the copies we possess differ in some areas. The textual critics, therefore, piece together the evidence to reconstruct the original text. In the case of the New Testament, three lines of evidence are available to reconstruct the original: the Greek manuscripts, early non-Greek versions, and the Church Fathers.

THE GREEK MANUSCRIPTS

How well have the Greek manuscripts of the New Testament been transmitted?

The problem with almost all ancient writings is the lack of extant (existing) manuscripts to reconstruct the text. Most ancient writings have the most paltry manuscript evidence by which experts attempt to establish the original.

In the case of the New Testament, however, we are not lacking manuscripts to reconstruct the text. On the contrary, we have an abundance of manuscripts.

In the history of the transmission of the Greek text we have found different lines of evidence: papyri, uncial manuscripts, minuscule manuscripts, and lectionaries.

The first line of evidence of the Greek manuscripts is the **papyri**. Papyrus is the material that the original copies of the New Testament were composed of. It is an extremely perishable material, surviving only in warm, dry climates. The papyrus fragments that have survived, however, contain some of the earliest witnesses to the New Testament text. Of the ninety-six surviving New Testament papyri, about half date earlier than the fourth century. The most significant papyri are the Oxyrhynchus Papyri (about twenty-five manuscripts of New Testament portions), the Chester Beatty Papyri (three early manuscripts—one with the four Gospels and Acts, another with the Pauline Epistles, and one with Revelation), and the Bodmer Papyri (three early manuscripts—one with John, another with 1 and 2 Peter and Jude, and one with Luke and John). The papyri were written with the uncial script.

Uncial writing, which consisted of uppercase letters (all capitals) that were deliberately and carefully written, is the type of writing used at the time of the composition of the New Testament. The uncial manuscripts were written between the fourth and tenth centuries. Among the most important and reliable uncial manuscripts are Codex Vaticanus (fourth century), Codex Sinaiticus (fourth century), Codex Alexandrinus (fifth century), and Codex Ephraemi Rescriptus (fifth century). In the ninth century, uncial writing began to be replaced with minuscule writing.

Minuscule writing was a script of smaller letters not as carefully executed as uncials; books could be turned out much faster by the employment of minuscule writing. Minuscule writing was in vogue from the ninth to the sixteenth centuries.

Lectionaries were the result of the Christian church following the custom of synagogue. Every Sabbath different portions of the Law and Prophets were read. The church developed a similar practice, reading a different portion of the Gospels and Epistles according to a fixed order of Sundays and holy days. These readings are known as lectionaries.

The earliest fragments of lectionaries come from the sixth century A.D. Complete manuscripts are found as early as the eighth century.

We catalogue the surviving Greek manuscripts along the following lines: papyri, uncial manuscripts, minuscule manuscripts, and lectionaries.

Type of Manuscript	*Number Surviving*
Papyri	96 or 97
Uncial	267
Minuscule	2,764
Lectionaries	2,143
Recent finds not catalogued	47
Total	5,317 or 5,318

The total number of surviving Greek manuscripts upon which the original New Testament text can be reconstructed dwarfs all other ancient works. Yet Greek manuscripts are not the only line of evidence available for this reconstruction.

VERSIONS

Another line of evidence by which the New Testament text can be established comes from the versions. Versions are translations of the different New Testament books into other languages. Although ancient literature was rarely translated into another language, the New Testament was an exception. From the second century, Christian missionaries, in an attempt to propagate their faith, translated the New Testament into the various languages of the people they encountered. Some of those translations, made as early as the middle of the second century, give us an important witness to the text of that early time.

When the copies of the manuscripts of the versions are catalogued, we are again faced with an overwhelming number. (It should be noted that when we speak of manuscripts or copies we are referring to any part of a manuscript or copy that has survived. Thus the copies could be anything from a single fragment to a complete text.) The following breakdown illustrates this:

Versions	*Number of Manuscripts*
Latin Vulgate	10,000+ (may be as high as 25,000)
Ethiopic	2,000+
Slavic	4,101+
Armenian	2,587
Syriac Peshitta	350+
Bohairic	100
Total	19,000+

Since the versions are translations from the Greek, they are not as valuable as the Greek manuscripts in reconstructing the original text. They are, however, an important witness to the text's basic reliability.

THE CHURCH FATHERS

A third line of evidence can be consulted in establishing the New Testament text, quotations from the writings of men known as the "Church Fathers." In their writings the Church Fathers would often quote from the New Testament text. Every time we find a biblical quotation in their writings, we have another witness to the New Testament text.

For example, Ignatius (A.D. 70–110) wrote seven letters in which he quoted from eighteen different books of the New Testament. Every time he quotes a text, we can observe what Greek text he was using by his quotation. Thus, the early Church Fathers provide us with an excellent early witness to the text.

The number of quotations of the Fathers is overwhelming, so much so that, if every other source for the New Testament (Greek manuscripts, versions) were destroyed, the text could be reconstructed merely on the writings of the Fathers. Consequently, when the evidence from the Greek manuscripts, the versions, and the Church Fathers is considered, any impartial person cannot help but be impressed.

VARIANT READINGS

What is a variant reading? Simply stated, when two manuscripts differ on a particular word or phrase in the text, the result is a variant reading. The difference may be of spelling, word order or different words employed. The variations in the text arose both unintentionally and intentionally.

UNINTENTIONAL VARIATIONS

The greatest number of variants in the New Testament manuscripts were of the unintentional variety. They could creep into the text through faulty sight, hearing, writing, memory, or judgment on the part of the scribe. Bruce Metzger writes:

> In the earliest days of the Christian church after an apostolic letter was sent to a congregation or an individual, or after a gospel was written to meet the needs of a particular reading public, copies would be made in order to extend its influence and to enable others to profit from it as well. It was inevitable that such handwritten copies would contain a greater or lesser number of differences in wording from the original. Most of the divergencies arose from quite accidental causes, such as mistaking a letter or a word for another that looked like it. If two neighboring lines of a manuscript began or ended with the same group of letters or if two similar words stood near each other in the same line, it was easy for the eye of the copyist to jump from the first group of letters to the second, and so for a portion of the text to be omitted (called *homeoarchton* [like beginning] or *homoeoteleuton* [like ending], depending upon whether the similarity of letters occurred at the beginning or the ending of the words). Conversely the scribe might go back from the second to the first group and unwittingly copy one or more words twice (called dittography). Letters that were pronounced alike were sometimes confused (called itascism). Such accidental errors are almost unavoidable whenever lengthy passages are copied by hand.[1]

INTENTIONAL VARIATIONS

Some variations in the text came about intentionally. J. Harold Greenlee writes:

---

[1]Bruce Metzger, *A Textual Commentary on the Greek New Testament* (London: United Bible Societies, 1971), pp. XV-XVI.

These comprise a significant, although a much less numerous, group of errors than the unintentional changes. They derive for the most part from attempts by scribes to improve the text in various ways. Few indeed are the evidences that heretical or destructive variants have been deliberately introduced into the mss.[2]

Bruce Metzger expands upon the intentional variations:

Other divergencies in wording arose from deliberate attempts to smooth out grammatical or stylistic harshness, or to eliminate real or imagined obscurities of meaning in the text. Sometimes a copyist would add what seemed to him to be a more appropriate word or form, perhaps derived from a parallel passage (called harmonization or assimilation). Thus, during the years immediately following the composition of the several documents that eventually were collected to form the New Testament, hundreds if not thousands of variant readings arose.[3]

It is often charged by those opposed to Christianity that the variant readings in the manuscripts undermine the reliability of the text. These people point to some two hundred thousand variants in the existing manuscripts, so it is impossible to recover the New Testament's exact text. Nothing could be further from the truth because we have so many early, reliable manuscripts that have enabled textual scholars to make great advances in recovering the original wording of the New Testament.

The great scholar Samuel Tregelles stated, "We possess so many mss, and we are aided by so many versions, that we are never left to the need to conjecture as the means of removing errata."[4]

---

[2]J. Harold Greenlee, *Introduction to New Testament Textual Criticism* (Grand Rapids: Eerdmans, 1964), p. 66.

[3] Metzger, *Textual Commentary*, p. XVI.

[4]Samuel Tregelles, *Greek New Testament*, prolegomena.

SUMMARY AND CONCLUSION

Although we do not possess the original manuscripts of any of the books of the New Testament, the evidence that it has been transcribed accurately through history is overwhelming. We conclude that the New Testament has been transcribed accurately throughout history. Any contrary conclusion is based either on ignorance of the evidence or on a willful desire not to accept the facts. The late Sir Frederic Kenyon, director of the British Museum, was a respected authority on ancient manuscripts. After a lifetime of studying ancient documents he came to the following conclusions:

> The text of the Bible is certain; especially is this the case with the New Testament. The number of manuscripts of the New Testament, of early translations from it, and of quotations from it in the oldest writers of the church, is so large that it is practically certain that the true reading of every doubtful passage is preserved in some one or other of these ancient authorities. This can be said of no other ancient book.[5]

---

[5] Sir Frederick Kenyon, *Our Bible and the Ancient Manuscripts* (New York: Harper and Row, 1941), p. 23.

CHAPTER 4

The Canon and the Apocrypha

Now that we have determined that the texts of both the Old and New Testaments have been transmitted accurately through the ages, let's move on to the next logical step—the right of these documents to be considered part of the biblical canon, or list of approved books. How do we know we have the right books in our Bible? Are they adequate witnesses to the events they attempt to record? What about other books that claim (or have had claimed for them) the right to be considered Scripture, yet are missing from our Bible?

THE CANON

Scholars speak of the Old and New Testament books as belonging to the *canon of Scripture*. The word *canon* comes from the Greek word *kanon*, which referred to a reed or cane used as a measuring rod. The canon is thus the "measuring rod" or standard we use to judge a work's inspiration, authenticity, and veracity.

OLD TESTAMENT BOOKS

We have already mentioned (in chapter 2) that the Old Testament has three sections: the Law, the Prophets, and the Writings. We also showed that the Protestant church has the same books in its Old Testament as have the Jews throughout their history (although the Jewish order and numbering are different). We will now show that those books had been established as authentic and deserving of inclusion in the canon of

Scripture long before the time of Jesus. They have every right to be considered the Word of God.

Jesus affirmed the canon of the Old Testament. Jesus never disagreed with the writings we find in our Old Testament today, but he did disagree with some of the oral traditions handed down in Israel (Matthew 15:3). Jesus Christ accepted the books of the Old Testament in the same threefold division that was common to the Jews of his day. This is clear in his statement to his disciples: "These are My words which I spoke to you while I was still with you, that all things which are written about Me in the Law of Moses and the Prophets and the Psalms must be fulfilled" (Luke 24:44).

Jesus Christ also testified to the extent of the Old Testament canon. In Luke 11:51 he spoke of "the blood of Abel to the blood of Zechariah." Abel was the first martyr in Scripture (Genesis 4:8), and Zechariah was the last martyr named in the Jewish arrangement of the Old Testament (where 2 Chronicles is listed as the last book of the Old Testament: 2 Chronicles 24:21). Jesus thus gave his approval to the entire canon of the Old Testament with the same contents we have today.

OLD TESTAMENT APOCRYPHA

Comments made previously in my book *Answers to Tough Questions* concerning the Old Testament Apocryphal books are appropriate here:

Today the word *Apocrypha* is synonymous with the 14 or 15 books of doubtful authenticity and authority. These writings are not found in the Hebrew Old Testament, but they are in some manuscripts of the Septuagint, the Greek translation of the Hebrew Old Testament, which was completed around 250 B.C. in Alexandria, Egypt.

Most of these books were declared to be Scripture by the Roman Catholic church at the Council of Trent (1545–1563), though the Protestant churches reject any divine authority attached to them.

Those who say these books are Scripture argue that the writers of the New Testament quote mostly from the Septuagint, which contains the Apocrypha. They also cite some of the Church

Fathers, notably Irenaeus, Tertullian, and Clement of Alexandria, who used the Apocrypha in public worship and accepted it as Scripture, as did the Syriac church in the fourth century.

Augustine, who presided over the councils of Hippo and Carthage, concurred with their decision that the books of the Apocrypha were inspired. The Greek church adds its weight to the list of believers in the inspiration of the Apocrypha.

The advocates point also to the Dead Sea Scrolls to add further weight to their belief in the Apocrypha. Among the fragments at Qumran are copies of some of the Apocryphal books written in Hebrew. These have been discovered alongside the Old Testament works.

The case for including the Apocrypha as holy Scripture completely breaks down when examined. The New Testament writers may allude to the Apocrypha, but they do not quote from it as holy Scripture or give the slightest hint that any of the books are inspired. (The only exception is Jude, who alludes to "The Assumption of Moses" and quotes from the book of Enoch—see Jude 9, 14.) If the Septuagint in the first century contained these books, which is by no means a proven fact, Jesus and his disciples completely ignored them.

Appealing to certain Church Fathers as proof of the inspiration of the books is a weak argument, since many of the Fathers, notably Origen, Jerome, and others denied their inspiration.

The Syriac church waited until the fourth century A.D. to accept these books as canonical. It is notable that the Peshitta, the Syriac Bible of the second century A.D., did not contain them.

The early writings of Augustine did acknowledge the Apocrypha, at least in part. But Augustine's later writings reject these books as outside the canon and inferior to the Hebrew Scriptures.

The Jewish community also rejected these writings. At the Jewish Council of Jamnia (c. A.D. 90), nine of the books of our Old Testament canon were debated for differing reasons whether they were to be included. Eventually they ruled that only the Hebrew Old Testament books of our present canon were canonical.

Citing the presence of the Apocrypha among the Old Testament fragments proves little regarding inspiration, as numerous fragments of other, nonscriptural documents were also found.

It cannot be overemphasized that the Roman Catholic church

itself did not officially declare these books Holy Scripture until 1545–1563 at the Council of Trent.

The acceptance of certain books in the Apocrypha as canonical by the Roman Catholic church was to a great extent a reaction to the Protestant Reformation. By canonizing these books, they legitimized their reference to them in doctrinal matters.

The arguments that advocate the scriptural authority of the Apocrypha obviously leave a great deal to be desired.[1]

THE DEAD SEA SCROLLS

The Dead Sea Scrolls contribute to our knowledge of the canon.

The canon is the collection of biblical books received as genuine and inspired. The Jewish synagogue and the Protestant church have the same canon of the Old Testament. The Roman Catholic church accepts the thirty-nine books of this canon as inspired, but it also accepts the collection of books that are known as the Apocrypha as part of the Catholic Bible.

We would like to know what books were deemed canonical by the Qumran community. A simple answer cannot be given because of the very nature of ancient writing materials. Each book existed as a single scroll. There is no bound collection of writings—such as our Bible—of which one could say, "These are our sacred books." The leaders of the Qumran community could have told us which of the scrolls were considered inspired Scripture, but no list of such writings has come down to us. In some sense all the documents kept in the library were considered authoritative—even the commentaries—but as Jews faithful to the tradition of the fathers there was doubtless a special regard for the law (or Torah).

Indicative of the fact that the Old Testament as we have it was regarded as sacred Scripture at Qumran is the fact that every book except Esther is represented, at least in the form of fragments. Thus every book of the Old Testament is found either in manuscript, quotation, or allusion in the Qumran literature. The

[1]Josh McDowell and Don Stewart, *Answers to Tough Questions* (San Bernardino, Calif.: Here's Life, 1980), pp. 36-38.

absence of Esther from the Qumran library may be because it was not composed among Palestinian Jews. Since its locale is Persia, it may not have been well known by the Qumranians. It is not quoted in the New Testament.

While Apocryphal literature is found in abundance among the Qumran documents, it is worthy of note that all of the commentaries thus far identified are of canonical books. It would appear that only the canonical books were considered important enough to warrant interpretative commentaries.

NEW TESTAMENT BOOKS: PRIMARY SOURCE TESTIMONY

As we investigate the New Testament, we are struck by the fact that the writers of the New Testament books claimed to be either eyewitnesses of the events recorded or those who gathered eyewitness testimony concerning them.

What was from the beginning, what we have heard, what we have seen with our eyes, what we beheld and our hands handled, concerning the Word of Life—and the life was manifested, and we have seen and bear witness and proclaim to you the eternal life, which was with the Father and was manifested to us—what we have seen and heard we proclaim to you also, that you also may have fellowship with us; and indeed our fellowship is with the Father, and with His Son Jesus Christ. (The testimony of the apostle John in 1 John 1:1-3)

Inasmuch as many have undertaken to compile an account of the things accomplished among us, just as those who from the beginning were eyewitnesses and servants of the Word have handed them down to us, it seemed fitting for me as well, having investigated everything carefully from the beginning, to write it out for you in consecutive order, most excellent Theophilus; so that you might know the exact truth about the things you have been taught. (The testimony of Luke in Luke 1:1-4)

For we did not follow cleverly devised tales when we made known to you the power and coming of our Lord Jesus Christ, but we were eyewitnesses of His majesty. (The testimony of Peter in 2 Peter 1:16)

The fact that the New Testament writers claimed such objective, complete, and firsthand evidence concerning Jesus Christ is of crucial importance in helping to determine the New Testament canon. Their evidence is not hearsay or imaginary; it is direct and reliable. Biblical scholar F. F. Bruce observes:

> The earliest preachers of the gospel knew the value of . . . firsthand testimony, and appealed to it time and again. "We are witnesses of these things," was their constant and confident assertion. And it can have been by no means so easy as some writers seem to think to invent words and deeds of Jesus in those early years, when so many of his disciples were about, who could remember what had and had not happened.
>
> And it was not only friendly eyewitnesses that the early preachers had to reckon with. There were others less well disposed who were also conversant with the main facts of the ministry and death of Jesus. The disciples could not afford to risk inaccuracies (not to speak of willful manipulation of the facts), which would at once be exposed by those who would be only too glad to do so. On the contrary, one of the strong points in the original apostolic preaching is the confident appeal to the knowledge of the hearers; they not only said, "We are witnesses of these things," but also, "As you yourselves also know" (Acts 2:22). Had there been any tendency to depart from the facts in any material respect, the possible presence of hostile witnesses in the audience would have served as a further corrective.[2]

DATING OF THE NEW TESTAMENT

When all the historical and textual evidence is amassed, it becomes clear that the New Testament was composed at a very

---

[2] F. F. Bruce, *The New Testament Documents: Are They Reliable?* (Downers Grove, Ill.: InterVarsity, 1960), pp. 45-46.

early date by eyewitnesses and/or by those who recorded eyewitness testimony. Eminent archaeologist William F. Albright concluded: "In my opinion, every book of the New Testament was written by a baptized Jew between the forties and the eighties of the first century A.D. (very probably sometime between A.D. 50 and 75)."[3]

Albright also reported: "Thanks to the Qumran discoveries, the New Testament proves to be in fact what it was formerly believed to be: the teaching of Christ and his immediate followers between c. 24 and c. 80 A.D."[4]

OTHER WRITINGS

There are other writings that have not been placed in the New Testament canon but for which some individuals have claimed divine inspiration.

Close examination shows that these books lack the necessary integrity to be included in the New Testament canon. These include the Letter of Barnabas, the Shepherd of Hermas, the Didache, the Letter of Clement, and others.

Although these writings are of historical interest, they are not of the spiritual, historical, or inspirational caliber of the canonical books. They do not contain eyewitness testimony.

Some books, rejected by all, are outright forgeries. These are called "pseudepigrapha." They were produced by heretics and cultists seeking to validate their heresies with pseudo-apostolic blessing. Among these are many false "Gospels" giving fanciful accounts of Jesus' childhood miracles.

After examining the evidence for the inclusion of our New Testament books in the canon and the evidence against including the Apocrypha and pseudepigrapha in the canon, we can safely conclude that the New Testament we have today is the complete complement of books God wants us to read.

---

[3] "An Interview with William F. Albright," *Christianity Today*, 18 January 1963.

[4] William F. Albright, *From the Stone Age to Christianity* (Baltimore: Johns Hopkins, 1946), p. 29.

CHAPTER 5
The Bible and Inspiration

We have seen that the books of the Bible have been transmitted accurately and are reliable witnesses to the events they portray. Now two questions will be addressed: Are the books of the Bible more than reliable historical literature? Are the books of the Bible the Word of God?

THE NATURE OF INSPIRATION:
FOUR PERSPECTIVES

One can view the Bible and its inspiration from several different perspectives. We will take a brief look at four of those perspectives before we produce a workable definition of the nature of biblical inspiration.

1. The Bible is an inspiring book but no different from other great literary works of the past. This view places the Scriptures on the same level as other human productions. It denies the possibility of God's providing a revelation of himself through the books of the Bible.

2. The Bible is "in part" the Word of God. This view limits the manner and quantity in which a revelation of God can be contained in the books of the Bible. Proponents of this view say, "The Bible *contains* the Word of God," or "The Bible *becomes* the Word of God."

The idea that the Bible *contains* the Word of God makes the individual reader the final determiner of inspiration. How is one to determine which parts of the Bible are part of God's revelation and which parts are of only human origin? When the individual, or even a community of individuals (as in a church), becomes the

49

determiner of inspiration, he becomes entangled in his own system. He has no adequate way of discerning whether the inspiration is inherent in certain parts of Scripture (and thus recognizable in some way by him), or perhaps he determines what is inspired, making biblical inspiration subjective rather than inherent.

3. The Bible is the divine Word of God dictated by God to selected human authors. This view leaves no room for the personal diversities of the various individual writers, diversities clearly evident in the Bible. Although it is popular among liberals and nonreligious persons to accuse all serious or conservative Christians (evangelicals) of holding this position, it is actually not a tenable position. Dr. James I. Packer notes:

> This "dictation theory" is a man of straw. It is safe to say that no Protestant theologian, from the Reformation till now, has ever held it; and certainly modern Evangelicals do not hold it. . . . It is true that many sixteenth and seventeenth-century theologians spoke of Scripture as "dictated by the Holy Ghost." But all they meant was that the authors wrote word for word what God intended. . . . The use of the term "dictation" was always figurative. . . . The proof of this lies in the fact that, when these theologians addressed themselves to the question, What was the Spirit's mode of operating in the writers' minds? they all gave their answer in terms not of dictation, but of accommodation, and rightly maintained that God completely adapted his inspiring activity to the cast of mind, outlook, temperament, interests, literary habits, and stylistic idiosyncrasies of each writer.[1]

4. The Bible is a book that is both divine and human. In expanded form, this view reflects the biblical teaching that the Bible itself, in all that it states, is a product of divine revelation, channeled through, but not corrupted by, human agency, by which the unique talents, backgrounds, and perspectives of the authors complement rather than restrict what God intended to reveal.

---

[1]James I. Packer, *Fundamentalism and the Word of God* (Grand Rapids: Eerdmans, 1958), p. 78ff.

All Scripture is inspired by God and profitable for teaching, for reproof, for correction, for training in righteousness. (2 Timothy 3:16)

But know this first of all, that no prophecy of Scripture is a matter of one's own interpretation, for no prophecy was ever made by an act of human will, but men moved by the Holy Spirit spoke from God. (2 Peter 1:20-21)

Our English word *inspired* comes from a Greek term, *theopneustos*, meaning "God-breathed." The source of all Scripture is God. The Scriptures, while inspired by God, are also the product of being channeled through men. These men recorded divine truth as they were led by the Holy Spirit.

It is important to understand that this claim of inspiration is made by the Scriptures themselves. It is not something imposed on them by the church. From Genesis through Revelation the writers of Scriptures believed they were recording the Word of God. Consistently we find phrases like "Thus saith the Lord," "God said," "The Word of the Lord came unto . . . ," and so on.

EXTENT OF INSPIRATION

We repeat our citation of 2 Timothy 3:16 in preface to our discussion of the extent of inspiration:

All Scripture is inspired by God and profitable for teaching, for reproof, for correction, for training in righteousness.

An important principle can be drawn from this passage: Inspiration of Scripture is plenary, meaning that it includes the entire body of Scripture. In context, Paul was speaking of the Old Testament. By inference, we extend the "Scriptures" to include also the New Testament because they were also read in the churches and were taught as God's Word.

PLENARY INSPIRATION

"All" Scripture—the entire corpus of Scripture—is inspired by God. Inspiration is plenary, or "full." Every portion is "God-breathed."

Some verses alluding to this are Revelation 22:18-19; Matthew 5:17-18; Romans 15:4; Jeremiah 15:19; 26:2; 36:2; and Luke 24:44, which is reproduced here:

Now He said to them, "These are My words which I spoke to you while I was still with you, that all things which are written about Me in the Law of Moses and the Prophets and the Psalms must be fulfilled."

The clear teaching of Scripture is that the whole of it is inspired by God. Everything is considered accurate. That does not mean, however, that every statement in the Bible itself teaches truth. Satan's words, for example, are recorded accurately and are there because God wanted them there. But Satan did not tell the truth (John 8:44).

VERBAL INSPIRATION

The Scripture indicates that inspiration extends not only to all of Scripture as a whole but to every word. It is not merely the thoughts or intentions of Scripture that are divinely inspired. Some of the verses upholding verbal inspiration include Jeremiah 1:7, 9; Exodus 34:27; John 6:63; and Matthew 4:4, where Jesus says, "It is written, 'Man shall not live on bread alone, but on every word that proceeds out of the mouth of God.'"

The truth of this teaching can be found in the fact that the apostles sometimes based their arguments on just one word of Scripture. For example, the apostle Paul cited a prophecy from the Old Testament and argued on the basis of one word in the Old Testament passage:

Now the promises were spoken to Abraham and to his seed. He does not say, "And to seeds," as referring to many, but rather to one, "And to your seed," that is, Christ. (Galatians 3:16)

FALLIBLE PEOPLE VERSUS INFALLIBLE BIBLE

An obvious question arises. How could fallible people produce an infallible Bible?

One of the most frequent arguments leveled against the infallibility of the Bible is based upon the fact that the Bible was written by human authors. Human beings are fallible. Since the Bible was written by these fallible human beings, it necessarily follows that the Bible is fallible. Or so the argument goes. As Roman Catholic scholar Bruce Vawter writes, "A human literature containing no error would indeed be a contradiction in terms, since nothing is more human than to err."[2]

Although we often hear this accusation, it is not correct. Here is an illustration: A teacher types a one-page outline of a course he is teaching. The finished product was inerrant; it had no typographical errors, no mistakes in copying from the handwritten original. Although the author was human and was prone to make mistakes, he was, in fact, infallible in this instance.

The point is this: It is possible for a human being to perform a mistake-free act. It is possible for fallible people to correctly record sayings and events.

John Warwick Montgomery, lawyer and theologian, illustrates this truth:

> The directions for operating my washing machine, for example, are literally infallible; if I do just what they say, the machine will respond. Euclid's *Geometry* is a book of perfect internal consistency; grant the axioms and the proofs follow inexorably. From such examples (and they could readily be multiplied) we must conclude that human beings, though they often err, need not err in all particular instances.[3]

The testimony of Scripture is clear. God used fallible people to receive and record his infallible Word so that it would reach us correct and without error.

WHAT ABOUT CONTRADICTIONS?

If the Bible is the divinely inspired Word of God, then God is the one who is eventually responsible for its content. This being

---

[2] Bruce Vawter, *Biblical Inspiration* (Philadelphia: Westminster, 1972).

[3] John Warwick Montgomery, ed. *God's Inerrant Word: An International Symposium on the Trustworthiness of Scripture* (Minneapolis: Bethany Fellowship, 1974), p. 33.

the case, we need to address the matter of so-called contradictions that are contained within its pages. A Bible containing errors or contradictions is inconsistent with the God it reveals. We will observe that a close evaluation of the matter shows that the Bible does not disagree with itself.

One of the things for which we appeal with regard to possible contradictions is fairness. We should not minimize or exaggerate the problem, and we must always begin by giving the author the benefit of the doubt. This is the rule in other literature, and we ask that it also be the rule here. We find so often that people want to employ a different set of rules when it comes to examining the Bible, and to this we immediately object.

What constitutes a contradiction? The law of noncontradiction, which is the basis of all logical thinking, states that a thing cannot be both *A* and *non-A* at the same time. In other words, it cannot be both raining and not raining at the same time.

If one can demonstrate a violation of this principle from Scripture, then and only then can he prove a contradiction. For example, if the Bible said—which it does not—that Jesus died by crucifixion both at Jerusalem and at Nazareth at the same time, this would be a provable error.

When facing possible contradictions, it is of the highest importance to remember that two statements may differ from each other without being contradictory. Some fail to make a distinction between contradiction and difference.

For example, the case of the blind men at Jericho. Matthew relates how two blind men met Jesus, while both Mark and Luke mention only one. However, neither of these statements denies the other, but rather they are complementary.

Suppose you were talking to the mayor of your city and the chief of police at city hall. Later, you see your friend, Jim, and tell him you talked to the mayor today. An hour later, you see your friend, John, and tell him you talked to both the mayor and the chief of police.

When your friends compare notes, there is a seeming contradiction. But there is no contradiction. If you had told Jim that you talked *only* to the mayor, you would have contradicted that statement by what you told John.

The statements you actually made to Jim and John are different, but not contradictory. Likewise, many biblical statements fall into this category. Many think they find errors in passages that they have not correctly read.

In the book of Judges we have the account of the death of Sisera. Judges 5:25-27 is supposed to represent Jael as having slain him with her hammer and tent peg while he was drinking milk. Judges 4:21 says she did it while he was asleep. However, a closer reading of Judges 5:25-27 will reveal that it is not stated that he was drinking milk at the moment of impact. Thus, the discrepancy disappears.

Sometimes two passages appear to be contradictory because the translation is not as accurate as it could be. A knowledge of the original languages of the Bible can immediately solve these difficulties, for both Greek and Hebrew—as all languages—have their peculiarities that make them difficult to render into English or any other language.

A classic example concerns the accounts of Paul's conversion as recorded in the book of Acts. Acts 9:7 (King James Version) states, "The men which journeyed with him stood speechless, hearing a voice, but seeing no man." Acts 22:9 (King James Version) reads, "And they that were with me saw indeed the light, and were afraid; but they heard not the voice of him that spake to me."

These statements seem contradictory, with one saying that Paul's companions heard a voice, while the other account says no voice was heard. However, a knowledge of Greek solves this difficulty. As the Greek scholar W. F. Arndt explained:

> The construction of the verb "to hear" (akouo) is not the same in both accounts. In Acts 9:7 it is used with the genitive, in Acts 22:9 with the accusative. The construction with the genitive simply expresses that something is being heard or that certain sounds reach the ear; nothing is indicated as to whether a person understands what he hears or not.
>
> The construction with the accusative, however, describes a hearing which includes mental apprehension of the message spoken. From this it becomes evident that the two passages are not contradictory.
>
> Acts 22:9 does not deny that the associates of Paul heard certain sounds; it simply declares that they did not hear in

such a way as to understand what was being said. Our English idiom in this case simply is not so expressive as the Greek.

It must also be stressed that when a possible explanation is given to a Bible difficulty, it is unreasonable to state that the passage contains a demonstrable error. Some difficulties in Scripture result from our inadequate knowledge about the circumstances and do not necessarily involve an error. These only prove that we are ignorant of the background.

While all Bible difficulties and discrepancies have not yet been cleared up, it is our firm conviction that as more knowledge is gained of the Bible's past, these problems will fade away.

THE AUTHORITY OF JESUS CHRIST

When it comes to determining whether or not the Bible is the inspired Word of God we can rest confidently on the authority of Jesus Christ. We arrive at this conclusion by the following logic:

1. We have already shown that the New Testament can be trusted as an accurate historical document, giving firsthand information on the life of Jesus Christ.

2. In this accurate, historical document Jesus Christ is presented as having made certain claims about himself. He claimed to be the Messiah, the Son of God, the Way, the Truth, and the Life, the only way by which anyone can approach God.

3. Jesus Christ demonstrated that he had the right to make those Old Testament claims by fulfilling prophecies about the Messiah. He performed miracles, showing he had power over nature. The most significant miracle of all was his rising from the dead (John 2:19-21). The resurrection confirmed his claims to deity.

4. Since Jesus is the Messiah, God in human flesh, he is the last word on all matters. He had the divine authority to endorse all Scripture or some. He universally affirmed all Scripture, in every part, as the divine Word of God. The crucial issue of the inspiration of the Old Testament is solved by Jesus Christ and his attitude toward it. We see Jesus viewing the Old Testament with total trust, considering it the Word of God. See Matthew 15:3, 6; 22:31-32; John 10:35; and Matthew 5:18.

If Jesus is who he claimed to be, God in human flesh, then his view of Scripture is of paramount importance. We see him constantly referring to it as sacred in his teachings and in discussions with the religious leaders of his day.

The conclusion is clear: since Jesus is God and authenticates the whole body and every portion of the Old Testament, we can conclude that it is the inspired Word of God.

CHAPTER 6
The Historical Reliability of the Old Testament

Is the Bible accurate in its description of persons, places, and events? That question is crucial. If the Bible is to be taken seriously, then the recording of historical events must be accurate. We cannot trust the theological observations of writers who cannot report historical events correctly.

The great biblical scholar F. F. Bruce echoed these thoughts:

> That Christianity has its roots in history is emphasized in the church's earliest creeds, which fix the supreme revelation of God at a particular point in time, when "Jesus Christ, his only Son our Lord . . . suffered under Pontius Pilate." This historical "once-for-all-ness" of Christianity, which distinguishes it from those religious and philosophical systems which are not specially related to any particular time, makes the reliability of the writings which purport to record this revelation a question of first-rate importance.[1]

In this chapter we will see that historical events recorded in the Old Testament are accurate as far as we can determine from present external evidence. (There are some events described in the Bible for which there is as yet no external

---

[1] F. F. Bruce, *The New Testament Documents: Are They Reliable?* (Downers Grove, Ill.: InterVarsity, 1960), p. 8.

historical evidence. Obviously the lack of evidence cannot be seen as a mark against the historical reliability of the Old Testament.)

The chronology of the history of ancient Israel is an issue that is hotly debated by archaeologists, historians, and others, and there is no consensus about these matters. We will review several possible chronologies in this section. But whatever view you follow, one thing is clear: The historical facts that the Bible mentions are totally reliable, and the model must be started by taking into account these facts rather than criticizing them from some outside position. The examples given in this chapter will confirm the accuracy of the Bible in the more or less generally accepted chronology.

We must emphasize that we do not believe that the Bible is the Word of God merely because it records history accurately. Correct historical reporting does not determine inspiration. One cannot have credible inspiration, however, with faulty historical records.

OLD TESTAMENT HISTORY

Biblical scholar John Bright correctly points out the Bible's own high view of history:

The genius of the Old Testament faith does not lie in its idea of God or in the elevation of its ethical teachings. Rather, it lies in its understanding of history, specifically of Israel's history, as the theatre of God's purposive activity. The Old Testament offers a theological interpretation of history. A concern with the meaning of history, and of specific events within history, is one of its most characteristic features. It records a real history, and it interprets every detail of that history in the light of Yahweh's sovereign purpose and righteous will. . . . The Old Testament consistently views Israel's history as one that is guided on to a destination by the word and will of her God.[2]

---

[2]John Bright, *The Authority of the Old Testament* (London: SCM, 1967), p. 130.

ARCHAEOLOGY AND OLD TESTAMENT TIMES

Approx. Date B.C.	Palestine/ Syria/Jordan	Also Called	Assyria/ Babylonia	Egypt
		I. PREHISTORIC		
–8000	Paleolithic	(Old) Stone Age		
8000–6000	Mesolithic	Middle Stone Age Natufian Tahunian/ Jerichoan		
6000–4000	Neolithic	Prepottery N. Pottery N. (5000–)	Ubaid	Prehistoric
4000–3200	Chalcolithic	Ghassulian (end)	Uruk	Tasian
3200–3000	Esdraelon		Proto-Literate	Badarian Naquada I–II
		II. BRONZE AGE		
3000–2800	Early Bronze (Age) I (= EB)	Early Canaanite (= EC)	Early Dynastic (= ED) I	Pre-Dynastic I
2800–2600	EB II		ED II	Archaic Period Dyn. I–III
2600–2300	EB III		ED III	Old Kingdom Dyn. III–IV
2300–2200	EB IV	EB IIIb	Sargonid	Dyn. V–VI
2200–1950	Intermediate Bronze (= IB)	EB-MB MB I/MCI	Ur III	First Intermediate Period
1950–1750	Middle Bronze (= MB) I	Middle Canaanite (= MC) IIa	Early Old Babylonian	Dyn. VII–XI Middle Kingdom (XII)
1750–1600	MB IIa	MB/MC IIb	Late Old Babylonian	Second Intermediate Dyn. XII–XVII
1600–1550	MB IIb	MB/MC IIc	Kassite	
1550–1400	Late Bronze (= LB)	Late Canaanite (= LC)	Middle Assyrian Middle Babylonian	New Kingdom (XVIII–)
1400–1300	LB IIa	LC IIa		
1300–1200	LB IIc	LC IIc		Dyn. XIX
		III. IRON AGE		
1200–1150	Iron (Age) Ia (= I)	(Early) Israelite Early Iron (= EI) I		
1150–1025	Ib			Dyn. XX Late Period
1025–950	Ic	EI II	Neo-Assyrian	Dyn. XXI
950–900	Id			Dyn. XXII (Libyan)
900–800	IIa	Middle Iron Middle Israelite (= MI) I Israelite II (970–840)		
800–700	IIb			Dyn. XXIII–XXV
700–600	IIc	MI II Israelite III (840–580)		Dyn. XXVI (Saite)
600–330	III	Late Iron Late Israelite (= LI) Israelite IV Persian	Neo-Babylonian (Chaldean)	Dyn. XXVII–
		IV. HELLENISTIC AGE		
330–165	Hellenistic I		Hellenistic	Hellenistic Egypt Dyn. XXVIII–XXX
165–63	Hellenistic II	Hellenistic-Herodian Maccabean		
63–A.D. 70	Hellenistic-Roman			Roman

R. K. Harrison, noted Old Testament scholar and historian, emphasized the important role of archaeology in affirming the historical reliability of the Old Testament:

Archaeology must not be regarded as the sole determining consideration in matters of historical criticism, since it, too, is beset with its own kind of problems. These include poor excavating techniques in earlier days, the varied interpretation of specific artifacts, and the difficulty of establishing an assured chronological framework into which events can be placed with confidence. Archaeology is in no sense an adequate "control" mechanism by which OT historic sequences stand or fall.

Nevertheless, archaeological discoveries have helped enormously in proving the historicity of certain OT events and personages, and in other areas have furnished an authentic social and cultural background against which many OT narratives can be set with assurance.[3]

Now we will briefly survey the Old Testament, showing some historical and archaeological evidence that gives further testimony to the reliability of biblical events. We will separate our survey into three major historical periods: the Middle Bronze Age (1950–1550 B.C.), the Late Bronze Age (1550–1200 B.C.), and the Iron Age (1200–330 B.C.).

THE MIDDLE BRONZE AGE
Old Testament scholar D. J. Wiseman shows how archaeology has helped confirm early biblical history from the Middle Bronze Age:

The Patriarchs fit best into the early Middle Bronze Age (MBA I), though their association with the Amorites or other folk-movements (including early Hapiru) known from contemporary texts cannot be proved. The Genesis narrative accords well with the archaeologically known occupation of the city-states that were then a dominant

---

[3] R. K. Harrison, B. K. Waltke, Donald Guthrie, and Gordon Fee, *Biblical Criticism: Historical, Literary and Textual* (Grand Rapids: Zondervan, 1978), pp. 6-7.

feature of Palestine. The occupation of Bethel, Shechem, Hebron (Kirjath-Arba), and the Dead Sea region of Sodom and Gomorrah is confirmed, as is that of the Negeb in southwest Palestine where flocks and herds (cf. Genesis 18:7; 20:1; 24:62) and grain crops (Genesis 26:12; 37:7) are traced in MBA I. There is valuable evidence of the verisimilitude [quality of appearing to be true] of the patriarchal personal and place names at this time. Thus, the name "Abram" occurs in a text from Dilbat (*Aba[m]rama*) and Aburahana (Abraham) and Zabilan (Zebulon) in Egyptian execration texts. . . . Other texts from these towns and from Alalah (from the eighteenth to the fifteenth century), Ur, Ras Shamra (fourteenth century), and Nuzi in Assyria (fifteenth century) throw considerable light on the patriarchal social customs. They show that it was usual for a childless couple to adopt an heir and then displace him at the birth of a real son (Genesis 15:4). According to her marriage contract, a barren woman was to provide her husband with a slave-girl to bear a son. Marriages were arranged for public purposes by the rulers of Ugarit and Qatna, as well as by Egyptian kings, and this may be reflected in the adventures of Sarah (Genesis 20) and Rebekah (Genesis 26). The special position of the first-born son (cf. Genesis 21:10ff.; 48:14ff.), the bridegroom "asking" for a daughter as bride, the use of betrothal and bride-gifts (Genesis 34:12), and the stipulation of marriage contracts that a man might take a third wife only if the first two were barren or take a second wife only if the first failed to give birth within seven years explain incidents in Genesis.[4]

Biblical archaeologist William F. Albright confirmed the historical and archaeological accuracy of the Old Testament during the patriarchal period:

> Until recently it was the fashion among biblical historians to treat the patriarchal sagas of Genesis as though they

---

[4] D. J. Wiseman and Edwin Yamauchi, *Archaeology and the Bible* (Grand Rapids: Zondervan), pp. 16-17.

were artificial creations of Israelite scribes of the Divided Monarchy or tales told by imaginative rhapsodists around Israelite campfires during the centuries following their occupation of the country. Eminent names among scholars can be cited for regarding every item of Genesis 11–50 as reflecting late invention, or at least retrojection of events and conditions under the Monarchy into the remote past, about which nothing was thought to have been really known to the writers of later days. . . .

Archaeological discoveries since 1925 have changed all this. Aside from a few diehards among older scholars, there is scarcely a single biblical historian who has not been impressed by the data supporting the historicity of patriarchal tradition.[5]

THE LATE BRONZE AGE

The Late Bronze Age deals with the period from 1550–1200 B.C. This is one area in which archaeology has been able to confirm the conquest of Canaan by the Israelites. The Bible records that Joshua conquered Canaan through a series of battles.

In the past many liberal scholars believed that the Israelites slowly and peacefully infiltrated the central hill country of Canaan. Those scholars rejected the biblical account. Paul Lapp gives the background of the situation.

The [Canaan] conquest provides another example of the search for connections between biblical and historical-archaeological material. This concerns an event for which there is a considerable amount of archaeological evidence, a great amount of detailed description in the biblical sources, and volumes of diverse opinions and hypotheses produced by modern scholars.[6]

Excavation in the cities of Bethel, Lachish, and Debir showed that the biblical account was correct. Canaan was taken through

---

[5] William F. Albright, *The Biblical Period from Abraham to Ezra* (New York: Harper and Row, 1960), pp. 1-2.

[6] Paul W. Lapp, *Biblical Archaeology and History* (New York: World, 1969), p. 107.

conquest; all of those sites revealed destruction around 1200 B.C. Lapp concludes:

> The archaeological evidence supports the view that the biblical traditions developed from an actual historical conquest under Joshua in the late thirteenth century B.C.[7]

THE IRON AGE

Since the Iron Age is so much closer to our time period, there is much more historical and archaeological evidence in support of the biblical events recorded of that time period (1200–330 B.C.). Below we have reproduced a summary of significant archaeological finds confirming biblical narratives:

> From this period onward, historical confirmation of the OT narratives is a much simpler matter, due to the comparative availability of extra-biblical evidence. The inscribed stele of Benhadad I, found in 1940 at a north Syrian site, has furnished general confirmation of the Syrian list in 1 Kings 15:18, without, however, identifying the Rezon who founded the Damascene dynasty or being specific about the number of Benhadads who ruled in Damascus. The discovery of the Moabite Stone in 1868 illustrated the vigor that Omri of Israel (c. 880–873 B.C.) displayed toward neighboring nations, and not least toward the Moabites. At this time Israel was referred to in Assyrian records at *Bit-Humri* (House of Omri). Omri's successors were known as *mar-Humri* or "offspring of Omri." "Ahab the Israelite" was mentioned in the Monolith Inscription of Shalmaneser III (c. 858–824 B.C.) as the leader of a powerful military group. . . .

The discovery of D. J. Wiseman in 1956 of four additional tablets of the Babylonian Chronicle in the archives of the British Museum provided the first extrabiblical confirmation of the capture of Jerusalem in 597 B.C., dating it precisely on the second of Adar (March 15-16). Besides mentioning the defeat of the Egyptian forces at

---

[7] Ibid., p. 111.

Carchemish in 605, the tablets preserved an account of a previously unrecorded battle between Egypt and Babylon in 601, in which both sides suffered heavy losses. This material thus confirms the OT tradition that Jerusalem fell to Babylon in 597 and again in 587.[8]

Clifford Wilson observes how archaeological discoveries have confirmed the biblical account of the Syrian invasion of Israel:

> It is interesting that in 1 Chronicles 5:26 we read that God stirred up the spirit of Tiglath-pileser, king of Assyria, but he is also referred to there by the name Pul. At first this seems to be a mistake; then we look again and notice that a singular verb is used in association with the two names. It turns out that Pullu was the throne name adopted by Tiglath-pileser when he became king of Babylon. He took this Babylonian name to avoid giving offense to the Babylonian people. The casual Bible reference is a remarkable piece of local color, and it is this sort of evidence that consistently reminds us that the Bible prophets and recorders lived against the backgrounds claimed for them. They confidently referred to kings and customs of the people with whom they and their leaders were in direct contact. . . .

Let's change contexts for a moment. Who would know the titles of army officers in World War II, or in the wars fought in Korea or Vietnam? Only those who had been in those conflicts or who had direct contact with those who had been there. The way these Bible writers confidently and consistently use the titles of the enemy is a clear pointer to the fact that they were writing against the backgrounds claimed for them by the Bible.[9]

SOME REVERSALS IN OLD TESTAMENT CRITICISM

Until this century with its archaeological discoveries, it was believed that Moses could not have written the first five books of the

---

[8] R. K. Harrison, et al., *Biblical Criticism*, pp. 14-15.

[9] Clifford Wilson, *Rocks, Relics, and Biblical Reliability* (Grand Rapids: Zondervan, 1977), pp. 88-90.

Old Testament because writing was said to be virtually unknown. The consensus was that Moses could not have written the first five books of the Old Testament because of the lack of the widespread use of writing or his lack of interest in recording Israel's history.

Modern discoveries, however, show that writing was in common use prior to the time of Moses. Moses did have the capacity to write the first five books. D. J. Wiseman observes:

Well before the end of the second millennium the pressures of trade and need for communication led to the widespread use of this simple form of writing (e.g., in marking personal objects; cf. stone inscriptions of Ahiram). Thus, by the time of the entry of the Hebrews into Canaan in the Late Bronze Age they would be confronted, if not already familiar, with at least five different forms of writing systems used for eight or more languages: (1) Egyptian hieroglyphs (Beth-shan, Chinnereth); (2) the Byblos syllabic script; (3) "Proto-Hebrew" (Lachish, Hazor); (4) Akkadian (Mesopotamian) cuneiform; and (5) the Ugaritic alphabetic script (found also at Beth-Shemesh).[10]

This is echoed by Old Testament authority Cyrus Gordon, who wrote:

The excavations at Ugarit have revealed a high material and literary culture in Canaan prior to the emergence of the Hebrews. The educational system was so advanced that dictionaries in four languages were compiled for the use of scribes, and the individual words were listed in their Ugaritic, Babylonian, Sumerian, and Hurrian equivalents. The beginnings of Israel are rooted in a highly cultural Canaan. . . . Canaan in the days of the Patriarchs was the hub of a great international culture.[11]

THE HITTITES

The Hittites, mentioned some fifty times in the Old Testament, were considered for a long time to be a biblically fabricated

---

[10]Wiseman and Yamauchi, *Archaeology*, p. 25.

[11] Cyrus Gordon, "Higher Critics and Forbidden Fruit," *Christianity Today*, 23 November 1959.

people. That is, the biblical references to the Hittites used to be regarded as historically worthless. John Elder comments on modern confirmation of the Hittites:

One of the striking confirmations of Bible history to come from the science of archaeology is the "recovery" of the Hittite peoples and their empires. Here is a people whose name appears again and again in the Old Testament, but who in secular history had been completely forgotten and whose very existence was considered to be extremely doubtful. . . . In Genesis 23:10, it is told that Abraham bought a parcel of land for a burying place from Ephron the Hittite. In Genesis 26:34, Esau takes a Hittite girl for a wife, to the great grief of his mother. In the Book of Exodus, the Hittites are frequently mentioned in the lists of people whose land the Hebrews set out to conquer. In Joshua 11:1-9, the Hittites join in the confederation of nations that try to resist Joshua's advance, only to be defeated by the waters of Merom. In Judges, intermarriage occurs between the Hebrews and the Hittites. In 1 Samuel 26, Hittites enroll in David's army, and during the reign of Solomon he makes slaves of the Hittite element in his kingdom and allows his people to take Hittite wives. But until the investigations of modern archaeologists, the Hittites remained a shadowy and undefined people.[12]

Archaeologist A. H. Sayce was the first scholar to identify the Hittite people from a nonbiblical source, the monuments. In 1876 he released his information and revolutionized critical theory concerning the Hittites.

Since Sayce's time in the last century, much information about the Hittites has been discovered, confirming again the historical accuracy of the Old Testament. Fred H. Wight concludes:

Now the Bible picture of this people fits in perfectly with what we know of the Hittite nation from the monuments. As an empire they never conquered the land of Canaan it-

[12]John Elder, *Prophets, Idols, and Diggers* (New York: Bobbs-Merrill, 1960), p. 75.

self, although Hittite local tribes did settle there at an early date. Nothing discovered by the excavators has in any way discredited the biblical account. Scripture accuracy has once more been proved by the archaeologists.[13]

SUMMARY AND CONCLUSION

After examining some of the historical and archaeological evidence in favor of the historical reliability of the Old Testament, we conclude with several observations:

1. The persons, places, and events listed during the different periods of Old Testament history match up well with the facts and evidence from history and archaeology.

2. Recent developments in textual criticism give examples of reversals by liberal critics who dismissed Old Testament passages for lack of evidence and then were forced by new evidence to accept them as historically reliable.

3. We first believe the Old Testament to be historically reliable because of the testimony of Jesus Christ, God in human flesh, whose claims were validated by his resurrection from the dead. Old Testament authority John Bright summarized it like this:

I am quite unable to get around the fact . . . that the Old Testament was authoritative Scripture for Jesus himself. Jesus knew no Scripture save the Old Testament, no God save its God; it was this God whom he addressed as "Father." . . . The very fact that the Old Testament was normative Scripture to Jesus, from which he understood both his God and (however we interpret his self-consciousness) himself, means that it must in some way be normative Scripture for us too.[14]

---

[13]Fred H. Wight, *Highlights of Archaeology in Bible Lands* (Chicago: Moody, 1955), pp. 94-95.

[14]Bright, *Old Testament*, p. 77.

CHAPTER 7
The Historical Reliability of the New Testament

The New Testament is primarily a record of the salvation work of Jesus Christ, the Son of God. It is not primarily a historical record. Yet when the New Testament addresses itself to historical issues, it is accurate and reliable.

Much of the older New Testament criticism did not have the vital testimony of archaeological evidence available today. Archaeologist William F. Albright observed:

> The form-critical school founded by M. Dibelius and R. Bultmann a generation before the discovery of the Dead Sea Scrolls has continued to flourish without the slightest regard for the Dead Sea Scrolls. In other words, all radical schools in New Testament criticism which have existed in the past or which exist today are prearchaeological, and are, therefore, since they were built *in der Luft* ["in the air"], quite antiquated today.[1]

This chapter reviews some of the important archaeological discoveries that confirm the New Testament view of the first-century world. We will first discuss the life and work of New Testament archaeologist-historian Sir William Ramsey and then review several important archaeological and historical finds that affirm the reliability of the New Testament.

---

[1] William F. Albright, *Archaeology*, in *The Teacher's Yoke*, ed. E. J. Vardaman (Waco, Tex.: Baylor University Press, 1964), p. 29.

SIR WILLIAM RAMSEY

Sir William Ramsey is an example of how an honest scholar of history can change his entire presuppositional perspective when faced by incontrovertible evidence from history and archaeology. Ramsey began his historical research toward the end of the nineteenth century. When he began his research he based it on the German (Tübingen) liberal/critical school of thought, which taught that the New Testament was not written in the first century and was not historically reliable. Instead, it was an invention of the second-century church. Although the New Testament book of Acts contained a variety of supposedly present-tense historical references, liberal critics rejected its historicity and declared it a fabrication.

As a young historian, Ramsey determined to develop an independent historical and geographical study of first-century Asia Minor. Assuming the unreliability of the book of Acts, he ignored its historical allusions in his studies. The amount of usable historical information concerning first-century Asia Minor, however, was too little for him to proceed very far with his work. That led him, almost in desperation, to consult the book of Acts. He discovered that it was true to first-century history. Here are Ramsey's own words chronicling his change of mind:

> I may fairly claim to have entered on this investigation without prejudice in favor of the conclusion which I shall now seek to justify to the reader. On the contrary, I began with a mind unfavorable to it, for the ingenuity and apparent completeness of the Tubingen theory had at one time quite convinced me. It did not then lie in my line of life to investigate the subject minutely, but more recently I found myself brought into contact with the Book of Acts as an authority for the topography, antiquities and society of Asia Minor. It was gradually borne upon me that in various details the narrative showed marvelous truth.[2]

---

[2]Sir William Ramsey, *St. Paul: The Traveler and Roman Citizen* (Grand Rapids: Baker, 1962), p. 36.

Ramsey's studies led him to conclude that "Luke's history is unsurpassed in respect of its trustworthiness,[3] and "Luke is a historian of the first rank; not merely are his statements of fact trustworthy . . . this author should be placed along with the very greatest of historians."[4]

From the experience of Ramsey we see that the New Testament writer Luke, author of a large portion of the New Testament (Luke and Acts) and an eyewitness of many events during the growth of the first-century church, was a careful historian.

The fact that many historical details, national boundaries, and government structures in Asia Minor were different in the second century from what they had been in the first makes it still more reasonable to conclude that the accurate author of Luke and Acts was a first-century author, not a second-century one.

Acts 14:1-6, for example, was in disrepute historically for many years. The passage implies that Lystra and Derbe were in Lycaonia but Iconium was not. Later Roman writers (such as Cicero) contradicted the passage, asserting that Iconium was in Lycaonia. For years this was used by the critical school to show the historical unreliability of Acts.

In 1910, however, Sir William Ramsey discovered a first-century inscription declaring that the first-century Iconium was under the authority of Phrygia, not Lycaonia. It was only in the second century that territorial boundaries changed and Iconium came under Lycaonian rule. A first-century writer would be aware of this historical detail; a second-century writer could have been ignorant of it. Ramsey's discovery was another confirmation of the historical reliability of the New Testament.

THE CENSUS IN THE GOSPEL OF LUKE

For years New Testament critics denied the historical reliability of the account about the Roman census recorded in Luke 2. Critics saw this as an excuse invented for Mary and Joseph to be in Bethlehem at the birth of Jesus. They believed that second-

---

[3]Ibid., p. 81.

[4]Sir William Ramsey, *The Bearing of Recent Discoveries on the Trustworthiness of the New Testament* (Grand Rapids: Baker, 1953), p. 222.

century New Testament writers had to fabricate a fulfillment to the Old Testament prophecy that the Messiah was to be born in Bethlehem. Luke wrote:

Now it came about in those days that a decree went out from Caesar Augustus, that a census be taken of all the inhabited earth. This was the first census taken while Quirinius was governor of Syria. And all were proceeding to register for the census, everyone to his own city. And Joseph also went up from Galilee, from the city of Nazareth, to Judea, to the city of David, which is called Bethlehem, because he was of the house and family of David; in order to register, along with Mary, who was engaged to him, and was with child. (Luke 2:1-5)

For many years there was no evidence of a census at that time. Jesus was born sometime before 4 B.C. A census was taken under Quirinius in A.D. 6 or 7, but there was no evidence for an earlier one that could correspond with the date of Jesus' birth. Many critics assumed that this was another historical error of some second-century writer who called himself Luke and claimed to have "checked his facts." However, what was eventually discovered revealed Luke's integrity and reflected poorly on the critics. Biblical scholar Gleason L. Archer chronicles the problem and its solution:

Luke 2:1 tells of a decree from Caesar Augustus to have the whole "world" (*oikoumene* actually means all the world under the authority of Rome) enrolled in a census report for taxation purposes. Verse 2 specifies which census taking was involved at the time Joseph and Mary went down to Bethlehem, to fill out the census forms as descendants of the Bethlehemite family of King David. This was the first census undertaken by Quirinius (or "Cyrenius") as governor (or at least as acting governor) of Syria. Josephus mentions no census in the reign of Herod the Great (who died in 4 B.C.) but he does mention one taken by "Cyrenius" (*Antiquities* 17.13.5) soon after Herod Archelaus was deposed in A.D. 6: "Cyrenius, one that had been consul, was sent by Caesar to take account of people's effects in Syria, and to sell the house of Archelaus." (Apparently the palace of the deposed king was to be sold and the proceeds turned over to the Roman government.)

If Luke dates the census in 8 or 7 B.C., and if Josephus dates it in A.D. 6 or 7, there appears to be a discrepancy of about fourteen years. Also, since Saturninus (according to Tertullian in *Contra Marcion* 4:19) was legate of Syria from 9 B.C. to 6 B.C., and Quintilius Varus was legate from 7 B.C. to A.D. 4 (note the one-year overlap in these two terms!), there is doubt as to whether Quirinius was ever governor of Syria at all.

By way of solution, let it be noted first of all that Luke says this was a "first" enrollment that took place under Quirinius (*haute apographe prote egeneto*). A "first" surely implies a *second* one sometime later. Luke was therefore well aware of that second census, taken by Quirinius again in A.D. 7, which Josephus alludes to in the passage cited above. We know this because Luke (who lived much closer to the time than Josephus did) also quotes Gamaliel as alluding to the insurrection of Judas of Galilee "in the days of the census taking" (Acts 5:27). The Romans tended to conduct a census every fourteen years, and so this comes out right for a first census in 7 B.C. and a second in A.D. 7.[5]

THE BURIAL PLACE OF JESUS CHRIST

Another detail of New Testament history that has been confirmed concerns the burial place of Jesus Christ. Contemporary archaeologist and historian Edwin Yamauchi reports:

The traditional site of Calvary and the associate tomb of Christ was desecrated by Hadrian in A.D. 135. In the fourth century, Helena, the mother of Constantine, was led to the site, where she then built the church of the Holy Sepulcher. Excavations in and around the church have helped demonstrate that it lay outside the wall in Jesus' day. Shafts dug in the church show that the area was used as a quarry and

---

[5]Gleason L. Archer, Jr., *An Encylopedia of Bible Difficulties* (Grand Rapids: Zondervan, 1981), pp. 365-366.

was therefore extramural, a conclusion also supported by Kenyon's excavations in the adjoining Muristan area. Thus there is no reason to doubt the general authenticity of the site. In the course of repairs since 1954 remains of the original Constantinian structure have been exposed. In 1975 M. Broshi found near St. Helena's chapel in the church a red and black picture of a Roman sailing ship and a Latin phrase *Domine iuimus*, "Lord, we went" (cf. Ps. 122:1). These words and the drawing were placed there by a pilgrim A.D. 330.

As for the actual tomb of Christ, quarrying operations may have obliterated the grave. A bench *arcosolium* (flat surface under a recessed arch) must have been used for Jesus. But early Christian pilgrims seem to have seen a trough *arcololium* (rock-cut sarcophagus); this raises the question of whether they saw the actual tomb.

In 1842 Otto Thenius, a German pastor, was attracted to a hill 150 yards north of the present walled city because of two cavities that give it a skull-like appearance. The hill was popularized among Protestants as an alternative site for Calvary by General Gordon in 1883. A seventeenth-century sketch of the hill demonstrates, however, that the cavities were not yet present then. The nearby "Garden Tomb" likewise has no claim to be the authentic tomb of Christ.[6]

SUMMARY AND CONCLUSION

After reviewing some highlights of the overwhelming evidence supporting the historical reliability of the New Testament, we can come to the following conclusions:

1. Archaeological and historical evidence concerning the historical events, places, names, and concepts mentioned in the New Testament conclusively affirms the basic historical reliability of the text. In addition, the nature of much of the evidence supports the biblical assertion that the New Testament writers

---

[6] D. J. Wiseman and Edwin Yamauchi, *Archaeology and the Bible* (Grand Rapids: Zondervan), pp. 84-86.

wrote during the first century and were either eyewitnesses of the events they described, or had carefully checked the facts and evidence with eyewitnesses. Luke reminds us of this concern for historical accuracy.

2. Not only are the New Testament authors accurate in their general historical observations, they are also accurate and meticulous in their recording of details.

3. Such concern for accuracy in general and in particular, which is exhibited by the New Testament writers for their historical accounts, is commensurate with a fidelity for truth in matters of teachings, moral, and spiritually significant issues. While historical accuracy does not guarantee such fidelity, it is a correlative necessity that one who claims to bring truth should tell the truth in all matters with which he or she deals. We should expect no less than historical accuracy from those who wrote the New Testament and claimed to represent the one who is the Way, the Truth, and the Life (John 14:6).

4. If we accept the promise of Jesus Christ to send the Holy Spirit as our guide, teacher, and comforter, then we should not be surprised that the Holy Spirit guided the disciples and New Testament writers. "But the Helper, the Holy Spirit, whom the Father will send in My name, He will teach you all things, and bring to your remembrance all that I said to you" (John 14:26).

We can trust the New Testament. Such accuracy is consistent with the inspiration and fidelity to truth claimed by the writers of the New Testament.

CHAPTER 8

The Contents of the Old Testament

We have shown that there are definite reasons to believe that the Bible is more than an accurate historical document. It is the Word of God. The contents of the Bible are therefore of utmost importance. Chapters 8 and 9 will give a short summary of each of the books of the Bible in order to familiarize readers with the contents as well as give the historical flow of the biblical narration.

The following chart lists the books of the Old Testament in the order found in the English Bible. The human authorship of some books is uncertain; the dates given are approximate.

Book	Author	Approximate Date of Composition (B.C.)
Genesis	Moses	1440
Exodus	Moses	1440
Leviticus	Moses	1440
Numbers	Moses	1410
Deuteronomy	Moses	1410
Joshua	Joshua	1350
Judges	Unknown—possibly Samuel	1050
Ruth	Unknown—possibly Samuel	1050
1 and 2 Samuel	Compiled	900
1 and 2 Kings	Compiled	550
1 and 2 Chronicles	Compiled	450
Ezra	Ezra	450
Nehemiah	Nehemiah	450
Esther	Unknown—possibly Mordecai	475
Job	Unknown—possibly Moses	1450
Psalms	David and others	550
Proverbs	Solomon and others	950

Ecclesiastes	Solomon	950
Song of Solomon	Solomon	950
Isaiah	Isaiah	675
Jeremiah	Jeremiah	580
Lamentations	Jeremiah	586
Ezekiel	Ezekiel	570
Daniel	Daniel	530
Hosea	Hosea	725
Joel	Joel	800
Amos	Amos	755
Obadiah	Obadiah	580
Jonah	Jonah	760
Micah	Micah	725
Nahum	Nahum	650
Habakkuk	Habakkuk	606
Zephaniah	Zephaniah	620
Haggai	Haggai	520
Zechariah	Zechariah	475
Malachi	Malachi	435

GENESIS

The book of Genesis is one of the most important books in the Bible. Genesis means *beginning* and this is the record of beginnings.

CREATION

Genesis introduces an infinite and personal God who created all things: "In the beginning God created the heavens and the earth" (1:1). The crown of God's creation was man and woman, whom God made in his own image (1:26-27).

THE FALL

Genesis describes how humanity failed in its responsibility, rebelled against God, and became totally dependent on his mercy (3). The rebellion that occurred placed a separation between God and humankind. God therefore promised that a Savior would someday be sent to bring mankind back into a perfect relationship with God. Until that Savior would come along, God instituted a sacrificial system that would be a symbol of what Jesus Christ would later do to enable human beings to approach God. Jesus Christ eventually would appear as Savior, providing himself as the ultimate sacrifice for sin.

THE FLOOD

After the human fall into sin occurred, people continued to do evil. God decided to destroy all the earth's inhabitants, except faithful Noah and his family, by a great flood (6–9). After the flood, there was a new beginning; but humanity continued to rebel, symbolized by the forbidden building of the tower of Babel (11). God spread humankind throughout the earth by confounding the languages people spoke.

THE ABRAHAMIC COVENANT

After the tower of Babel incident, God established a covenant with one man named Abraham, whom he called out from an idolatrous culture for the purpose of establishing a great and special nation (12:1-3). God also promised Abraham a land that would belong forever to his descendants (12–25). The rest of the book of Genesis deals with the descendants of Abraham: Isaac (21–27), Jacob (25–50) and Jacob's twelve sons, from whom came the twelve tribes of Israel. The book of Genesis closes with Jacob and his twelve sons in the land of Egypt, waiting for the fulfillment of God's promises.

EXODUS

The book of Exodus records how Jacob's descendants began to multiply, thus fulfilling God's promise that a great nation would descend from Abraham. A pharaoh arose in Egypt who was threatened by the great number of the people of Israel and made slaves of them.

DELIVERANCE

The people cried out to God to deliver them from this Egyptian bondage. God heard their cry and raised up Moses as their deliverer. The pharaoh did not want to let the people leave Egypt to go to the promised land, so God brought ten plagues upon Egypt (7–12). The last plague finally resulted in Pharaoh's allowing the Israelites' *exodus*, or going out, from Egypt. Through that plague, Israel was reminded of the need for blood to be shed as the basis of forgiveness of sin (12). In instituting the *Passover*, God passed over and did not punish families in houses that had blood placed on the doorposts. The houses that did not have blood on the doorposts lost their firstborn sons through God's judgment. After the children of Israel left Egypt, they were miraculously delivered by God from the pursuing Egyptian army at the Red Sea (14).

GIVING OF THE LAW

Under God's protection they arrived at Mount Sinai (13–19), where, through Moses, God gave them the law, including the Ten Commandments (20). The law would be the perfect standard of God, teaching the people that they could not measure up to what God required of them on their own and demonstrating their need for God's mercy and forgiveness. Exodus also records the laws of social and religious life that God's people were to observe (20–24).

THE TABERNACLE

God then gave Moses the design of a tent (*tabernacle*) which he was to build. The tabernacle would be a holy place, representing God's dwelling in the midst of his special people. Through the priest the people could approach God with their sacrifices (25–31). The tabernacle and its furnishing symbolized the person and work of the Messiah who was to come. The need for God's grace became evident during this time when the people rebelled; they designed and worshiped a golden calf. Moses interceded with God on their behalf, and most of them were saved from God's just wrath (32–33). The tabernacle was then built, solemnly dedicated, and visibly filled with the glory of God (40).

LEVITICUS

The book of Leviticus records the instructions God gave Moses at the door of his tent on Mount Sinai. God first gave instruction about five offerings the people were to present to God: the burnt offering, the grain offering, the peace offering, the sin offering, and the trespass offering (1–7). Then Aaron and his sons were consecrated as the priests who would present these offerings (8–10).

LAWS AND REGULATIONS

After that, God gave further laws dealing with purity (11–22). These laws tell what food was to be eaten and what was not, along with regulations for a pure nation, pure marriages, pure morals, and pure priests. Following this section are the laws of the feasts (23–25). Israel's seven high holy days are explained. The book closes with special laws on blessings and cursing, taking vows, and giving of tithes (26–27).

NUMBERS

The book of Numbers deals with the journeys of the children of Israel on their way to the promised land. A census of the people was taken, and the tribes were arranged for traveling, with particular attention being given to the priests (1–4). Laws were given for the purity of the camp (5–6) and for the offerings for worship (7–8). The remembrance of the Passover was celebrated for the first time since the Israelites left Egypt, and God supernaturally guided his people with a cloud by day and a pillar of fire by night (9). Special signals were given to the people for marching and assembling (10).

COMPLAINTS AND UNBELIEF
As the people began their journey, they continually complained against God (10–12). Reaching the borders of the promised land, twelve spies were sent out; all except Joshua and Caleb brought back a negative report, which caused the people to complain even more. God punished this unbelief by sending them to wander aimlessly forty years through the wilderness, with everyone over twenty years of age, except Joshua and Caleb, dying in the desert (13–14). During this period Moses and Aaron also sinned and were forbidden by God to enter the promised land.

YEARS OF WANDERING
The remainder of the book chronicles the events of the period of wandering, including the rebellion of Korah (16) and the plague of serpents sent upon the camp for unbelief (21). Israel, with God's help, conquered the Midianites while coming again to the borders of the promised land. The tribes of Reuben, Gad, and half the tribe of Manasseh preferred to settle on the east side of the Jordan River rather than to enter the promised land (32). The book closes with a review of the years of wandering and precautionary instructions to the people about the conquest and division of the promised land (33–36).

DEUTERONOMY

Deuteronomy is known as the Second Law. It contains the final words of Moses, probably delivered during the last week of his life. It is not merely a repetition of the Law, but rather an application of it as the people were about to possess the Land of Promise. Moses began by reviewing the history of the forty years of wandering in the wilderness since leaving Egypt (1-4).

LAWS FOR THE NEW LAND

In Deuteronomy, Moses repeated and elaborated on the Ten Commandments, preparing the people for obeying them in the new land (4–11). He continued with the repetition of other laws that would have special application in the promised land: laws about idolatry, the eating of meat, the sabbatical year, the feasts, and the administration of justice (12–18). There is also a prophecy about a special prophet who would come (18). Laws were given dealing with criminals, the military, and civil responsibility. Moses concluded his discourse with directions about the thank offering of the "first fruits" to the Lord (26). He gave instructions on how the Law was to be confirmed upon entering the land (27–30).

PROPHECIES

This last discourse is one of the most important sections in Scripture: it prophesies the future course of the nation of Israel. Through Moses, God spoke of the blessing his people would receive as long as they remained obedient. He warned of judgments to come if they disobeyed, God promised that disobedience would cause removal from their land and a scattering of the people among the nations. However, faithful to his promises, God would bring a remnant back to the land. This prophecy has been fulfilled twice in Israel's history. The first removal was completed in 586 B.C., with a remnant returning in 536 B.C. The second time the people were scattered was in A.D. 70 with the remnant returning as a nation almost nineteen hundred years later, in May 1948. History has borne out the fact that God is true to his Word. The remainder of Deuteronomy (31–33) records the appointing of Joshua as Moses' successor, a song, and a prophetic blessing given by Moses to the nation, mentioning each tribe. The final chapter (34) records Moses' death.

JOSHUA

Deuteronomy closes with the Israelites about to enter the promised land. The book of Joshua describes how the Israelites entered Canaan under Moses' successor Joshua and began to conquer it. Joshua led the children of Israel across the Jordan River after sending out spies to explore the land. The crossing of the Jordan occurred in a miraculous fashion, with flood waters rolling back to let the people, led by those carrying the ark of the covenant, cross to the other side. Two monuments were erected (one in the riverbed and another right beside it) to commemorate this event. The males were circumcised, something neglected during the wilderness wanderings, and the first Passover in the promised land was celebrated.

OCCUPYING THE NEW LAND

The city of Jericho was the first to be conquered. The next city to be taken was Ai, but not until after the Israelites suffered a resounding defeat because of the sin of Achan (6–8).

Then followed the solemn confirmation of the law in accordance with the instructions given by Moses. The ungodly inhabitants living in the south and north were destroyed; only the people of Gibeon escaped, because of a clever trick they pulled on the Israelites (8–12). The land was then divided among the remaining nine and a half tribes, with faithful Caleb given a special portion (13–19). Within the land itself, and also east of the Jordan River, a number of cities were designated "Cities of Refuge," designed to give refuge to anyone who unintentionally committed manslaughter. Forty-eight cities were set aside for the priestly class, the Levites (20–21). The two and a half tribes erected an altar across the Jordan against God's designation of the Jordan as the boundary of the promised land (22).

JOSHUA'S CHARGE

Joshua then addressed the people and charged them to keep God's law. The covenant was renewed. The book closes with the death of Joshua.

JUDGES

The book of Judges covers a three-hundred-year period between the death of Joshua and the institution of the monarchy in Israel. This was one of the darkest periods in Israel's history. During this time the people were ruled by judges, or magistrates, who not only administered justice, but also delivered Israel from its enemies. A cycle that happened seven times in the book of Judges went like this: the people had a good relationship with God, then fell into idolatry. Consequently, they were conquered by another people, which made them cry out to God for help. God heard their cry and sent a judge to deliver them and restore them to fellowship. Then the cycle began again.

INCOMPLETE CONQUEST
The book begins with the angel of the Lord coming from Gilgal to Bochim to rebuke the people for not driving the enemies completely out of the land. The conquest of the land was incomplete—one of Israel's most troublesome enemies, the Philistines, were allowed by the Israelites to live within the borders of the land in violation of the direct command of God. Consequently there was a need for a judge.

LED BY JUDGES
The judges for the most part were insignificant people, not known for their greatness. One of the most courageous was a woman named Deborah (4–5). Other judges included Gideon, who defeated a great company of Midianites with only three hundred men (6–8); Jephthah, who made a rash vow (11–12); and Samson, who completely wasted the powers given him by God (13–16).

SPIRITUAL CHAOS
The last part of the book (17–21) describes the introduction of idolatry into the tribe of Dan and a horrible deed done to the tribe of Benjamin. All these were because of the Israelites' failure to obey the commandments of God and because of the lack of strong leadership during this period. The last verse of the book sums up the era: "In those days there was no king in Israel; everyone did what was right in his own eyes" (21:25).

RUTH
The book of Ruth presents a lovely episode that occurred during the dark reign of the judges. Ruth, a Moabitess, married an

Israelite man, who later died. Ruth decided to follow her mother-in-law, Naomi, back to the promised land, where she learned to know and serve the true God. She then fell in love and married Boaz, a relative of her deceased husband. One of their children was the grandfather of King David, making Ruth one of the ancestors of Jesus Christ of Nazareth, the promised Messiah.

GRACE OF GOD
The book not only gives us certain links in the ancestry of David and Jesus; it is also a wonderful demonstration of God's grace reaching down to a Gentile (non-Jewish) woman, who, after learning about the true God, became a spiritual Jew and a part of the Messiah's human ancestry.

FIRST SAMUEL

First Samuel follows chronologically after the book of Judges. It opens by describing Eli, the last of the judges, and the birth of Samuel the prophet. The continual sin of Israel made it necessary for God to call Samuel, the first of the great prophets. The book tells of the circumstances surrounding the birth of Samuel and how, as a young child, he was dedicated to the Lord.

The book describes the ungodly sons of Eli and their sins against God, which led to the capture of the ark of the covenant by the raiding Philistines (1–6). The Lord caused the Philistines to bring back the ark (7), and Samuel, the man of God, ruled the people.

THE FIRST KING
The people, however, were not satisfied and rebelliously asked the Lord for a king. God gave them a king named Saul, according to their desire (8–12). Saul achieved victories over his enemies, but in his own strength, not the Lord's, and was a constant problem to the Lord (13–15).

DAVID CHOSEN
God then commissioned Samuel to anoint "a man after his own heart" to be king. That man was David. That development led to jealousy on the part of Saul, who repeatedly tried to kill David. David was forced to flee and to hide out as a fugitive as long as

Saul was alive (19–30). Saul eventually died in a battle with the Philistines, opening the way for David, the divinely chosen king, to reign in Israel. The first book of Samuel closes with Saul's death.

SECOND SAMUEL

Second Samuel relates the history of the reign of King David. After Saul's death, David was proclaimed king over the tribe of Judah in the city of Hebron (1–2). One of the generals of the deceased king placed one of Saul's sons on the throne of all Israel. Although David attempted to achieve a peaceful settlement with that son, his efforts failed because of the plots of others.

DAVID'S REIGN

Finally, David ascended to the throne as king over all the Israelite people. He made Jerusalem his residence and brought the ark of the covenant there. David wanted to build a temple in Jerusalem to the Lord, but because he was a warrior and not a man of peace, God would not permit him to do that (5–7). This job was to be accomplished by David's son Solomon. During his reign, David defeated his enemies and established Israel as a mighty nation (8–10).

DAVID'S SIN

Yet he fell into the sins of adultery and murder (11–12), for which God punished him severely: his family was torn with strife and feuding, his illegitimate child by Bathsheba died, and his eldest son Amnon was murdered by his brother Absalom (13). David banished Absalom from his kingdom, but Absalom led an insurrection and proclaimed himself king, forcing David again to flee. David amassed an army and retook his kingdom, but his son Absalom died in the battle. The death of Absalom broke David's heart. He had truly loved his wayward son. David put down another uprising by a man named Sheba and settled an old feud between himself and the house of Saul (20–21). The book concludes with another failure of David, his prideful numbering of the people of Israel, which resulted in a plague brought upon them as God's judgment (24).

FIRST KINGS

The book of Kings, divided into 1 and 2 Kings in the English Bible, continues the story that was started in 2 Samuel. The two books describe the monarchy from the death of David to its eventual fall. First Kings begins with the last days in the life of David, now an old man.

SOLOMON'S REIGN

After his death the kingdom went to his son Solomon, but not without an attempt by some people to make David's son Adonijah the king. Solomon followed his father's advice and made peace with various enemies, something his father had failed to do. God promised to grant Solomon any request, and Solomon chose to ask not for riches or fame, but rather for wisdom. God gave Solomon wisdom, but he also added riches, with which Solomon built a permanent temple to the Lord (5–8). God allowed Solomon's fame to increase, which caused the Queen of Sheba to come and admire his splendor and wisdom. Regrettably, Solomon did not obey God fully; he took many pagan wives, which led to his downfall. These women brought along their idols, and Solomon began to worship them. Therefore God removed the kingdom from him (11).

KINGDOM DIVIDED

Solomon was succeeded by his son Rehoboam, under whom the kingdom was divided into two parts. Rehoboam reigned over two tribes, the southern kingdom of Judah (the tribes of Judah and Benjamin), while the ten northern tribes became subject to the reign of Jeroboam. First and 2 Kings deal mainly with the history of the northern kingdom of Israel; the two books of Chronicles are concerned with the history of Judah.

GODLESS KINGS OF ISRAEL; ELIJAH'S PROPHECIES

First Kings centers on the dynasty of the godless kings Jeroboam (11–14) and Omri and Ahab (16–22). The people of the northern kingdom became deeply involved in idolatry and immorality, which led God to send the prophet Elijah to demonstrate in a miraculous way that the God of Israel was greater than the idols the people were worshiping (18). The many confrontations of Elijah with the evil king Ahab constitute the remainder of 2 Kings, with Ahab meeting his death in battle (22).

SECOND KINGS

Second Kings continues the account of the inglorious history of the northern kingdom. It begins by describing Elijah's ascension into heaven and his succession by the prophet Elisha. Elijah and Elisha were sent to bring the idolatrous northern kingdom back to God. Although they worked many miracles, the northern kingdom, as recorded in 2 Kings, included nine dynasties (some of only one king).

COLLAPSE OF ISRAEL

Each new dynasty ascended to power by the murder of the previous king. For example, Ahab's house was destroyed by Jehu, who also incurred the wrath of the Lord because of his sins (9–15). Interspersed is information about the kings of the southern kingdom (1, 3, 8, 11–12, 14, 16, 18–25). After the rapid succession of their kings, the northern kingdom came to an unceremonious end at the hand of the Assyrians. Many of the people were taken in exile to Assyria, and certain Assyrians were brought to Palestine to live. The Assyrians in Palestine intermarried with the Israelites who were left behind; these became the Samaritans (17).

COLLAPSE OF JUDAH

The remainder of 2 Kings deals with the battles of the kingdom of Judah, first against the Assyrians (18–19) and then after the great revival under King Josiah, against King Nebuchadnezzar of Babylon (22–24). Jerusalem was eventually captured, and the city and magnificent temple were destroyed. The majority of the inhabitants of Judah (the Jews) went into exile in Babylon. Second Kings closes with the murder of Gedaliah, who had been appointed governor of those still living in Palestine, and with the elevation in Babylon of Jehoiachin, the former king of Judah.

FIRST CHRONICLES

The books of Chronicles, like Samuel and Kings, are also divided into two books in our English Bible. First Chronicles begins by listing Israel's most important genealogies, going all the way back to Adam. It goes on to describe the history of King David and his descendants ruling in Jerusalem.

GOD'S VIEW

Chronicles, as opposed to Kings, gives God's view of history, showing that this period was not one entirely of rebellion but of many positive aspects. Consequently, very little is said about the northern kingdom of Israel, or the sins of David, Solomon, and the other kings. The things revealed point to the positive developments during this period. First Chronicles goes into detail about how the ark of the covenant was brought to Jerusalem (13–16), about the valiant deeds of David's mighty men (11–12, 18–20), and about the preparations made by David for building the temple (17, 21–29).

Thus, the book centers around God's work in Judah and Israel, represented by the kings in the line of David who obeyed the Lord's commandments.

SECOND CHRONICLES

Second Chronicles follows the pattern of 1 Chronicles, outlining the history of the kings of the house of David from Solomon to the exile. Emphasis is placed on how Solomon built the temple (2–8) rather than on the personal aspects of his life as described in 1 Kings.

GODLY KINGS

After Solomon, the emphasis is on the kings who obeyed the Lord and promoted worship of him in the land. They include: Asa (14–16); Jehoshaphat (17–21); the reformation under the priest Jehoiada in the time of King Joash (22–24); Amaziah (25); the revival under Hezekiah (29–32); and the revival under Josiah (34–35). The sins of Judah, which led to the fall of Jerusalem and the Babylonian captivity, are mentioned only briefly. The book concludes with a proclamation by Cyrus ending the exile and the subsequent return of some of the Jewish people to Judah (36).

EZRA

Ezra begins with the words with which 2 Chronicles ends, the proclamation of King Cyrus that ended the exile. Ezra gives details about the religious and political restoration of the Jewish nation after the exile in Babylon. The first of the exiles returned under the leadership of Joshua and Zerubbabel (3). They courageously rebuilt the altar in Jerusalem, reintroduced the sacrifices, and celebrated the Feast of Tabernacles.

REBUILDING THE TEMPLE
They began rebuilding the temple even though there was opposition from their enemies. The work, in fact, had to be interrupted several times for fairly long periods (3–5). During that time, the prophets Haggai and Zechariah encouraged the people to return to work on the temple. When the work was completed, the new temple was dedicated and the Passover was celebrated (6).

INFLUENCE OF EZRA
Years later another group of exiles arrived in the land under the leadership of the scribe Ezra (7–8). Ezra called the people to follow the law of Moses. The people heeded the Word of God, confessed their sin, and were restored to fellowship (10). The book of Ezra closes by describing how the people abandoned their ungodly practices.

NEHEMIAH

Nehemiah takes up the account where Ezra left off. Nehemiah, a cupbearer of King Artaxerxes of Persia, longed for the rebuilding of Jerusalem, its walls, and the altar and temple. The king gave his permission; and Nehemiah, despite intense opposition from the Samaritans, saw that this difficult work was carried out (1–7).

RENEWAL
The account reveals the faithfulness and trust that Nehemiah placed in God and the eventual reformation of the people under both Ezra and Nehemiah. Ezra publicly read the law to the people, the Feast of Tabernacles was observed, and the covenant with God was renewed (8–10). The book lists the residents of Jerusalem, the priests and Levites, and describes the dedication of the city walls (11–12).

REFORMATION
After a twelve-year absence Nehemiah returned to the land and instituted reforms. The people had strayed from the commandments of the

92

law. The book closes with Nehemiah's account of the reforms he made among the people (13).

ESTHER

The story of Esther is a story of the providence of God. God's people were in a strange land and were no longer visibly his people. Yet God protected them. This book is characterized by the total omission of God's name, but his care is evident. God's providence brought a young Jewish woman named Esther to the Persian court, where as the queen of Persia she was presented with an opportunity to save her people from destruction.

JEWS SAVED

A plot to destroy the Jews was made by an evil man named Haman, who was eventually hanged when his plot backfired. The Jews were allowed to avenge their enemies, and this victory was celebrated with the establishment of the Feast of Purim to be observed in commemoration of their being saved from total destruction.

JOB

The book of Job has been called a literary masterpiece. The exact time of the events is uncertain, but it probably took place around the time of Abraham, some two thousand years before Christ.

JOB'S LOSS

The account concerns a rich, God-fearing man named Job, who with God's permission was tested by Satan. Job lost everything he possessed, including his health, and he wished himself dead.

Three of his friends visited him and attempted to answer the profound question, Why do the righteous suffer? Although the book of Job never directly answers that question, it gives insight into the providence of God, who allows suffering in order to instruct his people. Only Job's young friend Elihu grasped something of this truth (32–37).

RESTORATION

But it was finally God himself who answered Job (38–41). God's answer was, in effect, that if Job and his friends could not tell the methods God had used to create the physical universe, they had no right to assume that he was unjust to allow a part of that creation to suffer. Job then humbled himself for judging God for the events that had transpired, and God restored to Job much more than he had lost. Although the book of Job is very old, the universal problem it deals with faces people in all ages, making Job's story ever relevant.

PSALMS

The book of Psalms is a collection of 150 songs, prayers, and wisdom. In the Psalms the full range of human emotions, such as pain, joy, fear, hope, and trust, are expressed to God. This book is helpful to believers of all ages. The Psalms can be divided into five sections.

In the first section (1–41) a faithful and righteous remnant of men and women put their hope and trust in the Messiah—described variously as the Son of God (2), the Son of Man (8), the one who would be resurrected from the dead (16), the suffering and glorified Servant (22) and the true sacrifice (40).

SUFFERING
The next section (42–72) deals with the suffering of the faithful and of the Messiah (69). It also shows the Messiah's final glorification and reign (72).

HISTORY
The third section (73–89) reflects the history from the beginning of the twelve tribes of Israel.

MESSIAH'S REIGN
The fourth section (90–106) deals with the reign of the Lord that would be established by the Messiah. This section also points to the ultimate salvation of God's people in accordance with the promises he made to the patriarchs (105–106).

RESTORATION
The fifth section (107–150) gives more details about the Messiah and the restoration of God's people. The ascent to Jerusalem is covered in the Songs of Ascent (120–134), and the book closes with magnificent anthems of praise to the Lord God.

PROVERBS

The book of Proverbs is a collection of short wise sayings on a variety of subjects dealing with human experience. They emphasize external religious life, teaching individuals how to live and overcome daily temptation. The Proverbs express a belief in God who is ruling over the universe; they seek to make the religion he has revealed become the controlling motive in everyday life and conduct.

ECCLESIASTES

The book of Ecclesiastes is the attempt of a wise man (King Solomon) to find the meaning of life and true happiness *apart* from divine revelation. He has a limited perspective, and consequently he sees everything as senseless and hopeless. This pessimistic book shows the futility of trying to live one's life apart from God. No matter how wise a person may be, he or she will not find lasting meaning apart from divine revelation. Wisdom without God is foolishness. Only God gives meaning to life.

THE SONG OF SOLOMON

The Song of Solomon is a collection of beautiful love songs from King Solomon, the bridegroom-shepherd, and his Shulammite bride. The book is more than a collection of love songs, however. It can also be seen as typifying the love between God and his people. Thus, spiritual truths can be gained from reading and applying its insights to one's own life.

ISAIAH

The book of Isaiah has a wide scope. Isaiah prophesied from around 720 to 675 B.C.

WARNINGS, AND PROMISES OF THE MESSIAH

Isaiah began by warning the people of the fall of Judah and Jeru- salem and the coming judgments. Yet there is also a promise of restoration under the Messiah (1–4). Isaiah then records a sevenfold "woe" against the people, comparing them to a vineyard that had disappointed God. Isaiah also proclaims his own woe when he realizes his own unholiness (5–6). Next comes the prophecy about the virgin birth of the coming Messiah. He would be the hope of those who were faithful to God. Though judgment was imminent, the Messiah would someday establish his kingdom (7–9). Isaiah then talks about the previous warnings the nation had received and about their greatest threat, the Assyrians. The Messiah would conquer their enemies and establish his glorious kingdom of peace (9–12).

EXILE AND RESTORATION
The second part of the book (13–27) announces judgment against the surrounding nations, especially Israel's new enemy, Babylon. The exile of Israel is prophesied but also a future restoration. A future resurrection is predicted for God's people (24–27).

REDEMPTION
The third main section (28–35) prophesies the attacks of different nations against the people of God. Spiritual lessons are drawn and applied to Israel who, according to these prophecies, eventually would become a redeemed people enjoying the full blessing of God.

HISTORY
The next section (36–39) is purely historical but is vital for understanding the different prophecies.

THE FUTURE
The last main section (40–66) concerns God's preparation for the certain deliverance of his people. They will be restored and the messianic kingdom will be set up (58–66).

JEREMIAH
The book of Jeremiah chronicles the long history of the prophet Jeremiah and the courageous prophecies he uttered against successive kings of Judah. Jeremiah witnessed the fall of Jerusalem, which was followed by his forced departure for Egypt with part of the defeated nation.

JEREMIAH'S LIFE
Jeremiah's entire life consisted of a series of admonitions to Judah; he kept prophesying the imminent judgment that would

strike the people because of their sin. The judgment, to be carried out by the Babylonians, could no longer be postponed. Zedekiah, the final king, was told repeatedly to turn the city over to those besieging it; his refusal finally led to his fall and the city's total devastation. The book is punctuated by distressing episodes in the life of Jeremiah (7, 11, 13, 18–22, 26–29, 32–44).

PROPHECIES
The book also contains messianic prophecies about the restoration of the repentant people (3), about the "Branch" from the line of David (23), and about God's everlasting love for the twelve tribes. It tells of Israel's restoration under the Son of David, the new covenant made with the people in the end-time, and their blessed future in a restored land and a restored city (30–33).

FALL OF JERUSALEM
After that, the book describes the history of Zedekiah, the fall of Jerusalem, and the flight into Egypt (where the people were still practicing idolatry). It closes by pronouncing judgment on a number of nations, including Babylon (46–51). Chapter 52 is a historical appendix.

LAMENTATIONS
The book of Lamentations contains Jeremiah's words of grief over the destruction of Jerusalem and the captivity of God's chosen people.

TRAGEDY
It was a terrible thing that God had to destroy the city he had chosen for his people, along with the temple and the altar. Jeremiah recognized that God's justice could not do otherwise since the people had sinned grievously against him.

HOPE
Yet as always there was the hope and assurance that someday all that was destroyed would be restored to those who repented and turned to the Lord.

EZEKIEL

The book of Ezekiel was written by a prophet who was also a priest in Jerusalem. He was among the first to be deported to Babylon, where the people settled by the river Chebar. It was there that Ezekiel prophesied for over twenty years to those in exile, both before and after the fall of Jerusalem under Zedekiah. Ezekiel did in Babylon what Jeremiah had done in Jerusalem. He pointed out to the people that the judgments that fell upon them were a result of their sins.

PROPHESIES

The first section (1–24) contains prophesies that date before the fall of Jerusalem, starting with Ezekiel's vision of the glory of the Lord, followed by the devastation of the city and land. Ezekiel also sees the idolatry being committed in the temple itself and the subsequent departure of the glory of the Lord from the temple and the city (1–11).

ADMONITIONS

Ezekiel sternly admonishes the leaders and false prophets and warns about the city and successive kings of Judah (12–19). The prophet emphasizes that Judah had placed itself in the same position as the ten tribes of the northern kingdom and would therefore meet the same fate (20–24). Though Judah was to be judged, the surrounding nations were also to experience the wrath of the Lord, with God using as his instrument King Nebuchadnezzar of Babylon (25–32).

PROMISES

Next comes a series of messianic predictions (33–39) announcing the true Shepherd, the Messiah, the Son of David. Ezekiel prophesies the devastation of Edom, an archenemy of Israel. There is also the prediction of a future restoration of Israel when the twelve tribes will again be united, and their enemies, Gog and Magog, will be destroyed. The final part of the book (40–48) describes the new temple, which will function when order is restored in the land.

DANIEL

The book of Daniel deals with the history of the Jews as captives of the Babylonians and the Persians.

WORLD EMPIRES

It also deals with the destiny of four successive world kingdoms that would arise. Daniel lived at the time of two of these kingdoms, the Babylonian Empire and the empire of the Medes and Persians. He also prophesied about the coming Greek and Roman empires. Because of the wisdom God gave him, he was kept at the Babylonian court by successive rulers as an adviser and even as a government official. But all the time he kept himself faithful to the one true God. The four world empires were first introduced in the form of a huge statue shown to King Nebuchadnezzar in a dream. The last empire would be destroyed by the Messiah at his coming. Daniel also saw the four empires in a dream, but he saw them in their true character, as four beasts.

SEVENTY WEEKS

Interwoven with the history of those kingdoms is the history of rejected Israel, which hoped for restoration. That hope was confirmed to them by the prophecy of the "Seventy Weeks," which concerned Israel and Jerusalem and foretold the Messiah's future reign. The book closes with a prediction of the nation's restoration.

HOSEA

Hosea is the first of the so-called Minor Prophets. They are designated such, not because their message was inferior to the Major Prophets but because of the size of their books. Hosea records the rejection of both the northern kingdom of Israel and the southern kingdom of Judah. Israel would be left without a king, without their unique relationship with God, until the last days when they again come to acknowledge both the Lord and his Messiah. At that time Israel will be converted and restored with the blessings of the Lord.

JOEL

The book of Joel predicts the destruction of the Assyrian army by means of a famine bound up with the day of the Lord, the coming time when the enemies of God would be destroyed. A remnant of God's people will be converted, and God's Spirit will be poured out upon all who are his own. In the end all the nations will be judged and God's people will receive his blessings.

AMOS

The book of Amos pronounces judgment on the surrounding nations because of their sins. At the same time the prophet Amos also declares that the long-suffering God will not bear with Israel's own unrighteousness any longer. Judgment will come to them as well. As always predicted, however, a righteous remnant will be preserved and blessed under the Messiah.

OBADIAH

Obadiah is a prophecy against Edom, a brother nation of Israel known for its jealousy and hatred of the people of God. Obadiah's prophecy is extended to all the nations and points ahead to the day of the Lord when the Messiah will judge the earth and redeem Zion, the Holy Mountain of Jerusalem.

JONAH

The book of Jonah demonstrates that even though the Lord had chosen Israel to be his people, his care and concern extended to all humankind. Jonah was sent to the godless Assyrians to pronounce judgment on the capital city, Nineveh. After running away from his calling and being swallowed by a large fish, Jonah, miraculously still alive, was able to proceed to fulfill his mission.

REPENTANCE

Although the message was one of doom, the people of Nineveh repented, throwing themselves on the mercy of God, who decided to spare their city. The message of the book teaches that God's grace extends to everyone, whether Jew or Gentile.

MICAH

Micah, a younger contemporary of the prophet Isaiah, pronounces judgment from God on both Israel and Judah. The land had been so thoroughly polluted with their sin that it could no longer be a haven for godly people. God, through Micah, denounced the leaders and the false prophets in Jerusalem, predicting their destruction. Micah proclaimed that the city would be restored in the last days, but before that would occur, Jerusalem would be destroyed and the people would be scattered.

DELIVERANCE

Micah also predicted that the Messiah would someday come, deliver his people, bless them, and rule over them. All unrighteousness would be removed. After those predictions, Micah again warned the people against serving idols. He laments the sinful condition of the people, but at the same time looks for the fulfillment of God's promises.

NAHUM

Nahum predicts the destruction of one of Israel's enemies, the people of Nineveh (the Assyrians). Nineveh not only would be destroyed—it would never be restored. The Assyrians, who had troubled God's people for a long time, were regarded as the most brutal of all ancient heathen nations, and Nahum prophesied God's vengeance on them for their terrible acts. Nahum reminds his readers that wickedness will be judged, but the righteous will be saved. God is the sovereign ruler in all human affairs.

HABAKKUK

Habakkuk relates some of his personal experiences. He was troubled by the unrighteousness of God's people, wondering why their sins were going unpunished. God showed him that he did intend to punish the people for their sins: he would send the Babylonians against them. Consequently, Habakkuk took pity on the people and asked the Lord to be merciful.

GOD'S REASSURANCES

He then brought before the Lord accusations against the sinful Babylonians, God's intended instrument of judgment. God told

Habukkuk that the Babylonians would also be punished, but that meanwhile the righteous would live by faith. The day of the Lord was coming and all the earth would be filled with the knowledge of his glory. The book ends with Habakkuk rejoicing at recalling God's earlier deliverances and looking forward to the glorious future.

ZEPHANIAH

The prophet Zephaniah announces imminent judgment on the land because of unrighteousness, hypocrisy and idolatry. This day of judgment, the day of the Lord, would also come upon the surrounding nations. Zephaniah also spoke of a remnant of people in Jerusalem who had trusted in the Lord; he called on these faithful men and women to watch and wait. The destiny of these people was connected with the End Times.

GENTILE BELIEVERS

Zephaniah foresaw believers coming from the Gentile nations, along with a spiritual and natural restoration for Israel. God's love for his people would be made manifest, making Israel renowned among all the peoples of the earth.

HAGGAI

Haggai is the first of the three prophetic books written after the exile. This prophet was one of the men who had encouraged the people to finish rebuilding the temple. After the temple was completed, Haggai declared that God would be with his people by his Word and Spirit and that he would one day shake the heavens and the earth. At that time the Gentiles would turn to the Messiah, and the temple would be filled with the glory of the Lord.

ZECHARIAH

The book of Zechariah can be divided into two sections.

DESTINY OF JERUSALEM

The first section (1–6) contains eight visions dealing with the destiny of Jerusalem. Jerusalem was at the mercy of four successive world empires (introduced as "horns" and "chariots," 1–6). Zechariah foresaw judgment for those nations along with a restoration of the city to its former splendor under the Messiah, the "Branch" (3, 6).

THE MESSIAH
The second section contains three "words of the Lord," again with Jerusalem and the Messiah as the theme. The first division (7–8) describes Jerusalem's future restoration under the Messiah. The second subdivision (9–11) introduces the same Messiah in the lowly estate that he would assume at the time of his first coming. After his rejection, Israel would be delivered into the hands of a "worthless shepherd."

The last of the three words of God (12–14) speaks of the redemption of Jerusalem at the time of the second coming of the Messiah, along with the conversion and reconciliation of the faithful. The book closes by prophesying the glorious final destiny of the city and its inhabitants.

MALACHI

Malachi, the last book of the Old Testament, describes the great moral decline of the Jewish people after their return from the Babylonian captivity. Despite God's unfailing love toward them, the people had forsaken his commandments. This caused Malachi to rebuke sharply their unholiness, faithless sacrifices, and unworthy priests.

FORERUNNERS AND THE MESSIAH
Malachi predicted the coming of a forerunner of the Messiah (fulfilled in John the Baptist). A prediction follows, about the coming of the Messiah, who would sift the people in judgment, sparing the faithful ones. The Old Testament here concludes with references to two of its greatest figures, Moses and Elijah. There is a call to return to the law of Moses and an announcement about the prophet Elijah, who will come before the day of the Lord.

CHAPTER 9
The Contents of the New Testament

Someone said concerning the two Testaments, "The New is in the Old contained; the Old is in the New explained." The Old Testament presents the promises and the law. The New Testament presents Jesus Christ as fulfilling the Old Testament law and promises. From the beginning the Old Testament predicted the coming Messiah who would save his people from their sins.

The following chart lists the books of the New Testament in the order given in the English Bible. As was true with the Old Testament chart, the dates are approximate.

Book	Author	Approximate Date of Composition (A.D.)
Matthew	Matthew	50–70
Mark	Mark	50–70
Luke	Luke	60
John	John	60–95
Acts	Luke	63
Romans	Paul	57
1 Corinthians	Paul	56
2 Corinthians	Paul	57
Galatians	Paul	49 or 56
Ephesians	Paul	62
Philippians	Paul	62
Colossians	Paul	62
1 Thessalonians	Paul	50
2 Thessalonians	Paul	51
1 Timothy	Paul	63–65
2 Timothy	Paul	66–67
Titus	Paul	63–65

Philemon	Paul	62
Hebrews	Unknown	65–69
James	James	45–55
1 Peter	Peter	62
2 Peter	Peter	65(?)
1 John	John	60–95
2 John	John	60–95
3 John	John	60–95
Jude	Jude	65–80
Revelation	John	60–95

MATTHEW

The Gospel according to Matthew, the first book of the New Testament, presents Jesus Christ as King of the Jews, the one who fulfilled the Old Testament prophecies about the Messiah.

TRANSITION

In charting Jesus' ministry, Matthew regards Jesus' miracles as a sign that he was indeed the long-awaited Messiah. But the people rejected both him and his testimony. Still, Jesus talked about building his church, which would consist of both Jews and Gentiles. Thus, Matthew's Gospel is a fitting transition between the Old and New Testaments.

Matthew began his book by linking Jesus with David the king and with Abraham, the father of the faithful. He gave an account of the birth of Jesus, conceived by the Holy Spirit and born of the virgin Mary. He was *Immanuel*, "God with us." Writing of Jesus' genealogy, birth, and the preparations for his ministry, Matthew consistently emphasized that prophecy was being fulfilled (1:1–4:11).

MINISTRY

After Jesus' baptism, he began his work in northern Galilee, where he delivered the Sermon on the Mount to expound the principles of the kingdom of heaven (4:12–7:29). Jesus sent out his disciples, who were given ability to perform miracles (8–10). Then followed the rejection of Jesus' forerunner, John the Baptist, and soon of Jesus himself (11–12). Jesus told seven parables pointing out the future character of the unified kingdom of heaven (13). His ministry as Savior of the world would extend beyond Israel.

DEATH AND RESURRECTION
Jesus began to predict his suffering, death, and resurrection (14–18). He concluded his teaching ministry in Judea and entered Jerusalem (19–22). Matthew's Gospel concludes with an account of Jesus' betrayal, death, resurrection, and his commission to his disciples to preach the gospel to all the world (28).

MARK
The Gospel according to Mark is the shortest of the four Gospels, giving a straightforward account of the ministry of Jesus Christ.

SERVANT
Mark portrays Jesus as both the Servant of the Lord and the Son of God. His emphasis is not so much on the statements and discourses of Jesus as on the work Jesus accomplished as the Servant of the Lord.

After a brief introduction, Mark describes Jesus' ministry in Galilee, where he performed seven miracles of healing. Christ taught about hidden principles of the kingdom of God and showed signs of his power and authority (1:14–5:43).

REJECTION
During further travels in Galilee he encountered people who rejected his ministry. Jesus prophesied his future suffering (6–9). He continued to minister to people on the way to Judea, in Jericho, and finally in Jerusalem (10–13). He was crucified in Jerusalem, yet three days later he rose from the dead.

LUKE
The Gospel according to Luke presents Jesus as the perfect man. Jesus designated himself the Son of Man, the man from God for all humanity, the Savior of the entire world.

HUMANITY
Luke's account stresses his humanity, giving details of his birth and boyhood (1–2). He describes Jesus' preparation for his ministry, his

baptism, and his temptation (3:1–4:13). Next came his work in Galilee (4:19–9:50), which included the calling of his disciples. Jesus explained his task and purpose, and predicted his suffering. Luke gives detailed descriptions of happenings on the way to Jerusalem (9:51–19:28). He records events in Samaria, Jesus' conversations with the Pharisees, and his miraculous healings.

BETRAYAL

The closing part (19:24–24:53) covers Jesus' entry into Jerusalem, the conflicts he faced, the Last Supper, his betrayal, arrest, trials, crucifixion, burial, resurrection, appearances, commissioning of his disciples, and ascension.

JOHN

The Gospel according to John was the last of the four Gospels to be written. It shows, by inference, acquaintance with the other three. John presents Jesus as God in human flesh. He is the one who was in the beginning, the creator of all things. John's purpose in writing this Gospel is to reveal Jesus as God's Son, the one who gives life to everyone who believes (20:31).

In the prologue (1:1-18) Jesus is presented as the eternal Word who became flesh. Later he is depicted as the Lamb of God, the one who will take away the sin of the world (1:29). John records Jesus' first miracle, turning water into wine at a wedding in Cana (2). He reports the conversation between Jesus and Nicodemus, a religious ruler. Nicodemus was told that he had to be "born again" (3). Afterward Jesus went to Samaria, where he talked with a Samaritan woman about the true worship of God (4). In the next section (5–7) Jesus explained more about who he was: the Son of God who gives life (5), the Son of Man offers himself as the bread of life (6), and the one who later will give the Spirit of life (7).

LIGHT OF THE WORLD

The next main section (8–12) pictures Christ as the light of the world, but rejected in his person, words (8), and works (9). John also describes him as the Good Shepherd who lays down his life for his sheep (10). Jesus showed his power by raising Lazarus from the dead (11). Still rejected by the Jews, he began talking about his coming death (12). That ended his public witness; from then on he is seen in the midst of his disciples.

WITH DISCIPLES
The next section (13–17) shows Jesus in the upper room where he celebrated the Passover. He washed the feet of his disciples and predicted his death on the cross (13). About to return to the Father and to send the Holy Spirit as the Comforter, Jesus explained the disciples' future blessings (14–16). He prayed, asking the Father to glorify the Son and to unify all the believers by their union with God (17).

ARREST
Then John told the passion story: the arrest of Christ, his appearance before Anna, Caiaphas, and Pilate; his crucifixion, burial, resurrection, and appearances at the Sea of Galilee (18–21).

THE ACTS OF THE APOSTLES

The Acts of the Apostles is a direct continuation of Luke's Gospel, giving the history of the early church in Palestine, Asia Minor, and Europe. The book is basically limited to the ministries of Peter and Paul and, because of the prominence given to Paul's travels, it provides significant background for understanding Paul's epistles.

CHURCH GROWTH
After a foreword, where Luke connects Acts with his Gospel, he repeats the account of Christ's ascension. While the disciples waited for the outpouring of the Holy Spirit, they appointed a replacement for Judas (1). At Pentecost, fifty days after the resurrection, the Holy Spirit descended, authenticating the New Testament manifestation of the church. The power of the Holy Spirit became evident through the disciples, and the church grew quickly despite intense opposition (2–5). Persecution set in with the martyrdom of Stephen (6–7). The gospel reached Samaria and an Ethiopian eunuch (8). Saul of Tarsus was converted and became the apostle Paul (9). The gospel also went to the Gentiles (10) and continued to spread throughout pagan lands (11–12).

PAUL

The next section contains the three missionary journeys of Paul. During the first journey (13:1–15:39) Paul ministered in Cyprus, in Pisidia (Asia Minor) and in the Galatian cities of Iconium, Lystra, and Derbe. He returned to Antioch. Then followed the council at Jerusalem, where the relationship of Christian believers to the Jewish law was discussed. On his second journey (15:40–18:22) Paul revisited Derbe and Lystra, traveled through Asia Minor to Troas, and crossed over to Europe. He ministered in Philippi, Thessalonica, Berea, Athens, Corinth, and made a brief visit to Palestine and Antioch.

On his third journey (18:23–21:16) Paul passed through Galatia and Phrygia, spending a long time in Ephesus, where he encountered much opposition. He crossed over to Macedonia and journeyed to Greece. After staying in Corinth, where he probably wrote the book of Romans, he returned to Macedonia. He crossed over to Troas, where Eutychus was raised from the dead. Paul bade farewell to the elders at Ephesus on the coast by Miletus, crossed over to Tyre, and went to Jerusalem via Caesarea.

He was arrested in Jerusalem and appeared before the Sanhedrin, before the governors Felix and Festus, and before King Agrippa. He was then taken to Rome as a prisoner, where he wrote the books of Philemon, Ephesians, Colossians, and Philippians. The book of Acts ends with Paul's stay and preaching in Rome.

ROMANS

The epistle to the Romans is addressed to a church that was not founded by Paul. He had never been in Rome, although he longed to visit the believers there (1:13; 15:22-23). He wrote the letter because he wanted to take the gospel to the Roman believers (1:15) and because he wished to announce his planned stopover in Rome on a journey to Spain (15:24-29).

TEACHINGS

After the introduction, Paul, in a long doctrinal section, shows how all of humanity has failed God. Human beings have no righteousness (ability to be right in God's eyes) except through faith in the work of Christ. That is the only basis through which anyone can know God and find forgiveness of sin. Paul illustrates that truth by giving the example of Abraham, who was considered righteous apart from the law—that is, by faith alone. Abraham believed that God could indeed bring life out of death (as God has proven through the resurrection of Jesus Christ) (3:21–4:25). Great blessings are attached to "justification by faith": Not only are a believer's sins forgiven, but that person is also saved from the power of sin. Hence, believers no longer belong to the family of Adam, but to the family of Christ (5).

Paul applied this freedom to practical areas of life. Because believers died with Christ on the cross, sin no longer rules over them. Its power has been broken. They have become bondservants of God (6), no longer under the yoke of the law (7). Consequently, believers can live for Christ by the power of the Spirit and have a glorious hope for the future (8).

ISRAEL
In the second main section (9–11) Paul deals with the special position of Israel. Although Israel has been set aside temporarily, there will be full reinstatement in the future.

EXHORTATIONS
The third section (12–16) includes admonitions about the believer's attitude toward God, neighbors, those in authority (13), and the weak in faith who do not fully understand Christian liberty (14–15). The epistle closes with many greetings along with final exhortations and a beautiful doxology (15–16).

1 CORINTHIANS
This is the apostle Paul's response to a letter brought to him that detailed some of the problems in the church of Corinth.

REBUKE
After expressing thankfulness, Paul discusses the abuses reported to him: a spirit of contentiousness and the rise of factions. He contrasts such attitudes with the "foolishness of the cross" and the true character of Christian service, pointing to himself as an example (1–4). Immorality had been condoned within the church (5–6),

and pagan courts were used to settle quarrels between Christians (6). Paul rebukes both of those practices.

QUESTIONS
In the next section Paul deals with questions the Corinthians had asked about marriage and celibacy (7); eating meat that had been offered to idols (which issue the apostle then incorporates into an important explanation of the communion service) (8–11); the question of the gifts of the Spirit and their orderly use in church meetings (12–14); and the question of the Resurrection, on which the entire Christian faith is based (15). Paul concludes with practical advice, admonitions, and greetings (16).

2 CORINTHIANS
The occasion of 2 Corinthians was a meeting in Macedonia between Paul and Titus. Titus had brought good news from Corinth, which led Paul to write another letter to that church. Second Corinthians begins with the customary greeting and thanksgiving for the comfort Paul had received during his recent persecution and affliction.

DEFENSE OF MINISTRY
Then follows the main section of the letter (1:12–7:16) in which Paul, in detail, defends his apostolic ministry. He reveals the purpose in changing his plans and the nature of his ministry (3–7). He is the minister of the New Covenant, which fulfills the Old Covenant under the law of Moses (3). That ministry consists of administering an immense treasure, although the ministers themselves are but "earthen vessels" (4). This ministry is carried out in light of the judgment seat of Christ, and contains God's offer of reconciliation based on Jesus Christ's death on the cross (5). Paul carried out this ministry in much affliction and prays that the Corinthians would walk in the light and live pure lives (6). Then follows a report on his meeting with Titus (7). In the next section (8–9) Paul reveals the necessity of collecting money for the poor in Judea.

DEFENSE OF SELF
In the last section (10–13) he gives a personal defense of himself as an apostle against those who challenged his authority (10). Paul

refutes their arguments and shows that Christ considered his apostleship important in that he allowed Paul to suffer so much (11). The apostle reveals some of the unique revelations he has received from God (12). He closes with remarks about his planned visit with them, pronouncing his well-known benediction (12–13).

GALATIANS

The letter to the Galatians is a strong protest by Paul against the influence of certain Judaizers who were undermining the churches by attempting to rob them of their freedom in Christ. These Judaizers were trying to impose the law of Moses, including circumcision, on the people. They also sought to discredit Paul's apostleship. The letter can be divided into three parts: historical (1–2), doctrinal (3–4), and practical (5–6).

PAUL'S CALL

Paul begins with an emphatic assertion that he has been called by God, not man, to be an apostle. He goes on to condemn those who would undermine the gospel. He himself had once fought for the traditions of the fathers, yet God called him to preach the gospel to the Gentiles. The other apostles confirmed this calling. Paul even had to rebuke Peter for being inconsistent in the matter of law and Christian liberty.

LAW VERSUS FAITH

In the next section, the apostle explains in greater detail why a legalistic Christianity is wrong. The Galatians had become believers not through the law, but through faith in Christ. Paul reminds them that the blessings received by Abraham did not come to him through the law, but through faith. The law can bring only condemnation for sinners, but Christ freed believers from condemnation by becoming a curse in their stead. Similarly, the law did not cancel the promise given earlier, but was added to it as a "tutor" to convict humanity of sinfulness and to point them to the coming Christ. Now that Christ had come, "infancy" under the law was to give way to liberty and to responsibility in sonship. Paul illustrates this idea by an allegorical application of the Old Testament story of Sarah, Hagar, and their sons.

LIBERTY
In his concluding section Paul makes it clear that Christian freedom excludes circumcision and other ritualistic practices of Judaism. At the same time he shows that liberty of the Spirit is not the same as liberty of the flesh (our sinful nature). Spiritual liberty in Christ makes one compassionate and gives him a desire to reach out to others. In his epilogue, Paul underscores the importance of this letter, written with his own hand. He contrasts the false motives of the Judaizers with his boasting solely in the cross of Christ. This letter closes with a general greeting.

EPHESIANS
The letter to the Ephesians is a profound treatise by Paul dealing with the special position and privileges of the church in connection with its head, Jesus Christ.

SPIRITUAL BLESSINGS
The letter begins with words of praise to God who has blessed his children with all spiritual blessings in Christ Jesus. Believers possess these blessings because they are the chosen ones, redeemed by the blood of Christ. They have become joint heirs with him, having received the Holy Spirit as a "down payment" or "pledge" of their inheritance. Paul prayed that his readers would be granted wisdom to understand the riches of this revelation. He also prayed that they would grasp the power by which God raised Christ from the dead. By that same power he has raised them up spiritually and seated them in the heavenly realm. This is the believer's position in Christ (1:1–2:10).

ONE BODY
Paul then goes on to mention the collective blessings of Christ's sacrifice. The Gentiles, who formerly were strangers to the news of the covenant and the promises, have now been joined in one church, one body, with the spiritual Jews. Similarly, the Jews, formerly separated from other nations by the law, are now one in Christ with the believing Gentiles. That revelation, which had not been fully understood in former ages, now is revealed, and Paul here sheds light on God's plan for the church. This truth led Paul

to another prayer. He asked Christ to dwell in the hearts of believers (2:11–3:21).

APPLICATIONS

The second part of the letter (4–6) is a practical application of these teachings, dealing with maintaining unity, the different gifts within the church, and the old and new life as worked out in the lives of believers, in marriage, in the family, and in the vocational sphere. These truths are to be implemented in people's lives. The letter closes with practical remarks and a benediction.

PHILIPPIANS

The letter to the Philippians is Paul's warm reply to the love expressed to him by the church of Philippi during his Roman imprisonment. Epaphroditus, the one who had brought their gifts to Paul, had been very ill, but had recovered. Paul was now sending him back to Philippi with this letter (2:25-30).

ENCOURAGEMENTS

After the opening greeting and words of thanksgiving for the Philippians' generosity and an assurance that he is praying for them, Paul describes his personal circumstances. He rejoices in his present situation, despite unfavorable news and uncertain prospects for his future. He encourages his readers to do likewise (1). He admonishes them to be of one mind and to display a humble, Christlike attitude. Paul then explains how Christ humbled himself on our behalf so that someday we could be exalted with him. The apostle shows from his own example, along with the examples of Timothy and Epaphroditus, that such humility is indeed possible (2).

WARNINGS

Next he warns against the Judaizers. He contrasts pseudo-Christians, enemies of the cross, with the genuine citizens of heaven who are looking forward to Christ's second coming (3). In closing, Paul gives a general exhortation to the Philippians to be of one mind, to have joy and peace in the Lord and to keep their consciences pure. He repeats his appreciation for their generosity and sends final greetings (4).

COLOSSIANS
The occasion for Paul's letter to the Colossians was a report that dangerous heresies had gained a foothold in the church at Colossae. Those heresies, which included elements of Greek philosophy (asceticism) and Jewish ritual (circumcision, angel worship), were drawing believers away from Christ.

PRAISE
Paul opens with the usual thanksgiving and then records his prayer that the Colossians would walk in a manner worthy of the Lord, giving thanks to the Father who has richly blessed them in Christ. Paul then praises Christ as the Son of God's love, the Creator of all things, the firstborn from the dead, the head of all things and especially the head of the body (the church). Christ laid the foundation for the reconciliation of all things. All wisdom and knowledge are in Christ, in whom dwells all the fullness of the Godhead and through whom believers also possess that fullness (1–2).

APPLICATION
The second part of the letter (3–4) applies these truths to practical matters of marriage, the family, and society. The life of the believer is hidden with Christ in God. The letter closes with practical hints, greetings and messages, and a brief reference to Paul's own life.

1 THESSALONIANS
This letter is Paul's answer to news brought by Timothy, his co-worker and traveling companion, from Thessalonica. Paul praises the Thessalonians for their perseverance, but also admonishes them for certain false teachings and misunderstandings, especially about the return of Christ.

DEVOTION
He begins by giving thanks for their testimony and devotion to God and for their eager expectation of Christ's return. Paul reminds them of the work he did among them and how they had received his word as the Word of God in spite of persecution. He describes how he longs for them and prays for their further growth (1–3).

CHRIST'S RETURN

In the next part of the letter, Paul encourages purity in marriage, brotherly love, and honest work. He then takes up the question of those who die before the return of the Lord. He assures the Thessalonians that those who die believing in Christ will be present when he returns. All believers, whether living or dead, will meet the Lord in the air when he comes for his church. Paul also explains that the time of Christ's return is not known. Christ's return will mean judgment for unbelievers. Christians will not be subject to judgment; nevertheless they must wait and be sober. The letter closes with practical admonitions and greetings.

2 THESSALONIANS

Paul sent his second letter to the Thessalonians shortly after his first in answer to a misconception on the part of the church in Thessalonica, namely, that the day of the Lord had already come.

JUDGMENT DAY

The apostle begins by pointing out that although the believers had suffered persecution, this was not a sign that the judgment day had already come. It will be just the opposite when that day actually does come. Believers will be rewarded; oppressors will be condemned (1). Further, the day of the Lord could not possibly have arrived yet, because it would be preceded by a falling away from the faith and the appearance of the man of lawlessness (known also as the son of perdition, the man of sin, or the antichrist). Although the antichrist will lead many astray, he will be destroyed by Christ at his coming (2).

The letter draws to a close with further thanksgiving and admonitions concerning prayer, ungodly living, and disobedience. There is also a greeting written in Paul's own handwriting.

1 TIMOTHY

Paul's first letter to Timothy was probably written after his first imprisonment in Rome. He gives instructions to Timothy about his work in Ephesus, encouraging him to take a firm stand and not be ashamed of the gospel.

After the opening greeting and words of caution about the situation in Ephesus, the apostle talks about his own experiences and reaffirms Timothy's commission (1).

INSTRUCTIONS
The next part of the letter (2–4) contains instructions about a variety of subjects including prayer, the position and attitude of women (2), and the qualifications of overseers and deacons. Paul then describes the church, the mystery of Christ's first coming and subsequent glorification (3), and certain threats to the church (4). He outlines correct church disciplinary procedure (5) and closes with various instructions about slaves, false teachers, the dangers of wealth, and Timothy's behavior as a "man of God."

2 TIMOTHY
Paul's second letter to Timothy was written after he had been taken prisoner again, shortly before his martyrdom in Rome.

ENCOURAGEMENTS
Looking back on what he had accomplished and ahead to his reward, Paul begins with his customary greetings and thanksgiving. He encourages Timothy by appealing to his gift of grace and the responsibility entrusted to him (1). Timothy is to persevere, the way good soldiers, athletes, and farmers have to persevere, keeping the final goal and reward in view. He must take a firm stand against false teachers and separate himself from all who continue to act unrighteously, identifying himself with those who call on the Lord from pure hearts (2). Paul then talks about the "last days," when the moral strength of Christianity fails in large measure (3).

FINAL TESTIMONY
Then, knowing his death is imminent, Paul gives one last commission, one final testimony, several personal requests, and a report on his defense before his judges. The letter closes with greetings and benedictions (4).

TITUS

The letter to Titus is addressed to another fellow worker and spiritual son of the apostle Paul. On one missionary journey Paul had left Titus behind in Crete so that he could ordain elders in the churches and clear up certain problems that had resulted from the laziness of the Cretans and the influence of Jewish heretics. After reaffirming his own apostleship, Paul mentions the proper qualifications to be employed in choosing elders and then goes on to expose false teachers (1).

CHRISTIAN LIVING

Paul then speaks about the true Christian walk to which young and old are called, including men, women, and slaves. This leads to a short summary of Christian doctrine (2). Finally the apostle writes about the proper attitude for Christians to take toward others. He reminds the Christians that they were once just like their sinful neighbors but have been saved solely by the grace of God. The letter closes with practical admonitions, plans and greetings.

PHILEMON

The letter to Philemon was written after Paul became acquainted with Onesimus, a slave who had fled from his master, Philemon. After Onesimus came to know the Lord, Paul sent him back to his master in Colossae, who was already a believer and a friend of Paul.

Paul sent this letter with him to persuade Philemon to take back his runaway slave and to forgive him. Paul promised to reimburse Philemon for any financial loss he might have suffered because of Onesimus.

HEBREWS

The letter to the Hebrews, whose author is unknown, was addressed to Jews and Jewish Christians who were familiar with the Old Testament as well as with the gospel. They were, however, still clinging to the Jewish law, worship services, and nationalistic character of Jewish ceremonies.

These Jews were admonished to give up this external, national brand of religion. It was useless to hold on to something that was a mere shadow of better things to come. Instead, they should trust the one who is the perfect fulfillment of the Old Testament sacrificial system.

BETTER THINGS

Hebrews, then, is a letter about the superiority of Christ over everything in Judaism. He is better than the angels (1); as the Son of Man, he is better than all creation (2); as the Son over the house of God, he is better than Moses (3); as the one who leads his people into true rest, he is better than Joshua (4); and as the high priest for his people, he is better than Aaron (5). Christ instituted a complete covenant founded on better promises and based on his own sacrifice (8–10).

LOOK BY FAITH

Thus the Hebrews had to learn not to look to external things any longer, but to look by faith to the invisible, glorified Christ—just as the patriarchs had in essence lived by this faith. But the greatest example was Christ himself. The Hebrews were to look to him and to better things he had initiated (11–12). That viewpoint is applied to practical circumstances. The letter closes with admonitions and greetings (13).

JAMES

The book of James was written by the brother of Jesus who for a long time was leader of the Jerusalem church. It was addressed to Jewish Christians who were still connected with the synagogue (2:2) and who still clung to the Jewish law (1:25; 2:8) and customs.

THE BELIEVER'S ATTITUDE

James begins with a discourse on the meaning of trials and testing and the attitude a believer should take at such times. Readers are not only to hear his words, but also to do them (1). True religion fosters no discrimination between rich and poor and does not degenerate into dead orthodoxy. Rather, it expresses itself in good works that are the fruit of real faith (2). Teachers must be able to control their tongues and must show proper wisdom (3). Believers must guard against overestimation of self (4). In closing, the writer exposes the rich oppressors and points out the need for patience in times of trouble. James also talks about swearing falsely, interceding for the sick, and helping brothers and sisters who go astray or need help (5).

1 PETER

The first letter of Peter is addressed to Jewish Christians who had believed in Jesus as their Messiah. Peter points repeatedly to the example set by Christ during his life on earth. He describes the nature of salvation as the outcome of faith, the theme of the prophets, and the result of trials and suffering (1:1–2:10).

CHRISTIANS' RELATIONSHIPS

The next section (2:11–3:12) deals with relationships of Christians to the world, to the state, to their daily work, to their marriage partners, to other believers, and to their calling in the world. The last chapter (5) describes the relationship between the elders and the "flock" and comments on the personal faithfulness of believers. Peter closes with practical details and greetings.

2 PETER

In the second letter of Peter, realizing his own death is near, the apostle warns believers against false teachers creeping into the churches.

TRUE KNOWLEDGE

Peter cautions them against giving up the true knowledge that is a possession of all who are partakers of the divine nature. That knowledge has been confirmed by the eyewitness testimony of Peter and others who saw the life of Christ—and also through fulfilled prophecy. Peter warns against false knowledge that would come into the churches: God will uproot those false teachers, just as he has overthrown his enemies in the past. Peter explains the activities and dangers of false teachers and warns against those who scoff at Christ's return. God will destroy the godless in a flood of judgment that ushers in new heavens and a new earth. Believers are to walk in the light of that truth, growing and maturing in the grace and knowledge of God.

1 JOHN

This epistle was written to expose certain heresies that were undermining the truth about the person of Christ—namely, that he is truly God in human flesh—and to expose fallacious suppositions about the Christian life.

John begins with testimony that the Son, who was eternally with the Father, lived visibly on earth in the form of flesh and blood. Believers have fellowship with the Son and the Father by possessing eternal life, which brings with it responsibilities.

LOVE IS THE BASIS

Believers must recognize in their daily walk that God is light and that they must therefore obey his commandments and love one another (1:5–2:11). John applies this to fathers, young men, and children in the faith (2). The love of the Father is evident in that they have become children of God; this ought to be made visible in their obedience and love for all (3). Believers are to guard against false teachings about the person of Christ. They are to recognize that God is love, which he demonstrated by sending his Son (4). God's love gives believers security and a basis for obedience (5).

2 JOHN

This is addressed to a "chosen lady" and her children. Similar in character to 1 John, its key word is *truth*, used three times in the introduction. Then follows an admonition to walk in truth, an appeal for a life of love and obedience. John warns against those who pervert the truth by preaching a different doctrine about Christ. Such persons are to be avoided. The letter closes with John's plans to visit this family.

3 JOHN

This is addressed to Gaius, an elder in the church. John praises him for walking in the truth and gives instructions about the hospitality to be shown to traveling ministers. Anyone who receives such persons into his house becomes a fellow worker for the truth. By way of contrast John reports that a certain Diotrephes should be rebuked because of his ambition and arrogance. By contrast, Demetrius receives words of praise from the apostle. The letter closes with visitation plans and greetings.

JUDE

The letter of Jude, written by the brother of James, bears a strong resemblance to 2 Peter. The book gives a defense of the faith because of deceivers who are trying to undermine it.

Jude describes those people who are rebelling against God's truth. He cites historical examples of divine judgment and compares the deceivers with past figures by depicting their depravity. Admonishing the believers to lead a positive Christian life, he closes with a doxology.

REVELATION

The book of Revelation is a revelation from Jesus Christ and concerning Jesus Christ. Unique in the New Testament, it is addressed to seven churches in Asia Minor and is written against the background of their conflicts with the Roman Empire. Against such problems the book gives a message of hope for a glorious future. John wrote the book while suffering persecution as a prisoner on the island of Patmos. He was given a vision of Christ as judge, who commanded him to write in a book "the things which you have seen."

John also describes "the things which are," that is, the present circumstances, and "the things which shall take place after these things."

INTERPRETATION

There are several ways to interpret the final and longest part of the book (4–22), which deals with future events. Some people apply these chapters to the history of Christianity on earth, including such events as the fall of Rome. Others see chapters 2 and 3, the seven letters, as seven time periods of church history before the rapture—when Christ will come again to take away his church—and chapters 4–19 as a description of the events to take place up to the time of Christ's return. These events include the Millennium, Christ's thousand-year reign on earth.

WHAT SHALL BE

In the introductory vision (4–5), the Lamb that was slain (Christ) is given a scroll with seven seals. With the opening of each seal, new judgments are unleashed on parts of the earth. But 144,000 from Israel, along with a great multitude from all peoples, are spared the judgments (6–7). The seventh seal launches seven judgments, each of which is announced by a trumpet. The last three of these judgments are called "woes." The last "woe" (the last trumpet) signals the return of Christ and the beginning of his glorious kingdom (8–11).

The remainder of the book deals with certain aspects of this period in more detail, in particular the "two signs." The first sign depicts three anti-Christian "beasts," which represent powers: the dragon, the beast from the sea and the beast out of the earth. Connected with all this are seven scenes drawn from the period of the "Great Tribulation" (12–14). The second sign depicts seven new judgments (seven bowls), which are poured out over the earth (15–16). An expanded sequence follows regarding the "great harlot" or "Babylon the Great" (17–18). From there, the book proceeds directly to the return of Christ and the establishment of his kingdom, followed by the last judgment and the creation of a new heaven and a new earth (15–21). A separate vision describes the glorified state of the church, the new Jerusalem, after Christ's return.

The epilogue contains specific exhortations and expresses longing for the return of Jesus, the Bridegroom. It also includes the promises of Christ and gives a closing benediction (22).

PART TWO
Creation and Evolution

INTRODUCTION

In Part 1 we discussed the Bible. The scope of the Bible includes the history of all creation. The first book of the Bible, Genesis, describes the beginning of all things—when God "spoke forth" the universe and its component parts.

In Part 2, *Creation and Evolution*, we will look at the Bible's account of the beginning of time—creation itself. The concern here is with *origins*. How did the universe begin? Has it always been there? Is it an illusion? If it had a beginning, what sort of beginning was it? We will use the Genesis account of creation as the basis for this study, but we also will delve into related areas of philosophy and science. We will see that the Genesis account of creation, far from being an ancient and fanciful myth, is an accurate, historical summary of the original creation of this universe.

Because much of secular science presupposes that there is no God, no design, no creative pattern, we will also discuss those ideas. We will show the harmony between true scientific evidence (not just scientific interpretation or speculation) and the Genesis account. Also, since much secular science is preoccupied with the theory of evolution (the view that all contemporary life forms evolved from earlier, simpler life forms), a significant portion of Part 2 will deal with evolution. After reading this section, you should be able to answer for yourself this question: What should I believe about evolution?

We have been very careful to ensure that the material presented is accurate and is based on a broad framework of research and study. Therefore, although we will discuss ideas about the origin and nature of the universe, we will not present complicated philosophical arguments. We will discuss theories of origins, but we will not engage in comprehensive surveys of scientific data. We will provide a framework for analyzing and assessing evolutionary theories in the light of biblical revelation, but we will not presume to set forth thorough argumentation in each of the areas

127

under debate. This section is designed to equip Christians with the tools necessary to defend their Christian commitment against contemporary secular thought.

Note that I am addressing these issues from certain perspectives. I believe in a universal Flood and lean toward (though am not necessarily convinced by) the recent creationist view (that is, the earth is much younger than the 4.6 billion years that many scientists need in order to hold an evolutionary point of view). There are good Christian scholars, both scientific and biblical, who differ in perspective and argue for a local flood or an old earth or for a progressive creationism. It must be understood clearly that *there is room for a difference of opinion here, and I do not consider either view the "Christian" view.* Both are viable options. But it is beyond the scope of this book to deal with all the arguments for and against the age of the earth and the extent of the Flood. Bible-believing Christians can disagree upon these issues. But one thing we all agree on is this: The universe came into existence by a series of creative acts by an infinite, personal God.

Travel with me, then, as we go back past recorded history to the beginning of it all—to the time when God, the eternal King, first created everything through the power of his word.

CHAPTER 1
Science and Society Move Away from God

Many people believe that religion and science are mutually exclusive, even contradictory to each other. That belief, however, is not required either by scientific fact or by the Bible. If we as Christians believe that the God of Creation is also the God of salvation, then such conflict is impossible. The same God will not create one testimony in the material record of the universe and then create a completely contradictory testimony in the written record of the Bible.

We do not want to return to the scientifically naive worldview of those like Ptolemy (ca. A.D. 85–160), who believed the universe was *geo*-centric—that is, with the earth at the center of it. The Bible nowhere teaches that the earth is the center of the universe. The Bible, although accurate in the science it does express, is not primarily concerned with science but with salvation. The location of the earth in relationship to the rest of the universe is irrelevant when compared to the spiritual concerns of the Bible. As we shall see in this section, there is no ultimate conflict between the reasonable and objective observation and interpretation of data (science) and a reasonable and objective interpretation of the Bible (theology).

From a biblical perspective, the story of the relationship of God and mankind is at the center of all existence. Quite properly, then, the Bible deals extensively with moral and philosophical ideas and only incidentally mentions scientific topics.

As we shall see in the following chapters, the few biblical passages that appear to contradict science in no way contradict reasonably interpreted and accurately observed scientific data. We shall see that the primary "conflict" between science and the Bible is in reality a conflict between atheistic presuppositions of many scientists and the theistic assertions of the Bible.

A SCIENTIFIC WORLDVIEW WITHOUT GOD

The contemporary scientific worldview is a worldview that has abandoned any belief in God. Three thinkers in the nineteenth century represent the bias against religion that helped to oust God from the scientific worldview.

Charles Darwin (1809–1882) revolutionized biology. Rather than accepting the special creation of all earthly life by God, Darwin chose to observe a vast quantity of biological data. From that he developed a theory of its origin based on naturalism (rather than allowing for any supernatural intervention).

He proposed that organisms change and develop in fundamental complexity through random variation, adaptation, and natural selection from one species to another or within species. The key to this system was that the changes were by adaptation and natural selection. There was no need for God in this system of change. (When Darwin first started writing, he attributed the beginning of the evolutionary process to the Creator. Later, however, he was not at all certain that there was a God.) Darwin's interpretation of his data, however, was not as far-reaching and all-encompassing as today's evolutionary model. When later scientists expanded Darwin's theory to include the origin and development of all life over a vast period of time, the agency and ultimate source for this evolution was chance, not God. We will discuss Darwin and his theory to a greater extent in chapters 4 and 5.

Karl Marx (1818–1883) revolutionized political science and sociology. Until his time, most political science, economics, and social structures depended on some sort of assumed or explicit divine absolute for their structure and values. Marx, however, was atheistic. He viewed belief in God as a hindrance to economic, political, and social development. He did not orient his system around any divine absolute. Instead, he proposed a political system (communism) oriented around the impersonal and arbitrary absolute of dialectical materialism. There was not only no need for

God in Marx's system, any idea of God was detrimental to human progress.

Sigmund Freud (1856–1939) revolutionized the social sciences through his unique form of psychology, called psychoanalysis. Freud was a forerunner of social scientists who orient their therapy and values subjectively, abandoning the concept that right and wrong are objectively and absolutely determined by God. Right and wrong, indeed all morals and values, become subjective and relative. Psychotherapy did not have as its goal the reconciliation of the individual to the laws of God, which previously was seen as the path to personal happiness. Rather, Freud's psychotherapy had as its goal the reconciliation of the individual's facts of personality to each other. With the advent of relativistic therapy and values (ethics), Freud and his followers believed they had no need for God.

These three thinkers are now gone. Their influence, however, has pervaded every facet of modern science. Contemporary science is a science without absolutes, and, as we shall see in subsequent chapters, without adequate answers to the *whys* and *hows* of the universe and of mankind.

PARTNERSHIP BETWEEN FAITH AND EVIDENCE

The *whys* and *hows* of the universe are answered by the revelation of God in the Bible and in his Son, Jesus Christ. Hebrews 1:1-2 declares, "God, after He spoke long ago to the fathers in the prophets in many portions and in many ways, in these last days has spoken to us in His Son." Contrary to the humanists, there is no absolute contradiction between the Bible and the evidence of science. There is, in fact, a partnership between faith and evidence. This partnership is illustrated in the book of Hebrews: "Now faith is the substance of things hoped for, the evidence of things not seen. . . . Through faith we understand that the worlds were framed by the word of God, so that things which are seen were not made of things which do appear" (Hebrews 11:1, 3, KJV). The following chapters in this section describe the partnership between faith and evidence mentioned by the writer of Hebrews. We will find that faith, as described in the Bible, complements and is confirmed by the evidence we find in physical reality around us.

The entire Christian faith, the gospel of truth, couples faith and evidence. The apostle Paul defined the gospel as the death, burial, and resurrection of Jesus Christ (1 Corinthians 15:1-3). He declared that faith and evidence were so closely related that "if Christ has not been raised, your faith is worthless; you are still in your sins" (1 Corinthians 15:17). The tomb was empty. The angel testified that its occupant had risen (Matthew 28:5-6). That was the consistent theme of the New Testament writers as they preached the gospel (the word means *good news*) and defended their faith.

Peter preached the first recorded evangelistic message after the resurrection of Christ. In it he pointed to the evidence. He pointed to the world of reality to confirm the reality of the resurrection of Jesus Christ. Peter appealed to the knowledge of his listeners: "Men of Israel, listen to these words: Jesus the Nazarene, a man *attested to you* by God with miracles and wonders and signs which God performed through Him *in your midst, just as you yourselves know—.* . . . This Jesus God raised up again, to which *we are all witnesses*" (Acts 2:22, 32; emphasis mine). Later he emphasized the corroborating value of evidence in his first epistle: "For we did not follow cleverly devised tales when we made known to you the power and coming of our Lord Jesus Christ, but *we were eyewitnesses* of His majesty" (2 Peter 1:16; emphasis mine).

The apostle Paul was one of the most intellectual of the early Christians. Some of his arguments in defense of the faith have been preserved for us in the New Testament. From them we can see Paul's emphasis on the use of reason, evidence, and common sense in testing and understanding reality. One of Paul's greatest speeches was before some Greek philosophers on Mars Hill in Athens (Acts 17). When Paul arrived in a new place he always began preaching the gospel in the Jewish synagogue. Then he also preached in the area marketplace or anywhere else he was sure to find a crowd to talk to. When he came to the synagogue of the Jews in Thessalonica, the Scripture records that "he went to them, and for three Sabbaths *reasoned* with them from the Scriptures, *explaining and giving evidence* that the Christ had to suffer and rise again from the dead, and saying, 'This Jesus whom I am proclaiming to you is the Christ'" (Acts 17:2-3; emphasis mine).

The same chapter records Paul's actions in Athens. It says that since he was "provoked within him as he was beholding the city full of idols," he was *reasoning* in the synagogue with the Jews and the God-fearing Gentiles, and in the marketplace every day with those who happened to be present" (Acts 17:16-17; emphasis mine). Some Greek philosophers observed Paul preaching in this manner and invited him to address their gathering. Paul's speech is one of the greatest short summations asserting the existence of God and the gospel of Jesus Christ (Acts 17:22-31).

What Paul had to say about "science" is interesting too. Many humanists would like to believe that the New Testament concept of God is primitive, that the biblical God's creative agency is vastly inferior to a complex naturalistic scientific model. But the Creator God asserted by Paul in Acts 17 is very sophisticated; his creative act fits modern scientific evidence much better than do the myths of the crude Greek deities. Paul called his God "the God who made the world and all things in it, . . . Lord of heaven and earth [not dwelling] in temples made with hands; neither is He served by human hands, as though He needed anything, since He Himself gives to all life and breath and all things" (Acts 17:24-25). As we shall see in this section, the God of the Bible, the God proclaimed by and revealed fully in Jesus Christ, has a far better explanation for the origin of the universe than does modern atheistic science.

CHAPTER 2
The Origin of the Universe

In this chapter we will see how scientific investigation of the universe presents us with a cosmology absolutely consistent with the biblical cosmology. No ancient religious system other than the biblical one corresponds so closely to the scientific evidence uncovered in the last two centuries.

ANCIENT RELIGIOUS COSMOLOGIES
Many ancient religions attributed supernatural qualities to natural forces and bodies. Some, for example, attributed the creation of the earth to the sun, often referred to as the Supreme God. In general, ancient religions saw the sun as the supernatural source and sustainer of life. That view is not completely off the mark scientifically, since science has shown us the dependence of earthly life on the sun. The ancient religions, however, erred in a significant way: they usually attributed supernatural power to the sun itself, seeing the sun as a god. Scientists reject that hypothesis as "primitive" or "superstitious," postulating instead "natural law" or the "inherent order in the universe," or the "interdependency of the universe" as proper descriptions of the relationship between the sun and earth.

The Bible does not contradict the scientific evidence. It, too, rejects the idea of a supernatural sun god. It sees law, order, and interdependency in the universe. But the Bible goes beyond science and asserts the source of the law, order, and interdependency evident in the universe: an intelligent, benevolent, all-powerful, personal God. The Bible recognizes the futility of locating the source of the universe within or as a part of the universe. At the same time, it goes beyond the scientific model, which is unable to define the cause of the order it observes.

ORIGINS: WHERE DID THE UNIVERSE COME FROM?

As we examine the origin of the universe, we will be discussing science and the Bible. Many times both will agree. That is not always the case, however. While all truth proceeds from God, who is truth, and while scientific truth can never contradict biblical truth, scientific suppositions and theories can contradict truth in numerous ways. The author of the Bible is the God of truth; scientists are not infallible. Likewise, when fallible humans interpret the Bible incorrectly, their views may contradict accurate science. Where science and the Bible appear to conflict concerning origins, we will discuss those conflicts and show why science is, at that point, in error, and why the Bible is true, or how the two coincide. There can be times when there appears to be a conflict, and the evidence does not clear it up at present. This is when time is the common denominator between the two. We do, though, want to reiterate that scientific truth is *not* in conflict with biblical truth.

In theory, it is the job of science to *observe* the natural world and seek to understand the natural world through that *observation*. It can often say, "This happens," or "This is the *value* of such-and-such event or process." *Why* and *value* are usually terms more properly associated with philosophy or religion than with science. In practice, scientists often overstep science's domain and attempt to deliver pronouncements on subjects with which science by definition is unable to deal. Biologist Jack Wood Sears notes:

> Science deals only with that which is timeless, repeatable at will, dependable, and universal. By this I mean that a scientist doing an experiment works only with those phenomena that are the same today as they were yesterday and as they will be tomorrow. He cannot deal with the unique, the thing that happens only once, for science relies for verification not upon one experiment but on repeated experiments. A scientist

in the laboratory does his experiment today and expects to be able to do it again tomorrow with the same results.[1]

POSSIBLE ORIGINS OF THE UNIVERSE

Although one at first might think that there are dozens of possible origins of the universe, there are actually only three. Once we have dispensed with the idea that the universe doesn't exist at all but is some sort of illusion, we are faced with three basic alternatives for its origin. No matter which of the hundreds of theories of origins one picks, any theory will fit into one of three possible origins. It does not take great scientific knowledge to figure out those three alternatives: it takes only logic and common sense. The three alternatives are:

1. The universe is not eternal but just popped into existence with no preexistent cause;

2. The universe is itself eternal, although it may have changed form at various times; or

3. The universe is not eternal but came into existence at a point in time and was caused by something or someone other than itself.

As a matter of fact, possibilities one and three are variations of the same idea, and so we could narrow the possibilities to two: the universe is either eternal or not eternal. We shall first deal with the idea that the universe is an illusion, and then we will be concerned primarily with ideas two and three, since science and the Bible both agree that a thing cannot cause itself or have a finite (not eternal) existence without any cause at all.

Is the universe an illusion? Most people would laugh at the idea that the universe is an illusion, but some philosophers and religious thinkers have argued for the idea that the universe, or all of existence as we know it, is illusory. Some assert that the world we see around us and in which we live is not a real world after all but is either a shadow or dream or hallucination or thought of the eternal and all-pervading god. Such thinkers often say that talk about the origin of the universe is silly since the universe doesn't really exist anyway.

We can answer such a thinker simply. Does he believe *anything*

---

[1]Jack Wood Sears, *Conflict and Harmony in Science and the Bible* (Grand Rapids: Baker, 1969), pp. 22-23.

exists? If he does, then what does he believe really exists (God, himself, etc.)? As soon as he tells us what he believes that has real existence, then we ask him, "Where did that real thing come from? What is its origin?" We have now faced him with the same alternatives we shall explore here: this real thing was created spontaneously with no cause; it is eternal; or it was created by something or someone outside itself.

Did the universe cause itself? Returning to our three viable options for the origin of the universe, we see that option one can be dealt with easily because it postulates the unscientific and unbiblical hypothesis that something (the universe) can come from nothing (self-caused). Christian philosopher Richard Purtill comments on the obvious problems with alternative one:

> The real choice, of course, is between the second and third alternatives, for hardly anyone takes the first alternative seriously. Because it will be useful later, we will briefly see why the first alternative is so implausible. One thing we could say about the possibility of the universe simply coming into existence from nothing is to declare that nothing comes from nothing . . . but suppose that someone denies the inconceivability of something from nothing. What can we say to him? We can, of course, challenge him to cite an instance of something coming from nothing, and if he does so he may reveal a misunderstanding of what he is denying. He may, for example, cite the theory of continuous creation held by some scientific cosmologists. But this theory does not claim that matter comes into existence from nothing, but says that in certain areas of space matter is formed from energy, rather as drops of dew condense from water vapor. Even if this theory were true it would no more contradict the principle that nothing comes from nothing than the creation of dewdrops from water vapor.
>
> Suppose, however, that the denial did not rest on a misunderstanding and the objector seriously maintained that things can just pop into existence for no reason at all. We could point out that if this happened at the beginning of the universe, there would be no reason why it should not happen now. We could point out that no one would take seriously

the idea that anything—a baseball, a planet, even a snow-flake—had simply popped into existence from nothing. The impossibility of this sort of thing is a basic assumption of any coherent thinking about the universe. For if any expla-nation of the existence of any particular thing may be it just popped into existence for no reason, and if the ultimate ex-planation of everything is just that, then all explanation is undermined. So to hold the pop theory of the origin of the universe is to give up any hope of rationality, or under-standability in the universe. If someone claims to hold this view then he cannot be reached by rational argument, for he has abandoned rationality. But if someone abandons ra-tionality he can have no reason for holding any view, and no reason for action except momentary passion or appetite. He has, in effect, stepped out of the human race down to the animal level. This is a solution of sorts to some prob-lems, but then so is suicide.[2]

So, then, our actual choices concerning the origin of the universe are that it is either *eternal,* or that it had a *beginning.*

Is the universe eternal? Most people who declare that the universe is eternal do not actually believe that the universe had no beginning. Usually they say it is "eternal" because they cannot imagine a time when the universe was not in existence. This universe is the only dimension with which they are familiar, and it seems impossible to think of a time when what is, wasn't. But when one thinks more deeply, it is just as mind-stretching to conceive of an eternal universe as it is to try and imagine what might have existed before our universe. Both postulate states completely beyond our finite experi-ence.

However, as we shall see, scientific research is mounting in sup-port of a clear beginning to our present universe. But before we deal with that evidence, on what basis do some still postulate an eternal universe? Such people are usually of one of two persuasions: they have a religious presupposition that assumes an eternal universe, or, they mistakenly think that scientific evidence supports an eternal universe theory.

---

[2]Richard Purtill, *Reason to Believe* (Grand Rapids: Eerdmans, 1974), pp. 81-82.

Those who accept an eternal universe because of a misunderstanding of scientific evidence show ignorance of the two most fundamental laws of physics: the law of conservation of energy ("The sum total of mass and energy in this universe is neither created nor destroyed") and the law of entropy ("Every process in the universe tends toward nonrecoverable energy loss"). Dr. Henry Morris describes these two laws and their relevance to the question of the origin of the universe:

The basic principle of all physical science is that of the conservation and deterioration of energy. The law of energy conservation states that in any transformation of energy in a closed system from one sort into another, the total amount of energy remains unchanged. A similar law is the law of mass conservation, which states that although matter may be changed in size, state, form, etc., the total mass cannot be changed. In other words, these laws teach that no creation or destruction of matter or energy is now being accomplished anywhere in the physical universe.[3] . . . This law of mass and energy conservation is also known as the first law of thermodynamics and is almost without controversy the most important and basic law of all physical science. . . .

The second law of thermodynamics, of almost as great significance, enunciates the corollary law of energy deterioration. In any energy transfer or change, although the total amount of energy remains unchanged, the amount of usefulness and availability that the energy possesses is always decreased. This principle is also called the law of entropy increase, entropy being a sort of mathematical abstraction which is actually a measure of the nonavailability of the energy of a system. . . . The same principle applies to all the stars of the universe, so that the physical universe is, beyond question, growing old, wearing out and running down.

But this law certainly testifies equally to the necessary truth that the universe had a definite beginning. If it is growing old, it must once have been young; if it is wearing

---

[3]Mass and energy are not necessarily independently constant, but the sum total of mass and energy together is constant.

out, it must once have been new; if it is running down, it must first have been wound up.[4]

THE "BIG BANG" THEORY

Modern scientific cosmology centers on the Big Bang theory for the origin of the universe. This theory, which says that the universe began with a huge explosion, provides convincing explanations for certain observable phenomena. First, the red shifts in the light coming from different galaxies indicate (via the Doppler effect) that those more distant are traveling away from us at a faster speed than closer ones. When one calculates these speeds backwards, it appears that all the galaxies originated from the same point in space and time. Second, in 1965 astronomers detected faint radio waves coming equally from all directions of the universe. This is now thought to be the "echo" of the Big Bang.

Though the idea of the universe having a beginning was repugnant to many atheistic scientists, they began to admit that, taken together, these facts compelled the abandonment of the Steady State theory of the universe. Noted agnostic astronomer Robert Jastrow said the evidence points to one conclusion: "The universe had a beginning."[5]

This conclusion did not go down easily. Phillip Morrison of MIT said in a BBC film on cosmology, "I find it hard to accept the Big Bang theory; I would like to reject it." And many other scientists said much the same thing. But the facts cannot be ignored, and Jastrow goes on to say,

This is an exceedingly strange development, unexpected by all but the theologians. They have always accepted the word of the Bible: In the beginning God created heaven and earth. . . . For the scientist who has lived by his faith in the power of reason, the story ends like a bad dream. He has scaled the mountains of ignorance; he is about to conquer the highest peak; as he pulls himself over the final rock, he

[4]Henry M. Morris, *The Bible and Modern Science* (Chicago: Moody, 1968), pp. 11-13.
[5]Robert Jastrow, *God and the Astronomers* (New York: W. W. Norton and Company, Inc., 1978), p. 111.

is greeted by a band of theologians who have been sitting there for centuries.[6]

But the Big Bang theory is not entirely satisfactory for many Christians. First, it suggests the universe is 10 to 15 billion years old, certainly much older than is favored by advocates of a recent creation. Second, the theory can be extended to suggest that there really was no "beginning"; merely we are in one phase of the universe's oscillation. For instance, if there is enough mass in the universe, the gravitational pull will slow its expansion to the point—in about 70 billion years—when everything will stop its outward fling and begin to contract. Ultimately it will collapse down to its pre-bang mass and explode again. While such cycles do not preclude a creator, atheists have staked out this sliver of theoretical real estate to claim that a perpetually oscillating universe does not *require* one either. On the other hand, if the universe does not contain enough mass for gravitation to stop its expansion (and current observation has not detected enough),[7] then there has been only one universe . . . with a beginning.

So we see that scientific evidence points to two facts: matter is neither created nor destroyed, and every process in the universe tends toward a loss of available energy. The phenomena that testify to these two laws is testimony to the fact that the universe is not eternal but had a beginning.

The universe had a beginning. We have made several biblically and scientifically important observations in this chapter. We have asserted that the biblical and scientific cosmologies have more in common with each other and with truth than either has with any other religious or nonreligious cosmology. A lot has been written about "biblical cosmology." Many have tried to say that the Bible is a geocentric cosmology. Others have said, "No, but we can't say what it is." I think most today would say that the Bible does not offer a cosmology, though it is clear that it does teach a cosmogony. A *cosmology* is the way it is technically supposed to be understood and has to do with the structure and the organization of the universe. A

---

[6]Ibid., pp. 115-116.
[7]Michael W. Friedlander, *Astronomy: From Stonehenge to Quasars* (Englewood Cliffs, N.J.: Prentice-Hall, Inc., 1985), p. 536.

cosmogomy has to do with its origin (see Rejer Hooykaas, *Religion and the Rise of Modern Science,* Eerdmans).

We have seen that it is illogical to believe that the universe is illusory. We then saw that it does not make sense scientifically or logically to say that the universe caused itself. We have just discussed the scientific reasoning behind a rejection of the eternal universe theory. We are left finally with the alternative that makes scientific and biblical sense: the universe was created (had an origin), and was created by something or someone outside itself. The remainder of this book will deal with this observation.

CHAPTER 3
The Universe: A Grand Design

We ended the last chapter with the reasonable conclusion that the universe really exists, it is not eternal, and it did not create itself. In this chapter we will observe the design apparent in the universe, which tells us something about the creator of the universe. Because of the grand, intelligent, ordered, and purposeful design and the structure and organization we see imprinted in the universe and its parts, we can extrapolate the existence of a creator who is infinite, intelligent, and purposeful.

Remember, science *observes*, it does not answer *why* questions, and so science can never really *prove* the existence of God. If we assume that there is a God, however, and that he did create the universe, and that he is the infinite, intelligent, powerful, and benevolent God the Bible says he is, then he would leave just such "traces" or "evidences" in his world as we find in our universe. We could almost say that the universe bears the "signature" of God. (See Hugh Ross's book *The Fingerprints of God* for the latest scientific evidence of the dimensions and origins of the universe.)

WHAT ABOUT THE DISORDER
IN THE UNIVERSE?

If order, structure, and organization imply a creator, does disorder imply that, perhaps, "chance" created some things while God created others?

Not at all. When the vast reaches of the universe display such sophisticated intelligent design as scientists can observe today, the proportionately smaller degree of disorder serves as testimony to an

145

interruption or *corruption* of the grand design of the universe. That is exactly what the Bible declares. God is the Creator of the universe, but he gave mankind the highest honor possible in the created order.

> When I consider Thy heavens, the work of Thy fingers, the moon and the stars, which Thou hast ordained; what is man, that Thou dost take thought of him? And the son of man, that Thou dost care for him? Yet Thou hast made him a little lower than God, and dost crown him with glory and majesty! Thou dost make him to rule over the works of Thy hands; Thou hast put all things under his feet. (Psalm 8:3-6)

It is no wonder, then, that when mankind deliberately broke their relationship with God, the entire creation felt and continues to feel the effects of that corruption. From the time that Adam and Eve sinned and were banished from God's presence, the effects of corruption have manifested themselves throughout the creation. The apostle Paul, in his letter to the Romans, said:

> For the anxious longing of the creation waits eagerly for the revealing of the sons of God. For the creation was subjected to futility, not of its own will, but because of Him who subjected it, in hope that the creation itself also will be set free from its slavery to corruption into the freedom of the glory of the children of God. For we know that the whole creation groans and suffers the pains of childbirth together until now. (Romans 8:19-22)

So, then, the presence of corruption or disorganization in the universe does not negate the testimony of the overall design and organization in the universe to the existence of an intelligent and all-powerful creator.

WHO IS THE CREATOR?

We can turn to the Bible for a clear description of the Creator of the universe, and of the manner in which he created everything. The Bible is not primarily a science text, but rather the revelation of God to mankind. It is our faith that it doesn't err scientifically.

In addition, the creation of the universe is one of the mighty acts of God and so is alluded to in several places in Scripture. The apostle Paul described the Creator as "the God who made the world and all things in it, since He is Lord of heaven and earth, does not dwell in temples made with hands; neither is He served by human hands, as though He needed anything, since He Himself gives all life and breath and all things" (Acts 17:24-25). This is how the Creator has described himself: "I, the Lord, am the maker of all things, stretching out the heavens by Myself, and spreading out the earth all alone" (Isaiah 44:24).

In later chapters we will discuss science and the biblical account of human creation. Here we will concern ourselves with the major claims of Genesis 1 regarding the origin of the universe.

DATING AND THE BIBLE

There are Christian scholars who believe that the Bible sets very definite limits on the age of the universe, the earth, and mankind. There are also many non-Christian scholars who dismiss any biblical notion of creation because they believe the Bible specifically limits the age of the universe, the earth, and mankind. Before we deal specifically with Genesis 1, we need to explain our own understanding of the Bible's dating of origins.

In my opinion, the age of the universe, the earth, and mankind is not specifically limited or determined by Scripture. I believe that every valid and reasonable interpretation of relevant Scripture passages can argue either for a very ancient creation or a more recent one. We respect serious Bible scholars on both sides of the argument, as long as those scholars hold to reasonable explanations for their convictions, and as long as their convictions are based on belief in the inerrancy of Scripture. The important thing is that no biblical interpretation should deny the *evidence* (not necessarily the *assumptions*) of science. Christian author James Jauncey presents a reasonable summary:

Although there has been some conflict between science and religion for centuries, the problem did not come out into clear relief until the end of the eighteenth century and the beginning of the nineteenth. That was the time when the

147

new geological discoveries were being made. It soon became possible that instead of an earth six thousand years old, as it had been generally believed, it could have gone back millions of years. This seemed to many people a direct challenge to the biblical message.

As we see it now, this point of conflict was rather unnecessary. Most of it was due to the rather unfortunate researches of an Irish archbishop named Ussher in the seventeenth century. Apparently he was also an amateur mathematician. As the result of his calculations, he concluded that creation occurred in 4004 B.C. Since he was an archbishop, most Christian people assumed he was correct. The date soon appeared in the margins of Bibles and still exists in many Bibles today.

The Bible makes no such stipulation. It simply says that in the beginning God created the heavens and the earth. According to this it could just as easily have been millions of years ago as just a few thousand years ago. You can see that the problem was science versus Ussher rather than science versus the Bible. The point no longer raises serious difficulty.

CREATION REFLECTS GOD'S DESIGN

For the rest of the chapter, we will examine the first creative claims of Genesis 1 concerning the origin of the universe. That will give us an outline of the biblical creation of cosmology and its harmony with the scientific creation cosmology. We believe there is no final conflict between scientific evidence and the biblical record. But there is often conflict between flawed scientific theories and the biblical record, and/or between scientific evidence and faulty interpretation of the Bible.

In the beginning God created the heavens and the earth. And the earth was formless and void, and darkness was over the surface of the deep; and the Spirit of God was moving over the surface of the waters. Then God said, "Let there be light"; and there was light. And God saw that the light was good; and God separated the light from the darkness. And God called the light day, and the darkness He called night. . . . Then God said, "Let there be an expanse in the midst of the waters, and let it separate the waters from the waters." And God made the expanse, and separated the waters which were below the expanse from the waters which were above the expanse; and it was so. . . . Then God said, "Let the waters below the heavens be gathered into one place, and let the dry land appear"; and it was so. (Genesis 1:1-9)

That statement of God's order of creation on the earth, offering a kind of harmony between the biblical account and scientific evidence, is a testimony to the creative power of God. (The origin of life will be discussed in the next chapter.)

GOD CREATED THE PHYSICAL UNIVERSE

Genesis 1 rejects the view that the universe is eternal. The heavens and the earth (the universe) are not eternal. They "began to be," or were created. If one looks at one postulate of science ("matter can neither be created nor destroyed"[1] one could assume falsely that the universe is eternal. However, that postulate must be understood with its requisite presupposition and in conjunction with another fundamental postulate of science. The presupposition to the first postulate is that within this system, the universe, matter can neither be created nor destroyed. It says nothing about the origin of the matter that now exists and does not deny that the matter that now exists did come into being some time. The second postulate of science which correlates to this first one is that of *entropy,* or the scientific observation that every process in the universe results in a product with less usable energy than was available before the process. In other words, everything is slowing down, cooling off, losing its dynamic potential. If the matter we have now cannot be created or destroyed, and if all matter is losing its available energy, then the claim of Genesis 1:1 that the heavens and the earth (the universe) were created is substantiated by scientific observation.

---

[1]The discovery that matter and energy are interconvertible means that matter can disappear if an equivalent amount of energy appears and vice-versa. Albert Einstein expressed the equivalence of matter and energy in a now-famous equation, $E=mc^2$, where E is energy, m is the mass of equivalent matter, and c is the speed of light.

In 1944, Christian scientist Peter W. Stoner noted the correlation between Genesis 1:1 and the newly emerging scientific evidence that became known as the "Big Bang" theory:

All Stars Had a Beginning. The radiation of our sun is apparently produced by the loss of about 4,200,000 tons of mass a second. Only about 1/200th part of this is recovered. This means that the sun is running down. The same can be said for all of the other stars. If the stars are all running down, they must have had a beginning. They could not have always existed, for if four million tons of mass are added to the sun each second for an infinite period of past time you would have an infinite mass and our sun would have started by filling all space. The same can be said for each of the one hundred billion stars in each of the trillions of galaxies. This is impossible. Therefore, every star had a beginning.

Genesis 1:1 does not state a time when the universe was created. As far as scriptural evidence is concerned it does not matter whether everything started five or six billion years ago, ten billion years ago, one hundred billion years ago, or any other assigned time. . . .

This evidence is so strong that many astronomers are freely talking about the *day* of creation. They are even forming theories as to how the universe was created. Some speculation seems to hinge about the concept that the universe was created from a tremendous amount of energy, probably in the form of light. One of these theories would have this energy change to matter in a remarkably short time, requiring no longer than one-half hour.

Thus Genesis 1:1 is no longer contradictory to science, but completely agrees with both the best facts and theories of science today.[2]

Genesis 1 goes on to state that the earth was without form, and void. While scientific theory has gone back and forth with myriad ideas about the formation of the solar system, the theories that

---

[2]Peter W. Stoner, *Science Speaks* (Chicago: Moody, 1969), pp. 25-26. See also Hugh Ross, *Fingerprints of God.*

appear to fit the evidence best, and appear to be most reasonable, are also those theories in harmony with this statement in Genesis. For instance, the statement in Genesis 1:3 where God said, "Let there be light," could be seen to dovetail with a universe born in a fiery explosion with matter only condensing out later.

Similarly the Nebular Hypothesis theorizes that solar systems developed as rotating gaseous bodies in space slowly cooled. As they cooled, they rotated more and more quickly, reducing their area and increasing their mass, until they were able to form separate rotating of planets.

One popular theory is that star systems or planetary systems are descendants or developments of dark (or black) nebulas. This is in harmony with Genesis 1:2. Having our earth produced from a dark nebula would also account for the evidence that the earth was once much hotter than it is now, and is continually cooling. For example, igneous rock is rock that was once molten (lava) and then cooled to a solid form.

Peter W. Stoner summarized his ideas concerning the scientific veracity of Genesis 1 in this way:

> We have shown that by very recent developments of science Genesis 1 agrees perfectly with all of the sciences concerned. There does not appear to be a contradiction of any magnitude still remaining. There is, however, this extremely strong argument, or proof, for the Bible's truth.[3]

The grand design of the universe is mirrored in the creation of the earth. We have seen from our brief survey of the origin section of Genesis 1 and from our comparison of that section with today's science, that an intelligent, benevolent, all-powerful creator, outside this universe, is the author of both the universe and the Bible.

The scientist who postulates chance alone as responsible for the origin of the universe in all its complexity is negating any idea of real order, design, predictability, or pattern in the universe. The best that such a person can postulate is a random and meaningless universe that gives a false *illusion* of order, design, predictability, and pattern. And yet that same scientist presupposes and relies on

---

[3]Ibid., pp. 114-115.

the existence of logic and order in almost everything he does or thinks. Science is based on the premise that there is order in the universe and that the order in the universe can be observed, measured, and used to understand the world in which we live. If there were no order in the universe, there could be no science.

If, however, an intelligent designer, God, created the universe with inherent design and order, then the scientist's task is *not* futile; we can learn a lot from science about our fascinating world.

CHAPTER 4
The Origin of Life

The wonders of new life! The beginning of new human life is breathtakingly beautiful. After the egg is fertilized by the sperm, everything that the new person will become develops from that one initial cell. Just twenty-one days after fertilization, the embryo has the basic form of a human being. Two months after fertilization the face appears; arms and legs, with their finger and toe buds, are clearly discernible. Three months after fertilization, at twelve weeks, tiny fingernails and genitalia are distinct.

At the end of an average nine months' gestation, the new little person is born, a living, breathing, growing, and, most uniquely, a thinking individual. New life, especially human life, is a miracle. The fascinating intricacy of reproduction cannot be the result of chance.

Scientists can't answer the *why* of life. Why did life develop? Why did life differentiate? Why do various life forms resemble each other? Why are there distinctions among life forms? Those who give the answer "evolution" are not *explaining*, they are only *describing* one possible chain of events. They are not answering *why*. In the final analysis, life remains a mystery to the scientist.

CELLULAR LIFE
When we look at a cell, we find an incredibly complex structure. The cell absorbs food, secretes waste, and even can produce by division. In the center of the cell is the nucleus, which contains at least part of the information the cell needs to function properly. The nucleus contains the chromosomes, long strands whose most

important component is DNA (deoxyribonucleic acid). DNA is the actual genetic material that determines hereditary characteristics. A DNA molecule looks somewhat like a twisted ladder. When the cell divides, the "ladder" splits lengthwise down the center, and each half forms a separate ladder.

Chromosomes consist of molecules; each molecule consists of a number of atoms. Most living cells contain molecules that consist of combinations of six elements: carbon, hydrogen, oxygen, nitrogen, phosphorus, and sulfur. The amazing complexity, diversity, and order we see in the living world around us has these six basic elements as its building blocks.

The Bible does not contradict this scientific observation, as we see in Genesis 2:7 ("the Lord God formed man of dust from the ground") and Genesis 3:19 (". . . till you return to the ground, because from it you were taken; for you are dust, and to dust you shall return").

But living organisms are more than just chemical elements arranged in particular patterns. A corpse, for example, still consists of the same chromosomes, the same molecules, the same atoms, the same elements, as a living person. But the corpse is not living. Life is gone. Scientists can observe differences between living and nonliving things. But they cannot *explain* what life is.

Human life is different from other forms of life, no matter how much modern materialists may insist that a human being is no more than a sophisticated machine. Only humans have self-cognizance, the ability to recognize themselves and their relationship to the rest of reality. That capacity is part of what the Bible means when it says we are made in God's *image*:

> Then God said, "Let Us make man in Our image, according to Our likeness; and let them rule over the fish of the sea and over the birds of the sky and over the cattle and over all the earth, and over every creeping thing that creeps on the earth." And God created man in His own image, in the image of God He created him, male and female He created them. (Genesis 1:26-27)

According to the Bible, only humans are made "in God's image." Only humans possess the will and self-consciousness that distinguish us so sharply from even the most intelligent animals. In this chapter we will explore the scientific and biblical scenarios for the origin of life. How did life begin on earth? What kind of life was it? What was required for life to begin? How do scientific speculations on the origin of life compare to the biblical account of the origin of life?

THE BIBLICAL ACCOUNT
OF THE ORIGIN OF LIFE

According to Genesis, life was created by God on the third "day" of creation. (It is not necessary here to determine the length of the "days" of Genesis. We refer interested readers to the Recommended Reading for books on that subject.) As we saw in chapter 3, God first created the heavens and the earth, dark and formless. He created light, and he brought light to the earth. As the earth cooled, some of the water vapor in which the earth was enveloped condensed, forming the oceans. Further cooling variegated the earth's surface, producing continents, mountains, valleys, and oceans. On the third day God created the first life on earth.

> Then God said, "Let the earth sprout vegetation, plants yielding seed, and fruit trees bearing fruit after their kind, with seed in them, on the earth"; and it was so. And the earth brought forth vegetation, plants yielding seed after their kind, and trees bearing fruit, with seed in them, after their kind. (Genesis 1:11-12)

Even though Genesis records that light first shone from the sun on the fourth day, after the creation of plant life, there was already light by which photosynthesis could take place (Genesis 1:3-5). Also, plants were created with reproductive capability from the beginning.

Before God created plant life, he created the environment that was capable of supporting that life. He created cycles of light and darkness, water, and atmosphere. Although the Bible clearly states that God *created* the first plant life, most scientists dissent sharply. Starting with the same friendly environment as described above, scientists postulate the spontaneous creation of life, by natural processes alone.

EVOLUTIONARY THEORY
OF THE ORIGIN OF LIFE

According to evolutionary theory, a few billion years ago the then young earth had an atmosphere completely different from ours. Since it lacked free oxygen, scientists at first thought it contained methane, ammonia, hydrogen, and water vapor. Most have since revised their theories to suggest that the atmosphere primarily consisted of carbon dioxide, water vapor, and nitrogen. By the action of ultraviolet rays, electrical discharges, and a continuous bombardment of highly charged particles, molecules were formed spontaneously and randomly. The molecules included sugars, amino acids, and pieces of DNA. More and more pieces clustered together and formed increasingly larger molecules and molecular chains. These giant molecules then reacted until a primitive cell stage was reached, again through a random process. Finally, those gelatinous clusters of proto-cells absorbed other molecules which, in combination with the gelatinous substances, at some point began to reproduce. Thus developed the first living cells. Those first living cells fed on the molecules still left in the "primeval soup."

Soon photosynthetic cells developed that produced and released into the atmosphere a necessary ingredient for virtually all life forms: oxygen. That oxygen, and the metabolism of those first living cells, destroyed the primitive molecules and changed the primeval atmosphere into the atmosphere as we know it. Once life had formed, the earth's environment was so altered by the introduction of large amounts of oxygen that life could no longer develop spontaneously on earth. On the other hand, some scientists argue for a primeval *oxidizing* atmosphere that would have oxidized organic molecules as soon as they formed.

What are the chances that life could have developed spontaneously in the hypothetical primeval soup by chance? Take a single bacteria cell. One bacterium contains some fifteen hundred different enzymes, each of which in turn consist of several hundred amino acids. Those various amino acids must be arranged in precisely the right sequence. The chance that a given enzyme, consisting of two hundred amino acids (of which there are twenty different kinds) could develop by chance is one in 20^{200}. In other words, the chance is practically nil. And that is only one of the necessary fifteen hundred enzymes for *one* bacterium. Even if the original bacterium were much less complex than modern ones (some theorize that they had as few as seventy proteins about one hundred amino acids long), the chances are nearly zero. Furthermore, the origin of a single living cell, then, would require billions of kilos of each of the many different enzymes and DNA molecules, combining and recombining randomly, until, against all probability, the right random combination occurred.

SPONTANEOUS GENERATION

A few centuries ago, people generally were convinced that life developed spontaneously everywhere. This is known as the theory of spontaneous generation. It was believed, for example, that flies could develop from rotting meat. It took two centuries for the scientific opponents of this idea to convince everyone that life can come only from life. Numerous experiments showed that if the proper sanitary precautions were taken, such as preventing flies from laying eggs in the meat, no new life developed. Finally, in the 1860s Louis Pasteur took broth, thoroughly boiled it, then sealed it off to prevent contamination by new microbes. The broth stayed clear and sterile. There was no new life. The universally accepted scientific postulate became: Life comes only from living things.

Curiously, the same scientists who dogmatically support that postulate also believe that life *did* develop from nonlife several billion years ago. Such scientists realize the inconsistency of assuming its past possibility while denying its present possibility. Their solution: Conditions must have been radically different then from what they are now. It is important to note that there is no conclusive evidence that conditions then were radically different. Such a difference is totally unverified by any evidence. Yet most introductory science texts present the existence of such a primeval soup and primeval atmosphere as *fact*.

But certainly some have *tried* to prove that life can still come from nonlife.

LIFE IN A TEST TUBE?

During the 1950s, the work of scientist Stanley Miller attracted attention. He was attempting to create the simple building blocks of life, amino acids. To do that was a necessary preliminary to attempting to create life from nonlife in a laboratory setting. Miller duplicated the atmosphere that evolutionists had postulated as providing the setting for the origin of life. Then he succeeded in producing certain molecules that are important building blocks of life. He accomplished that by subjecting the atmosphere of methane, ammonia, hydrogen, and water vapor to electrical charges.

Miller's experiments not only produced molecules that are important building blocks for life, they also produced the biologically unusable "right-handed" molecules. Miller's experiments complicated rather than simplified matters for evolutionists. Did the primeval atmosphere also produce both kinds of molecules? If so, how did any life-building molecules dissociate themselves from the other molecules long enough to react and produce the first living cell? And if the atmosphere was not the same as that in Miller's experiments, how do we know what it was and why it produced only life-building molecules? The problems with Miller's experiments proved greater than the solution he sought to provide for the origin of life.

As mentioned earlier, most scientists now agree that the primeval atmosphere contained, not the methane, ammonia, hydrogen, and water vapor used by Miller, but carbon dioxide, water vapor, and nitrogen, and some argue for the presence of free oxygen. Furthermore, remember that *Miller never produced one single living cell.* He produced a diversity of organic molecules, far removed from the complexity of a living cell.

Philosopher Robert Augros and theoretical physicist George Stanciu point out the significance of this complexity:

> Matter has many capacities but also definite limitations. We can distinguish two categories of forms that matter is able to assume. One kind of form is produced by an agency within matter itself according to recognized laws of physics and chemistry. . . .
>
> Another category of form is that which does not originate from any agency within the matter itself. For example, a block of ice is carved into a statue of Poseidon. The ice receives this form in a purely passive way, having no natural

inclination to it. . . . The determination to this particular form of Poseidon must come from an outside cause—the artist in this case. All human artifacts are examples of this kind of form imposed on matter from without.

Into which of these categories falls organic matter? Where shall we place the form of the adult horse or the mature oak tree? The forms of the elements or compounds arise by physical or chemical necessity. For example, hydrogen and oxygen have a natural inclination to form water. Organic forms are not produced in this way but are built according to genetic instructions. Matter has of itself no innate inclination to produce a horse or an oak tree, any more than it has an innate inclination to produce a chair or a microchip. It must be told how to produce a horse or an oak tree cell by cell, protein by protein, through chemically coded instructions. Matter can be shaped into an unlimited number of organic forms and is indifferent to all of them. Therefore, organic forms are not the product of physical or chemical necessity like the forms of compounds and elements. . . .

Thus the organism has something in common with artistic forms. . . . The major difference is that artistic forms have an external cause while organic forms have an internal cause. There is, therefore, in each living thing something analogous to human art. . . .

Matter does not need special instructions to manufacture snowflakes or sodium chloride. These forms are within its power. Not so with organic forms. Thus living forms transcend all other natural forms, not merely because of their unique activities but also because the laws of physics and chemistry alone cannot produce them.

What does produce them? What cause is responsible for the origin of the genetic code and directs it to produce animal and plant species? It cannot be matter because of itself matter has no inclination to these forms, any more than it has to the form Poseidon or to the form of a microchip or any other artifact. There must be a cause apart from matter that is able to shape and direct matter. Is there anything in our experience like this? Yes, there is: our own minds. The statue's form originates in the mind of the artist, who then subsequently shapes matter, in the appropriate way. The artist's mind is the ultimate cause of that form existing in matter, even if he or she invents a machine to manufacture the statues. For the same reason there must be a mind that directs and shapes the organic forms. Even if it does so by creating chemical mechanisms [DNA] to carry out the task with autonomy, this artist will be the ultimate cause of those forms existing in matter. This matter is God, and nature is God's handiwork.[1]

Even if biochemists could succeed in producing something that resembles life or even was life, this would not prove that life originated spontaneously as the result of random processes. Instead, they would have shown that life can be produced from matter and energy when that matter and energy is *directed* and *controlled* by intellectual effort and great technological skill.

HOW DOES ENTROPY RELATE TO EVOLUTION?

As we discussed before, one of the fundamental laws of the universe is that of *entropy*, the second law of thermodynamics. Briefly stated, this means that in any general process, the amount of available or usable energy decreases or is less than what was available before the process. In cosmological terms this means that eventually the entire universe will cool, slow down, and be unable to use any more energy. Entropy means that processes tend toward disorganization rather than organization, toward more randomness rather than more order. Bolton Davidheiser gives this as an illustration of entropy:

When a spring-type clock is wound, energy is put into the spring as it is coiled tighter and tighter. As the spring uncoils, this energy operates the clock. But less energy is available for running the clock than was put into the spring during the winding because some of the energy dissipates as heat. In any operation, some energy is lost as heat or in some other way so

---

[1]Robert Augros and George Stanciu, *The New Biology* (Boston: Shambhala Publications, Inc., 1987), pp. 188-191.

that it is not useful to the process. Thus the total amount of useful energy becomes less. Scientists are certain that unless there is a creative force operating in the universe, a time will come when the sun and all the stars will burn out and the universe will have "run down" completely.

The "running down" of the universe poses a real problem for the atheists, for how could it have gotten "wound up" in the first place so that it can now be in the process of "running down"?[2]

When we look at evolution, we see the problem evolutionists have with reconciling evolutionary theory with the law of entropy. The development of a living cell would require that nonliving matter spontaneously organize itself "upward" to much higher degrees of order, complexity, and purposefulness. But the second law of thermodynamics counters such a trend, evidencing instead that matter never increases in the organization of life.

Evolutionists, aware of the thermodynamic dichotomy, nonetheless believe in the spontaneous development of life. They attempt to reconcile the problem by objecting that the second law is applicable in a "closed system," i.e., a system that does not exchange or receive energy from outside itself. The earth, they maintain, is not a closed system. It is an open system that constantly receives abundant amounts of energy from the sun.

That, however, is a totally inadequate answer. Energy in and of itself contributes nothing to organization or design. Simply adding energy from the sun gives no developmental input to the random processes evolutionists describe for the origin of life. A pile of bricks and wood never would spontaneously develop into a building, no matter if the energy from the sun radiated on it for a trillion years. Matter and energy are insufficient causes of the complexity, design, and development we see around us. Walter L. Bradley of Texas A&M University demonstrates this:

It is sometimes argued that there are self-ordering tendencies in nature that may account for the observed order in

<hr>

[2]Bolton Davidheiser, *Evolution and Christian Faith* (Nutley, N.J.: Presbyterian and Reformed, 1969), p. 220.

living systems. Crystal formation as well as vortices (as in your bathtub when it is nearly empty) or convective heat currents are offered as examples of the self-ordering tendencies in nature. Such analogies fail to recognize that the ordering in vortices, crystals, etc. is very redundant compared to the observed ordering in living systems which is quite diverse and information intensive. The three sequences of letters below illustrate a random arrangement, a highly ordered but redundant arrangement, and a highly ordered, information intensive arrangement:

(a) random:
ACDBGEF ADGEBFC CBFGEAD
(b) ordered but redundant (like a crystal):
ABCDEFG ABCDEFG ABCDEFG
(c) ordered and information intensive (like DNA or protein):
THIS SEQUENCE OF LETTERS CONTAINS A MESSAGE![3]

In order for a system to become more complex, it must have complexity added to it, not just energy. When Christians say that God is the Creator, they are asserting the Designer behind the design, the Intelligence behind the intelligence, the Purposer behind the purpose, and the Mind behind the complexity of the universe. The heart of our argument, and the total defect in the evolutionary argument, is that Christians have an *adequate source* for the development and complexity in the universe, while evolutionists have *no adequate source* for the world they see around them. Energy is inadequate to account for the order, complexity, purpose, and design we see in the created world around us.

WHERE DID LIFE COME FROM?

Evolution is incapable of accounting for the complexity and design everywhere evident in living organisms. Evolutionists

---

[3]Walter L. Bradley, "The Trustworthiness of Scripture in Areas Relating to Natural Science," in *Hermeneutics, Inerrancy, and the Bible*, ed. Earl D. Radmacher and Robert D. Preus (Grand Rapids.: Zondervan, 1984), p. 293.

who take matter and energy, and to it add time, have still not answered the problem. Matter, energy, and time cannot accomplish any more than redundant order with relatively small complexity when compared to living organisms. What is needed is a designer or programmer. Christians know that Designer as God.

Following is a comparison of two common philosophical perspectives in interpreting the world and its origins.[4]

Nontheistic Evolutionist

Naturalism: Nature is the sum total of reality. Knowledge of the world can be obtained entirely through the methods of science. There is no need to seek to explain the world in any other way.

Uniformity: The Uniform Process Theory states that knowledge of the present is sufficient to explain the past and to predict the future. This is done on the basis of certain natural laws which are said to be changeless. There is no divine intervention in history.

Chance (Causalism): Life began as the result of chance events. The end result of a chance event is a consequence rather than the achievement of a purpose. Because the present forms of life originated by chance, they could easily have arisen in some other form or not at all.

Creationist

Theism: Natural science is not sufficient by itself to provide answers to life's questions (1 Corinthians 2:12-14). Part of reality can be explained only in spiritual terms (John 4:24). A complete view of reality recognizes both the natural and supernatural aspects.

Sovereignty: The world was created by God (Hebrews 11:3; Genesis 1:1; 2 Peter 3:5-6). God does not change and has created a world which obeys certain uniform natural laws (Hebrews 13:8; Proverbs 3:19-20). But the history of the universe is not explicable in terms of natural laws alone because God is not bound by those laws (Matthew 19:26).

---

[4]L. Duane Thurman, *How to Think about Evolution* (Downers Grove, Ill.: Inter-Varsity, 1978), p. 54.

Purpose (Teleology): The world was created by God for his purpose. All history is a working out of God's plan (Colossians 1:16-17; Ephesians 1:9-12). Mankind was made in the image of God's own divine personality (Genesis 1:26; Romans 8:28-29).

CHAPTER 5
Evolution or Creation?

Although modern evolutionary theory is much more sophisticated than what Charles Darwin devised, his name is still the one that for most people evokes ideas of the "ape-to-man" theory. In this chapter we will discuss how the theory developed and how it contrasts with biblical creationism.

Some readers may be surprised to learn that not everything labeled with the word *evolution* is necessarily opposed to Christianity. First of all, some Christian scientists feel that there is ample evidence of *microevolution*, insofar as it describes relatively minute changes within species, while rejecting what might be called *macroevolution*, the development of a new, higher specie from an older, less complex specie. Also, some Christians in science regard themselves as "theistic evolutionists"—although I do not regard "theistic evolution" as a biblically faithful position. Some well-qualified, intelligent scientists reject evolution in favor of the biblical creation account. Although we will not exhaust the study of the evolution/creation controversy in these few pages, we will try to provide a general background to the subject, along with some useful ways of looking at the controversy.

LIFE OF CHARLES DARWIN

Charles Darwin, the father of evolutionary theory, was born in 1809 in England. He began his university studies in medicine, following in his physician father's footsteps. Then he changed his major to theology, looking forward to enjoying life as a quiet country clergyman. At Cambridge, Darwin studied geology with Adam Sedgwick and botany with John Stevens Henslow. When his theological studies did not inspire him to seek a pastorate after graduation, he returned to his father's house with few concrete plans for the future. Then Darwin was offered a post as botanist on the ship *Beagle*, which was embarking on a five-year voyage to prepare navigational charts. During that voyage, which began in 1831, Darwin's religious beliefs were replaced by a general materialism, which undoubtedly influenced his developing thesis of evolution. Bolton Davidheiser quotes Darwin's description of his loss of religious belief:

> I had gradually come by this time to see that the Old Testament from its manifestly false history of the world . . . was no more to be trusted than the sacred books of the Hindus, or the beliefs of the barbarian. . . . I gradually came to disbelieve in Christianity as a divine revelation.[1]

The part of his journey that had the most impact on Darwin's evolutionary scheme was the time the ship spent in the Galapagos Islands off the west coast of South America. There Darwin observed finches that were similar to mainland finches, but different enough that they were unable to interbreed with mainland birds or even with birds on neighboring islands. Later Darwin used these finches as examples of adaptive evolution, a microcosm of the grand evolutionary design by which he believed all life had developed to its current complexity.

Darwin believed that the finches had been blown by storm winds from the mainland to the islands and there developed significant differences through isolation and interbreeding.

> The idea is that the birds got to the islands accidentally from the mainland, by the action of a storm or some freak of nature, and developed differently because they were isolated on separate islands. It is strange indeed, though apparently overlooked for convenience, that they would accidentally cross

---

[1]Quoted in Bolton Davidheiser, *Evolution and Christian Faith* (Nutley, N.J.: Presbyterian and Reformed, 1969), p. 67.

hundreds of miles of ocean and then remain isolated on small islands within sight of each other. If a storm carried them so far to sea, it is to be expected that sooner or later other storms would mix them up on the islands. William Beebe, the noted naturalist, did not believe the birds came to the islands by accident from South America, but that they came by way of a former land bridge from Central America.[2]

Darwin did not publish his complete theory of evolution until he was fifty. The theory was described in *The Origin of Species by Means of Natural Selection or the Preservation of Favored Races in the Struggle for Life* (1859).

Darwin died in 1882, years after the first furor over his revolutionary new ideas had died down. He spent the last third of his life refining and promoting his theory of evolution.

DARWIN'S EVOLUTIONARY THEORY

Darwin's general theory of evolution, as first described in his *Origin of Species,* can be summarized in six points (here somewhat simplified).

First, Darwin recognized, as all observant people would, that species differ. Second, he observed that the mortality rate among the infants of species was extremely high, and appeared to be compensated for by large numbers of births. Third, Darwin proposed his now-famous "struggle for existence" theory: Offspring struggle to be of the survivor class instead of dying. Fourth, given that this struggle exists, it stands to reason that those individuals who survive must be more fit than those who die. (This Darwinian concept is usually referred to as "survival of the fittest.") Fifth, Darwin assumed that fit individuals who reproduced passed on the genetic characteristics that had made them better able to survive to their offspring. Sixth, Darwin concluded that new species arise by the continued survival and reproduction of the individuals best fitted or adapted to their own particular environment.[3]

---

[2]Ibid., p. 61.
[3]Adapted from John W. Klotz, *Genes, Genesis, and Evolution* (St. Louis: Concordia, 1970), pp. 34-35.

Most reasonable people would not disagree with all of Darwin's points; one cannot really argue with the first two. There are many species, and most populations produce more offspring than actually survive to maturity. There is strong disagreement, however, even among non-Christian scientists, as to whether there is a true "struggle" for existence of the sort Darwin deemed vital to his conclusions. It is also generally *not* true that only the fittest survive. John W. Klotz refers to this criticism of Darwin's theory:

> There are also many instances in which the fittest individual does not survive. Often the survival of one individual and the death of another is a matter of chance. This criticism of Darwin's theory was pointed out very early. It may be that one individual is not exposed to the same environmental stresses as another member of the same species. In this way he may survive, even though he may not be as fit as his less fortunate neighbor. This is especially true where animals are the victims of predators. Here it is often a matter of chance which individual supplies the predator with his dinner.[4]

The most significant problem with Darwin's theory is his conclusion that fitness characteristics are passed on to an individual's descendants. Many different characteristics might make an individual more fit than another of the same species group. However, some of those characteristics usually do *not* represent *genetic*, or inheritable, characteristics. As a simple example, we could think of an Olympic runner. While some portion of his fitness for running could be genetic and therefore inheritable (being born with large lung capacity, etc.), the most significant factor in his achieving Olympic status is what he *does* with his "raw materials." Large lung capacity is totally irrelevant if he never uses it but instead whiles away his time watching television. Many of his runner's advantages arise from training, self-discipline, and hard work. Such factors are not inheritable.

Although Darwin produced a comparatively well-researched, well-thought-out proposal, it is reasonable to take issue with

---

[4]Ibid., p. 34.

some of his most important propositions and conclusions. His theory has consequently undergone many modifications.

HUGO DE VRIES—THE MUTATION THEORY

A Dutch botanist, Hugo de Vries, built on the genetic studies of a monk named Gregor Mendel, who had experimented with crossbreeding garden peas. De Vries' work concerning mutations is still used by many evolutionists today. In 1905 he published *Species and Varieties: Their Origin by Mutation*. This book described his work with a species of evening primrose. He cultivated several previously wild varieties and produced what he called a completely new species.

De Vries was convinced that new species arise by beneficial mutations, which are then passed on to succeeding generations. However, many scientists today agree that the different kinds of plants produced in de Vries' experiments were not new species but merely varieties of the same species. In addition, his theory was open to even more severe criticism, as Klotz notes:

Most, if not all, of de Vries' "mutations" were not mutations as we know them today, but were due to the breeding out of recessive characters present in the stock but not showing themselves (similar to the birth of an albino child to two normal parents both of whom were "carriers" of the trait) and to chromosomal rearrangements within the cells. . . .

Today we do see mutations in various plants and animals. These are sudden, abrupt changes in the organism which are due to changes in the genes. They are inherited, and hence are passed down from generation to generation. For instance, in the latter part of the eighteenth century there appeared in a purebred New England flock of sheep a lamb with very short, bowed legs. This lamb was bred and gave rise to the Ancon breed of sheep. It is obvious that this character would be one desirable to the breeder. Such an animal cannot jump fences and cannot run fast and thus lose weight. Incidentally, it is also obvious that such a character is unfavorable to the sheep.

Such a sudden inheritable variation is known as a mutation. There have been literally thousands of such mutations, some striking and significant, and others insignificant. Like the Ancon mutation in the sheep, however, most of these mutations have proved to be harmful to the organism.[5]

In the modern theory of evolution, natural selection and genetic manipulation (through breeding and/or mutations) are the basic mechanisms by which change and development are accomplished. Evolution, in that view, is the general cause of all development and differentiation among plant and animal life throughout the history of life on earth.

TERMINOLOGY

We should define some terms we are using. Much of the conflict between the evolution and creation views arises because both evolutionists and creationists tend to misunderstand what the other is saying.

Evolution generally means a process of change in a certain direction. When we refer to evolution, we mean that life as we know it today has come through a process (and is still in the process) of development from simple to more complex, single to multiple, "lower" to "higher" forms of life. Scientists also use the term *evolution* to describe a variety of lesser degrees of change. Some scientists use *evolution* to refer to what most people think of as individual variations within a "family" grouping of a particular species. Those smaller changes are often referred to as *microevolution*.

Finally, evolution can refer to our initial definition above, where there is change from one species to another, or changes in other major categories of organisms. Such major change is often referred to as *macroevolution*.

It is also important to understand the terms *species* and *mutation*. In further discussion, in fact, we will find that some evolutionary arguments fall because of a faulty understanding of what a species is or what a mutation is. Duane Thurman has a good, concise definition of *species*.

---

[5]Ibid., pp. 38-39.

A species is a basic unit of classification which can be recognized and placed in a classification system without even considering evolution. The concept originated independent of evolutionary theory. It is defined in several different ways, depending upon the backgrounds and purposes of the investigators. Some, such as Linnaeus, defined a species as a group of individuals which looked alike. He said there was an unbridged gap (that is, a lack of common characteristics) between species. . . .

A species may be characterized in several different ways, but most definitions agree on the following: a species has certain designated characteristics in common; it usually does not interbreed with other species in nature; and if members of one species do breed with members of another, they usually will not produce fertile offspring.[6]

Most scientists agree on the basic definition of a *mutation:* an abrupt change in the genetic code of an individual that can then be passed on to successive generations (as either a dominant or recessive trait). Disagreement occurs, however, when one discusses the significance of mutations in (1) the development of new varieties and/or species and in (2) whether a particular "new" characteristic is the result of a true mutation, i.e., it is not just an unobserved normal genetic trait.

Mutations are important to evolutionists because the presence of mutations is used to account for a small divergent group within a species being able to survive and adapt to a hostile change in the environment. We must remember, however, that the vast majority of mutations observed in the laboratory and field are *harmful* mutations. Far from promoting survival, they often ensure the demise of the affected individuals.

An example from language may be helpful in demonstrating how an organism may undergo certain dramatic mutations within its kind while being unable to evolve into a new kind.[7]

---

[6]L. Duane Thurman, *How to Think about Evolution* (Downers Grove, Ill.: Inter-Varsity, 1978), pp. 90-91.
[7]This example is adapted and expanded by Dave and Neta Jackson in *Hot Topics Youth Electives* (Elgin, Ill.: David C. Cook Publishing Co., 1990), pp. 54-55. It was originally from Michael Denton, *Evolution: a Theory in Crisis* (Bethesda, Md.: Alder and Alder, 1985), pp. 88-89.

A sentence, like an organism, is a complex system. To be functional, a sentence must avoid ungrammatical or nonsense strings of letters just as an organism must avoid nonfunctional variations.

Consider the sentence, "He sat on the bed," and all the possible variations that one could make while changing only *one* letter at a time. Each change must create a logical and grammatically correct sentence.

> *He sat on the bed.*
> She sat on the bed.
> She sat in the bed.
> We sat on the bed.
> We sat in the bed.
> We sit in the bed.
> We sit on the bed.
> We sit on the beds.
> We sat on the beds.
> He sat in the bed.

If you were to change *bed* to *bid* (as in delaying a financial transaction), you could get another set of variations. *Bid* could then be changed to *bit* (as in drill bit—it would be rather uncomfortable to sit on one, but logically and grammatically correct) for another round. *Bed* could also be changed to *bud* (as in flower bud).

The options are quite impressive. On the other hand, notice that limits are clearly reached rather quickly. For instance, it is impossible to evolve such a closely related sentence as "He sat on the chair" without passing through four, nonfunctional mutations:

> *He sat on the bed.*
> He sat on the ced.
> He sat on the chd.
> He sat on the cha.
> He sat on the chai.
> He sat on the chair.

From a biological perspective, four such mutants couldn't survive any better than the four intermediate sentences communicate anything meaningful. It's the futility of intermediary stages that limit macroevolution. A change must be functionally beneficial— or at least not a handicap—for it to last.

THE EVOLUTIONARY PICTURE

By *macroevolution* we mean the process by which simple organisms developed into complex organisms over a long period of time, transforming primitive life forms into the complex and varied life forms in our world today. If we were to draw a word picture of macroevolution, it would be something like this:

We start with the primitive, nonliving early earth environment. Macroevolutionists assume that nonliving things developed into living things. (See chapter 4 for further information on the origin of life.) Since they believe that all living forms in evidence today developed from common original ancestors, macroevolutionists assume that all plants and animals are somehow germinally related. Macroevolutionists see the progress of evolution as a sort of tree or family lineage, with just a few main branches. For example, all of the invertebrates are related; they represent an ancient part of the tree of life. From the invertebrates developed the vertebrates, all of whom are closely interrelated (and related by ancestry to the invertebrates). Finally, macroevolutionists divide the vertebrates into their own chronologically occurring "families" of amphibians, reptiles, birds, and mammals. This is often referred to as the "General Theory of Evolution."

Macroevolutionists describe this tree in detail and yet *have no hard evidence of its actual development*. Almost all aspects of the general theory are supported only by inference or by interpreting the data with the presupposition that evolution is already an established fact.

To summarize the most important features of and the contrasts between the evolutionary model and the creation model, we reproduce below a concise chart.[8]

---

[8]Duane T. Gish, *Evolution: The Fossils Say No* (San Diego: Creation-Life, 1978), p. 50.

Creation Model	Evolution Model
By acts of a creator	By naturalistic mechanistic processes due to properties inherent in inanimate matter
Creation of basic plant and animal kinds with ordinal characteristics complete in first representatives	Origin of all living things from a single living source which itself arose from inanimate matter. Origin of each kind from an ancestral form by slow gradual change.
Variation and speciation limited within each kind	Unlimited variation. All forms genetically related.

Can new species develop, which are clearly defined and separated from other similar groups? That would be consistent with creation. Or does genetic evidence support the possibility of the formation of new species *ad infinitum*, and across the boundaries of existing groups? That would be consistent with evolution.

The findings of genetics do not point in the direction of evolution, but rather that the families must have come into being independently of each other. Molecular genetics especially has provided strong support for this conclusion. Molecular research has brought to light certain kinds of "shifts" in the relationship of genetic factors. Such shifts can form the basis of the development of new species (i.e., within a family—which is consistent with the biblical account). Nowhere, however, have scientists been able to observe consistent and major sequences of genetic changes that would mirror macroevolutional development in the past. In fact, the most significant and species-changing genetic trends are usually produced artificially by the direct intervention of humans who interbreed and hybridize plants and other organisms for various purposes. The deliberate manipulation of genetic material for a designed end does not reflect blind chance and random development.

SPECIES DEVELOPMENT AND THE GENESIS ACCOUNT OF CREATION

We do not believe that the biblical account of creation denies any change in species as the result of human intervention or

174

selective adaptation or crossbreeding. That is neither the intent nor the vocabulary of Genesis. When Genesis 1 states that God created the plants and animals to reproduce "after their own kind," it does not mean that the species type and limits are always inviolate. The Genesis word *kind* is a general term, having application in different contexts to species or families. Klotz discusses the Hebrew term in Genesis and its relationship to the scientific term species:

> We shall have to agree that the Bible does not use the term "species." The Hebrew word used is *min*, which is probably best translated "kind." The word does not mean species in the same sense that we use the term today. . . .
>
> Accepting the definition of species given [previously], we shall certainly have to admit that there have been new species. . . . True, most of the demonstrable instances have arisen in very artificial situations and under laboratory conditions, so that it is unlikely that they could have arisen in that way out in nature. Nevertheless they are new species in the generally accepted sense of the term. And it is not correct to say that no new species have arisen since Creation.[9]

Understanding the Genesis *kind* and the ambiguity in scientific classification systems removes the artificial dichotomy between *limited speciation* and *special creation*.

CONCLUSION

We conclude our survey of evolution and creation by stating that *there is no direct evidence of the macroevolution proposed by scientists who presuppose a naturalistic and mechanistic world*. On the contrary, many pieces of evidence pointed to by evolutionists can be used by creationists to support the creation model. Thurman provides a summary for our present discussion:

> Recent research still has not produced the evidence called for. . . . The evolutionist crosses these gaps by faith in

---

[9]Klotz, *Genes*, pp. 72-73.

evolution in the same way that a creationist crosses the gaps by faith in God. It is not a matter of whether or not one has faith, because either choice requires it. It should be understood that the object of faith is one of the biggest differences between evolutionists and creationists.[10]

---

[10]Thurman, *Evolution*, p. 112.

CHAPTER 6
The Testimony of the Fossils

Over the last 150 years, scientists have found and catalogued millions of fossils (remains of plants and animals). Many fossils are records of plants and animals that are now extinct. Many others are identical to plants and animals alive today. Fossils are scattered through many different rock formations. Klotz gives a good description of fossils:

> Fossils are the hard parts of plants and animals which have been preserved by petrification. Sometimes bones and teeth are preserved by having their pores filled with mineral matter, and in this case the hard material of the bone or tooth remains intact and unaltered. In other cases the original substance of the hard part is dissolved away and replaced, often particle by particle, by mineral matter, such as silica or carbonate of lime. Wood is commonly preserved in this way, and the process may be so delicate that the cells and other microscopic structures of the wood are preserved even after all the organic matter has disappeared.[1]

Evolutionists assume that the rock strata (layers) containing fossils developed gradually over a period of millions of years. For a fossil to form from a dead organism, that organism must be preserved from corruption by forces that would otherwise disintegrate it long before its physical components could be replaced, almost molecule by molecule, by mineral (rock) deposits. That so

---

[1]John W. Klotz, *Genes, Genesis, and Evolution* (St. Louis: Concordia, 1970), p. 185.

many millions of plants and animals were preserved this way is remarkable. Some fossils represent the entire organism, even its soft parts, which would typically decay long before calcification could take place. How did that remarkable preservation take place? And how do we account for the huge deposits of fossils that seem almost like mass graves because of the abundance of fossils?

Klotz offers a theory of fossilization consistent with the creation model:

> Immediate burial is a first prerequisite for fossilization, and it should be such as to exclude the air so as to prevent oxidation of the organism. Usually this burial is effected by water-borne sediment, so that fossil remains of creatures making their homes in the shallower regions of the seas, rivers, and lakes are the most common. Thus the record is not truly representative of all habitats. Deep sea organisms are comparatively unknown, because so little of these deposits have been elevated onto land. Deposits formed near the mouths of rivers sometimes contain the remains of land animals, but these inclusions are purely accidental and, like the fossils of deep sea organisms, not too common. Windborne materials, such as loess or volcanic ash, sometimes yield fossils of land-living animals, and miring in bogs and quicksands has also provided fossils of land animals. Yet they are still relatively uncommon.[2]

Many fossil beds could have been formed through catastrophic means rather than by the "thousands of years in the making" evolutionary explanation. In a cave in Maryland, fossil remains of dozens of different mammals were found, together with those of many reptiles and birds. These fossils represent animals from tropical, moderate, and polar regions together in one "grave." In Germany there are lignite beds (a form of brown coal) containing large numbers of fossil plants, animals, and insects from various regions and climates of the world. The remarkable preservation of these animals is striking proof of sudden burial. Near Lompoc, California, enormous diatomite deposits were found containing millions

---

[2]Ibid., pp. 203-204.

of beautifully preserved fossil fish, usually in a position indicating sudden death.

The fossilization of such large organisms as whole trees presents another problem to the traditional evolutionary approach to fossilization. These gigantic fossils frequently have been found complete and intact, piercing two or more coal seams. Yet organisms of that size could never have been fossilized if they had been covered slowly during the slow deposition and subsequent coalification of peat bogs. They would have decayed first. We must conclude that they were covered almost immediately, as with sand and water.

FOSSILS "ACCORDING TO THEIR KINDS"

According to the theory of evolution, all life forms have developed gradually and progressively. The fossil record does not support that. In nature there are a number of well-defined main groups of plants and animals without intermediate forms clearly linking them. The fossil record shows the same gaps, in spite of the fact that, according to evolution, all organisms, living or dead (fossilized), represent a continuous "family tree" development without any major gaps among the various groups. These very same gaps, however, are used by evolutionists to classify living forms, distinguishing among family groups, classes, species, etc. The inconsistency of the presence of complicated invertebrates in the Cambrian level is summarized by J. Kerby Anderson and Harold G. Coffin:

> We have also seen that those invertebrates that first appear in the Cambrian period have been complex invertebrates. In no way can these early multicellular organisms be considered primitive. The later appearance of other invertebrates, groups such as the ammonites and insects, also do not give us any support for the various models of evolution. In summary, we should note that the explosion of life in the Cambrian period and the systematic gaps between major invertebrate "kinds" are much more supportive evidence for the creation model than for the various models of evolution.[3]

---

[3]J. Kerby Anderson and Harold G. Coffin, *Fossils in Focus* (Grand Rapids: Zondervan, 1977), p. 44.

The oldest fossil-bearing strata (that is, of multicellular life forms), are those of the Cambrian period. In those strata, fossil remains of *highly* developed life forms have been found also (corals, sponges, worms, crustacea, etc.). Highly developed representatives of several main classifications, even of animal classes, have been found in the Cambrian layer without any trace of common or more simple ancestors. Evolutionists believe that these highly developed life forms required millions of years to evolve. Yet not a single authenticated multicellular fossil has been found in any strata earlier than the Cambrian.

Not a single proof in the fossil record supports the assumption that the single- and multiple-cell organisms are related in their germinal origins, or that all subsequent life forms are developed from earlier, more simple life forms. The theory of evolution is not documented by the fossil record. On the contrary, the oldest documentation we have shows that the main classifications of life forms existed side by side *from the beginning*. Rather than picturing the history of life as a gigantic family tree, we instead can picture it as a large graph of more or less closely associated bars, representing the history of major classes as separate from the beginning.

TRANSITIONAL FORMS IN THE FOSSIL RECORD

Evolutionists are quick to point out that many orders and families of the animal kingdom are not represented in the Cambrian strata but appear only in more recent strata. This is used as evidence that those recent life forms developed or evolved from the earlier life forms so abundant in the Cambrian Age.

Part of the creationist's answer to the above is to question the evolutionist's methods of dating the different strata. We will discuss that at length later. For now we will merely say that without exception the animal and plant families, orders, and classes appear suddenly in "more recent" strata, without any intermediate forms. If they did develop from the Cambrian life forms, where are the *transition* fossils? There simply are no intermediates between invertebrates and vertebrates.

When fossil "proofs" for general evolution are presented, it is usually within the vertebrate classification, since the fish, amphibians, reptiles, birds, and mammals seem to appear in successive strata. Each of those classes, however, in their various orders, always appears suddenly in the fossil record, without intermediate forms. There are four classes of fish: the jawless, the placoderms (armored fish, now extinct), the cartilaginous fish (such as sharks), and the bony fish. The first two groups, which are alleged to be the ancestors of modern fish, contain several orders that are very different from one another and for which no common ancestors have been found among the fossils. The placoderms appear in strata where we would expect, according to the evolution model, to find the ancestors of the cartilaginous and bony fish. However, the placoderms themselves are a widely varied group with their own species, and any derivation of the higher fish from the placoderms is anatomically impossible. Then, too, the cartilaginous and bony fish appear suddenly, with no transitionary forms in the fossil record.

According to evolutionists, the amphibians evolved from the fish, a process that must have taken millions of years and a tremendously large number of transitional forms to accomplish such a great transformation through minute adaptive and mutational changes. Several groups of fossil fish have been suggested as providing the transitional forms that led to amphibians. But it does not appear that any fossils have been found that can be authenticated as a transitional form between any of these fish and any amphibian fossil. Instead, we find that the various amphibian orders appear simultaneously, with marked differences among them and no known common ancestors. It needs to be pointed out that many evolutionists would take issue with the creationists' view of the fossil record.

The lineage of amphibians becomes more confused when we discover that during the Mesozoic Age there are no fossil amphibians at all. Between the various extinct amphibians of the Paleozoic Age and the three living subclasses of amphibians today, no fossil link exists. We propose that the dating system of the evolutionists is completely unreliable, and that the various forms of amphibians developed relatively quickly from the original amphibious prototypes, created by God.

Gish has an interesting discussion of the "fish to amphibian" hypothesis:

For a long time it was assumed that the fish that evolutionists believe gave rise to the amphibians became extinct
about 70 million years ago. In rocks which evolutionists
assume are 70 million years or younger, no fossils of the
fish have ever been found. In about 1939, however, this
type of fish was found to be alive and well off the coast of
Africa. It is a cross-opterygian fish of the genus *Latimeria*. It
was taken from a depth of about 5,000 feet. Here he is still
very much the same fish that is supposed to have given
rise to the amphibians multiplied millions of years ago. It
would certainly be astounding to believe that he has remained so genetically and morphologically stable for all
those millions of years while his cousin was evolving all the
way to man! Furthermore, how could any creature be on
this earth for 70 million years without leaving a trace in the
fossil record? Perhaps there is something wrong with evolutionary assumptions![4]

Evolutionists have fewer problems asserting their belief that
amphibians evolved into reptiles. This is not because there exists
clear fossil evidence of such an evolution, but because amphibian
and reptilian skeletal structures are so similar. The major differences between amphibians and reptiles are in their soft parts,
which are generally not fossilized. The evolutionists have the
comparatively simple task of finding similar fossil skeletal parts
and proclaiming them related or transitionary forms.

THE ORIGIN OF WARM-BLOODED ANIMALS

The warm-blooded animals are the only ones able to maintain a stable, relatively high body temperature. The origin of
warm-bloodedness is one problem with which evolutionists are
unable to cope by the use of fossil evidence. Mammals are also
skeletally similar to the reptiles, but their soft parts are very different (hair, skin, mammary glands for the nursing of young, etc.).

The two most striking differences between the skeletal parts of

---

[4]Duane T. Gish, *Evolution: The Fossils Say No* (San Diego: Creation-Life, 1978),
p. 65.

mammals and reptiles are ears and jaws. All mammals (both fossil and living) have a single lower jawbone. All reptiles (fossil or living) have at least four bones on either side of the lower jaw. All mammals have three middle ear bones on each side. All reptiles have only one ear bone on each side. Not a single fossil exists with transitionary forms of jaws and/or ears. But evolution tells us that the transitionary forms must have existed. (Perhaps two of the lower jaw bones of some reptiles moved to their ears!) If evolutionists insist on a gradual transition, then how did the transitional forms chew with lower jaws that were not properly hinged, or how could they hear during the complete reorganization of the bones in their ears?

The evolution from reptiles to birds is also an enigma, despite the fact that evolutionists believe they can produce the fossil of a true transitionary form, *Archaeopteryx*. However, *Archaeopteryx* is fully a bird, not a birdlike reptile. The development of a flying animal requires changes in virtually every structure of the nonflying ancestor. We would expect to find numerous transitional forms in a process that requires so many changes. When we consider that this must have taken place at least four times in the evolutionary process (insects, flying reptiles, birds, and bats), then the fossil remnants should be especially numerous. But no transitional series have been found leading to any of the four flying animal types we have today. All four kinds of flying animals appear suddenly in the fossil record, complete, and frequently in varying forms. Nevertheless, *Archaeopteryx*, a fossil bird from the Jurassic strata, is presented as the closest thing to a transitional form evolutionists have found yet. However, as Gish remarked, the *Archaeopteryx* was no true transitional form:

> In not a single instance concerning the origin of flight can a transitional series be documented, and in only one case has a single intermediate form been alleged. In the latter case, the so-called intermediate is no real intermediate at all because, as paleontologists acknowledge, *Archaeopteryx* was a true bird—it had wings, it was completely feathered, it *flew*. . . . It was not a halfway bird, it *was* a bird.[5]

---

[5]Ibid., p. 84.

The so-called reptile features of the *Archaeopteryx* fossils consist of clawlike appendages on the edges of the wings, teeth, vertebrae that are turned outward along the tail, and a small breastbone. However, those characteristics do not prove that *Archaeopteryx* is a transitionary form between reptiles and birds, since some birds living today possess similar traits, such as claws on the wings.

EVOLUTION AMONG MAMMALS

We have surveyed a few of the indications that plant and animal life was created in several groups or "kinds," from which limited adaptation and development occurred. We reject the macro-evolution model. When we look at the lack of evidence for the evolution of orders within the class of mammals, we come to the same conclusion.

Consider bats, which are said by evolutionists to have developed from insectivores (moles, shrews, etc.). It should be obvious that major changes must occur necessarily for a molelike animal to become a bat. The "hands" of the insectivore would have to grow enormously, since the flying web of the bat is stretched between the four elongated "fingers" and the hind legs. Fossil bats have been found, some in the lower reaches of the Tertiary strata. But again, even the oldest bats are still bats. Anderson and Coffin discuss the lack of evolutionary evidence for the bat:

> If bats evolved from shrewlike ancestors, there is certainly no fossil evidence to support it. *Icaronycteris* is a very advanced flying mammal. Glenn Jepsen of Princeton University has stated that this Eocene bat "is not a 'missing link' between shrews or anything else and bats, but already a true bat."[6]

THE EVOLUTION AND CLASSIFICATION OF DIFFERENT MAMMALS

The various rodent families appear in the fossil record without any transitional forms. The evolutionary scheme has no explanation

---

[6]Ibid., pp. 62-63.

for the origin of beavers, old world porcupines, and others. Hares and rabbits used to be considered a suborder of the rodents, but today are considered a separate order. They are so intrinsically different that they cannot be classified with any other mammalian order. Even the oldest fossils of these animals exhibit all of the unique characteristics of the contemporary order. The same is true of all the thirty orders of primates.

This type of problem concerns the classification of man, too. Biologists consider man a part of the primate order, which also includes lemurs, monkeys, and apes. The evolutionists picture the primates as having developed from an order of insectivores. However, they have been unable to trace the true origin of the lower primates (lemurs, and tarsiers). The fossil record has no transitional forms; existing fossils of the lower primates are almost identical in form to living animals today. Any indication of transition from lower primates to other monkeys or the apes is absent.

DATING THE STRATA

Although many textbooks assume that strata dating is absolutely certain, such is not the case. Thurman has a helpful discussion of the dating problem:

Evolutionists use several methods of dating fossils, all based on untestable assumptions. The most widely used method is based on the decay rate of several kinds of radioactive materials, such as the uranium-lead or potassium-argon "atomic clocks." An age is estimated by measuring the amount of uranium remaining in a rock sample, comparing it to the amount of lead formed and multiplying this by the decay rate.

This method of dating fossils assumes several things, including: (1) only the radioactive material, and not any intermediate or final decay products (for example, lead) were initially present; (2) no intermediate or final product was added or lost since its initial formation (although some intermediate products are gases); and (3) the rate of radioactive decay has not varied since the beginning of time. Actually, what the scientists determine is only the amount of initial and decay products remaining in the sample. Determining the age requires calculations based on the above assumptions. If these assumptions are true, the calculated age is realistic. But until these assumptions can be supported, no dates based upon them can be known with certainty. There is some question as to just how far the present can be extended into the past, especially when billions of years are involved.[7]

CONCLUSION

Our survey of the fossil record has been necessarily brief and selective. (For a much more comprehensive view of the fossil record, see Dr. Philip Johnson's book *Darwin on Trial*.) We have seen consistently, however, that the objective record does not support the evolution model. Instead, the record is consistent with the creation model. If the general theory of evolution is true, the fossil record would almost certainly provide abundant confirmation, or at the least it would not testify to the inconsistencies of the system. However, we find that the fossil record lacks any significant objective verification of evolution and does point to inconsistencies in evolutionary theory.

We are convinced that no fact in science, including the objective evidence of fossils, will ever controvert the biblical account.

---

[7]L. Duane Thurman, *How to Think About Evolution* (Downers Grove, Ill.: Inter-Varsity, 1978), pp. 106-107.

CHAPTER 7
What Are Human Beings?

What are human beings? How are we like and different from animals? Are we a special creation of God, or did we evolve from lower life forms?

> God said, "Let the earth bring forth living creatures after their kind: cattle and creeping things and beasts of the earth after their kind"; and it was so. And God made the beasts of the earth after their kind, and the cattle after their kind, and everything that creeps on the ground after its kind; and God saw that it was good. Then God said, "Let Us make man in Our image, according to Our likeness; and let them rule over the fish of the sea and over the birds of the sky and over the cattle and over all the earth, and over every creeping thing that creeps on the earth." And God created man in His own image, in the image of God He created him; male and female He created them. And God blessed them; and God said to them, "Be fruitful and multiply, and fill the earth, and subdue it; and rule over the fish of the sea and over the birds of the sky, and over every living thing that moves on the earth." (Genesis 1:24-31)

The Bible does not specifically date the origin of the universe, the earth, life, or humans. The Bible does not require from its genealogies (in Genesis 11) that the creation took place in the year 4004 B.C. This date was initially based on the mid-seventeenth century calculations of James Ussher, an Irish bishop, and has been printed in the margin notes of many Bible editions since. With some minor modifications, some creationist scientists still accept this rendition of the biblical geneologies. But as A. E. Wilder-Smith points out, "The important geneology of Genesis 11 does not profess to be complete and does not sum up the total number of years elapsed from the start to finish. It looks as if Moses knew that his table was incomplete and that he therefore deliberately avoided his usual custom of totalling the years."[1] Therefore, much longer time spans are legitimately allowable on the basis of the biblical worldview and genealogies while still leaning toward a *relatively* young-earth view.

By acknowledging the inexact dating of the early chapters of Genesis, we are not denying that creation took place as Genesis describes it. However, we are acknowledging that Genesis does not strictly limit the date or duration of creation. As one evangelical writer says, "Many of the names mentioned in the OT genealogical tables stand for leading genealogical names, and that the lists cover much longer periods of time (and often cover hundreds of years) than at first thought."[2]

THE IMAGE OF GOD

The first human was very different from the rest of the life forms on the earth. Humans are spiritual beings, created in the image of God: God breathed *his* breath of life into the nostrils of that first person. Humans were an entirely new creation, the high point of God's creative work. The entire earth with its various life forms was made subject to humans. We resemble God in that which separates us from the animals: our spiritual and moral attributes give us the capacity for communion and fellowship with God.

DIFFERENCES BETWEEN HUMANS AND ANIMALS

We are different from all other animals in a number of ways, both immaterially and physically. Let us review just a few of those differences:

---

[1] A. E. Wilder-Smith, *Man's Origin, Man's Destiny* (Minneapolis, Minn.: Bethany Fellowship, Inc., 1968), p. 111.
[2] R. Allen Killen, "Anthropology," in *Wycliffe Bible Encyclopedia*, vol. 1 (Chicago: Moody, 1975), p. 101.

1. We can *think analytically;* we can reason and philosophize. A non-Christian writer, Julian Huxley, noted that only humans possess true language and conceptual thought, art, humor, science, and religion.

2. Another distinction, also noted by Huxley, is that only humans can *record and make history;* we produce and appreciate culture.

3. We can communicate by abstract symbols. We possess *language* capability. One of the first responsibilities given Adam by God was to name the animals (Genesis 2:19-23).

4. Humans are *social beings,* capable of conscious interaction and fellowship. Adam and Eve's union was much more significant than the mating of two animals. It was a spiritual and social union, a marriage, of which no animal is ever capable (Genesis 2:24).

5. We are *economic beings,* able to transact complicated business and to administer goods and services. God instructed Adam and Eve to take control over the earth and "subdue" it (Genesis 1:28).

6. We are *aesthetic beings,* capable of perceiving and appreciating beauty and intangible values. This is closely related to this *ethical* orientation (see number 8 below).

7. Only humans have an understanding of *justice,* more than just a simple awareness of right and wrong (which might be trained into a household pet with a few obedience lessons). Humans can understand and apply concepts of judgment and punishment.

8. Humans are *ethical beings.* We can distinguish between good and bad, right and wrong. We can and do make moral judgments. We have a conscience. Only to humans, of all the animals, could God talk of "good" and "evil." Because of Adam and Eve's sense of justice and this ethical orientation, God could fairly punish them for their willful disobedience in Eden.

9. Only humans can experience *faith.* We alone, of all earthly creation, can worship and trust our Creator.

HUMAN FOSSILS AND EVOLUTION

We have seen that human beings are the direct and special creation of God. But what is evolution's side of the picture? Does the fossil record concerning humans support the idea that *Homo sapiens* developed from lower life forms and are merely sophisticated animals?

Remember that the fossil record concerning human life is scanty, and what fossils do exist are most often fragmentary. We do not possess either the wealth or quality of fossils of humans and humanlike animals that we do of other life forms. Some argue that humans and other primates mostly lived near the equator, and the humid tropical climates were not conducive to fossil preservation. We do, however, possess human and primate fossils from non-tropical areas, and most evolutionists will agree that humans or "proto-humans" lived in a variety of environments, including environments where abundant numbers of other life forms were preserved as fossils. Klotz notes the fragmentary nature of most primate or human fossils:

> There are few complete skulls and even fewer complete skeletons. Often the entire find is represented by a piece of the skull or by a jawbone. Certainly any reconstruction based upon such fragmentary remains is extremely precarious. Hooton calls attention to this by saying that when we recall the fragmentary condition of most of these fossil skulls and when we remember that the faces are usually missing, we can readily see that even the reconstruction of the facial *skeletons* leaves room for a great deal of doubt as to details. To attempt to reconstruct the soft parts, he points out, is an even more hazardous undertaking. The lips, the eyes, the ears and the nasal tip leave no clues on the underlying bony parts. Hooton says that you can model on a Neanderthal skull either the features of a chimpanzee or those of a philosopher. He concludes by saying that the alleged restorations of ancient types of man have very little, if any, scientific value and are likely only to mislead the public.[3]

Another problem with the fossil record is even more serious than those already mentioned with typical fossil formations. Dating of any fossil remains, as we saw in the last two chapters, is at best a guess. When the subject is human or humanlike fossils, the problem is worse. That is because many human cultures bury their dead; ceremonial burial is one thing that has distinguished humans

---

[3] John W. Klotz, *Genes, Genesis, and Evolution* (St. Louis: Concordia, 1970), p. 384.

from other animals. Now, if an early human died during one time period, and his or her contemporaries buried the body at any appreciable depth below the surface of the ground, it would be very easy for a scientist, finding the remains thousands of years later, to assume that the individual had lived in the stratum in which the remains were found. Of course, sometimes there are telltale clues to the burial and its depth, which will aid in adjusting the age of some fossil remains. But the clues are not always there, and the chance of misdating a bone because of burial is real.

When Darwin's general theory of evolution gained popularity, evolutionists were eager to find fossil remains that would provide the "missing links" in the evolutionary chain from primate ancestor to modern human. One of the first finds was made in 1890 by a Dutchman, Eugene Dubois, who led an expedition to Java to find man's ancestors in the fossil record. In 1891 he discovered the upper part of a skull and a few teeth in a riverbank. A year later he found a human femur (leg bone) fifteen meters from the original discovery. Those two finds became the first fossil "evidence" of the apelike ancestor of modern human beings. The human prototype was called Java man (scientific name *Pithecanthropus erectus*; later *Homo erectus*). Had Dubois not associated the human femur with the teeth and skull portion, most scientists would have classified the skull piece and teeth as a true ape, not a proto-human. What is perhaps most startling about Dubois's work is that for thirty years he hid two other skulls that were found near the same location and at approximately the same level. The two skulls were almost identical to those of modern aborigines! Gish comments on Dubois's omission and gives an opinion as to the reason for it:

> To have revealed this fact at that time would have rendered it difficult, if not impossible, for his Java Man to have been accepted as a "missing link." . . . His failure to reveal this find [the two skulls] to the scientific world at the same time he exhibited the *Pithecanthropus* bones can only be labeled as an act of dishonesty and calculated to obtain acceptance of *Pithecanthropus* as an ape-man.[4]

---

[4]Duane T. Gish, *Evolution: The Fossils Say No* (San Diego: Creation-Life, 1978), p. 114.

Although it is not certain that Dubois was deliberately trying to be dishonest, his unethical concealment of the two human skulls shows the lengths to which some persons will go in an effort to substantiate their own convictions to others.

Other scattered discoveries of human or humanlike fossils were found in the 1920s and 1930s and were eventually classified as part of the general class of *Homo erectus*. In 1921 two molars were found at a fossil dig near the village of Choukoutien in China. In 1927 another molar was found. Over the years of the dig a total of almost forty individuals were said to be represented by the various tooth, skull, and bone fragments found. The fragments were found in a large fossil deposit of contemporaneous animals. Scientists surmised that the deposit represented the contents of a completely filled giant cavern. There were arguments over whether the cave was filled with a one time stratum of material (indicating a quick filling of the cavern) or with a multitude of strata (indicating an extremely slow filling of the cavern over perhaps thousands of years). However, regardless of how the cavern was filled or how long it took, all of the animal and supposed human fossil remains were closely related within their respective classifications and probably represented, given the evolution model, the same level of development.

The new fossil fragments were used to postulate a human ancestor that the scientists dubbed popularly, Peking man, or, more scientifically, *Sinanthropus*. There was debate about whether or not *Sinanthropus* should be classified as of approximately the same evolutionary stage as Java man (*Pithecanthropus*), and therefore labeled *Pithecanthropus pekinensis*. The outcome of the debate was to classify both *Pithecanthropus* and *Sinanthropus* as representatives of *Homo erectus*. During World War II all of the fossils disappeared and have not been seen since. However, photographs and plaster casts had been made of the fossils, and these continued to be studied by evolutionists. Of course, lacking the actual fossils makes it impossible to use new dating methods to verify the fossils' ages. Subsequent digging at the same site in 1949 yielded a humerus and a tibia that were related to modern humans, plus a jawbone and five teeth similar to the original find. Also found were chopper tools, fireplaces, and charred bones of animals; fire is only known to have been used by *humans*.

FAMOUS FOSSIL HOAXES AND MISTAKES

As we have said, dating and identification of fossil remains are very difficult. Often the scientist must admit that conclusions are just guesses. Among the humanlike fossil remains scientists have found are those that were later shown to be frauds or misidentifications. We will mention some of them here.

One mistake, which can probably be attributed to overzealous misidentification, concerns a molar found in Nebraska in 1922. It was identified as coming from an important transition form between humans and our primate ancestors by at least four well-known scientists. One of them, Osborn, declared on the day he first saw the tooth: "It looks one hundred percent anthropoid . . . it looks to me as if the first anthropoid ape of America has been found."[5] However, in 1927 the molar was correctly identified as that of a pig!

In the early 1900s two well-known British geologists were digging fossils at a quarry in the south of England. They claimed to have discovered a human skull next to an apelike jawbone. Their discovery became the famous Piltdown man. A second human skull was found in the same quarry later by Professor Arthur Smith-Woodward, a seeming confirmation of the first find. Many anthropologists had been skeptical of the first find, but the Smith-Woodward find convinced most of them that Piltdown man was a genuine example of the evolution of humans from more primitive primates. Piltdown man (*Eanthropus dawsoni*) was said to be around half a million years old.

However, by 1950 sophisticated dating and chemical analysis techniques were applied to the Piltdown remains. The findings were startling. The skull was dated at just a few thousand years old, certainly that of a "modern" human. The jawbone was not fossilized at all and was only about as old as the year of its "discovery." It was definitely identified as the jawbone of a modern ape. Gish summarizes the investigation and its results:

The bones were subjected to a thorough and critical examination. It was discovered that the bones had been treated with iron salts to make them look old, and scratch marks

---

[5]Quoted in Bolton Davidheiser, *Evolution and Christian Faith* (Nutley, N.J.: The Presbyterian and Reformed, 1969), p. 347.

were detected on the teeth, indicating that they had been filed. In other words, Piltdown Man was a complete fraud! A modern ape's jaw and a human skull had been doctored to resemble an ape-man, and the forgery had succeeded in fooling most of the world's greatest experts.[6]

Piltdown man and the Nebraska pig's tooth are just two of the blunders or hoaxes that have been exposed in the search for fossilized human ancestors. While we cannot discount all finds as hoaxes or misidentifications, we must learn a lesson from the frauds of the past. It is possible to be tricked or to make mistakes in identification and dating.

THE HUMAN FAMILY TREE

All of the anthropoid fossils that have not been discredited as frauds or misidentifications can be grouped under three main categories: (1) Neanderthal man, (2) Homo erectus, and (3) Australopithecus.

1. *Neanderthal man.* Many remains have been found of Neanderthal man. This, in fact, was the only fossil material available to Darwin when he wrote *The Descent of Man* (1871). While Neanderthal man used to be described as stooped, wild, hairy, and not very intelligent, today he is classified as belonging to our own species, *Homo sapiens.* (See "Pulling the Neanderthals Back into Our Family Tree," *Science,* 19 April 1991, pp. 376-378.) Davidheiser summarizes the importance of the later assessment of Neanderthal man's posture:

After a thorough examination of the skeleton they concluded, "He cannot in view of his manifest pathology, be used to provide us with a reliable picture of a healthy, normal Neanderthalian. Notwithstanding, if he could be reincarnated and placed in a New York subway—provided he were bathed, shaved, and dressed in modern clothing—it is doubtful whether he would attract any more attention than some of its other denizens." They

[6]Gish, *Evolution,* pp. 120-121.

194

affirm that "there is thus no valid reason for the assumption that the posture of Neanderthal man . . . differed significantly from that of present-day men."[7]

The first substantial Neanderthal skeleton was of a man who suffered from arthritis and rickets. No wonder he appeared stooped! So Neanderthal man was no more different from a modern human qualitatively than could be explained by differences such as racial characteristics we see today around the world. His proportionate brain size (percentage compared to body size) is within normal modern human parameters.

2. *Homo erectus.* Peking man and Java man (discussed above) are both classified as *Homo erectus,* which is thought to be a predecessor of *Homo sapiens* (modern humans). It is now recognized, however, that some examples of *Homo erectus* seem to be more recent than some examples of *Homo sapiens!* Such a time overlap tends to discredit the idea that *Homo erectus* developed into *Homo sapiens.*

Anthropologist F. Weidenreich was of the opinion that all so-called *erectus* types should be classified as a subgroup of *Homo sapiens.* Such a classification would assume considerable variability within the species *sapiens.* Weidenreich believed that the anatomical evidence offered no alternative but to unite all of the known human fossils and modern human beings in a single species, *Homo sapiens.* While he suggested that the South African forms may constitute a separate species not in the human line, *Pithecanthropus* and *Sinanthropus* are definitely included in *Homo sapiens.* Other scientists are of the opinion that some fossils classified as *erectus* should be identified more properly as true apes.

3. *Australopithecus.* Many different African finds, which originally had been given a wide variety of names, are now classified as *Australopithecus.* Especially rich finds have been made by the Leakey family in Tanzania. For thirty years Louis and Mary Leakey worked in the Olduvai Gorge in search of the fossil remains of transitional forms between primitive apes and modern humans. On the basis of their finds and other finds in Africa, *Australopithecus* had been divided into two categories: *Australopithecus robustus* and the lighter *Australopithecus habilis* (sometimes called *Australopithecus*

---

[7]Davidheiser, *Evolution,* p. 332.

africanus). A general description of this fossil includes a skull capacity just a little larger than a modern gorilla's but quite a bit smaller than that of modern humans. The jaw is shaped more like a human than an ape. The molars are massive and the jaw is very heavy. Most scientists agree that *Australopithecus* walked like other apes, with knuckles on the ground. Some believe *Australopithecus* is just that, an extinct form of ape, not directly related to human development at all. The "tools" (questioned as real tools by some) found in the proximity of the *Australopithecus* fossils could have been used by other humans rather than by *Australopithecus*. Also, monkeys and some other animals make use of very primitive tools—sticks and twigs to accomplish tasks.

The finds in 1974 by Donald Johanson ("Lucy" and her thirteen companions) are a subclass of *Australopithecus*. Although Johanson identifies them as the "missing links" between apes and humans, there is nothing in their appearance to distinguish them significantly from other *Australopithecus* finds. If we classify those as extinct apes instead of primitive humans, Johanson's finds present no problem to creationists. The only real connection between *Australopithecus* and human beings is the tools found in the vicinity of the fossils. The evolutionists assume, without evidence, that *Australopithecus* used the tools. Creationists are just as justified in assuming that the tools belonged to humans who hunted *Australopithecus*.

We conclude that we have been human from the beginning. We did not evolve from some other life form, and we are not related in origin to any primate.

Why do evolutionists continue to insist that human beings developed from more primitive life forms and that humans and modern primates have common ancestors? They do not base their insistence on the evidence because, as we have seen in our brief survey, the evidence is sketchy at best and certainly open to divergent explanations. No, the evolution of humans from lower life forms is necessary if one holds certain presuppositions that are opposed to Scripture. Many modern scientists are convinced absolutely that God does not exist, and that the universe we see around us is a product of chance (see chapter 2 for a discussion of that theory). Scientists with such presuppositions *must*, therefore, defend the evolution of humans from more simple life forms. With their theory all framed, and the details all filled in, such scientists then look at the physical evidence around them—scrambling, if necessary, to support their beliefs. An excellent book is *Darwin on Trial* by Philip Johnson of the University of California, Berkeley.

As Christians, we believe that human beings are a special creation by God, a fully developed and unique "kind" as described in Genesis 1. Christians believe that men and women are made "in the image of God" and reflect God in special ways. Only we are capable of having fellowship with God and worshiping him. Only we are capable of those thoughts and actions that make us unique among all life in the universe. Christians also believe that the physical evidence around us in the universe is consistent with the biblical revelation of God, the Creator, Sustainer, and Savior.

CHAPTER 8

Natural Disasters and the Design of God

As we have mentioned before, the earth's crust consists of a number of layers, or strata. These vary widely as to type, thickness, composition, distribution, combination, and fossil content. Rock, the general name for the material of which strata are made, can be of different composition. *Igneous* rocks are solidified magma, or lava, molten rock from beneath the earth that rose to or near the surface, cooled, and hardened. *Sedimentary* rocks are produced from the compression of sediments such as clay, sand, and gravel. *Metamorphic* rocks result from changes in preexisting rocks that are subject to (usually sudden) tremendous heat and/or pressure. Most rocks can be classified under these three main categories. Given that the strata exist and that we can determine the causes of the different kinds of rock, the questions before creationists and evolutionists are: When, how, and why did the strata come to be as we see them today?

Biblical data give us keys for understanding the formation of the strata. It is our belief that *biblical catastrophism* provides the most coherent explanation of the rock phenomena in our world. We will demonstrate this by constructing a catastrophic model (using the biblical outline), compare it to the evolutionist *(uniformitarian)* model, and then compare both with the geological record we see on the earth.

WHEN DID THE STRATA COME TO BE?

Our first question deals with the age of the strata. Here we will define the two terms we used above, *catastrophism* and *uniformitarianism*.

In geology, *catastrophism* is the view that the geological formations we see today are primarily the result of one or more large catastrophes. Catastrophism holds that the fossil records and the many strata could have been formed in a relatively short period of time. Geologists who are catastrophists assume that the disasters we see in the world today are very small in comparison to the enormous destructive forces that formed the geological record before recorded history. These local events, however, can give us explanations for how the solid geological data we have today came about. Catasrophists do not necessarily view the strata as a time line that chronicles the history of the earth and the evolution of life in sequence.

Geological *uniformitarianism* is the view that the geological formations we see today are the result of the same natural and environmental phenomena we have around us every day. Change happens only over a very long period of time. Fossils and different kinds of rock are formed over thousands, perhaps millions, of years. Uniformitarianism holds that the fossils and the many layers were formed over an extremely long period. Geologists who are uniformitarians say that "the present is the key to the past." They believe that the strata represent a time line that chronicles, in order, the history of the earth and the evolution of life.

Geological uniformitarians and biological evolutionists are kindred spirits. Both require enormous amounts of time as the only mechanism by which the geological strata could have accumulated and evolution could have taken place. It should be no wonder, then, that most evolutionists are uniformitarians, and most uniformitarians are evolutionists.

However, if catastrophism answers the *when, how,* and *why* questions of geology better than uniformitarianism does, then there is no need to assume an extremely old earth and extremely ancient life on earth. A young earth geologically and the relatively recent creation of life are consistent with the biblical account.

On the other hand, it should be acknowledged from the outset that the biblical record *can* be understood to describe an ancient earth, mostly formed in a uniformitarian pattern, with *occasional* catastrophes such as the Flood without also assuming an atheistic evolution for the origin of the species. Following are some of the other explanations that have been advanced that take the Bible record seriously while accepting an ancient earth. Each has its strengths and weaknesses, just as does the catastrophism and young earth theory we favor and will explain more fully in this chapter.

The *"day-age"* theory holds that each day of creation embraced extended periods of time. This theory turns on the definition of the word "day" for the six days of creation in Genesis 1. Does *day* mean twenty-four hours or a period of time in general, as in "the day of trouble"? Second Peter 3:8 says, "With the Lord one day is as a thousand years" and is often used to support this theory.

The *"gap"* theory postulates that aeons passed between Genesis 1:1 and Genesis 1:2—possibly leaving their own plant and animal remains in the fossils we now find. Usually those life forms are not thought to have been precursors to modern plants and animals but were completely destroyed when fallen Lucifer and his domain was punished, rendering the earth "formless and void" as described in Genesis 1:2. This theory is partially based on the assumption that God would never create something as chaotic as is described in the second verse of the chapter. Something (sin) must have occurred to require ruination of God's original creation. Some even suggest that God could have used a collision with a meteor or comet to destroy Satan's world, causing darkness and chaos much like the "nuclear winter" scientists warn of.

"Progressive creation" suggests that God may have guided a general evolutionary process and intervened at strategic points—such as breathing a soul into humanoids. This theory usually utilizes some form of the day-age theory to explain the six days of creation.

As Bible-believing Christians, we accept what the Bible says and are free to speculate on unspecified aspects of when or how. For instance, the Bible states (as we shall discuss below and in chapter 9) that the earth suffered a great flood in the time of Noah. The Bible also states that life was created by God in its various "kinds," and that humans were God's special creation, in his own image.

We do not so much insist on one interpretation for *how* or *when* God created as we want to show that there is harmony between the Genesis account and true scientific evidence.

HOW DID THE STRATA COME TO BE?

It seems that much of the strata that we now observe developed over a relatively short period of time, being precipitated by the universal flood that destroyed the world as it was known at that time. We accept the biblical account of Noah, the ark, and the Flood. We also accept the geological evidence of a cataclysmic flood that caused massive changes in the earth's crust and in life on earth. The Genesis account of the Flood gives us one picture of the universality of the Flood:

> In the six hundredth year of Noah's life, in the second month, on the seventeenth day of the month, on the same day all the fountains of the great deep burst open, and the flood-gates of the sky were opened. And the rain fell upon the earth for forty days and forty nights. On the very same day Noah and Shem and Ham and Japheth, the sons of Noah, and Noah's wife and the three wives of his sons with them, entered the ark, they and every beast after its kind, and all the cattle after their kind, and every creeping thing that creeps on the earth after its kind, and every bird after its kind, all sorts of birds. So they went into the ark to Noah, by twos of all flesh in which was the breath of life. And those that entered, male and female of all flesh, entered as God had commanded him; and the Lord closed it behind him. Then the flood came upon the earth for forty days; and the water increased and lifted up the ark, so that it rose above the earth. And the water prevailed and increased greatly upon the earth; and the ark floated on the surface of the water. And the water prevailed more and more upon the earth, so that all the high mountains everywhere under the heavens were covered. The water prevailed fifteen cubits higher, and the mountains were covered. And all flesh that moved on the earth perished, birds and cattle and beasts and every swarming thing that swarms upon the earth, and all mankind; of all that was on the dry land, all in whose nostrils was the breath of the spirit of life, died. Thus, He blotted out every living thing that was upon the face of the land, from man to animals to creeping things and to birds of the sky, and they were blotted out from the earth; and only Noah was left, together with those that were with him in the ark. And the water prevailed upon the earth one hundred and fifty days. (Genesis 7:11-24)

From the above passage we can gather the following evidence for a global deluge that destroyed all life except for that aboard the ark. First, God said that he would destroy all people everywhere for their wickedness. The Flood could not have been local or even regional and still destroy every human being as described in Genesis 6:7 (unless the distribution of humans were localized at that time). Second, the water was said to reach fifteen cubits (about thirty feet) higher than the highest mountains. Even if the local mountains around Mesopotamia were meant and if their elevation was similar to what they are today, the water would still have been deep enough to inundate the entire globe. Third, according to the Bible, the Flood was God's judgment against human wickedness (2 Peter 3, etc.). God's judgment was on the whole human race, and so the whole human race was destroyed.

There are also geological reasons for believing in a universal flood. The very strata and rock formations uniformitarians use to support their view more consistently and accurately support the biblical universal flood view.

FOSSILS

Three factors concerning the fossil record point to the universality of the Flood: the number of fossils, the formation of fossils, and the location of fossils.

Both scattered fossils and gigantic fossil beds are located around the world, in all climates and all altitudes. There are fossils in Death Valley in California, the lowest elevation in North America. There are fossils on the tops of high mountain ranges, in tropical jungles, in the polar regions. The presence of fossils, and often of large deposits, in almost every area of the world is a testimony to the universality of the Flood. (See chapter 6 for more on fossils.)

Uniformitarians believe that fossils are formed over an extremely long period of time, under stable conditions. Dead plants or animals are slowly covered with sediment, slowly have pressure exerted on them, and slowly petrify. This produces fossils—or so say the uniformitarians. However, with those same conditions in existence today, we should be able to see fossils forming today. Such is seldom the case. The reason is dead carcasses rapidly decay and disintegrate *unless* they are preserved from the air by a quick burial. The uniformitarians can point to nothing in the present world as the "key" to the past where fossils are concerned. In fact, the evidence points to catastrophe as the origin of fossils.

Henry Morris summarizes how fossilization points to catastrophism:

There are a number of different ways by which fossils can be produced and preserved. In every case, they must be formed rapidly, or else the forces of erosion, bacterial decay, weathering, or other disintegrative processes will destroy them before the fossilization process is complete. Fossil-forming processes include: (1) preservation of bones or soft parts by induration (compact burial); (2) formation of casts or molds; (3) petrification; (4) cementation of tracks or other impressions; (5) freezing; (6) carbonization (e.g., coal).

Although some have visualized fossilization as a slow process, brought about by gradual application of heat, pressure, chemical replacement, etc., it should be obvious that the actual formation of potential fossils in the first place, before other processes can start to work on them at all, requires rapid and compact burial of the organisms concerned, and this requires catastrophism.[1]

STRATA

Our second consideration is the formation of the strata, layers of rock built up on the crust of the earth. As we discussed at the beginning of the chapter, there are several different types of rock, formed in different ways. We will now discuss types of rock. How those types of rocks become layered refers to the types of strata we find. Since our discussion of strata as testimony to catastrophism rather than to uniformitarianism is necessarily short, we will refer only to two issues. We will discuss (1) the evidence that the strata were laid continuously, without interruption, and (2) the evidence that fossil forms, assigned by geologists and evolutionists to different geological "ages," are found in the same stratum, indicating that the life forms lived at the same time.

---

[1] Henry Morris, ed., *Scientific Creationism* (San Diego: Creation-Life, 1974), p. 97.

Each stratum varies in width from less than an inch to several inches. The only way geologists can differentiate between two adjoining strata (ignoring the fossil evidence) is by the "stratification planes," which are present at the intersection of the layers. Henry Morris notes how the stratification planes are formed:

> The adjacent strata may be of the same material, contain the same types of fossils and look very much like it. The planes between them, however, indicate that some slight difference must have intervened to denote a break—either a brief time-lapse in deposition, or a slight change in one or more of the characteristics of the sediment-forming flow.[2]

There are specific characteristics of stratification planes that separate strata from widely different time periods. Picture it this way: Sedimentary action, for example, deposits a layer of strata three inches thick. The cause of the sedimentation is taken away (the river changes course, the lake dries up, etc.). For a long period of time no sedimentation takes place at that location. A stratification plane is formed as the top surface of the stratum. If the stratum contains fossils, they will be fossils of animals and plants that were contemporaries during the time the stratum was deposited. After this long period, sedimentation resumes (the river changes back, rainfall and snow runoff refill the lake, etc.). The stratification plane separates the original stratum from this new stratum. The new stratum, if it contains fossils, will likewise contain fossils of contemporaneous animals and/or plants.

Given the above model, a geologist studying the strata thousands of years later should be able to "decode" the strata. One could assume that the higher stratum was formed after the lower one. If the fossils in the two strata are markedly different, it's logical that the strata were laid at different time periods. The geologist could assume a long separation between strata only if the stratification planes between the strata show evidence of erosion or wear (the geological terms for that are *disconformity, paraconformity,* or *unconformity*). The only way the stratification planes can be protected from erosion is by being covered with the next stratum.

---

[2]Ibid., pp. 112-113.

Is that what geologists find? No. On the contrary, most of the stratification planes between stratum layers are remarkably free from any deterioration at all.

There is abundant evidence, admitted by evolutionists and creationists alike, that fossilized life forms that are supposed to belong to different geologic ages are sometimes found together or in reverse order in the strata. Evolutionists and creationists differ in explaining those anomalies, however.

Evolutionists usually insist that under- or overthrusting of strata is responsible for finding fossil life forms in reverse order from the evolution model. They explain fossil life forms from different "ages" in the same strata by saying that mini-catastrophes occurred, which jumbled the strata and formed new anomalous strata. They still insist that their basic evolution and geologic model holds firm—simple plant forms first, complex plant forms second, marine invertebrates third, marine vertebrates fourth, amphibians fifth, reptiles sixth, and mammals (including humans) last.

Creationists reject the evolutionists' explanations. Creationists agree that the geologic column represents the normal manner or order in which fossil materials were deposited. But this can fit with the catastrophic model too. The waters of the Flood, rising swiftly, overtook different life forms at different times during a very short period. The marine plant life and marine microorganisms, simple to complex, were deposited first. As the waters became polluted from the flooding, the marine animal life succumbed and was deposited. Amphibians, being closest to the water, died and were deposited next. Reptiles, with little ability to escape and with mostly low-level habitats, were next. Warm-blooded animals, especially small ones that could not travel far or quickly, followed. Finally, large warm-blooded animals and humans who were unable to escape the initial reaches of the Flood were deposited last. The extensive amount of erosion accompanying such a flood would provide ample sediment to bury each life-group as it succumbed. Most others who died from the Flood probably were destroyed through decomposition and the destructive force of the waters before they could be deposited into sediment layers and fossilized.

However, as with any theory, not every question is answered.

For instance, how were clumsy sloths nimble enough to scamper to the high ground to die last just so they could be buried in the upper strata? Also, when we look at the way creatures die in modern floods, we find that though many of the stronger, swifter animals escape, that is not true for all. Some get caught on islands or by raging torrents and never make it to the high ground. So why isn't there a peppering of all creatures throughout all strata even if some are concentrated at different levels according to their "ability"?

Actually, there are irregularities in the fossil record, though not quite the way one might imagine. Another explanation for the irregularities could be that with such a violent upheaval it is not surprising that some layers would be upturned.

Finally, let us turn to the types of rocks formed. As we mentioned before, rocks can be described in three major categories: igneous, metamorphic, and sedimentary. We shall see that each kind of rock is formed very quickly and presents no problem to our catastrophic model.

Igneous rock is formed when magmas (rock materials heated to liquid forms) are pushed to or close to the surface of the earth's crust. There they quickly cool and become solid rock. Lava flows from modern volcanoes are contemporary evidence of this.

But geologists are unable to find metamorphic rocks being formed anywhere on the earth today. That fact makes it difficult to determine how they were formed in the past. A metamorphic rock is one that used to be a sedimentary rock (such as limestone), but which changed into a different form (as into marble). Geologists surmise that both tremendous heat and pressure were necessary for the formation of metamorphic rock. Some creation scientists think this is consistent with catastrophism. However, we must acknowledge that the Bible does not answer all the questions. For instance, how could a flood produce enough heat to create metamorphic rock? And certainly at the bottom of the ocean we currently have pressures similar to what was endured under much of the flood, and yet metamorphic rock is not noticeably being formed on the ocean floor.

Sedimentary rocks are most important to geological investigation both because they are the most numerous rock forms and because they are the rocks within which we find fossils. Uniformitarians assume that the normal, slow processes of sedimentation we observe around us today are the same processes that in times past produced sedimentary rock. Sedimentation today, however, does *not* solidify into rock.

So catastrophism is a strong explanation for most of the fossil records, the strata, and the types of rock. Certainly some catastrophism took place, according to the Bible, during the Flood. Whether it was violent enough to account for all the geologic record is a matter of speculation.

This is how the scenario presented by the Bible fits with catastrophism. Genesis 7:11 tells us that at the beginning of the Flood "all the fountains of the great deep burst open." Possibly across the entire ocean floor, which is the thinnest part of the earth's crust, the floor was lifted up, all on the same day. This could have included violent volcanic and earthquake convulsions.

The "floodgates of the sky" were opened and rain fell for forty days and forty nights, around the world. (The source of all of this water, much more than is present in our atmosphere today, is debated.)

Simple calculations reveal that the forty-day downpour did not account for all the floodwater, which covered the highest mountains (even though the mountains may not have been as high then). Most of the water probably came from subterranean water masses that burst forth from the "fountains of the great deep." The torrential downpour would have caused enormous erosion of the soil and rocks still above water. Soon the water began to run down the slopes to lower levels, carrying the first sedimentary materials, which created a "snowballing" effect and increased the erosion.

Floods today can give us a tiny picture of what it must have been like. Local floods can wipe out entire villages, cities, and countrysides in a remarkably short time. Boulders weighing several hundred tons can be transported over long distances in a short time. Thousands of tons of material per square kilometer can be picked up by floodwaters and deposited elsewhere. Rivers can quickly swell to a depth of several stories, destroying everything in their paths. If a localized catastrophe can do that, what would be the effects of a flood so enormous that it covered the highest mountains and ravaged the earth for almost a year and a half? And what would have been the geological aftermath of such a disaster?

Let's look at a plausible flood model. Such a gigantic cataclysm must have caused tremendous sedimentary activity. Because of the continuous rains, the bursting forth of the "fountains of the deep," the enormous magma eruptions, the tremendous earthquakes, the giant tidal waves, and the shifting of the land, the earth's crust would be brutally battered. The magma and sand churned up by the turbulent water and steam would bury millions of marine invertebrates alive on the bottom of the oceans. The first deposits, then, would contain the remains of marine invertebrates that lived on the ocean floor.

Immediately above these first strata we would expect to find the remains of fish, since they could escape a little longer. We would also find more marine invertebrates.

In the meantime, disaster also struck the land. Ultimately, all land animals would also perish. Although people would try to escape by running, climbing, and swimming, they too would drown in the end, in a few cases being buried relatively intact by the turbulent masses of earth and water. The earth's surface would be eroded by the waters. Uprooted trees and plant life in tangled masses would be shoved by the waters to the sea.

The land masses themselves would undergo tremendous changes. Rocks would bounce and crack in the turbulence, disintegrating into gravel and sand. Enormous seas of mud and rocks would race downstream and overtake plant and animal remains, dragging them along.

As the waters calmed, these sediments would slowly settle again. Dissolved chemicals would settle in thick layers at various times and places. Thick sedimentary layers would be formed all over the world. Under the great forces of cataclysm, they would form into fossil-bearing sedimentary rock.

CONCLUSION

This scenario does not account adequately for everything we find in the geological record. For instance, in the Gulf of Mexico one finds twenty-five thousand feet of strata in many, many layers. Some seem to have been formed by evaporation and precipitation, some from shells and bones that accumulated on the ocean floor, and some by sedimentation. How can all this be explained by the cataclysm of the Flood? And yet the Flood may be a better explanation for much of the world's strata than is uniformitarianism. Whether the earth is old or young, uniformitarians and evolutionists cannot adequately explain much of the geological evidence. But the Flood of the Bible does solve many of the mysteries.

CHAPTER 9
Noah and the Great Flood

The great Flood of Noah is a historical record of God's judgment and salvation. In this chapter we will discuss Flood traditions from around the world and their parallels to the biblical account, the ark of Noah, and the gathering and care of the animals.

FLOOD TRADITIONS

The Babylonian Gilgamesh epic, including its lengthy flood story, is the best-known story outside the Bible concerning the early history of the world. The Gilgamesh story tells how the gods decided to bring a flood on mankind, and how Ea, the god of wisdom, told Utnapishtim (corresponding to Noah) of this decision by saying: "Tear down thy house, and build a ship! Abandon thy possessions, seek to save life! Cause to go up into the ship the seed of all living creatures. The ship which thou shalt build, its measurements shall be accurately measured." The account then tells how Utnapishtim built his boat, loaded the animals on, and shut it up against the rains. After the rains subsided, Utnapishtim, like Noah, sent birds out as scouts, to see if it was safe to disembark. The last bird he sent was a raven.

We assume that the Gilgamesh account is an imperfectly transmitted tradition of a true occurrence that Moses, in writing Genesis, preserved perfectly because of the inspiration of God. Perhaps Moses and the writer of the Gilgamesh account had some common sources of information or tradition. That does not take away from the accuracy and inspiration of the biblical account.

Traditions of a global flood are found all over the world, which is strong evidence that all humanity once fell victim to a "judgment by water," and that the only survivors, Noah and his family, then repopulated the world.

FLOOD TRADITIONS WORLDWIDE

Asia. Flood stories are found in the folklore of remote tribes on the Indian peninsula, including those of the Kamars, those in Kashmir, and in Assam. The Karens of Thailand report that a brother and sister were saved on a boat and then repopulated the world. The Vietnamese tradition talks of a brother and sister, also, who were saved in a great "chest," which also contained two of every kind of animal. In a Chinese tradition, Fah-he escaped from the flood with his wife, three sons, and three daughters, from whom the entire population of the modern world was descended. Japanese tradition recounts that their islands rose like jewels from the Pacific, which achieved its present form after a great deluge. These are just a few of the Flood traditions abounding throughout Asia.

Australia and Pacific. The Australian aborigines have flood stories that say that God sent a flood as judgment on man's wickedness. The Hawaiians say that a long time after the first man, Kumukonna, all of mankind became completely wicked. The only righteous man was Nu-u, who was saved from the flood that inundated the land. God left the rainbow as a token of his forgiveness of Nu-u and his family. Natives of Fiji tell that only eight persons were saved from a devastating flood. The Battaks of Sumatra recite that their creator, Debata, was angry with mankind for its evil and determined to destroy it by flood. All of mankind died except for one couple, who took refuge on the peak of a high mountain and were forgiven by Debata. There are many other flood stories among the cultures of Australia and the Pacific.

North and South America. Alaskans tell the story that the "father" of their tribe was warned by a vision that a flood would destroy all life on the earth. He built a raft upon which he was able to save his family and all the animals. The Athapascan Indians on the west coast of North America have a flood tradition. They teach that it rained day and night until "the sky fell and the land was not." All life—plant, animal, and human—was destroyed. Then dry land and life were created again by the Earth-god Nagaitche. Arizona

Indians tell that a great flood destroyed all people except Montezuma and his friend, a coyote. After the flood subsided, the Great Spirit used Montezuma to help repopulate the earth with animals and people. That story is fairly representative of Indian myths across the Americas.

Europe. The ancient Druids taught that in judgment a great fire split the earth so that all of the seas swept over the earth and killed all life except for one wise man, his family, and the animals he had gathered in his barge. The ancient Greeks possessed a flood tradition: Homer wrote of the "rainbow that the son of Kronos set in the clouds" after a great flood. Latin poet Ovid preserved an ancient version of the Flood story in his *Metamorphoses.* Remnants of a Flood tradition survive in the legends of almost every culture in Europe.

Africa. Plato recorded a statement of an Egyptian priest that the gods purified the earth by covering it with a flood. In the Sudan, the natives call Lake Chad *Bahr el Nuh,* the Lake of Noah. Natives in western Nigeria believed that the chief of all the gods, Sango, destroyed all of mankind except for one of his servants because of their ingratitude toward him. Numerous tribal groups throughout the continent preserve a tradition of a great flood.

The parallels between the many stories are amazing. They generally agree that (1) there was some provision made (an ark, barge, etc.); (2) living things were destroyed by water; (3) only a few were saved through divine intervention; (4) the flood was judgment against the man's wickedness; (5) animals are often saved with the few humans, and birds are often used by the humans to report the end of the flood; (6) the vessel comes to rest on a mountaintop, or the people are saved on a mountaintop. Frederick Filby concludes: "The cumulative weight of this evidence is that the present human race has spread from one center and even from one family—a family who themselves experienced the great Deluge of which every story speaks."[1]

NOAH'S ARK

The Hebrew word translated "ark" is *tebah* and means chest or box. The biblical ark was an oblong, almost rectangular, boxlike

---

[1]Frederick Filby, *The Flood Reconsidered* (Grand Rapids: Zondervan, 1970), p. 56.

barge. The ancient *cubit* measurement varied from about 18 inches to perhaps as much as 24 inches. The dimensions of the ark were somewhere between a minimum of 138 meters by 22.5 meters with a height of 13.8 meters and a maximum of 180 meters by 30 meters with a height of 18 meters.

The ark had three decks, each divided into cubicles and compartments. While the dimensions of the compartments are not given in the biblical record, we know that their function was both to separate the animals and to provide what we would today call "bulkheading" for bracing the structure of the ark. It was made of wood and coated with pitch inside and out to waterproof it. It had a door and a window that probably ran around the under edge of the roof overhang.

Noah designed and built the ark over a 120-year period (probably hiring local help as well as using his family members to help). It was a well-built vessel, the perfect design for surviving cataclysmic waves with a heavy cargo.

Was the ark too large for Noah and his family to attempt to build? Would it have been possible for such "primitive" people to construct such a grand structure? Filby notes:

> Some may feel that the ark was too large for early man to have attempted. A survey of the ancient world shows in fact the very reverse. One is constantly amazed at the enormous tasks which our ancestors attempted. The Great Pyramid was not the work of the later pharaohs; it was the work of the 4th Dynasty—long before Abraham![2]

THE ANIMALS ON THE ARK

Many argue that even though the ark had an enormous cargo capacity, it was unequal to the task of carrying two of every single animal on the face of the earth, and enough food to sustain them for over one year. Such critics miss some important points.

First, Noah did not have to take two of *every single species of animal*. He had to take only two of each "kind" into the ark.

---

[2]Ibid., p. 92.

"Kind" is not necessarily the same as "species." (See the discussion in chapter 5; even scientists disagree on their definition of *species*.) Noah was charged with preserving the various "kinds" of animals living at the time of the Flood. He did not have to preserve marine animals, which already lived in water—though many of them died as a result of waters polluted with heavy sediment. He did not have to preserve animals that were already extinct. He did not have to preserve each type of animal within each "kind." For example, it would be reasonable to think that he had only one "dog kind" couple on the ark. From them could have descended (after the Flood) each of the varieties of "dog kinds" we see on earth today—domestic pets, wolves, foxes, jackals, etc. Some conservative scholars estimate that the entire animal kingdom would have been represented by "kinds" and have taken up no more than one-fifth of the storage space on the ark. (That figure even allows for the seven pairs of "clean" animals required for sacrifice.)

Second, Noah did not go out and gather the animals himself. The biblical record indicates that God caused the animals to come to Noah. Given supernatural intervention by God, it does not matter whether their transport was instantaneous or took any or all of the 120 years the ark was being built. Most scientists also believe that at one time there was only one land mass, and no separate continents. If that were the situation before the Flood of Noah, travel distances would have been much shorter. And if the earth's climate was very different from that after the Flood (see chapter 8), and there were no extremes in temperature and climate, then the differences among types of animals within kinds would have been less significant. Given that the earth's topography was much different before it was ravaged by the Flood, physical obstacles to the animals' traveling to Noah would be inconsequential.

Third, the food requirements of the animals could have been substantially less than one would think at first. Many of the younger animals would have required a smaller amount of food than full-sized adults. Some animals naturally hibernate or lower their metabolisms given adverse weather conditions (winter, or a year-long flood, for example). Reptiles are especially prone to slower metabolism in colder weather because they are cold-blooded. Such animals would require less food than normal. And, too, there was still four-fifths of the cargo capacity of the ark, which could accommodate the animals' food needs.

In short, there is no serious reason for not believing the Flood account in Genesis.

CHAPTER 10
The World in Which We Live

In this final chapter we will reflect on some of the wonderful aspects of creation and protection by our Creator, God. We will see the mighty power of God as described by the Bible. We will see that human beings were created by God for a spiritual purpose not given to any other earthly creation. Finally, we will glimpse the coming cataclysm which, like the Flood of Noah, will be the pronouncement of a holy God against sinfulness. And, most important, we will see how to escape that horrible catastrophe through faith in the Lord Jesus Christ.

GOD'S CREATION

The universe around us, the earth, the life, both plant and animal, with which we are surrounded, all testify to creation by God. There is order, design, purposefulness, beauty and complexity in the world around us. Blind force could never create a flower. Instinct could never explain the love of parents for their children. Randomness could never produce the complex living world around us.

The Scriptures abound with testimony to the creative power of God. For example, in the book of Job we find repeated reference to the creation by God, and God himself is quoted extensively concerning his creative power. Job talks of God's creation and even acknowledges the Lord's power to cause the great flood:

With Him are wisdom and might; to Him belong counsel and understanding. Behold, He tears down, and it cannot be rebuilt; He imprisons a man, and there can be no release.

217

Behold, He restrains the waters, and they dry up; and He
sends them out, and they inundate the earth. (Job 12:13-15)

In the latter chapters of Job, the Lord God himself declared his
almighty power in creating the world and everything in it:

Then the Lord answered Job out of the whirlwind and said,
"Who is this that darkens counsel by words without knowledge? Now gird up your loins like a man, and I will ask you,
and you instruct Me! Where were you when I laid the foundation of the earth? Tell Me, if you have understanding, who set
its measurements, since you know? Or who stretched the line
on it? On what were its bases sunk? Or who laid its cornerstone, when the morning stars sang together, and all the sons
of God shouted for joy? Or who enclosed the sea with doors,
when, bursting forth, it went out from the womb; when I
made a cloud its garment, and thick darkness its swaddling
band, and I placed boundaries on it, and I set a bolt and
doors, and I said, 'Thus far you shall come, but no farther;
and here shall your proud waves stop'? Have you ever in
your life commanded the morning, and caused the dawn to
know its place; that it might take hold of the ends of the earth,
and the wicked be shaken out of it?" (Job 38:1-13)

Here in the mighty proclamations of the Lord God we see the
majesty and power of his creation. The universe is not a senseless
jumble of mass and energy. The solar system is not a chance
relationship among pieces of matter in space. The earth is not a
product of random "nature," giving only the illusion of order,
design, and purpose. Plant and animal life is not a mass of evolutionary mistakes and "good tries," on the way to something better
through directionless trial and error. And human life is not just a
chemical process trapped in matter.

GOD'S PROTECTION
The same God who created everything also preserves, sus-
tains, and protects his creation. The same section of Job chronicles
God's work of control over the creation he has made:

> Can you bind the chains of the Pleiades, or loose the cords of
> Orion? Can you lead forth a constellation in its season, and
> guide the Bear with her satellites? Do you know the ordi-
> nances of the heavens, or fix their rule over the earth? Can
> you lift up your voice to the clouds, so that an abundance of
> water may cover you? Can you send forth lightnings that
> they may go and say to you, "Here we are"? Who has put wis-
> dom in the innermost being, or has given understanding to
> the mind? Who can count the clouds by wisdom, or tip the
> water jars of the heavens, when the dust hardens into a mass,
> and the clods stick together? (Job 38:31-38)

Everywhere in the creation we see the protective hand of God.
Although it is true that the world suffers from the effects of the Fall
and the Flood, God's handiwork is still in evidence. God has not
abandoned his creation. On the contrary, if it were not for his
continual preservation of the world, nothing could continue to
exist. The apostle Paul, in Acts 17, declared that in God "we live
and move and exist" (v. 28).

Because of the protective and preserving power of God, Noah
and we, his descendants, can trust God's promise, signed with the
rainbow, that he will never again destroy life as we know it by
flood. The universe is God's creation. Who else has better authority by which to control and direct it?

WHY ARE WE HERE?

On the previous page I quoted the book of Job for its insights
on God's creating the universe. Now I refer to that book again to
point out that humans are conscious, thinking, and worshiping
beings because of God's creative act. In Job 38:36, the Lord asks,
rhetorically, "Who has put wisdom in the innermost being, or has
given understanding to the mind?" As we discussed in more
depth in chapter 7, human life is more than a mass of chemicals in
reaction. Human thought is not based on random impulses that
merely imitate order and intelligence. Each of us really is a *personal
being,* made in God's image. We are the only part of the earth's
creation that can worship him. Only we have the capability for
rational thought. The first responsibility God gave to the first man

was to "name" the animals as they were brought before him by God's direction. Only human beings have inclination to *name* the life we see around us. (Even today, nontheistic scientists spend thousands of hours classifying and "naming" every living and nonliving thing they can observe.)

Man was made in God's image. But something happened after humankind was created. The first human beings, Adam and Eve, deliberately disobeyed their Creator and broke the bond of fellowship that had existed before that. From that point on, all creation was marred by their sin. Romans 5:12 declares that sin entered into the world through one man—Adam—and death from sin. By the time of Noah, humanity was so thoroughly evil that God's solution was a judgment that had catastrophic consequence for the earth, its plants and animals, and the entire human race. God destroyed all people except for Noah and his family by means of the Flood.

Never since has the earth seen destruction such as was wrought by the great Flood. But the day will come when further judgment will come on the whole earth. This judgment, the final judgment, will be on all who reject the truth of God.

That constant confrontation will have its final match during the cataclysm described by the apostle Peter (2 Peter 3). Peter first describes the earth and its inhabitants just before the judgment. His description reminds us of the world we see around us today:

> Know this first of all, that in the last days mockers will come with their mocking, following after their own lusts, and saying, "Where is the promise of His coming? For ever since the fathers fell asleep, all continues just as it was from the beginning of creation." For when they maintain this, it escapes their notice that by the word of God the heavens existed long ago and the earth was formed out of water and by water, through which the world at that time was destroyed, being flooded with water. (2 Peter 3:3-6)

According to Jesus and the apostles, the great flood was a prototype of the final judgment awaiting the present world. Alfred Rehwinkel notes the similarities between the world of Noah and today:

As in the days of Noah, so the world today has reached an unprecedented stage of material and technical progress. There never was a time in the history of man when physical advantages, comforts, luxuries, and leisure were so widely distributed as in our age. We harnessed the forces of nature and have compelled them to do our bidding. . . . Superstition, ignorance, and illiteracy are rapidly disappearing. Human suffering is being alleviated, life is prolonged, and men even speak of the time when death will be abolished.

But there is a counterpart to all this material progress. As of the first generation, so must it be said of the great masses today that they are flesh. They are no longer governed or guided by the Spirit of God. Our age is an age of worldliness, or carnal-mindedness, and secularism; violence and wickedness abound. The philosophy of the average man is decidedly a this-world philosophy. . . .

Such is a picture of the world today. In the chapter which gives the reasons why God brought the worldwide flood upon the first world, we read: "And God saw that the wickedness of man was great in the earth, and that every imagination of the thoughts of his heart was only evil continually. . . . The earth also was corrupt before God, and the earth was filled with violence. And God looked upon the earth, and, behold, it was corrupt, for all flesh had corrupted his way upon the earth" (Genesis 6:5, 11-12).

This description most certainly fits our own generation. The world is ripening fast for its final judgment. . . . "But the Day of the Lord shall come as a thief in the night, in which the heavens shall pass away with a great noise and the elements shall melt with fervent heat, the earth also and the works that are therein shall be burned up. Seeing, then, that all these things shall be dissolved, what manner of persons ought ye to be in all holy conversation and godliness, looking for and hasting unto the coming of the day of God, wherein the heavens, being on fire, shall be dissolved and the elements shall melt with fervent heat! Nevertheless, we, according to his promise, look for new heavens and a new earth wherein dwelleth righteousness. Wherefore, beloved, seeing that ye look for such things, be diligent that ye may

be found of him in peace, without spot and blameless"
(2 Peter 3:9-14).[1]

We, too, can be confident that we are in him, "in peace, without
spot and blameless." We, too, can be part of "Noah's family" and
know that God will rescue us from the coming judgment.

---

[1]Alfred M. Rehwinkel, *The Flood* (St. Louis: Concordia, 1951), pp. 343-350.

PART THREE
*Israel, the
Chosen People*

INTRODUCTION

God had a plan for his creation before anything was created. The history of the world reflects this plan and moves toward the fulfillment of God's purpose. This eternal purpose of God is the overall subject of this book.

In Part 3 we look at the Old Testament and Intertestamental period to see how God dealt with humankind from the beginning until the time of Jesus Christ. We will see that God cares about people. God loves us and wants us to be happy and fulfilled in our relationship to the Creator. The Old Testament is a record of God's relationship with different individuals, particularly of his relationship with a special group of people, the Jews. Is Israel God's chosen people? This section provides the answer.

As we study the people and events of the Old Testament, we are better equipped to judge our own lives and societies by the standards of God's law. Our study can also help us to see the clear evidence of God's mighty work in history. Each person who touched Israel's life was an actor on the great stage of civilization. In viewing their drama, we can see the unending conflicts between small rival clans, observe the collapse of societies that were dedicated to unbridled hedonism, and rejoice with the eternal triumph of those who were faithful to God when the vast majority of people were not.

Beyond all the values and lessons that may come from knowing this history lies the fact that the people and events of the Old Testament pointed to the coming of the Messiah, Jesus Christ, and to the fulfillment of history in him. The underlying theme of the Old Testament—as well as the New Testament—is the progression Creation-Fall-Redemption-Restoration. In the lives of the people and nations that fill its pages, we see this drama moving toward its fulfillment. Journey with me, then, as we relive the early history of God's people and trace his perfect design from the beginning of time, through the Old Testament centuries, to the coming of the promised Messiah, Jesus Christ—God's Son.

SOME DATES

The Old Testament spans history from the Creation to a few centuries before Jesus Christ. Its composition was long, occurring over a period of about a thousand years. Abraham, the first patriarch of Israel, probably lived around 2000 B.C. Approximately 1440 B.C., God entrusted to Moses his revelation of creation and history up through the Hebrew people's forty-year journey in the wilderness of Sinai. The third major Old Testament figure is David, who was king of Israel around 1000 B.C. The last prophecies of the Old Testament were recorded around 400 B.C. (see also LaSor, Hubbard, and Bush, *Old Testament Survey*, pp. 92ff.).

During this long period of history, communication and travel were limited. Most people in the Middle East, the locale of the Old Testament, spent their entire lives within one hundred miles of their birthplaces. Dynasties fought over control of prize lands and people. Small tribes of seminomads roamed the Fertile Crescent, operating under tight family control with relatively little actual control settling in villages but still allowing their flocks to roam (Genesis 13:12, 18; 37:12ff.). One group of seminomads became the source of the Hebrew people, the origin of the Jewish nation, and the seed of the coming Messiah, Jesus Christ.

THE STORY OF THE OLD TESTAMENT

The story of the Old Testament is one of God's relationship to human beings. God created the universe to display his glory and on the earth prepared a beautiful paradise for the first two humans, Adam and Eve, who were made in his image, fulfilling themselves with worship and love of their Creator. Being in God's image, Adam and Eve could make moral choices: they could choose to disobey their Maker. This they did, and that first act of sin plunged all of creation into cataclysmic changes that are still evident today (Romans 8:22).

Despite their faithlessness, however, God did not abandon his love for his people and his creation. In the pages of the Old Testament we have the eloquent testimony of God's love extended toward the men and women he created. God takes an active interest in human affairs and rules his creation, marred as it is by sin, with loving concern.

Near the beginning of the Old Testament we see God calling. We see Abraham, the father of the Hebrew race and of all believers, called by God from Ur of the Chaldees. Abraham was not perfect; his sins as well as his virtues are recorded in the Bible. But Abraham was a man of faith (Genesis 15:6). God's covenant relationship with Abraham is a picture of his relationship with believers throughout all time.

Later in the Old Testament we see God calling Moses to lead his special people, the Hebrews, out of bondage in Egypt and into freedom in Canaan, the promised land (Exodus 3). God entrusted the record of earth's earliest history to Moses, as well as his commands concerning holy worship, right doctrine (teaching), theocratic government, and godly living.

In the story of the Old Testament we see God also calling a special community to a covenant relationship. It, too, pictures the loving relationship between God and the person who responds in faith to his offer of salvation. The covenant community was to come through Abraham's unique son, Isaac. The twelve tribal heads of Israel came through Isaac's son Jacob. In the nation as a whole and in numerous individuals we see God's benevolent care of those who turn to him in trust. We also see God's judgment against sin and unrighteousness—his love working through justice in the midst of the corrupted world.

The Old Testament also records God's actions through his nation, Israel. The nations around Israel are judged for their idolatry, but God cares providentially for Israel as a testimony to his righteousness and faithfulness to his people. We see the establishment of a theocratic rule over Israel, first through the judges and prophets, and then through kings. Saul was the first king of Israel, but he was unwilling to fulfill his reign in harmony with the Lord's directives. By contrast, the kingdom of Israel experienced great glory under King David, the man "after God's heart." David's kingdom is a mirror of God's spiritual kingdom of believers when they inherit the new Jerusalem and the new earth to be prepared for them by God (Revelation 21).

But things are not easy for God's people. Unbelief and complacency take their toll on faithfulness. Sin grows stealthily among God's people until even Israel feels the judgment of the righteous God. The people are overrun by other nations, their possessions are seized, and they are taken captive to strange lands, far from the land promised them by their God. God's mercy is never ending, but it is coupled with his holiness and justice. Even in the midst of judgment against Israel meted out by other nations, however, the God of Abraham, Isaac, and Jacob does not forsake those who turn to him. The great message of the prophets of the Babylonian exile is that restoration would be granted by a merciful God to all who come to him for cleansing from sin.

With this background we turn now to the Old Testament, the record of God, his people, and his providential actions toward all who "call on his name."

CHAPTER 1
In the Beginning

The opening words of the book of Genesis set the tone for the entire Bible: "In the beginning God created. . . ." The author of Genesis does not start out by trying to prove that God exists, or that God created everything, or that this record is accurate. The text of Genesis assumes the existence of the God who is revealed from its first sentence until the last sentence of Revelation. This God is totally unlike any god of any other cultural, social, or religious system. The God of the Bible is pictured as transcendent, eternal, all-powerful, creative, intelligent, moral, personal, and dynamic. Such a God contrasts with ideas of deity in the cultures prominent at the time Genesis was written.

GOD THE CREATOR

Genesis 1:1 asserts that "God created the heavens and the earth." Besides assuming the existence of God, the Bible assumes that the universe has purpose and design. It did not just happen to exist by chance or random organization. The universe itself is not eternal but owes its origin, development, and present existence to the creative and sustaining power of God, who is neither a projection of nor an essential part of his creation. That, too, is contrary to the religious ideas about creation that were current when Genesis was written. The writer of Genesis did not assume the polytheistic views of the cultures surrounding him. (Polytheism says that there are many gods.) Instead, the writer of Genesis declared that the eternal God purposefully caused the existence of the world around us.

Genesis does not detail every aspect of God's original creative acts. After the summary title in verse 1, with verse 2 describing the conditions and circumstance when God began to create in verse 3, we are told what kinds of things God created when he formed the universe: light (v. 3), the earth's atmosphere (vv. 6-8), and the great land masses and oceans (v. 9).

Genesis 1 also pictures his filling the earth with life. God created vegetation (v. 11) that was designed to reproduce itself and pro-vide "fruit" (or sustenance) to the other life forms, animal and human, he would create.

Contrary to common scientific assumptions that there is no creator God, life did not evolve over millions of years of random development from nonlife to the sophisticated life forms—including humans—that we see today. Although one may endlessly debate the significance of alledged scientific evidence, a Christian cannot believe both the Bible and the antisupernatural belief of the general theory of evolution.

Verses 14-19 then describe the creation and earthly purpose of the heavenly bodies—the sun, moon, and stars. Here we observe that the God of the Bible is not the God of some small locality or even of the earth alone. Instead, he is the Creator of the entire universe. Even the stars in the remotest reaches of the universe were made by his word (Psalm 33:6).

The Genesis record turns next to the creation of water life (fish, shellfish, etc.) and birds. Verses 20-22 describe the profusion of this first animal life as God created it: "Then God said, 'Let the waters teem with swarms of living creatures, and let birds fly above the earth in the open expanse of the heavens.' And God created the great sea monsters [that is, large, powerful sea creatures], and every living creature that moves, with which the waters swarmed after their kind, and every winged bird after its kind; and God saw that it was good." In Canaanite mythology the sea monsters were dreaded. The Old Testament often uses them figuratively as the enemies of God (Jeremiah 51:34; Job 5:17; Psalm 74:13). Here, however, they are shown to be part of God's good creation and under his complete control. "And God blessed them, saying, 'Be fruitful and multiply, and fill the waters in the seas, and let birds multiply on the earth'" (Genesis 1:22).

This is the second occasion in Genesis 1 where God is said to have created life to reproduce "after its kind." This important concept is assumed throughout Scripture, even though ideas that one form of life could turn into or produce another form of life have been popular at many times in human history. In distinction, the Bible immediately asserts that the different life forms were created to reproduce offspring like themselves.

Genesis 1:24-25 speaks of the creation of land animals on the earth. Although the most common classifications of animals familiar to the Old Testament people are mentioned specifically, we should not assume that the author of Genesis was ignorant of any other types of animals. The Bible simply states that God created the living animals and then gives a few examples. Here, too, the author reiterates that the land animals were to reproduce "after their kind."

One of the most important distinctions in Genesis 1 is that between humankind and all other life forms. By physical description, a human being may be classified as an animal. But in God's sight and by virtue of being made in God's image, humans are qualitatively different from all other life forms, including animals. The creation of humankind is described separately from that of the animals.

> Then God said, "Let us make man in Our image, according to Our likeness; and let them rule over the fish of the sea and over the birds of the sky and over the cattle and over all the earth, and over every creeping thing that creeps on the earth." And God created man in His own image, in the image of God He created him; male and female He created them. And God blessed them; and God said to them, "Be fruitful and multiply, and fill the earth, and subdue it; and rule over the fish of the sea and over the birds of the sky, and over every living thing that moves on the earth. ...." And God saw all that he had made, and behold, it was very good. (vv. 26-28, 31)

Note several important facts from the above passage. First, man is created in God's image. Only man has a moral soul that is capable of self-knowledge, righteousness and worship and fellowship with his Creator (Ephesians 4:24; Colossians 3:10). No animal can participate in any of the above. Man is crowned as the ruler of God's creation. He is built to enjoy a personal relationship with his maker.

Image and *likeness* are synonyms reflecting the imprint of God left on humankind giving them dignity that should not be violated by murder (Genesis 9:6) or by cursing (James 3:9). The context links "image" with its function, the establishing of dominion over God's creation even as ancient kings left an image of themselves as a symbol representing their rule over their territory. So man was to rule as God's representative (Psalm 8:5-8; Genesis 1:26). This image has (Romans 8:29) and will have its ultimate realization in Christ (1 John 3:2), who will rule in righteousness. This image was not destroyed by the fall (Genesis 9:6; James 3:9).

Second, the above passage from Genesis notes that "man" was created male and female. Although the creation of the first two humans, Adam and Eve, is treated in more detail in Genesis 2, it is significant here that God's original design included both men and women as joint rulers of God's creation. The Hebrew word translated "man" in chapter 1 indicates a human being in general. Genesis 2 informs us that Adam was unfulfilled as a human being until he was in relationship with another, Eve, who is described as his "helper" even as God himself would be the psalmist's helper (Psalm 27:9).

Third, the Genesis 1 description of the creation of human beings asserts that they have a responsibility before God to care for the rest of the world and to cultivate the earth with authority and respect.

Finally, Genesis 1 concludes with God's evaluation of his creation: it was very good. Nothing in the original creation was less than perfect, less than exactly what God intended. For One who is all-powerful, infinite, all-good, and dynamic, creation could be nothing less.

ADAM AND EVE

Genesis 2 and 3 focus on God's relationship to his special creation, humankind. Chapter 2 pictures Adam and Eve in their original and perfect state, created in God's image, fulfilled in the interpersonal relationship of male and female, fellowshiping with their Creator, and assuming their moral responsibilities. Chapter 3 is an awful contrast, chronicling the first humans' deliberate choice to rebel against God's will. Through the fall of man, sin entered the world, which then underwent cataclysmic corruption (see Romans 5:12-21; 8:22).

As Genesis 2 begins, God has blessed the human couple with a perfect environment. Adam and Eve have each other as life partners, and they are in perfect relationship with God. They are not forced to obey God, however, and thus they have moral choice. Genesis 3 describes their deliberate disobedience of God as a free choice, made tempting by the suggestions of the serpent (Satan; Revelation 12:9; 20:2).

God gave Adam and Eve a monumental choice: obey him completely or fall into the depths of sin. The choice was represented very simply. Adam and Eve were not to eat of "the tree of the knowledge of good and evil." Genesis does not record whether God gave them a reason for his commandment. It is enough that the Creator commanded. The serpent, however, challenged God's command, enticing Eve with promises that she and her husband would gain divine knowledge through their disobedience. Both Adam and Eve chose to sin. They ate the fruit and immediately felt the guilt and shame of willful disobedience. Only human beings have the capability to react to make moral choices. Adam and Eve reacted to their sin by hiding their bodies (3:7) and then hiding themselves from God's holy presence (v. 8).

But one cannot hide from the Creator of the universe, the Judge of all life. God's communication with Adam and Eve was direct and to the point: the penalty for their moral irresponsibility, which changed the order of the created world, was judgment. And that judgment would fall upon all their descendants. They were cast out of the Garden of Eden, out of fellowship with God, and into the world now made harsh by the effects of their sin. This world is now a place characterized by physical pain, relational conflict (3:16), and fruitless labor (3:18).

The record is incomplete, however, without the mercy and grace of God displayed in his promise of deliverance. Genesis 3:15 provides a glimpse of the future resolution of sin that would come through the atonement of Jesus Christ, Son of God and Son of Man (Romans 16:20). God prophesies, "And I will put enmity between

233

you [Satan] and the woman, and between your seed and her seed [Christ]; He shall bruise you on the head, and you shall bruise him on the heel."

RESULTS OF THE FALL

The fall of man resulted in separation (1) between God and man, (2) between man and nature, and (3) between man and his fellows. Previous to the Fall, they were in unbroken harmony with him and with each other. The Fall broke that harmony, for no longer could Adam or Eve directly approach God. Their sin loomed large between them and God. Throughout the Old Testament the frequent mention of priests and temple worship reminds us of the necessity for mediation in sacrifices.

The Fall is recorded in Genesis 3. The rest of the Bible points to the ultimate redemption of the fallen world through the mediation of Jesus Christ, in his sacrifice (the atonement), his triumph over death (the resurrection), and his reestablishment of fellowship with God.

After Adam and Eve were banished from God's presence and the Garden of Eden, they had numerous children. Cain and Abel were their first. Abel was a sheepherder, and Cain was a farmer. Both were familiar with the concept of sacrifice in worship to God.

Genesis 4 describes the last sacrifice offered by the brothers together. Cain brought "the fruit of the ground" as his offering (cf. Leviticus 2), while Abel brought animal sacrifices from his flocks. Because of Cain's inner attitude, which was discerned by God, his sacrifice was rejected. Abel's sacrifice was accepted. In jealous anger, Cain killed Abel and then expressed denial when confronted by God. Consequently, God judged Cain and decreed that he would spend his days wandering as a fugitive.

Genesis 5:4 tells us that Adam had sons and daughters. Cain probably married a sister, niece, or grandniece. Considering the length of lives recorded in Genesis (around nine hundred years, on the average), a sizable population could have developed rapidly.

Genesis 4:16-17 provides in summary form the information that Cain traveled to the land of Nod, built a city, married a wife, and fathered a son, Enoch. The rest of Genesis 4 and 5 and the first part of Genesis 6 describe the growth of the human race, list a genealogy of significant descendants of Adam and Eve, and briefly mention both godly and sinful men. This short section serves as a bridge between the account of the first individuals and the problems faced by Noah's generation.

NOAH AND THE FLOOD

To demonstrate his judgment against sin and to check the human evil spreading throughout the world, God determined to destroy most of the human race and to cleanse the earth through a great flood. The "sons of God" marrying the "daughters of men" may refer either to angels (see Job 1:6) or more likely to intermarriage between the godly line with the ungodly (Hosea 1:10; 1 John 3:1). Genesis 6 describes God's plan and his choosing of Noah, who was "a righteous man, blameless in his time" (v. 9) to be the deliverer, or head of the remnant of the human race. The Bible declares that Noah was righteous (6:9). Noah's righteousness was based on his turning to God in repentance and his desire to please God, coupled with God's gracious forgiving of his sins (see D. Clines, *The Theme of the Pentateuch*, pp. 61-79). That coupling is symbolized in Noah's sacrifices, which typified the ultimate sacrifice of Jesus Christ on the cross for all sins, past and present.

God told Noah he would destroy life except for what was preserved in a giant ark, which Noah was commanded to build. During the long period of building, the wicked men and women around Noah could have heeded the Lord's warning and repented. The only people who survived the Flood were Noah and his family—eight people in all. In addition, at least two of every animal type were preserved in the ark. Consistently emphasizing the need for sacrifice or mediation in fallen man's relationship to God, God also commanded Noah to take extra clean animals necessary for sacrifices after the Flood.

After Noah, his family, and the animals entered the ark, the Bible records that God shut the door, leaving the rest of humankind outside to suffer his judgment. God then supernaturally intervened in the weather, causing cataclysmic raining and flooding that lasted for forty days and forty nights (Genesis 7:4). Even though the rains stopped after forty days, the flooding (perhaps increased by subterranean springs) continued for months. Only after sending birds out of the ark several times until one returned with a branch of fresh leaves did everyone leave the ark, which had been deposited on mountains of Ararat by the floodwaters (southeastern Turkey). Noah's first act after leaving the ark was to build an altar and offer sacrifice to God. God responds with a covenant: "I establish my covenant with you: Never again will all life be cut off by the waters of a flood; never again will there be a flood to destroy the earth." (Genesis 9:11, NIV) His rainbow was given as a sign of this unconditional covenant.

Genesis 9 summarizes Noah's activities after leaving the ark. His son Ham sinned, for which Noah prophesied the future servitude of Ham's son, Canaan. This was fulfilled when the nation of Israel entered Canaan, ravaged the inhabitants, and subjected that nation to Israelite rule (Genesis 15:16; Deuteronomy 7:1-6).

Genesis 10 presents a genealogy of Noah's descendants, a list that is probably not meant to be all-inclusive but highlights the most important families and individuals. Although God ordered Noah to populate the whole earth, chapter 11 indicates that people were slow in migrating to other areas. All people spoke the same language until God intervened supernaturally in judgment against the false worship instituted at the Tower of Babel, which many relate to the the ziggurat towers of Mesopotamia, viewed as stairways to heaven (11:1-9; see also 28:12).

Edersheim has described the spiritual significance of the tower and God's dispersion of humankind.

> Holy Scripture does not inform us whether "the tower" was allowed to stand after the dispersion of its builders; nor yet does it furnish any details as to the manner in which "Jehovah did there confound the language of all the earth." All this would have been beyond its purpose. But there, at the very outset, when the first attempt was made to found, in man's strength, a vast kingdom of this world, which God brought to naught by confounding the language of its builders, and by scattering them over the face of the earth, we see a typical judgment, of which the counterpart in blessing was granted on the day of Pentecost; when, by the outpouring of the Holy Spirit, another universal kingdom was to be founded, the first token of which was that gift of tongues, which pointed forward to a

reunion of the nations, when the promise would be fulfilled that they should all be gathered into the tents of Shem![1]

The next event of spiritual significance recorded in the Bible is God's calling of Abraham to be the father of a new nation. Israel would be a nation special in God's sight, God's kingdom people, believers who were to worship him forever.

---

[1] Alfred Edersheim, *Old Testament Bible History* (Grand Rapids: Eerdmans, 1975), pp. 63-64.

CHAPTER 2
Abraham and the Patriarchs

We now move into a new phase in God's plan. From among the people living on earth, God chose one person to whom he would reveal himself in a special way. He would follow God's plan to change the course of history through him and his descendants. From this one person God planned to create a new and mighty nation through which he would display his spiritual goals for humankind, his mercy and grace toward repentant sinners, his judgment against sin, and his ultimate design of a holy "nation" of believers with whom he would enjoy fellowship forever. Originally named Abram ("exalted father"), this man was given a new name, Abraham ("father of many"), in recognition of his new relationship with God and the revolutionary changes to be brought forth in his own life and in human history.

Chapters 12–50 in the book of Genesis tell the story of the patriarch Abraham and of the family that God miraculously gave to him. After reviewing the highlights of Abraham's life, we look also at his son Isaac, his grandson Jacob, and his great-grandson Joseph.

ABRAHAM

The call of Abraham is recorded in Genesis 12:1-3: "Now the Lord said to Abram, 'Go forth from your country, and from your relatives and from your father's house, to the land which I will show you; and I will make you a great nation, and I will bless you, and make your name great; and so you shall be a blessing; and I will bless those who bless you, and the one who curses you

I will curse. And in you all the families of the earth shall be blessed.'" Note that this covenant contains four promises: a great nation would descend from Abraham; Abraham's name would be made great; God would bless those who blessed him and curse those who cursed him; and through Abraham's descendants the whole world would be blessed. God also promised him a land (Genesis 12:7). As the story of Abraham and his descendants unfolds in Genesis, we see how all those promises move toward fulfillment.

Abraham did not doubt the promises of God, unlikely as they might have seemed to him, but immediately left his home in Haran. Abraham and his wife, Sarah (originally Sarai; both meaning "princess"), traveled to Canaan under the Lord's direction. Twice he built altars in recognition of God's sovereign power in directing their lives. Abraham truly believed that God would give him that land for the nation was to arise from his lineage.

Once they had arrived in Canaan, famine swept the land, affecting all of its inhabitants, including Abraham, his family, and those in his camp. Not surprisingly, Abraham's people fled starvation in Canaan by journeying to Egypt. But it was never Abraham's intention to disobey God's direction or to settle there permanently. He was simply coping with a temporary natural disaster.

During that time in Egypt, however, Abraham and Sarah both sinned before the Lord. Fearful that covetous Egyptians might kill him and appropriate Sarah for themselves, he instructed his wife to pretend they were brother and sister. As a consequence, the two were unable to avoid the pharaoh's invitation to Sarah to "join his household" (that is, become his concubine or wife). God's judgment on Abraham and Sarah's lie was to send plagues on the pharaoh and order him to return Sarah to Abraham. That development forcibly ended their brief sojourn in Egypt. Abraham returned to Canaan.

NEPHEW LOT

Abraham and Sarah's troubles were not over, however. Abraham's livestock proved to be a point of contention between him and Lot, his nephew. There was insufficient water and forage for both to supply all their livestock. The two agreed to separate, Abraham settling for more arid land in Canaan, and Lot choosing the best land on the Jordan plain, near the evil cities of Sodom and Gomorrah. Those choices of land would have serious consequences for Lot and his family.

All was still not peaceful in Canaan. War broke out between two confederations of kings and Lot and his possessions were taken captive. Loyal to his kinsman, Abraham prepared his army—318 trained men—to do battle. Remarkably, the battle went in Abraham's favor, and he was able to free Lot with his possessions.

Some time later, Abraham was instrumental in getting Lot's family out of Sodom and Gomorrah before God destroyed them in judgment. All types of sin, especially sexual sins, were rampant in those two cities. Represented by two angels, God intervened supernaturally, announcing imminent destruction for the two wicked cities. Because of Abraham's pleading with God, God gave Lot and his household time to leave the cities before they were destroyed. Lot's wife, however, disobeyed the angels' warnings not to look back and was caught in the destruction, turning to a "pillar of salt" (19:26).

God spared Lot and his daughters from destruction out of mercy rather than because they were without sin, which is illustrated by the daughters' actions immediately after they fled the city. Fearful that they would never find husbands in that strange wilderness and with their own city destroyed, the two conspired, got Lot drunk, and tricked him into impregnating them both. Their sons, Moab and Ammon, became the source of two nations that often plagued Israel. Ruth, the great-grandmother of David would be a Moabitess.

THE PROMISED SON
At the time Abraham rescued Lot from the kings, Abraham had a curious religious encounter with a king, Melchizedek, who was said to be a priest of "God Most High"—the true God, the God of Abraham (Genesis 14:18-20). Blessed by Melchizedek, Abraham gratefully gave 10 percent of his wealth to this representative of God. In the New Testament, Melchizedek is presented as a type of Christ, and Abraham's homage to him as indicative of spiritual Israel's submission to Jesus Christ (see Hebrews 7:1-10).

In commendation of Abraham's faithfulness, God again spoke

to him and reiterated the promises. Abraham responded to God by pointing out that he had been married for a long time and yet had no heir. How could his descendants be as numerous as the sands if he had no children? Perhaps, as he suggested to God, his descendants would be counted from his closest servant, Eliezer. It was common practice in that culture for a family's inheritance to be passed on through trusted household members who were adopted as legal heirs. No, God declared again, Abraham's descendants would come from his own body.

Abraham tried to be faithful to God's promise, but after years had passed, Sarah convinced him that he should produce an heir by having relations with her servant, Hagar, whose son would become an adopted heir. Abraham agreed, and the son born to that union, Ishmael, was considered by Abraham and Sarah as Abraham's heir, promised by God. That arrangement, too, was a common practice of the time (as found in tablets from Nuzu and a parallel in Hammurabi's code [# 146]).

Although many Old Testament figures, even some who were close to God, took concubines or had multiple wives, that was never God's design; the monogamous relationship was the way God intended things to be, and later this relationship was used to typify the relationship between Christ, the "bridegroom," and the church, the "bride." Eventually God appeared to Abraham and Sarah and clarified that the heir would come through Sarah. Finally, in old age, Sarah conceived, and Abraham received a male heir, Isaac. According to standard local practices, the late-born Isaac became the principal heir, supplanting the status of both Eliezer and Ishmael. Now Abraham's name means "father of many nations." Through Isaac and his descendants, God's promises to Abraham would be fulfilled.

Abraham and Sarah, with their son Isaac, were a true family and the progenitors of the nation of Israel. Ishmael and his mother, Hagar, were set free in lieu of receiving the inheritance, which is similar to the laws of Hammurabi. Ishmael was not forsaken by God. God promised Hagar that he would provide for their needs and that a great people would arise from Ishmael too. Ishmael in fact became the father of the Arabs, and the rivalry between the Jews and the Arabs can be traced to the circumstances recounted in Genesis 21. The two peoples became religious rivals as well, as the history of Jewish-Muslim relations reveals. (See part 4 for further discussion of Islam.)

Throughout both Old and New Testaments, Abraham is noted as the "man of faith" or the "father of the faithful." God knew Abraham's heart and called him to display that commitment even in his relationship to Isaac, commanding Abraham to sacrifice his unique son as a burnt offering (Genesis 22). Even at this request, Abraham did not falter in his commitment to God. He was willing to go through with the sacrifice and had just raised his knife to kill Isaac when God intervened and provided a wild ram for the sacrifice. Mount Moriah, the site of this special offering, became the location of the Jewish temple (2 Chronicles 3:1), typifying the future ultimate sacrifice of God's only Son, Jesus Christ.

Abraham died at the age of 175. His life had not been perfect or sinless, but it had exemplified faithfulness to God and his promises. From that time, approximately 2000 B.C., until today, Jews count Abraham as their father. Christians recognize the spiritual heritage of Abraham and believe that "if you belong to Christ, then you are Abraham's offspring, heirs according to promise" (Galatians 3:29).

ISAAC

Isaac and Rebekah inherited the promises of Abraham. As the new patriarch of the family, Isaac displayed the same faith that he had seen in his father. After twenty years of marriage, he and Rebekah had twin sons, Jacob and Esau. It was God's will that the nation of Israel would trace its heritage through Jacob, even though he was the younger of the twins.

There was often rivalry between the two brothers, and Genesis 25 records the sad consequences of such competition. Esau, hungry and out of food, approached Jacob and asked to share his food. Jacob, realizing his chance to become the chief heir of the family and knowing that Esau regarded the inheritance as of little value, agreed to feed his brother only if Esau would agree to sell his right as the chief heir. The sale of inheritance rights is also seen in the tablets from Nuzu. This Esau did. Although Esau tried to regain his former position in the family several times, God's promise had been to go through Jacob's descendants, not Esau's.

Isaac had his lapses of faith, just as his father, Abraham, sometimes sinned. During a famine, Isaac needed to move his tribe to more plentiful lands. God directed him to Gerar, the land of the Philistines. There Isaac prospered, but there he also committed the sin his father had committed years before in Egypt: Isaac pretended to the king that Rebekah was his sister instead of his wife. When Abimelech discovered Isaac's deception, he quickly warned everyone to leave Rebekah alone, lest God judge them for taking advantage of another man's wife. God used the king to rebuke Isaac for his faithlessness.

Isaac prospered so much in Gerar that the king asked him to leave the land and return to Canaan. Isaac moved away, opening some of the wells that had been dug originally by Abraham but had fallen into disuse. There was still contention with the Philistines so Isaac finally returned to Beersheba. Upon Isaac's return, God reaffirmed his commitment to the promises he had earlier made to Abraham concerning Abraham's descendants.

JACOB

Jacob, the favored younger son of Isaac, became the father of the twelve sons who originated the twelve tribes of Israel. The story of Jacob's life can be divided into four periods: (1) his time in Canaan, until he fled from there after deceiving his father; (2) his time in Mesopotamia, while he worked for Laban in payment for marrying first Leah and then Rachel, and then for flocks and herds; (3) his return to Canaan and life there until he reached 130 years of age; and (4) his sojourn to Egypt, where he spent the last seventeen years of his life.

IN CANAAN

Jacob's early years in Canaan were characterized by almost constant rivalry with Esau. God had promised that the inheritance would be passed to Jacob, and Jacob had coerced Esau into selling him his right as heir. In addition, Jacob was the favorite son of Rebekah. Isaac, however, preferred Esau, in spite of God's decision, and Esau continued to resent Jacob's preferred status.

The last major conflict occurred when Isaac, old and blind, wanted to give a final patriarchal blessing to Esau, whom he had designated as heir. Jacob and Rebekah, however, conspired to steal the blessing for Jacob. Jacob disguised himself as Esau and entered his father's room while Esau was gone. Although Isaac was suspicious, he blessed Jacob, thinking he was blessing Esau (Genesis 27:26-29). When Esau realized the deception his brother and mother had carried out, he demanded an additional blessing from Isaac. Isaac, realizing God's will but loving his son, responded repeating God's prophecy that Esau would serve Jacob, adding that Esau would be man of the sword and would eventually throw off his brother's yoke. In frustration Esau sought to kill Jacob, but Jacob, warned by his mother, planned to leave. Isaac sent Jacob to Mesopotamia to find a wife, diverting Esau's deadly plans.

That tragic scene illustrates the futility of trying to thwart God's plans as well as the sorrow that accompanies deception. None of the family was sinless in this affair. Rebekah was guilty of duplicity in the deception fostered on Isaac. Isaac was guilty of initially not supporting God's choice of Jacob as his heir (Hebrews 11:20). Esau was guilty of treating his inheritance so lightly that he would sell it to Jacob just because he was hungry (Hebrews 12:6). Jacob was guilty of deceiving his father and taking advantage of his brother. The entire family suffered for those sins. Rebekah had to see her favorite son sent away, Esau lost his inheritance, and Jacob became a twenty-year fugitive, estranged from his family.

IN MESOPOTAMIA

Jacob's exile was not without purpose, however. Isaac sent him to find a wife, and he returned twenty years later with two wives, Leah and Rachel, both the daughters of Laban. Jacob's marriage to Leah, who, although not favored, brought him six sons: Reuben, Simeon, Levi, Judah, Issachar, and Zebulun. Rachel, jealous because her sister was fertile and she was barren, sent her maidservant Bilhah to Jacob, much as Sarah had done with Abraham and Hagar. By Bilhah, Jacob had two sons, Dan and Naphtali. Leah retaliated by sending her maidservant Zilpah to Jacob, and two sons were born of that union: Gad and Asher. Finally, Rachel conceived and bore one son, Joseph. Joseph would become Jacob's favorite, since he was born from his beloved Rachel.

IN CANAAN AGAIN

Prompted by the Lord, and by then a very wealthy man with a large family and household, Jacob planned to return to his home in Canaan. He was in no hurry, however, to arrive in the land controlled by Esau, who, Jacob was convinced, was still bitter over Jacob's deception of Isaac. When Esau heard that Jacob was returning, he sent four hundred of his men to meet him. Jacob, fearing the worst, divided his tribe into two equal parts, hoping that Esau would not be able to massacre both groups at once.

In the dark of the night, Jacob called on the Lord. Reminding the Lord of his promises, Jacob threw himself on God's mercy, begging for protection during the coming confrontation. Through the night, Jacob vacillated concerning his relationship with God. In a dynamic supernatural encounter, the Lord himself seems to have appeared to Jacob in bodily form and wrestled with him, as he named the place "Peniel" claiming to have seen God face to face and lived (see also Hosea 12:4). Jacob is left limping, forcing him to depend on God for protection against Esau.

That was the major turning point in Jacob's life. To mark the occasion, God gave him a new name, dropping Jacob ("deceiver, supplanter") and honoring him as Israel ("he struggles with God"). This also became the name of God's nation, descended from Abraham, Isaac, and Jacob.

Fortified by his life-changing encounter with God, Jacob met Esau, and Esau's actions were surprising: the elder brother embraced Jacob, bowed to him, and accepted his gifts. Their relationship was restored. In accordance with God's prophecy, Esau had now deferred to Jacob.

Jacob finally arrived in Bethel and built an altar to the Lord. He cleansed his people from their idols and sacrificed to the Lord, repenting of his deceitfulness and rebellion. God answered Jacob's prayers, reminding him of God's promises, their origin in Abraham, and God's continuing protection over Jacob and his household. The special relationship between Jacob and God was thus cemented over the altar of Jacob's repentance and God's grace.

Finally Jacob and Rachel began the journey to visit Jacob's father, Isaac. On the way, Rachel died while giving birth to Jacob's youngest son, Benjamin. The sons of Jacob now stood to inherit God's promises of the coming nation of Israel. With the death of Isaac and his burial with Abraham in Hebron, Jacob moved from the center of God's stage to the side; Jacob's favorite son, Joseph, then took the forefront in God's miraculous dealings with his people.

JOSEPH

The story of the patriarch Joseph is one of the Old Testament's most significant and interesting chronicles (Genesis 37–50). Throughout his long life Joseph encountered diverse hardships, blessings, people, and places. From his story we learn about early Canaanite and Egyptian life. God uses the story of Joseph to teach us about faithfulness, love, mercy, and honesty. Joseph is a model of wisdom and above reproach.

Consistent with the rest of the Old Testament, the story of Joseph centers on the mighty conciliatory acts of God toward humankind, looking forward to our ultimate reconciliation with him in the sacrifice of Jesus Christ on the cross. Besides demonstrating God's wonderful providence, the story of Joseph forms a bridge in the fulfillment of God's promise to Abraham. God had warned Abraham that his people would be afflicted in Egypt for four hundred years before their deliverance. That affliction began during the story of Joseph. Irving L. Jensen describes the significance of Joseph:

Even though Joseph was not of the Messianic line . . . of the twelve sons of Jacob, God sovereignly chose him to be the benefactor of Israel during the next crucial years of dwelling in Egypt. While in Egypt, the descendants of Joseph and his brothers multiplied rapidly, and soon became a large nation."[1]

BETRAYAL BY HIS BROTHERS

As sons of Jacob's favorite wife, Joseph and Benjamin received more of Jacob's attention and love than did his other children. Jacob's other sons resented Joseph's favored position in the family, especially since he was much younger. They resented his receiving special favors and gifts from his father, including a richly ornamented regal robe. Joseph also had divinely given dreams, which he freely shared with his brothers. The theme of each dream

---

[1]Irving L. Jensen, *Survey of the Old Testament* (Chicago: Moody, 1978), pp. 77-78.

was the same: the elder brothers bowed to and served Joseph.

Joseph's life as a favored child ended abruptly when he was seventeen years old. He had been sent to meet his brothers, who were off tending the flocks. His brothers, seeing him approach, first plotted to kill him or leave him trapped in the wilderness to starve to death. However, in order to avoid direct responsibility for his death, they decided to take advantage of a Midianite caravan that was passing by on its way to Egypt. The brothers sold Joseph to the Midianites as a slave. They stained his valuable coat with animal blood and told Jacob that Joseph had been killed by a wild animal. Jacob mourned for his dead son, the brothers were free of their uppity sibling, and Joseph was on his way to Egypt as a slave. K. A. Kitchen notes the historical accuracy of the story as told in Genesis:

> Finally, the price of twenty shekels of silver paid for Joseph in Genesis 37:28 is the correct average price for a slave in about the eighteenth century B.C.. Earlier than this, slaves were cheaper (average, ten to fifteen shekels), and later they became steadily dearer. This is one more little detail true to its period in cultural history."[2]

IN EGYPT

The Midianites arrived in Egypt and sold Joseph to an Egyptian named Potiphar, who was captain of the pharaoh's guard. Genesis says that Joseph "found favor" from his new master and was eventually made overseer of Potiphar's household. At one point Potiphar's wife tried to seduce Joseph, but he refused her. In retaliation, the wife accused Joseph of attempting to seduce her, and her husband sent Joseph to prison. Yet God used this new calamity in Joseph's life to reveal his will and to give Joseph an even higher position after his release.

Joseph was imprisoned with the king's baker and cupbearer, who both had dreams that only Joseph could interpret. Pharaoh's cupbearer, grateful for Joseph's interpretive powers, promised to speak on Joseph's behalf when he was released from prison. But he forgot. Joseph was left in prison for more than two years before God

---

[2]K. A. Kitchen, *Ancient Orient and Old Testament* (Downers Grove, Ill.: Inter-Varsity, 1966), pp. 52-53.

orchestrated events outside the prison to bring about his release.

God caused Pharaoh to have two dreams. Pharaoh believed the dreams important, but neither he nor his spiritual counselors could interpret them. That jogged the memory of the cupbearer, who then remembered Joseph and his interpretive powers. Summoned from prison into Pharaoh's presence, Joseph, through the power of God, correctly interpreted both dreams. God was warning Pharaoh through the dreams that the next seven years of harvest would be good years; the following seven would be disastrous. Adequate preparation for the seven years of famine needed to begin immediately.

Impressed with Joseph's divine wisdom, Pharaoh appointed him as overseer of all Egypt. During the seven good years, then, Joseph prepared the surplus harvests for the seven lean years to follow. During the famine, he was in charge of dispersing the stockpiles. He had to supply not only the Egyptians but also the many foreigners who came to Egypt to buy food, since the famine covered a much larger area than Egypt alone.

Thus, through what seemed to be calamitous events, God set the stage to bring Jacob's people to Egypt, to preserve them through the coming famine, and to fulfill his prophecy to Abraham that the people would sojourn in Egypt for four hundred years (Genesis 15:13). The circumstances of Joseph's life from favored son to slave to prisoner to vice-regent were all part of God's plan for his people.

In Canaan, Jacob heard of the food available for sale in Egypt and sent his ten sons to buy enough to take care of his people. He kept Benjamin with him, for fear he might lose him as he had lost Joseph. The ten brothers appeared before Joseph but failed to recognize him. Bowing down to this Egyptian official (thereby fulfilling Joseph's boyhood dreams), they pled for food for their people. Joseph did not reveal his identity, but he did place restrictions on the sale: he threw Simeon into prison, sold the other brothers the grain they needed (returning the sale money by hiding it in the sack), and commanded them to return with Benjamin.

The brothers later had to return to Egypt a second time or face starvation of their whole people. This time, Joseph revealed his true identity, asserting God's sovereignty in the situation:

And now do not be grieved or angry with yourselves because you sold me here; for God sent me before you to preserve life.

For the famine has been in the land these two years, and there are still five years in which there will be neither plowing nor harvesting. And God sent me before you to preserve for you a remnant in the earth, and to keep you alive by a great deliverance. Now, therefore, it was not you who sent me here, but God; and He has made me a father to Pharaoh and lord of all his household and ruler over all the land of Egypt. (Genesis 45:5-8)

After weeping together, the brothers returned to Canaan with their money, provisions to feed the people and livestock, and Joseph's command for them to tell Jacob he was alive and wanted Jacob and all of his people to come to Egypt to wait out the famine. While Jacob at first did not believe his sons, the wealth of money and food finally convinced him, and he rejoiced that his lost son was found.

GOD'S PEOPLE MOVE TO EGYPT

The next period of Joseph's life saw the move of Jacob and his people to Egypt. Forced out of Canaan by the widespread famine, they willingly accepted Joseph's invitation to share in the bounty of Egypt, which was prepared for the famine because God had used Joseph to warn the nation. Through both ordinary and regrettable circumstances, God had intervened on behalf of his people and provided for their needs.

On the way to Egypt, Jacob sacrificed in Beersheba. The Lord revealed that he and his family should go to Egypt. Perhaps he remembered that both Abraham and Isaac had gone to Egypt (Genesis 26:1-2). God assured him in a dream that his people should not be afraid to journey to Egypt. Not only was the journey a safeguard against starvation, it was also God's way of providing his people with an environment in which they could multiply in numbers, strength, and wealth, and a fulfillment of God's prophecy to Abraham (Genesis 15:13). On arrival in Egypt, Jacob was presented to the pharaoh by Joseph and given land on which his people could live and prosper. This land of Goshen was the best pastureland in Egypt, and the people prospered beyond their greatest dreams.

Jacob lived in Egypt more than seventeen years. Nearing death, he commanded all his sons and Joseph's two sons, Ephraim and Manasseh, into his presence. He blessed them all, being used by God to designate the two grandsons as representatives with their uncles (except Levi) of the coming twelve tribes of Israel. They, too, would share in the inheritance promised Abraham by God.

Jacob's death was mourned by his family for seventy days. His sons carried his body back to Machpelah in Canaan, where he was buried with Abraham, Isaac, Sarah, Rebekah, and Leah. Then they returned to Egypt and lived the rest of their lives in that foreign land, protected by Joseph's position of power and blessed by God's providence. Joseph lived 110 years, and although most of his life had been spent in Egypt and it was in Egypt that he prospered, he still desired to be buried with his ancestors in Canaan. His desire was fulfilled only when the nation of Israel finally left Egypt hundreds of years later.

The age of the patriarchs ends with the death of Joseph, son of Jacob (or Israel), son of Isaac, son of Abraham. As we have seen, the lives of each of these great men of God demonstrate clearly God's amazing providence.

The accompanying chart lists some of the major events in the lives of the patriarchs. The chronological framework followed is based on a straightforward reading of the Masoretic Text.[3]

CHRONOLOGY OF THE PATRIARCHS

Event	Date	Abraham	Isaac	Jacob	Joseph
Entrance into Canaan (Genesis 12:5)	2091	75			
Ishmael born (16:15-16)	2080	86			
Isaac born (21:5)	2066	100	0		
Mount Moriah (22)	2051(?)	115	15		
Isaac marries Rebekah (25:20)	2026	140	40		
Jacob born (25:26)	2006	160	60	0	
Abraham dies (25:7)	1991	175	75	15	
Jacob goes to Haran (28:5)	1929		137	77	
Jacob marries Leah and Rachel (29:21-30)	1922		144	84	
Joseph born (30:25; 31:38-41)	1915		151	91	0
Jacob and family move to Canaan (31:17-21)	1909		157	97	6
Joseph sold into slavery (37)	1898		168	108	17
Isaac dies (35:28-29)	1886		180	120	29
Joseph given high position (41:39-40)	1885			121	30
Jacob and family move to Egypt (45:6; 47:9)	1876			130	39
Jacob dies (47:28)	1859			147	56
Joseph dies (50:26)	1805				110

---

[3]John H. Walton, *Chronological Charts of the Old Testament* (Grand Rapids: Zondervan, 1978), pp. 40-41.

CHAPTER 3
Moses and the New Nation

The Israelites lived in Egypt some four hundred years, at first
enjoying prosperous peace with their Egyptian benefactors as a
result of Joseph's service to the Egyptian pharaoh. After the advent
of the Hyksos, a line of non-Egyptian rulers, the Israelites' position
changed and they began to be used as a labor force. This development brings us to one of the greatest moments in the history of
Israel, the exodus from bondage in the land of Egypt. This event
marks the beginning of Israel's existence as an independent nation. The promises God made to the patriarch Abraham about the
coming nation were in the process of being fulfilled. The people of
God would soon be on their way to the Land of Promise.

MOSES
The human instrument God used to accomplish his divine
purpose was a Hebrew named Moses. Samuel J. Schultz introduces us to this period of Hebrew history:

> Centuries pass in silence from the death of Joseph to the dawn
> of national consciousness under Moses. Sacred history, how-
> ever, takes on new and exciting dimensions with the unique
> transition of the Israelites from the Pharaonic clutches of slav-
> ery to the status of an independent nation as God's chosen
> people. In less than a lifetime they undergo a miraculous
> deliverance from the mightiest emperor of the day, receive a
> divine revelation that makes them conscious of being God's
> covenant people, and have imparted to them a code of laws

253

in preparation for occupying the land of patriarchal promise. It is not surprising that this remarkable experience was retold and relived annually in the observance of the Passover. Repeatedly the prophets and psalmists acclaim Israel's deliverance from Egypt as the most significant miracle in their history.

So meaningful was this emancipation and so vital was this involvement between God and Israel for coming generations that four-fifths of the Pentateuch or more than one-sixth of the entire Old Testament is devoted to this short period in Israel's history.[1]

MOSES' EARLY YEARS

Moses' parents were from the tribe of Levi. Before Moses was born, they had a daughter, Miriam, and a son, Aaron. When Miriam and Aaron were children, Pharaoh increased the burden of the Israelites with bondage, persecution, and harassment. Frightened by the potential military strength of this populous nation in the midst of his kingdom, Pharaoh determined to do away with any such threat. He therefore decreed that all male children born to Israelite women should be killed at birth by the midwives.

The midwives, however, fearing the God of Israel, deceived Pharaoh. They reported that the Hebrew women gave birth before the midwives could intervene and so had hidden their male children away. Pharaoh then amended his order, directing his men to seize all male babies and throw them into the Nile River. He was determined to erase the Israelite threat to his kingdom.

After Moses was born, his mother hid him at home for three months, but the risk of his being discovered grew too great. What could be done? She decided to keep him in a small basket made of bulrushes and set him adrift among the reeds along the bank of the Nile. Her daughter Miriam would watch over him.

One day, Pharaoh's daughter went down to the river to that very place and found the infant. Taking pity on him, she decided to raise him as her own son. Miriam took the opportunity to volunteer her mother as nursemaid to the baby Moses. Moses, whose name

---

[1]Samuel J. Schultz, *The Old Testament Speaks* (New York: Harper & Brothers, 1960), p. 43.

means "drawn out," thus grew up as the son of Pharaoh's daughter and was schooled in the wisdom of the Egyptian court. Charles Pfeiffer notes the kind of education Moses probably received and comments on the circumstances of Moses' leaving Egypt.

Probably Moses' first task as a student was the mastery of the hieroglyphic system of writing. The name hieroglyphic (literally "sacred writing") is of Greek origin and it suggests that the priests were the first masters of the art of written communication. Hieroglyphic texts date back well over a millennium and a half before the time of Moses, but only the educated priest or scribe had the ability to read and write. . . .

As an Egyptian prince, Moses would have grown accustomed to the skillful music of court harpists and the sound of handmaids reading aloud the stories that had become a part of Egypt's literary heritage. He probably knew by heart the story of Sinuhe, an Egyptian courtier who left his homeland and spent years among the bedouin of the Syro-Palestinian country until he reached old age and was welcomed back to the wonderful land of Egypt.

Yet at some time in his life Moses learned that he was not an Egyptian. He grew increasingly resentful of the way in which the Egyptians treated his own people. As he visited royal construction projects he heard the sound of the taskmaster's whip and the cries of his kinsmen. Scripture gives no hint of the struggle that must have gone on in Moses' soul during those years. Should he forget his oppressed people and seek fame and office among the people who had adopted him? As the son of Pharaoh's daughter might he even succeed one day to the throne? While we do not know what went on in Moses' mind, we do know the choice that he made: "By faith, Moses, when he was grown up, refused to be called the son of Pharaoh's daughter, choosing rather to share ill-treatment with the people of God than to enjoy the fleeting pleasures of sin" (Hebrews 11:24-25).[2]

When Moses was forty (Acts 7:23), he chose to side with his

---

[2]Charles Pfeiffer, *Old Testament History* (Washington: Canon, 1973), pp. 151-153.

natural people, the Israelites, working against the Egyptian bureaucracy in an attempt to achieve some measure of mercy and justice for his people. In anger over the physical abuse of a Hebrew by an Egyptian, Moses killed the Egyptian. Pharaoh found out and attempted to seize Moses and have him killed, but Moses fled to the desert of Midian in Sinai. There he herded sheep for forty years, being seasoned by the Lord for his great calling—to lead the people of Israel out of bondage in Egypt and into the promised land. In Midian Moses married Zipporah, the daughter of Jethro, a priest of Midian who seems to have had some knowledge of Yahweh. They had two sons, Gershom and Eliezer.

CALLED BACK TO EGYPT

At the age of eighty, Moses finally received his call to leadership from the Lord. On Mount Horeb (that is, Sinai) the Lord spoke to Moses out of a burning bush, identifying himself as the great "I AM" and commissioning Moses to fulfill part of God's promise to Abraham. Moses was to be the instrument God used to deliver the Jews from Egypt into the land promised to Abraham so long ago.

In protest, Moses gave God five "good" reasons why he could not comply. God answered each objection, and eventually Moses agreed to obey. He would go to Pharaoh, taking Aaron along as his spokesman.

Moses and his family returned to the Israelite settlement in Egypt, where Aaron acted as Moses' spokesman before the elders. By divine intervention, Moses' staff was turned into a snake, a sign to the people of God's power being with Aaron and Moses. The people paid homage to God's men and looked forward to deliverance from Pharaoh's oppression.

Then Moses and Aaron went to Pharaoh and, as God had commanded, asked permission to celebrate a feast to the Lord in the wilderness. But Pharaoh ignored God's command and instead increased the persecution and exploitation of the Israelites, so that things were worse than before. Moses, now very discouraged, talked to the Lord and was reassured that God's plan would indeed be fulfilled: the people would be freed. Strengthened, Moses and Aaron repeated God's demand to Pharaoh, warning that God would judge Egypt for Pharaoh's disobedience. When Pharaoh challenged their words, Aaron threw down his staff, which miraculously turned into a snake, as God had said it would. However, the magicians of the Egyptian court, mocking Moses, did the same miracle themselves through their occult arts.

THE PLAGUES

Because Pharaoh refused to listen to Moses, God caused ten plagues to descend on the kingdom. Not until after the last one did Pharaoh finally agree to let the people leave Egypt.

1. The first plague was *the Nile turned to blood*. The Egyptians called this river the life of Egypt, and they could now see that the Hebrew God alone had true authority over the god of the Nile (Exodus 12:12).

2. A vast invasion of *frogs* covered the land, disrupting agriculture, commerce, and travel. The frog god was thus also shown to be under the control of the Hebrew God.

3. Next, *lice* infested the entire Egyptian land, afflicting "man and beast." At this point even the magicians recognized Moses' superior power, which they attributed to the true God.

4. Swarms of *flies* covered the land—except not in Goshen, where the children of Israel lived. This supernatural distinction impressed Pharaoh and his magicians, but still he refused to let anyone go.

5. Next came a *plague on the livestock*. This blow was both economic and religious, showing his sovereignty over the bull god of Egypt. As with the fourth plague, only Egyptian animals were affected, as God miraculously preserved Israel's livestock.

6. Painful *boils* afflicting both people (including Pharaoh's magicians) and animals struck next. Pharaoh still refused to let the people go off to sacrifice to their God in the desert.

7. The next plague—*hail*—destroyed livestock and agriculture throughout Egypt. Again, the land of Goshen, the dwelling place of God's people, was spared.

8. An invasion of *locusts* covered the whole land of Egypt so that even the ground could not be seen.

9. For three days *darkness* covered all of Egypt, again with the exception of Goshen making visible His victory over the esteemed Egytian sun god Re.

10. Finally, God caused *the death of the firstborn*, a judgment that Pharaoh and all the Egyptians could not ignore.

257

Moses was warned in detail about the fatal tenth plague, and he prepared the Hebrew people so they could protect themselves from it. At midnight, the Lord would sweep over Egypt, killing the firstborn of every living thing, man and beast, except for those who were protected. That protection was afforded by the sacrifice of a spotless lamb. Each family was to sacrifice such a lamb and to sprinkle its blood on the doorposts. The blood, symbol of God's protective power, would cause the angel of death to pass over.

Thus was instituted what is still one of the most holy Jewish holidays, the Passover. When Jesus Christ came, his followers realized the further significance of the Passover rites: they foreshadow the sacrifice of Jesus Christ as the true Passover Lamb. His blood shed on the cross is the true blood of atonement and protection, and God's judgment on sin "passes over" those who have been protected by that blood.

Pharaoh heard the cry of grief and mourning throughout his land. His household, too, had been affected: his firstborn son was dead, and now he was ready to give up the fight. The God of Israel was too powerful for him. Relenting from his stubbornness, he summoned Moses and Aaron and permitted them to lead the people, with all their possessions, out from the land of Goshen in Egypt and to their God in the wilderness.

Pfeiffer notes the significance of the plagues as indicators of the power of the true God and the impotence of the false Egyptian idols:

The events preceding the exodus may be looked upon as a contest between Yahweh, Israel's God, and the numerous gods of Egypt. The element of power is uppermost in the contest: Egypt's gods are powerless, but Yahweh is omnipotent. While Yahweh is specifically the God of Israel, he is concerned that his power be known among the Egyptians: "And the Egyptians shall know that I am Yahweh, when I stretch forth my hand upon Egypt and bring out the people of Israel from among them" (Exodus 7:5). When the Nile became putrid, and the sun (Re) was darkened, the Egyptians could see the impotence of their gods.

Centuries later the Greeks and Romans expressed contempt and scorn at finding primitive religious ideas in a race so admirable for its achievements. It is one of the

ironies of history that Israel, . . . and usually a pawn between the larger states, should have been the nation
through which the knowledge of the true God came, while
Egypt, at one time the major power in the East, never matured in religious thinking but worshiped a multitude of
gods and entertained crass theories of the universe until the
Jew, the Christian, and ultimately the Muslim put the death
blow to the religious concepts of ancient Egypt.[3]

THE EXODUS
After 430 years in a foreign land, the children of Israel now departed for the Promised Land. Their journey was guided supernaturally by a pillar of cloud by day and a pillar of fire by night. When
God instructed Moses to set up camp near the Reed Sea, Pharaoh
thought he might now ambush the people. When he sent his
chariots after them, the Hebrews fearfully complained to Moses,
who assured them of God's protection.

And indeed Israel saw the salvation of the Lord. He miraculously shielded the Hebrews from the Egyptians with a cloud of
darkness. Then Moses stretched forth his hand and, in the name of
the Lord, the sea parted and the people escaped across the dry sea
bed. When the Egyptians pursued, the waters returned, drowning
them all. That was the last the people saw of the Egyptians, and
after such a great victory and miraculous salvation, the people
sang a song of redemption in gratitude to their God.

Now that God had delivered Israel through his mighty hand,
the long trek across the desert began. Israel complained when they
lacked food and water, and God showed his power by providing
for their needs. At Marah, bitter undrinkable water was made
sweet. At Elim, they found water and shade. God caused supernatural food, *manna*, to rain down from heaven. He gave them
quail for meat and gushing water from the rock at Rephidim.

On the way to Mount Sinai, where God had originally called Moses,
the Israelites encountered the Amalekites, the descendants of Esau,
and fought the first of many battles on their way to the promised
land. Moses and his general, Joshua, went with the armies to battle
and by the power of God, the children of Israel defeated Amalek.

---

[3]Ibid., p. 143.

AT MOUNT SINAI

Three months after leaving Egypt, the Hebrews arrived at the holy mountain. They remained there at Sinai for eleven months. The time was meant to be for celebration and instruction, but the sin of the people turned it into a time of testing, judgment, and eventual repentance.

Moses climbed the mountain to speak with God. The Lord reminded Moses of his faithfulness and power in delivering the people from the Egyptians and assured Moses that Israel had a special covenant relationship with him. They were "a kingdom of priests and a holy nation" (Exodus 19:6). God would not forsake them in the desert. Moses returned and repeated the Lord's words to the people, who agreed to obey all that the Lord said to do. Finally, prepared and sanctified, the people were to wait to be further instructed in God's law.

God then gave the Ten Commandments to the people through Moses. The first four of these laws deal with man's relationship to God. The second six deal with man's relationship to others. The giving of the law was accompanied by thunder, lightning, and other phenomena that caused the people to stand far from Moses. Urged by the people, Moses again ascended the mountain to speak with the Lord.

Moses was with God on the mountain for forty days and forty nights. During that time God gave him detailed instructions concerning a *tabernacle*, or tent, which the Hebrew people were to build in his honor as a symbol of his presence among them (Exodus 25:8). That tabernacle would be the center of Israel's public worship during their wilderness wanderings. It would remain such until David would bring the ark to Jerusalem.

The tabernacle was the place where God would meet Israel and manifest his glory. That earthly tabernacle was beautifully designed to reflect the perfection of God in heaven. The tabernacle would contain the ark of the covenant (or "ark of the testimony"), in which would be kept the stone tablets on which the Ten Commandments were written. In addition, the Lord gave Moses explicit instructions for building an altar, for setting up a system of animal sacrifice, and for making the garments of the priests who would officiate at those rituals.

When Moses came down from the mountain after forty days, he

found the Hebrew camp in chaos. Although the Lord had alerted him to what had taken place there in his absence, Moses was enraged at the sight. The people were singing and dancing in the presence of a golden calf-idol. How could such a thing have happened?

When Moses was gone so long, the people felt leaderless and began to doubt that he would ever return. They requested that Aaron, who was in charge, make them gods to lead them. He collected their gold, melted it down and made it into a calf-idol reminiscent of Egypt and of their deliverance from bondage there. The people then made sacrifices, brought offerings, and celebrated their allegiance to that graven image. Edersheim explains how such a development came about:

> Their leader was gone, and the visible symbol of Jehovah was high up on the mountaintop, like "a devouring fire." They must have another leader; that would be Aaron. But they must also have another symbol of the Divine Presence. One only occurred to their carnal minds, besides that which had hitherto preceded them . . . , who, under the form of a calf, represented the powers of nature. To his worship they had always been accustomed; indeed, its principal seat was the immediate neighborhood of the district in Egypt where, for centuries, they and their fathers had been settled. . . .
>
> Their great sin consisted in not realizing the presence of an unseen God, while the fears of their unbelief led them back to their former idolatrous practices, unmindful that this involved a breach of the second of those commandments so lately proclaimed in their hearing, and of the whole covenant which had so solemnly been ratified.[4]

The true God, the Lord, was angry at the people's disobedience. They had seen his mighty works against the Egyptians and had enjoyed his protection and provision in their escape and subsequent journey through the wilderness. How could they think he was insignificant? Moses, returned from the mountain, interceded with

---

[4] Alfred Edersheim, *Old Testament Bible History* (Grand Rapids: Eerdmans, 1975), pp. 126-127.

the Lord for the people, as he had done earlier, begging him to forgive their sin.

Moses smashed the tablets God had given him and then destroyed the golden calf. His fury along with God's judgment resulted in many deaths. After intercessory prayer, Moses ascended the mountain again and returned with new tablets on which the Ten Commandments were rewritten. The people would now learn more about the law of God.

Besides the Ten Commandments, God gave many more laws to his people while they were camped at Mount Sinai. These are contained in the book of Leviticus, which is basically a rule book informing the people how to relate to a holy God. Laws of sacrifice and laws for daily life are given along with rules for the priests, the Day of Atonement, and the feasts. Together those laws gave the nation an understanding of how they were to act in the presence of a holy God (Leviticus 19:2).

Sometimes people think that God gave the law as a way of salvation for the Jews. Such a view implies that those who could follow the demands of the law would be saved by doing so. Such an understanding of the purpose of the Levitical law is wrong. The law was given first to show God's perfect will, which could never be fulfilled by fallen human beings. The apostle Paul clearly describes the purpose of the law:

> Why the Law then? It was added because of transgressions, having been ordained through angels by the agency of a mediator, until the seed should come to whom the promise had been made. . . . Is the Law then contrary to the promise of God? May it never be! For if a law had been given which was able to impart life, then righteousness would indeed have been based on law. . . . Therefore the Law has become our tutor to lead us to Christ, that we may be justified by faith. (Galatians 3:19, 21, 24)

Second, the law was given to provide the necessary basis for civil government and justice in the new Jewish nation, which was to be established in the promised land. The Jews had been living under Egyptian government for four hundred years. Before that, they had been a relatively small tribal-family unit and needed no large national government. However, God was sending them in to possess the whole land of Canaan, and they needed a workable and comprehensive civil code. The law provided that code.

Once the laws were laid down, the people left Mount Sinai and continued on the way to Canaan. Before leaving, they were numbered and organized according to tribe. They marched through the desert toward the Land of Promise as an ordered and well-regulated group.

MOSES' LAST YEARS

Moses had seemingly intended to lead the people directly from Egypt to the promised land. The Lord instructed Moses that twelve men be sent ahead to spy out the land before they all entered. Those spies then brought back fearsome reports of giants in the land. Only two of the twelve, Joshua and Caleb, encouraged the people to press ahead. The other ten spies convinced the people that they would never be able to defeat the inhabitants of Canaan. God punished the unbelief of the people by making them wander in the wilderness for the next forty years. All those above the age of twenty, except Joshua and Caleb, would die in the wilderness, never seeing the promised land. Instead, their children would be the generation entering the Land of Promise.

Thus the first generation gradually passed from the scene. When the new generation was on the border of Canaan and about to enter, Moses delivered a series of farewell addresses. In them he restated and reaffirmed the covenant God had made with them on Mount Sinai. He reminded them of the blessings that obedience would bring but warned of the consequences of unbelief, one of which would be removal from the land.

Because of disobedience, Moses himself was not allowed to enter the Land of Promise. The career of this great man was now over; leadership was turned over to Joshua. Then Moses went up to Mount Nebo where God permitted him to see the land before his death, and God personally buried him in the land of Moab. Deuteronomy concludes with this evaluation of Moses: "Since then, no prophet has risen in Israel like Moses, whom the Lord knew face to face, who did all those miraculous signs and wonders. . . . For no one has ever shown the mighty power or performed the awesome deeds that Moses did in the sight of all Israel" (Deuteronomy 34:10-12, NIV).

JOSHUA

A truth taught throughout the Bible is that when God says something, it comes to pass. His Word is true. We observe this truth as we read about the conquest of Canaan.

As we have seen, when God called Abraham out of Ur of the Chaldees, he made certain promises. One of those promises was that a great nation would descend from him. That promise was now fulfilled; from that one man a great nation had emerged.

Another part of the promise to Abraham was that God would give him the land of Canaan. The Lord had pledged to Abraham, "Lift up your eyes and look from the place where you are, northward and southward and eastward and westward; for all the land which you see, I will give it to you and to your descendants forever" (Genesis 13:14-15). God's time had now come to fulfill this promise as well. His choice to be leader was Joshua, one of Moses' assistants throughout the years in the wilderness.

THE CONQUEST OF CANAAN

The Lord was very clear in commissioning Joshua to lead the people into Canaan to conquer it, stating: "Every place on which the sole of your foot treads, I have given it to you, just as I spoke to Moses. From the wilderness and this Lebanon, even as far as the great river, the river Euphrates, all the land of the Hittites, and as far as the Great Sea toward the setting of the sun, will be your territory" (Joshua 1:3-4).

After Joshua delivered similar words of encouragement to the people, he sent out two spies to report on the conditions in the city of Jericho. The spies were hidden from the authorities by a prostitute named Rahab. Rahab had heard reports of the mighty works accomplished by the God of Israel, who had brought them to the promised land. She asked them to spare her life and the lives of her family when Jericho was taken. The spies agreed, and Rahab helped them escape safely back to their camp. Centuries later, the New Testament listed Rahab in the Messianic line (Matthew 1:5) and among the faithful because of her courage in protecting the spies (Hebrews 11:31).

The Lord then demonstrated to Joshua and the people that the land would be conquered by his mighty hand and not by their strength or cunning. First the Israelites would enter the land in a supernatural way. The people were led across the river Jordan by the priests bearing the ark of the covenant, which was a special evidence of God's presence with them. As soon as their feet touched the water, the Jordan miraculously rolled back, even though the river was then at flood stage. The priests who held the ark stood on the dry riverbed as the people crossed into Canaan. After all the people of Israel passed through the river, the waters returned to normal. Twelve stones taken from the Jordan were placed at Gilgal as a testimony that their entrance had come about supernaturally.

The first city to be conquered was Jericho. Does it come as a surprise that the method God asked the children of Israel to use is not to be found in any military manual? The priests, bearing the ark of the covenant, led the people around the city walls once each day for six days. One can imagine the bewilderment inside Jericho. On the seventh day, however, the strategy changed. Instead of marching around once, they made seven circuits. After the seventh trip the priests trumpeted with a ram's horn, and suddenly the walls fell down. The Israelites thus conquered the city, sparing only the family of Rahab. No one but God could take credit for such a victory.

After the victory of Jericho the overconfident children of Israel turned their attention to the small city of Ai, where they learned a valuable lesson. Joshua's spies reported that its destruction would be a simple task. But a small contingent of soldiers sent to do the job were summarily routed and chased away. The Lord revealed to Joshua that this setback occurred because of sin among the people. One of the soldiers, Achan, had taken spoils from the city of Jericho in violation of a command from God. Achan paid for his sin with his life, and the next Israelite attack on Ai was victorious.

The conquest of the southern part of Palestine began with the different armies of the Canaanites marshaling their forces against Israel. One group of people, the Gibeonites, decided to deceive the Israelites. Putting on old dusty clothes and carrying dry and moldy bread, they came to Joshua pretending to be from a distant land. Joshua fell for their ruse and made a treaty with them without bothering to consult the Lord. When the Israelites realized they had been tricked, they decided to make them their slaves.

When the other kings heard that the Gibeonites had made a pact with Israel, they decided to make war with them. Joshua defended the Gibeonites, winning a great victory from Beth Horon to Azekah. On that occasion, the Lord actually caused the sun to stand still to allow Joshua more time for fighting.

The northern kings joined forces against Joshua after he had destroyed the southern confederation. Those kings also were delivered into Joshua's hand.

DIVIDING THE LAND

By now Joshua was old, and the Lord again spoke to him. Much land still remained to be conquered. One such area was the land of the Philistines, who would be a source of constant warfare in Israel's future.

Nonetheless, the time had come to apportion the land among the tribes of Israel. The first region to be divided was the Transjordan, or the eastern side of the Jordan River. This was assigned to Reuben, Gad, and half the tribe of Manasseh. Faithful Caleb, along with Joshua, had been among the twelve spies; now they were the only survivors of the adults who had left Egypt. As a reward, Caleb received a special inheritance: territory of Hebron in the southern part of Judah. The central territories were assigned to Ephraim and the other half of the tribe of Manasseh.

The tabernacle was set up at Shiloh, and from that spot the remaining seven tribes divided the land. Simeon was assigned an area from the territory of Judah. Dan and Benjamin inherited land between Judah and Ephraim. The other four tribes—Asher, Simeon, Naphtali, and Issachar—received land in the northern part of Palestine. Joshua received his own inheritance in the territory of Ephraim. Forty-eight cities were given to the Levites along with three cities of refuge.

Joshua addressed the Israelites one final time in Shechem, exhorting them to keep the laws of God. He rehearsed their history and stressed the faithfulness and power of God. The aged leader then urged them to make a clear decision about whom they would serve: "And if it is disagreeable in your sight to serve the Lord, choose for yourselves today whom you will serve: whether the gods which your fathers served which were beyond the River, or the gods of the Amorites in whose land you are living; but as for me and my house, we will serve the Lord" (Joshua 24:15).

The people responded by saying they, too, would serve the Lord. The book of Joshua closes with his death and that of Eleazar, the high priest and successor to Aaron. Regrettably, the people did not keep the promise they made before the Lord that day. Despite the previous warnings of Moses and Joshua, the Israelites forgot the One who had brought them to this land of blessing.

THE JUDGES

We now encounter one of the darkest times in the history of Israel: the time of the judges. God raised up more than a dozen persons in the role of judge, but none were effective in guiding the whole nation such as Moses and Joshua had been. The chaos of Judges demonstrates Israel's need for a king.

THE CYCLE

During the time of the judges the same cycle of events repeated itself again and again. It began with the people in fellowship with God and enjoying his blessings. The nation then fell into sin and forsook God's commandments. This led God to bring judgment upon them by means of a conquering nation. Israel, in bondage, cried out to God for help. The Lord heard their cry and sent a deliverer to rescue them. They again enjoyed the blessing of God. And then the cycle started all over again: blessing, sin, judgment, cry for help, deliverer, and restoration of blessing. That cycle is repeated seven times in the book of Judges. It is a sad tale in the history of God's people.

Briefly, consider the work of the six so-called major judges of Israel. The problems began with the people of Israel forsaking the Lord and serving the Baals and Asherahs. That led God to deliver them into the hands of the Mesopotamian king. He held Israel in bondage eight years until Othniel, a nephew of Caleb, delivered the people. Othniel judged Israel for forty years.

But the Israelites did evil in the sight of the Lord, which caused God to deliver them into the hands of Eglon, king of Moab, for eighteen years. Hearing the cries of his people, the Lord raised up a left-handed man from the tribe of Benjamin named Ehud, who killed the Moabite king. There was peace then for eighty years.

Israel again did evil in the sight of the Lord, causing God to send

Jabin, king of Canaan, to enslave them. After a twenty-year period of bondage, God raised up the woman Deborah as prophet and judge. Deborah sent for Barak to deliver Israel. He, however, would not do battle with Jabin's general Sisera without the aid of Deborah. She consented, and Israel won a victory from its enemies. The land was at peace some forty years.

Afterward, the Israelites again fell into sin, and this time the Midianites were God's tool of judgment. After seven years of oppression and the people's prayers for deliverance, the Lord called Gideon to save Israel. With God's clear guidance, Gideon attacked a huge Midianite army with only three hundred Israelites and won the victory. The land then had rest for forty more years.

When Israel again did evil in God's sight, he delivered them into the hands of a coalition of several peoples including the Ammonites and the Philistines. Under bondage, Israel cried out to God, who raised up a man from Gilead named Jephthah. Jephthah, claiming Israel's right to the region of Gilead, sent messengers to the king of Ammon. When the Ammonite king refused to hear his claim, Jephthah defeated the Ammonites in battle.

Jephthah, however, had made a rash vow before that skirmish: If God would grant him victory, he would offer to the Lord the first thing that came out from his doors. After the victory his own daughter emerged first from his door. How great his sorrow was! But Jephthah fulfilled his vow and sacrificed his daughter. (Some have argued that Jephthah did not in fact perform this horrible deed. They suggest that she was dedicated to the Lord, meaning she should never marry.)

Finally, the dark period of the judges includes the sad story of Samson. Here was a man who had unrivaled strength and the anointing of the Lord, yet he frittered it away and largely made a waste of his life. The Philistines had ruled over Israel for years, and Samson was chosen by the Lord to be Israel's deliverer from Philistine oppression. Samson feuded with the Philistines, killing many of them with the jawbone of a donkey but never fully delivering his people. He spent time with prostitutes and performed feats of strength that had no real significance. In the end he was seduced by Delilah, who managed to get him to reveal the secret of his strength. Once his hair was shorn, his strength vanished, and he was taken captive by the Philistines. They blinded Samson and humiliated him by making him grind at the mill. Then, during a festival that honored their pagan god Dagon, they brought him out for ridicule. Samson prayed to God and was empowered one last time. He used his great strength to bring down the building, killing more in his death than while he lived.

The last verse of the book of Judges aptly sums up that epoch: "In those days there was no king in Israel; everyone did what was right in his own eyes" (21:25). Judges accurately records the history of rebellion that provided a background for Israel's need and cry for a king, which pointed forward to Saul. The book of Ruth provides a happy contrast to the chaos of Judges and points forward to David.

SAMUEL

As the period of the judges is ending, our attention is focused on Samuel, the last judge of Israel. The book that bears his name begins with the judgeship of Eli. During those years a childless woman named Hannah, the wife of Elkanah, came to the tabernacle in Shiloh to pray for a son. Eli promised Hannah that the Lord would answer her prayer, and, sure enough, she had a child whom she named Samuel ("heard of God"). Hannah dedicated him to the Lord at an early age and took him to Shiloh to be Eli's helper. The young boy grew into a God-fearing man, in spite of the bad influence that Eli's evil sons might have had on him. God then spoke to Eli through a prophet about his godless sons and later spoke to Samuel about judgment coming upon the house of Eli.

That judgment occurred when Israel went to war with the Philistines. Eli's sons took the ark of the covenant into battle with them, believing it would ensure their victory. The battle was lost, however, and the ark captured and the sons of Eli killed. Upon hearing the news that the ark had been captured, old Eli fell back off his chair and died of a broken neck.

The ark caused the Philistines nothing but problems, so they finally put it on a cart with two young cows that brought it back to Israel. Tragically, the men of Beth-shemesh looked inside the ark and were struck dead by God. The ark then rested some twenty years at a private residence in Kiriath-jearim while Israel was under Philistine bondage. Eventually Samuel rallied the people at Mizpah, where they repented of their sins and then marched off in the strength of the Lord and drove the Philistines out of the Jewish hill country.

As Samuel became advanced in years the people grew dissatisfied with him and his two sons who were to be his successors. They cried out for a king. When Samuel complained despondently to the Lord, God made it plain that Israel had rejected the Lord, not Samuel. God would give them a king as Moses had predicted they would (Deuteronomy 17:14), a man from the despised tribe of Benjamin named Saul.

Saul was introduced in the narrative as he was looking for some of his father's lost donkeys. He arrived in Ramah, Samuel's hometown, and was invited to stay the night. The next morning Samuel privately anointed him king. Then Samuel summoned the people together and officially proclaimed Saul as their king, an appointment that the people publicly confirmed. Finally Samuel, now far along in years, called the nation together in a farewell speech and exhorted them to remain faithful to the Lord. Even then, however, his influence was not at an end.

The reign of Saul was characterized by frequent fighting. He soon found himself warring against the Philistines. King Saul summoned the people together, but when they saw the large advancing Philistine army, many became frightened and hid themselves. Saul then waited for Samuel to bring the offering to the Lord before they went to battle. When Samuel was late, Saul grew impatient and performed the offering ritual himself. Samuel arrived just then and prophesied that the rulership would be taken away from Saul's family because he had disobeyed God's commandment in his impatience.

Then a war with Amalek led to another act of rebellion by Saul. That disobedience caused his kingship eventually to be stripped from him. When Saul fought the Amalekites by command of the Lord, he was told to destroy them utterly, along with all they possessed. Saul indeed won that battle, but disobeyed God's word by failing to destroy everything: he spared some of the best cattle, along with King Agag. Angrily, Samuel denounced Saul and again proclaimed God's judgment on him. The king repented, but Samuel informed him it was too late. Samuel then killed Agag in Gilgal and departed from Saul's presence, never to see him again.

Now that the Lord had rejected the disobedient Saul as king over his people, the stage was set for his next choice to arrive on the scene. His name was David, whose story we take up in the next chapter.

CHAPTER 4
David and the United Kingdom

Along with Abraham and Moses, David is one of the most important figures in the Old Testament. With each of these men, the Lord established a covenant that had a major effect on the history of Israel and that was, in different ways, related to the work of Jesus Christ and therefore relevant to all humankind.

DAVID

David, like Abraham and Moses, was not perfect; the Bible does not hesitate to record the sins of each of these great followers of God. David, though, typically acted as a man of great faith and, in fact, is described as a man after God's own heart (1 Samuel 13:14; Acts 13:22). His character, therefore, contrasts sharply with that of Saul, whom we have seen was often disobedient to the will of God and whom God therefore rejected as king of Israel.

Although God had given up on Saul and had selected David to succeed him, the Lord waited several years before actually removing Saul from the scene and installing David in his place. Those years were often times of great testing for David but no doubt were uniquely preparing him for the years ahead when he would lead Israel to national greatness.

DAVID AND SAUL

Samuel was still mourning over Saul's regrettable ways when God told him to go to Bethlehem and anoint one of the sons of Jesse as king. God's choice was the youngest son, David. At the request of Saul, David was brought to the king to play the harp in order to calm his unsettled nerves. As all this occurred, Saul was unaware that David was God's choice to succeed him.

Saul meanwhile continued to do the best he could against Israel's enemies—primarily, the Philistines. At one point the Philistines had camped across a valley from the Israelites to do battle with them. They sent their champion, a giant named Goliath, whose awesome size invariably struck fear into the hearts of the people. Goliath would come out daily and ridicule both them and the God of Israel. Although Saul had promised his daughter and exemption from taxation to whoever would fight Goliath, no one could be found. But David, while visiting his brothers, heard Goliath's insults and volunteered to fight the giant. With a stone from his sling, and the power of the Lord, David killed Goliath. That amazing development caused the Philistine army to scatter, and a great victory was won for Israel. This incident represents David's introduction to the nation of Israel.

David became best friends with Saul's son, Jonathan, and was greatly loved by all the people. Naturally Saul was jealous, and twice he personally tried to kill David. After those attempts failed, Saul sent David out to battle. David, however, won a great victory, which caused Saul to seek David's arrest. With the help of his wife, Saul's daughter, Michal, David escaped and went to be with Samuel. Although Saul pursued David, he did not capture him. Afterward Jonathan met David and told him that the matter was hopeless: as long as Saul reigned, David would have to remain a fugitive.

David's flight from Saul carried him to Nob, where the priests gave him bread and the sword of Goliath. In retaliation against that city, Saul killed all its inhabitants except Abiathar the priest, who escaped. He, along with other disenchanted followers, joined David—with Saul in hot pursuit. Saul was obsessed with killing David, and although David had a couple of chances to kill Saul, he refused out of respect for Saul as the Lord's anointed.

The Philistines again went to war with Israel. That turn of events put David in a difficult position, since, under false pretenses, he had joined with his enemies, the Philistines. But the Philistines did not trust him to fight against Israel. Upon seeing the Philistine army, Saul inquired of the Lord what to do, but the Lord did not answer him. In desperation, Saul consulted a medium for direction, a witch at the town of Endor. Saul disguised himself and asked the medium to call up Samuel. The spirit then told Saul of his upcoming death and of defeat for Israel. Saul was devastated by the news.

The Philistines indeed won a great victory against Israel, seriously wounding Saul and killing his three sons. The wounded Saul committed suicide, which caused the remainder of the Israelite army to scatter. So ended the life of Saul, the first king of Israel.

THE REIGN OF DAVID

Israel's period of greatest glory came during the kingships of David and Solomon. Apart from the disastrous reign of Saul, it was the only time in Israel's history when the entire country had one ruler. In some sense it was a golden age. Territorial expansion and religious ideals, as envisioned by Moses, were realized to a greater degree than ever before or after in Israel's history. In subsequent centuries the prophetic hopes for the restoration of Israel's fortunes repeatedly referred to the Davidic kingdom as ideal.

When David heard of the death of Saul, he mourned. Still faithful to his dead king, David first saw to it that an Amalekite who took credit for Saul's death was killed. He then lamented over Saul and Jonathan. The Lord instructed David to go to Hebron, and there he was anointed king of Judah. But before he could be king over the whole nation, he first had to do battle with the house of Saul. Abner, the commander of Saul's army, made Ish-bosheth, Saul's only surviving son, king over Israel while David reigned over Judah. Joab, commanding David's army, defeated the forces of Ish-bosheth, under Abner, and Joab personally murdered Abner. When Ish-bosheth was murdered by two corrupt men, David ordered those men executed also.

With Abner and Ish-bosheth dead, David could become king over Israel as well. As king, he led his men in the conquest of Jerusalem, which at that time was a Jebusite city. The city was taken and renamed the city of David. Jerusalem became the capital of Israel—and will eventually become the most important religious center in the world. When the Philistines heard that David was king, they attempted to attack him at Jerusalem but were routed by him and his men, who drove them out of their territory.

The ark of the covenant was then moved to its intended desti-nation, the city of Jerusalem. Long ago it had been with the Israel-ites in their wilderness wanderings. It had preceded them into the promised land at the river Jordan and had gone before them at the battle of Jericho. Once in the promised land, it moved from Gilgal to Shiloh. The ark was captured by the Philistines, remaining in their land for seven months. When it was returned to Israel, it was kept in Kiriath-jearim in the home of Abinadab. Now David had the ark brought from this residence to Jerusalem. He placed it on a new cart drawn by oxen. Unexpectedly the oxen began to stum-ble, causing the ark to tip. A man named Uzzah reached out to steady it, but when he touched the sacred vessel, he was immedi-ately struck dead. Despondently, David left the ark for three months at the house of Obed-edom.

That may seem harsh punishment for one who was trying to protect the ark, but it is an indication of the ark's important religious symbolism. It was not just a religious artifact. It was the repository of the word of the Lord, the law, and of the proofs of God's benevolent care, including some of the manna that had sustained the Israelites in the wilderness. God's revealed will was so important that it was etched by the finger of God into stone and then preserved in a vessel (the ark of the covenant) that typified or symbolized the presence and attributes of God. The death of Uzzah became, then, a symbol of the sanctity and holiness of God.

Afterward David had the ark carried in the correct manner to Jerusalem. Along the route there was much celebration, including a dance by the enthusiastic David. Seeing David dance like that before the ark annoyed his wife Michal, causing her to despise her husband and criticize him. But David's joy over the arrival of the ark in Jerusalem was undiminished.

David now lived safely in Jerusalem, since the Lord had given him rest from his enemies. Pensively he told the prophet Nathan that he the king lived in a house of cedar while the ark of God resided in a tent. David wanted to see a house built for the Lord and for the ark. The prophet Nathan confirmed to David that the Lord was with him in this desire, but that because David was a man of war, it would be David's son Solomon who would build the temple. Still, David received remarkable promises from God, including that of an everlasting kingdom for his descendants.

Those promises were fulfilled when the greater Son of David, Jesus Christ, came on the scene. (See Luke 1:32; Acts 2:29-31.)

One by one David conquered the surrounding nations: Philistia, Moab, Zobah, Aram, Hamath, Ammon, Amalek, and Edom. After successful battles against such foes, David had clearly demonstrated that he was a force to be reckoned with in that region. He had significantly extended the borders of Israel's territory, for the first time approximating the boundaries of Israel contained in the promise made to his ancestor Abraham (see Genesis 15:18-21).

During that era of arduous fighting by King David, we find a lovely episode with a remaining son of Jonathan named Mephibosheth. David wanted to know if anyone from the house of Saul still survived, in order that he might show them kindness because of the covenant made between David and Jonathan (1 Samuel 20:16-17). When he learned of Jonathan's crippled son, Mephibosheth, David summoned him and allowed him to eat continually at the king's table. That gracious act provides further insight into the love and respect David had for the house of Saul.

SIN AND REBELLION

Next we encounter one of the saddest deeds in the life of David. Instead of taking his rightful place in leading Israel to battle, the king stayed behind in Jerusalem. While he was in the wrong place, one night from his roof he noticed a beautiful woman bathing. Even though he knew she was married, he committed adultery with her, and she became pregnant. Trying to cover up his sinful deed, David ordered her husband, Uriah, back home from battle to be with her.

Uriah, however, was so loyal to the Lord and his fellow soldiers that he refused to be with his wife while Israel was in battle. David tried to get him drunk, but Uriah still would not sleep with his wife. The desperate king then sent Uriah back to the battle and ordered Joab to put him on the front lines and then retreat, ensuring his death. When Uriah's death was reported to David, he believed he had gotten away with his crime. Thereupon he married Bathsheba, feeling safe from any retribution. The Scripture says, however, "The thing that David had done was evil in the sight of the Lord" (2 Samuel 11:27).

The prophet Nathan then came to David and told him a parable about a rich man who had stolen the only ewe lamb that a poor man owned. Nathan's account angered David, who pronounced judgment on the rich man. The prophet then informed him that he, David, was the culprit.

Realizing his great sin, King David repented. Alexander Maclear comments:

> Unlike other kings of Israel and Judah, unlike any common Eastern despot, David did not slay or ill-treat the messenger of judgment; he acknowledged his sin and the justice of the sentence. On this Nathan went on to tell him that the Lord had put away his sin, and he himself was not to die. But future judgments soon appeared. The Lord struck the child that Uriah's wife bare unto him, and it died. But in the midst of judgment God remembered mercy; and in the course of time a second son was born to Bathsheba, whom Nathan named Jedidiah, beloved of the Lord, but David himself called him Solomon, the peaceful one (2 Samuel 12:15-25).[1]

The consequences of David's sin continued. One of David's sons, Amnon, raped Tamar, his half sister. Tamar told the episode to her brother Absalom, who after two years took revenge by murdering Amnon. Absalom then fled to his grandfather Talmai, the king of Geshur, where he remained three years. David mourned for his dead son Amnon but lamented even more the loss of his favorite son, Absalom. Because of David's relentless mourning Joab enlisted the aid of a wise woman, who convinced David to pardon his banished son. David consented but ordered that Absalom not see him face to face for two full years, even though they both lived in Jerusalem. Finally they met, but David was unaware of the evil desires against him that Absalom now harbored. Partial forgiveness had bred resentment.

Four years later, Absalom asked David if he could go to Hebron to pay a vow to the Lord. David gave his permission. Absalom,

---

[1] K. A. Kitchen, *The Bible in Its World* (Downers Grove, Ill.: InterVarsity, 1979), pp. 89-90.

however, used that opportunity to proclaim himself king. Absalom's conspiracy reached many people, including David's advisor Ahithophel. As a result, the king fled from Jerusalem with some of his followers. While leaving the city, David was further humiliated by Shimei, a relative of Saul, who cursed him and threw stones at him.

Battle soon began between the followers of David and the followers of Absalom. Although David wanted to be the victor, he did not want to see his son killed. But his army put Absalom's on the run, and Absalom found himself caught up in a tree by his long hair. Then he was discovered and killed by Joab, David's commander. Absalom's army was soon defeated, and David greatly mourned the death of Absalom. Shortly after, David was able to return to Jerusalem and reoccupy the throne.

DAVID'S FINAL YEARS

In the last years of his reign, David committed another grievous error. The Lord allowed Satan to tempt David to number the people. After he had taken the census, David repented, realizing his sin. God sent the prophet Gad to him with a choice of three punishments: seven years of famine, three months of being chased by his enemies, or three days of pestilence sent by the Lord. David's answer to those choices revealed his insight into the character of God: "Let us now fall into the hand of the Lord for His mercies are great, but do not let me fall into the hand of man" (2 Samuel 24:14). Thus three days of pestilence hit the land and caused many to die. The Lord stopped the hand of the avenging angel at the threshing floor of Araunah in the city of Jerusalem. The prophet Gad ordered David to construct an altar on that spot. The site of this threshing floor (and, earlier, of Abraham's altar for offering Isaac) was Mount Moriah, where the temple of Solomon was eventually built (2 Chronicles 3:1).

David was now old and about to die, yet he had not named his successor. Learning that his son Adonijah was preparing to take over the throne, David made it clear that Solomon was his choice. Before David died, he charged Solomon to obey the commandments of the Lord and walk in his ways. David also discussed with Solomon the plans for construction of the temple, imploring his son to carry them out exactly as prescribed.

David called the leaders together to make Solomon the king officially. He publicly handed over the temple plans to his son and announced that he had made a generous contribution from his vast treasury to construct the temple. When David urged the leaders to follow his example, the people responded by also giving great riches to the temple building fund (1 Chronicles 29). Overwhelmed by their response, David sang a song of gratitude. Soon thereafter, the great king went to his reward.

SOLOMON

Immediately after the death of David, Solomon established himself as king, dealing effectively with several who had been troublesome to David and who might challenge Solomon. During the reign of David the ark had been in Jerusalem, but the tabernacle had been moved from Shiloh to Gibeon. At Gibeon Solomon organized a ceremony to offer sacrifices to God. That night God appeared to him in a dream, inviting him to ask whatever he wanted from the Lord. Instead of asking for riches, Solomon asked for wisdom and knowledge. God granted that request, along with the riches, honor, and long life he did not ask for.

Solomon became both the wisest and the most powerful king in the history of Israel. Under his reign the borders were extended farther than any time past or present. There was also peace in the land. The reputation of Solomon spread far and wide, and people from many nations came to hear his wisdom. The wise king had riches, honor, and wisdom beyond all imagination.

BUILDING THE TEMPLE

Now came the time to build the temple that David had wanted to construct. Solomon contracted with Hiram, the king of Tyre, to hire servants to cut down timber. He also exchanged wheat and oil for the cedar wood of Lebanon. Huge stones were quarried and brought to the site. Scripture states that no sound of a hammer could be heard in the vicinity of the temple. It was a magnificent undertaking, one that took over one hundred thousand men to complete.

In architectural style it was typical of temples built in the Middle East during that period. Kenneth Kitchen states that the descriptions of Solomon's temple in Kings and Chronicles . . .

reflect recognizable architectural features of the Levant in the second/first millennia B.C., and beyond. The scheme of a pillared portico, vestibule and inner sanctuary (Holy of Holies) was current in Syria from at least the twenty-fourth/ nineteenth centuries B.C. at Ebla, and is attested at thirteenth-century Hazor in Canaan itself, and soon after Solomon's day again in Syria (at Tell Tayinat). The temple proper was of relatively modest size by Near-Eastern standards, hardly more than 120 feet long by 60 feet wide overall, of solid masonry. The wealth of gold, etc., used in its decoration (1 Kings 6:21ff.) is typical of the lavish ways of the ancient Near East.[2]

Although Solomon's temple had much in common with other Middle Eastern religious structures and architecture, it was also significantly different. Solomon's temple was built according to the Lord's exact specifications, similar to the plan of the tabernacle, given to Moses so long before in the wilderness. The temple had no graven images or false idols. The Israelite temple was a physical teacher or icon of God, his creation, and his plan of redemption. For example, the veil between the holy place and the Holy of Holies represented the impenetrable barrier between sinful man and the holy God, Yahweh. The veil could be passed through only once a year by the high priest offering atonement for the people, in prefigurement of the coming atonement by Jesus Christ. It is significant that when Christ died on the cross, God's power tore the veil in two, from top to bottom (Hebrews 10:20).

Alan Millard comments on the subsequent history of the temple.

Solomon's temple was destroyed by Nebuchadnezzar in 587 B.C. Much of its glory had already been torn away and paid as tribute when foreign conquerors menaced Judah. The disconsolate exiles in Babylonia were heartened by Ezekiel's vision of a new temple (Ezekiel 40–43), described with minute attention, and including facts about the courtyard which

---

[2]Ibid., p. 125.

hardly occur in the account of Solomon's work. This sanctuary was never built, but the exiles who returned about 537 B.C., after some delay, completed the rebuilding of the old one in 515 B.C. The little we know about it shows it followed the old design closely, however inferior its appearance. Nothing has survived from the first temple. But a length of stone walling above the Kidron Valley, on the east of the site, may be a part of the platform on which this second temple was erected, and which Herod incorporated into his walls. . . .

Herod's temple was the Idumaean king's attempt to curry favor with his Jewish subjects. Most of it was built between 19 and 9 B.C., although work continued until A.D. 64. The Romans destroyed it in A.D. 70. Parts of its massive substructure are still visible on the west (the "Wailing Wall") and east sides, and some blocks from the parapets have been recovered in excavations.

Descriptions by the Jewish historian Josephus, and notes in rabbinic writings, supply us with information about this splendid building. The great courtyard was surrounded by a portico where schools were held, and business transacted (John 10:23; Luke 19:47; John 2:14-16). Beyond the barrier mentioned was the Women's Court where the money-boxes stood (Mark 12:41-44), then the Court of Israel, and finally the Priests' Court in which the altar and the temple proper stood. This last was a larger version of Solomon's design.

The "holiest place," however, was empty, as in the second temple. The ark holding the terms of the covenant, upon whose covering lid (the "mercy-seat") God had appeared, was no longer in existence. Significantly, the temple, too, disappeared with the establishment of the new covenant and the new Israel.[3]

Once Solomon's magnificent temple was completed, it had to be dedicated. The first act was to bring the ark of the covenant into the temple. It was borne by the priests and put into the Holy of

---

[3]Alan Millard, "The Temples," in *The Lion Handbook to the Bible*, edited by David and Pat Alexander (Tring, Herts, England: Lion, 1973), pp. 253-254.

Holies. Immediately the "glory of the Lord" visibly filled the temple. This was followed by the dedication ceremony, in which Solomon rehearsed the history of Israel, which clearly showed the faithfulness of God. Solomon then offered a long magnificent prayer to the Lord, in which he extolled God's greatness. He also realized that this building did not contain God but was a place where his glory could be manifest. Solomon prayed, "But will God indeed dwell on the earth? Behold, heaven and the highest heaven cannot contain Thee, how much less this house which I have built!" (1 Kings 8:27).

Solomon asked the Lord to hear the people's prayers in the newly constructed temple. Following a hymn of praise sung to the Lord at the altar, the consecration of the temple occurred, with an unparalleled number of offerings along with a great week-long feast. Thus the dedication of the magnificent temple conceived by David and built by Solomon was concluded.

The temple took seven years to construct, while Solomon's own palace, built adjacent to the temple, was thirteen years in the making. After all the construction was completed, God appeared to Solomon and promised continued blessing if Solomon would serve him faithfully. However, the temple would be destroyed and the people removed, warned God, if they were disobedient.

Solomon continued to build. He enlarged Jerusalem along with other cities. He built cities for his horses and chariots, along with cities for storage. Although Israel's power and might flourished, forced labor along with heavy taxes levied on the people to pay for this expansion caused Solomon to lose some of his popularity.

Because of the great building program, the enlargement of Israel's navy, and the wisdom God had given him, Solomon's fame continued to spread. One person who came to hear his wisdom and view his wealth was the queen of Sheba in southwest Arabia. She came to see for herself and test Solomon with questions. She arrived in Jerusalem with a great procession and found even more than she anticipated. The queen exclaimed, "It was a true report which I heard in my own land about your words and your wisdom. Nevertheless I did not believe the reports, until I came and my eyes had seen it. And behold, the half was not told me. You exceed in wisdom and prosperity the report which I heard" (1 Kings 10:6-7).

SOLOMON'S DECLINE

Those great blessings from God—wisdom and untold wealth—were not all that Solomon possessed. He made a grievous mistake, one the Scripture warned about (Deuteronomy 17:17): he married many foreign wives. This tragic statement was then made concerning Solomon: "For it came about when Solomon was old, his wives turned his heart away after other gods; and his heart was not wholly devoted to the Lord his God, as the heart of David his father had been" (1 Kings 11:4).

When the idols worshiped by these foreign wives were brought to Israel, Solomon not only bowed before them, he built temples to them. The Lord rebuked him for his idolatry, but Solomon paid no attention. God then announced that upon Solomon's death his kingdom would be divided; the great majority of the nation would not be loyal to the house of Solomon. God then stirred up Solomon's enemies, including Hadad the Edomite, who had earlier fled from Edom when David and Joab had slain his people. Hadad, the king's young son, had gone to Egypt and found favor with the pharaoh. Another enemy was stirred up, Rezon of Zobah.

Both Rezon and Hadad gave Israel trouble, but the nation's most dangerous enemy was one of their own, an Ephraimite named Jeroboam. There had been rivalry between Ephraim and Judah. Jeroboam had been made ruler of the house of Joseph by Solomon, who trusted him. The prophet Ahijah met Jeroboam outside Jerusalem, where he tore a new robe into twelve pieces and gave Jeroboam ten of them. The prophet announced that because of Solomon's sins, Jeroboam would rule the ten tribes after Solomon's death. Jeroboam, however, attempted to take over the ten tribes before the king's death. When Solomon attempted to kill him, Jeroboam fled to Egypt.

After ruling Israel for forty years, Solomon died. His kingdom was given to his son Rehoboam.

CHAPTER 5
Division and Captivity

After the glorious reigns of David and Solomon, the history of God's people took a downward turn. The nation was divided, and the people of God experienced difficult times.

The kingdom was split in two parts: the northern kingdom was called Israel, and the southern kingdom Judah. Sometimes the Old Testament uses the term *Israelite* to signify a person in the northern kingdom, and the term *Jew* to signify a person in the southern kingdom. At other times, either term can refer to any descendant of Jacob.

First the northern kingdom and then the southern kingdom were conquered, and God's people passed into years of slavery. At no later time in Israel's history would all twelve tribes again dwell together in Canaan. The exile of the tribes became the beginning of the Diaspora, or the dispersing of the Jews through-out the world.

After the death of Solomon the prophecy of a divided kingdom began to be fulfilled. Solomon was succeeded by his foolish son Rehoboam, who went to Shechem to be anointed king. The men of Israel sent for Jeroboam in Egypt, and then contacted the new king, informing him that the people would serve him because of the heavy tax burden his father had put on them. Rehoboam unwisely listened to the advice of his younger, inexperienced counselors, who urged him to increase the people's burden; that ill-thought counsel led to the division of the nation. Only two tribes, Benjamin and Judah, remained faithful to the house of Solomon. The other ten tribes followed Jeroboam.

Alexander Maclear has compared the kingdoms of Israel and

Judah in three respects (his dates have to be updated to reflect modern chronology).

I. *Their respective duration.* The kingdom of Israel lasted from 930 B.C. to 722 B.C., or 208 years. The kingdom of Judah lasted from 930 B.C. to 586 B.C., or 344 years, thus outliving her more populous and powerful rival by 136 years.

II. *Their mutual relations.* These . . . were dictated by three different lines of policy: (a) Mutual animosity from 930 to 869 B.C. The first three kings of Judah, Rehoboam, Abijah, and Asa, persisted in the hope of regaining their authority over the Ten Tribes, and for nearly sixty years there was war between the two kingdoms. (b) Close alliance, united hostility to Syria, 869–835 B.C. With the accession of Jehoshaphat there sprang up an alliance between the two kingdoms, cemented by intermarriage, and prompted probably the necessity of joint action in resisting the encroaching power of Syria. (c) Fresh animosity, and the gradual decline of both kingdoms before the advancing power of the Assyrian Empire, 869–612 B.C. The alliance between the kingdoms was rudely shattered by the accession of Jehu to the throne of Israel. He put Ahaziah to death, and the hostility thus begun reached its highest pitch under Amaziah, Jehoash, and Pekah.

III. *Their contrasts.* In the kingdom of Judah, (a) there was always a fixed capital and a venerated centre of religion; (b) the army was always subordinate; (c) the succession was interrupted by no revolution; (d) the priests remained faithful to the crown.

In the kingdom of Israel, (a) there was no fixed capital and no real religious centre; (b) the army was often insubordinate; (c) the succession was constantly interrupted, so that out of nineteen kings there were no less than nine dynasties, each ushered in by a revolution; (d) the authorized priests left the kingdom in a body, and the priesthood established by Jeroboam had no divine sanction and no promise; it was corrupt in its very source. Hence in the kingdom of Israel the prophets were the regular ministers of God, and, especially during the second of the two periods above mentioned, their ministry was distinguished by far more extraordinary events than in the kingdom of Judah, whose annals offer no prophetical deeds like those of Elijah and Elisha.[1]

We treat here separately the history of the two kingdoms. In Israel, as Maclear has noted, nine different dynasties succeeded one another. Below we list together the kings of each northern dynasty and comment briefly on some of them. Their story appears primarily in the biblical books of 1–2 Kings. The story of the southern kings, who preserved an unbroken line from King David, is told most fully in 2 Chronicles. We comment here on each one, again only briefly. It is noteworthy that while some of the southern rulers were righteous and some evil, the kings of the northern tribes were, to a man, evil.

ISRAEL, THE NORTHERN KINGDOM

Jeroboam, Nadab. After Jeroboam severed the political unity of the nation, he decided also to break the religious unity that bonded them together. The fact that the people journeyed to Jerusalem three times a year for the feasts caused him concern. His solution was to create two new centers of worship, complete with two golden calves—one placed on the southern border in Bethel, the other at the northern border in Dan. The people were told they no longer needed to go to Jerusalem to worship; now they had their own religious centers. Jeroboam instituted a counterfeit temple, altar, priesthood, and Feast of Tabernacles and thus ruled both politically and religiously. Because Jeroboam perverted the true worship of God, God rejected him, sending a prophecy that the house of Jeroboam would not continue its rule. After his son had ruled only two years, Baasha assassinated him and the entire house of Jeroboam, thus fulfilling God's word.

Baasha, Elah. Baasha was no better as a ruler than the man he murdered. The prophet Jehu, from Judah, pronounced judgment on the house of Baasha. Like Jeroboam, Baasha also fought against

---

[1] A. Maclear, *A Class Book of Old Testament History* (Grand Rapids: Eerdmans, 1952), pp. 453-454.

Judah. After Baasha's death his son Elah ruled in his stead, and he in turn was soon destroyed by Zimri, one of his generals.

Zimri. This evil king reigned a mere seven days. Trapped by Omri, another army leader, Zimri committed suicide.

Omri, Ahab, Ahaziah, Jehoram. The house of Omri was one of the most powerful of the northern kingdom. Omri built Samaria, the new capital for the divided kingdom, where he established his godless rule. His son, Ahab, married a Sidonian princess named Jezebel, who introduced the idols of the Phoenicians to the people. Up until that time, idol worship—specifically worship of the golden calves—took place under careful restrictions. Ahab, along with Jezebel, now promoted open worship of the various pagan deities, including Baal. The Israelites had been familiar with those false gods for some time, but Ahab made them part of the religious life of the northern kingdom.

The prophet Elijah confronted Ahab and the prophets of Baal on Mount Carmel, where the Lord dramatically showed his superiority to Baal. Later, Elijah appeared before Ahab again and announced judgment upon his house for his dastardly deeds. Surprisingly, Ahab humbled himself and repented, which caused God to be merciful and to delay judgment. After three years of peace, war broke out with Syria, and Ahab was killed.

Jehu, Jehoahaz, Jehoash, Jeroboam II, Zechariah. Jehu was anointed king by Elisha's messenger. Jehu subsequently killed Jehoram, the last of the house of Omri, and Ahaziah, king of Judah. In Jezreel, Jehu also killed Jezebel. He then convinced the elders of Samaria to put to death the remaining sons and grandsons of Ahab. Jehu, however, continued in the sins of Jeroboam.

Jeroboam II ruled for forty-one years, longer than any other king of Israel. During his reign, he recaptured a large area in the north, as predicted by the prophet Jonah. Jeroboam also recovered the city of Damascus. During that time Israel prospered but remained sinful, and God sent the prophet Amos to warn them of judgment for their sins.

Shallum. Murderer of Zechariah, last king of the house of Jehu, Shallum ruled for only a month before being assassinated.

Menahem, Pekahiah. During Menahem's time on the throne, a new factor came onto the scene: the nation of Assyria. Menahem paid tribute to Pul (Tiglath-Pileser III), the Assyrian king, and was saved from his invading army for the time being.

Pekah. The rule of Pekah marked the beginning of the end of the northern kingdom. When the Assyrians conquered the Transjordan region and the northern part of Canaan, the captivity of Israel began, with the deportation of some of its inhabitants.

Hoshea. After at first paying heavy tribute to the Assyrians, Hoshea aligned himself instead with the pharaoh of Egypt. That led the Assyrian king, Shalmaneser V, to march against Hoshea and capture Samaria. Some Israelites fled to Jerusalem, but the remainder were deported, never to return. Those who remained behind interbred with a variety of different people brought in by Assyria, producing a mixed race known as Samaritans. The idolatrous northern kingdom of Israel had come to an end.

ELIJAH AND ELISHA

Whenever there is a great sin, God sends someone to warn of judgment and call the nation to repentance. This action was needed particularly in the northern kingdom, where no faithful priests were serving. The primary spokesmen for God there were the colorful prophets Elijah and Elisha.

We are introduced to Elijah when he appeared to Ahab and told the king that it would not rain in the land for three years. A spiritual battle was being waged, since Baal was the god of rain. After a three-year famine, God told Elijah to tell Ahab it would rain again.

Elijah then told the godless king to summon the prophets of Baal to Mount Carmel for a contest to determine who was the true God. Elijah gave the terms of the contest: "Elijah went before the people and said, 'How long will you waver between two opinions? If the Lord is God, follow him; but if Baal is God, follow him.' But the poeple said nothing. Then Elijah said to them, 'I am the only one of the Lord's prophets left, but Baal has four hundred and fifty prophets. Get two bulls for us. . . . Then you call on the name of your god, and I will call on the name of the Lord. The god who answers by fire—he is God'" (1 Kings 18:21-24, NIV).

The people gathered at Mount Carmel to watch the outcome, but it was no contest. The priests of Baal cried out all day, but nothing happened. Elijah then prayed a simple prayer to the Lord, and the "fire of the Lord" (v. 38) fell. The sacrifice was consumed, and the people acknowledged that the Lord was God. Elijah then ordered the priests of Baal to be put to death. Soon thereafter Elijah announced it would rain again.

Elisha's prophetic work also included the miraculous. At the end of Elijah's ministry, Elisha, his successor, desired that a double portion, the inheritance right of the firstborn, of Elijah's spirit might fall on him. A chariot of fire drawn by horses of fire appeared, taking Elijah up into heaven. Seeing Elijah taken was an indication that the Lord was granting Elisha's request. As Elisha left the scene, he took the cloak of Elijah and hit the water of the Jordan River with it, causing it to part. The company of prophets who witnessed this recognized Elisha as the legitimate successor to Elijah.

During war between Israel and Syria, the Syrian king tried to kidnap Elisha by surrounding his house in Dothan. Elisha prayed, and God struck the Syrians with blindness. Elisha then led the would-be kidnappers to Samaria, where he showed them mercy by providing bread and water and then sent them on their way.

Syrian king Ben-hadad II was not that appreciative of the gesture and soon besieged Samaria again. A great famine resulted that caused the people to resort to cannibalism. Jehoram wanted to kill Elisha for that tragedy, but the prophet pronounced correctly that the famine would end the next day.

Another famine occurred, which lasted seven years. During that time, Elisha went to Damascus to anoint Hazael to succeed Ben-hadad II as king of Syria. Elisha also sent his servant to anoint Jehu to be king of Israel and to carry out the destruction of the house of Ahab.

JUDAH, THE SOUTHERN KINGDOM

We now focus attention on the southern kingdom of Judah. Unlike the ten northern tribes, whose kings were only evil, Judah had some glorious moments: some of its kings walked in the ways of the Lord.

Solomon's son **Rehoboam** ruled when the kingdom divided. His kingdom had been greatly diminished compared to that of his father, so his task was to strengthen what was left. After walking in the ways of the Lord for three years, Rehoboam did an about-face, forsaking God and turning to idols. In judgment, God sent Pharaoh Shishak of Egypt, who attacked the fortified cities of Judah and Jerusalem and plundered the treasures of the temple. At that point Rehoboam and his princes humbled themselves and repented, causing God to stay the hand of judgment. Shishak left without destroying everything, but Judah became a vassal to Egypt. Rehoboam reigned seventeen years in Jerusalem, warring continually with Jeroboam and the northern kingdom—but worship of the Lord continued.

Rehoboam was succeeded by his son **Abijam** (or Abijah). As war with Israel continued, Abijam made many of the same mistakes as his father. The Scripture, however, says that for David's sake, God allowed Judah to prosper and not be defeated by the idolatrous northern kingdom.

After Abijam's death, his son **Asa** reigned in his place. Asa did not make the mistakes of his father or grandfather but for the most part walked uprightly with the Lord. He rid the country of idols and made the cities secure, bringing peace in his time. Asa achieved victory over the Egyptians and Israel and also purified the land of the idols that had been brought down from Israel.

Asa was succeeded by his son, **Jehoshaphat,** who was another king faithful to the Lord. He fortified the cities of Judah, strengthening the kingdom. During the reign of Asa, some "high places" (for idol worship) and idolatrous groups had appeared, but Jehoshaphat had them destroyed. The king then sent princes and Levites throughout the land to instruct the people in the law of God. The surrounding kingdoms became afraid of Judah and sought to make peace. Because Jehoshaphat trusted the Lord, he prospered, earning the respect and fear of Israel and her neighbors. Yet, unwisely, he made a pact with the evil king Ahab of Israel. God used the Moabites to invade Judah to chastise Jehoshaphat for that sin. A Moabite, Ammonite and Edomite alliance came against Jehoshaphat and after praying Jehoshaphat was granted a miraculous victory.

After the succession of good kings reigning in Judah, there came a bad one, Jehoshaphat's son **Jehoram.** After Jehoram was made king, he murdered all of his brothers. He also caused the inhabitants of Judah to sin by erecting high places for idol worship in the land. Consequently, Elijah the prophet wrote Jehoram a letter pointing out that he was behaving like the godless kings of Israel. God would therefore send a plague on the people because of their sin, and Jehoram would die with a horrible intestinal disease. But before that occurred, invaders came into the land and carried off all of Jehoram's family except his son Ahaziah (also called Jehoahaz) and his mother, Athaliah. Jehoram died as prophesied.

Ahaziah, the only son the invading army had left behind, succeeded his father as king. He was also evil and was greatly influenced by his mother, Athaliah. His ungodly reign lasted only one year, for he was killed in Jehu's purge.

The next ruler was **Athaliah,** the mother of Ahaziah and the only woman to rule in either north or south. She was the daughter of the ungodly Ahab and, like her father, was evil. As soon as she found out that her son Ahaziah was dead, she attempted to destroy the remaining royal heirs of the house of Judah. But Joash, a young son of Ahaziah, was taken by his aunt and hidden in the temple for six years. In the seventh year of Athaliah's reign, Jehoiada the priest managed to overthrow the evil queen. He made a covenant with the people to obey the word of the Lord. They broke down the temple of Baal, destroyed the altars, and reinstated the temple service.

Joash was a child of seven when he assumed the throne. Jehoiada the priest became his tutor while the young king grew up. One of Joash's acts was to repair the temple, which had fallen into disrepair during the time of Athaliah. A collection was taken among the people to accomplish this task, and the temple once again functioned properly with Jehoiada's guidance. After Jehoiada's death, however, some of the princes of Judah induced Joash to practice idolatry. Groves were built where all types of false worship and sexual debauchery were practiced. God sent prophets to warn the people, but they would not listen. In punishment, a small Syrian regiment came into Judah and spoiled the land. Joash died at the hands of his servants.

Joash was succeeded by his son **Amaziah,** who, unlike his father, was a good king—although he also had lapses of faith. Amaziah challenged King Jehoash (also spelled Joash) of Israel, whose army sent the soldiers of Judah running. The king was taken captive, obviously a heavy defeat for Amaziah, since it was the first time a king in David's line had been captured. The temple was again plundered, and part of the walls of Jerusalem were broken down. Amaziah eventually fled to Lachish, where he was killed.

Uzziah, Amaziah's son, had much in common with his grandfather Joash. As long as his mentor was alive, he remained a good king. He began to rule at the age of sixteen, and did what was honorable in God's sight. He went to war with the Philistines and Arabians, soundly defeating them. By fortifying Jerusalem and the cities of Judah, he strengthened his kingdom. He overstepped his bounds, however, and entered the temple to burn incense on the altar of incense, something only priests could do. For that, Uzziah was rebuked by the priest Azariah and became a leper right before the priest's eyes. Because of his leprosy and transgression against the Lord, he was banished and stripped of his kingship.

Uzziah's son **Jotham** was a good king who walked upright in God's sight. He was a great builder and fortified the cities of Judah. He warred against the Ammonites and defeated them, causing the conquered to pay him tribute.

We now arrive at another black spot in the history of Judah—the reign of **Ahaz.** Because of his abominable practices, God delivered him into the hand of Syria (Aram). Ahaz then foolishly aligned himself with the Assyrian king, Tiglath-Pileser III, in spite of the stern warnings of Isaiah—a move that had disastrous results. The Assyrians conquered Damascus and a large part of Israel and also conquered Judah, making it a vassal state. The evil king Ahaz then believed he must acknowledge the Syrians' gods as greater than the Lord, so he decided to sacrifice to them. He destroyed the vessels of the house of God and erected pagan altars in Jerusalem. It was during his reign that the northern kingdom of Israel went into captivity.

After the death of Ahaz, the rulership in Judah went to his son **Hezekiah,** whose reign was one of the bright spots in Judah's history. Hezekiah removed the idols and altars built by his godless father. He reopened the temple and restored it according to the law of the Lord. Hezekiah rallied the people together in Jerusalem to celebrate the Passover, the first time it had been celebrated as a national holiday since the time of Solomon. When Hezekiah attempted to free himself from Assyrian influence, Sennacherib,

Sargon's son, occupied Judah's fortified cities. Even though the Assyrian army was surrounding Jerusalem, Isaiah assured Hezekiah that the city would not fall. That same night, the angel of the Lord struck down a very large number of the Assyrian army, causing the remainder to return home in shame. Immediately afterward, Hezekiah had a serious illness and was informed that it was his time to die. When the king pleaded with the Lord to prolong his life, God granted him another fifteen years.

When Hezekiah finally died, the heir to the throne was his son **Manasseh,** an evil king. Manasseh brought back the worship of Baal. He even sacrificed his own son and murdered his opponents. His monstrous conduct caused prophets to come and predict inevitable judgment against Judah. Later, a rebellion against the Assyrian king Ashurbanipal occurred. Manasseh was suspected of complicity and was taken to Babylon in chains by the Assyrians. As a result, the evil king humbled himself before God and repented. God allowed him to return to Jerusalem, where he instituted some reforms.

Sadly, the turnabout of Manasseh did not have lasting effects. His son **Amon,** who succeeded him, continued in the sinful ways of his father. Amon was assassinated by his servants.

The next king in Judah was **Josiah,** the last good one the nation had. He assumed the throne at eight years of age and at twenty brought about a final reformation in the land, destroying idols, pagan temples, prostitute quarters, and altars. During this period of reformation, the Assyrian influence was declining, and Babylon became the new nation to be reckoned with. During the eighteenth year of his reign, Josiah started to collect money to repair the temple. In the process of doing so, the high priest Hilkiah found the "Book of the Law." On hearing it read, Josiah realized the extent of sin into which the nation had fallen, repented, and had it read to all the people. Josiah restored the Passover and the Levitical priesthood. The king died when he foolishly tried to intervene between Pharaoh Neco of Egypt and the Babylonians.

Jehoahaz ruled in the place of Josiah. Judah had come under Egypt's dominion after Josiah's death, and the people from outside Jerusalem proclaimed Josiah's middle son, Jehoahaz, as king. Three months later, Pharaoh Neco canceled that arrangement, installed Jehoahaz's half brother Eliakim as king and put Jehoahaz in prison. Neco changed Eliakim's name to Jehoiakim and levied a heavy tribute on Judah.

Jehoiakim reigned in Judah for eleven years. This unjust king sanctioned idolatry and imposed heavy taxes on the people to pay tribute to Egypt. The Babylonian king Nebuchadnezzar defeated Neco at Carchemish, which broke the Egyptian stranglehold on Judah. Babylon next turned its attention toward Jerusalem, deporting a number of the Jews from noble families in 605 B.C., along with the temple furnishings. Shortly after, Jehoiakim tried to rid himself of the Babylonian bondage. Nebuchadnezzar sent an occupation force to break up the king's insurrection. In 597 B.C., Nebuchadnezzar came personally to Jerusalem and laid siege to the city. He wanted to take Jehoiakim to Babylon as his prisoner, but Jehoiakim died during the siege.

Jehoiachin (or Coniah) succeeded his father as king during the Babylonian siege of Jerusalem. He reigned just over three months before surrendering the city, which resulted in the second deportation. The king and his mother and all except the poorest people were taken to Babylon, along with treasures from the palace and temple. Jehoiachin remained in exile in Babylon for over thirty years before he was granted amnesty.

The last king of Judah before the captivity was **Zedekiah,** the youngest son of Josiah. He swore an oath of loyalty to Nebuchadnezzar but rebelled against the king by secretly sending messengers to Egypt to ask help from the pharaoh. Nebuchadnezzar responded to this insurrection by sending his army against Zedekiah. After a long siege, the Babylonians entered the city. Zedekiah was blinded and taken to Babylon. Nebuchadnezzar's men burned down the entire city, including Solomon's temple. This time people who were left, except for the poorest of the poor, were deported. Again the treasures of the temple were plundered and taken to Babylon (586 B.C.).

Thus the kingdom of Judah came to an inglorious end because of its sins against the Lord. That, however, was not the permanent end of the kingdom. The northern kingdom never returned, but Judah did, because of the promises of a faithful God. The prophets predicted removal from the land for a seventy-year period (Jeremiah 25:11; 29:10), which is exactly what occurred.

CAPTIVITY IN BABYLON

When King Nebuchadnezzar descended for the third time on Judah, he destroyed the city of Jerusalem along with the temple and took most of the people captive to Babylon. Before looking at the Jews who were thus taken to Babylon, we will consider the few who were allowed to remain in Palestine.

This group came under the strict control of the Babylonians. Among those who remained in the land was the prophet Jeremiah, who had warned the people in vain of the coming captivity. Nebuchadnezzar appointed Gedaliah to govern those who remained, making him responsible to restore agriculture in order that a tribute could be paid to Babylon. Ishmael, a descendant of King David, murdered Gedaliah along with many others. He then took Jeremiah and others to go to Ammon; at Gibeon they were freed by a man named Johanan.

The entire population, now under Johanan's direction, decided the best thing to do was to move to Egypt. They also approached Jeremiah, however, to seek his advice on the matter; this time, they assured him, they would listen to whatever he said. Ten days later the prophet announced God's word: If the people remained in Judah, they would have nothing to fear from the Babylonians. If they decided to go down to Egypt, great misfortune would overtake them.

The people had not learned their lesson. They had refused to listen to Jeremiah when he predicted the Babylonian captivity, and on this occasion they again refused to hear the word of the Lord. Because they were afraid of the Babylonians, they disobeyed God's wishes and went to Egypt—taking a reluctant Jeremiah with them. Of course Jeremiah used this further act of rebellion to pronounce judgment on them. He reminded them that Jerusalem fell to Babylon because of the idolatry of the people. The foolish leaders disagreed with Jeremiah, laying blame for the captivity on the kings who had reigned since Josiah. Those kings had stopped the idolatry, they said, and the cessation of idolatry was the cause for their captivity. Jeremiah contended that soon everyone would know the true reason for the deportation.

This is the last we hear from the prophet and the Jews who unwisely decided to go to Egypt. Ironically, Nebuchadnezzar soon thereafter invaded Egypt and captured many Jews who had thought themselves safe from the yoke of Babylon. It was another example of judgment coming on those who do not obey God's commandments.

REASONS FOR THE EXILE

Although a minority of Jews had permission to stay in Palestine, most of the inhabitants of Israel were taken from the promised land for a seventy-year period of captivity. At least four factors contributed to this divine punishment.

Idolatry. The first commandment read, "You shall have no other gods before Me" (Exodus 20:3). But the people of Judah disobeyed the Lord and worshiped gods made out of wood and stone. The prophets warned that such idolatry would cause their removal from the land.

Immorality. One of the inevitable fruits of idol worship was the decline of morality among the people. As the people turned from worshiping the true God to idols, immorality increased (Jeremiah 17:2; see also 7:9-15; 19:4-9; Ezekiel 8:9-18). Immorality was rampant among the people from the highest to the lowest, including also many of the priests and prophets. The voices of moral prophets like Jeremiah, Uriah, and Habakkuk, who rose up in protest, often were not heeded. Their outcry frequently brought them only persecution and martyrdom.

Corrupt rule. Many rulers were corrupt, oppressive, and heartless, with only their own selfish desires in mind. While the land was poverty stricken, King Jehoiakim lived in luxury and built great palaces for himself through the forced labor of the people. Many workers died while performing slave labor; others went unpaid. The prophets spoke out against such wrongs (Jeremiah 22:13-17; Habakkuk 2:9-17).

Sabbath neglect. A further reason for the removal of the people from the land was their neglecting to observe the Sabbath year. Leviticus 26:34-35 commanded that a Sabbath year was to be observed every seventh year. The people would work the land for six years, and on the seventh year they were to allow it to rest. For 490 years this commandment was neglected, making a total of seventy years that the land needed to rest. Therefore God would remove them from their land for seventy years to make up for those years that the land was to go uncultivated.

God's people were originally placed in the land to be a witness to him; their lives and actions were to testify to his holy character. Their idolatry, immorality, corruption, and Sabbath neglect made them ripe for judgment. As God had warned before they entered the promised land, such disobedience would cause their removal (Deuteronomy 28:15-68). The Babylonian captivity again proved that God was true to his word.

Yet we also see the great and merciful God who judges his people but does not abandon them. God would bring his people back to the Land of Promise when justice had been meted out.

DANIEL

Most of the Jews were deported to Babylon. When the remainder fled from Palestine to Egypt, the land was left virtually empty. The southern part, known as the Negev, was occupied by the Edomites, who had cheered loudly when Jerusalem fell. The northern portion was placed under the governorship of the Samaritans and was kept devoid of people.

Of the Jews who went to Babylon, some became slaves; others, like the prophet Ezekiel, were given places to live. The exiled Jews lived in their own communities and enjoyed a certain amount of freedom. Those who were skilled craftsmen were used by Nebuchadnezzar in his building program. A small group was given important positions in the court of Nebuchadnezzar. Among this select group was a man who would prosper for six decades under the political leadership of the Babylonian and Medo-Persian kingdoms: Daniel.The pages of Scripture are filled with the exploits of great men and women of God, and ranking high on that list is Daniel. A prophet and statesman, Daniel was born in Judah, but while young he was taken captive in the first deportation to Babylon. The pressure on him to conform to the pagan Babylonian system was enormous, but Daniel would not betray the God of Israel. Consequently God blessed Daniel and allowed him to be promoted to positions of prominence in both the Babylonian and Medo-Persian kingdoms.

The first glimpse we have of Daniel is in the court of Nebuchadnezzar. Along with three of his friends, Daniel was among the first hostages taken. Talented young men were to be instructed in Babylonian customs and religion. Once they adopted that mind-set, they could be returned to their own people to teach them the ways of Babylon. Daniel and his friends had a choice: Would they defile themselves with the Babylonian life-style, or would they honor the Lord? They chose to honor the Lord, and it soon became evident to all that these four young Hebrews were superior in wisdom to all the wise men in the Babylonian court.

Once Daniel demonstrated his unwillingness to compromise, the stage was set for God to use him in a remarkable way. The king had a dream that troubled him, and none of his wise men could tell him what he had dreamed or what it meant. Frustrated, Nebuchadnezzar wanted to put to death all the wise men, which included Daniel and his three friends. The godly Hebrew youths prayed for the answer, and God granted their request. Daniel then approached Nebuchadnezzar and revealed to him both the dream and the interpretation.

In his dream Nebuchadnezzar had seen a brilliant image with a head of gold, a chest and arms of silver, a stomach and thighs of bronze, legs of iron, and feet of iron mixed with clay. The image was destroyed by a stone that struck it in its feet.

The image represented four successive kingdoms. Nebuchadnezzar was the head of gold, and his kingdom would be replaced by a kingdom inferior to his. Similarly, the second kingdom would be supplanted by a third kingdom inferior to it. The fourth kingdom, which would conquer the third, would ultimately become divided. While the fourth kingdom was in power, the kingdom of God would come like a large stone and crush that kingdom. Then the eternal kingdom of God would be established.

The dream of Nebuchadnezzar, along with the interpretation given by Daniel, has been fulfilled—once again demonstrating that God's word is true. The head of gold was *Babylon*. In the ancient way of thinking, Babylon's kingdom was superior to the other three in that it was an autocratic, one-man rule. There were no committees, no legislature, and no governing body to answer to. Nebuchadnezzar was the sole ruler.

The *Medes and Persians*, though stronger than Babylon, were (in the above sense) inferior in rulership. Leadership was dually held by the Medes and the Persians, making their government inferior to the Babylonian one-man rule. As we study the image, we observe that the metal becomes increasingly inferior yet stronger. The

Medo-Persian kingdom was stronger than the Babylonian kingdom, having conquered more territory than its predecessor.

The third kingdom, *Greece,* conquered the Medo-Persians under the brilliant leadership of Alexander the Great. Greece expanded the borders of its kingdom beyond that of Medo-Persia, but soon after obtaining that vast amount of territory, Alexander the Great died. His mighty kingdom was divided into four parts, each ruled by one of his generals.

The last Gentile world kingdom was *Rome.* Rome was the most ferocious of the four kingdoms. Rome held sway longer than any of the other kingdoms, eventually being divided into east and west (the two legs).

Finally, *God's kingdom* will appear in the days when the fourth kingdom is in power. Rome was never really conquered as the previous three kingdoms had been; it fell apart. However, because we have the image portrayed as having feet of iron mixed with clay, we should expect to see a revival of some form of the Roman Empire in the last days, before the kingdom of God is established on earth. (See part 5 for more discussion of these prophecies.)

After Daniel had finished giving Nebuchadnezzar the interpretation of his dream, the king blessed the God of Israel and promoted Daniel and his three friends to significant positions. Because these men would not compromise their convictions, God blessed them and allowed them to be in positions of authority in the midst of this pagan kingdom. In this and other ways, the Lord protected and preserved his people until the time came for their return to the promised land.

CHAPTER 6
Return and the Messianic Hope

As the seventy years of captivity drew to a close, the Lord was orchestrating events so his people could return to Jerusalem. Once the Jews had returned, God would allow several centuries to pass before it was time to send the Messiah. At the right time, however, God's Anointed would indeed come, fulfilling numerous Old Testament prophecies and, in his sacrificial death, solving completely the problem of separation that sin had caused between God and man.

RETURN
The return of the Jews to Israel depended on political events that the Lord was carefully overseeing. We begin with the fall of Babylon to the Medes and Persians.

THE FALL OF BABYLON
The book of Daniel records the changing of power from the Babylonian Empire to the Medo-Persian Empire. Belshazzar, who was ruling in Babylon at the time, held a great banquet. At the time of the banquet the city of Babylon was under siege by the Medo-Persian army, but the Babylonians thought themselves invincible. As the banquet progressed, the drunken King Belshazzar called for the sacred vessels that had been taken from the temple of the Lord. The king then profaned the holy vessels by using them to drink wine and to praise the gods of gold and silver. By doing this, he was directly attacking the God of Israel. God was not about to stand for such profanity.

In the midst of that drunken revelry, a large hand suddenly appeared and began to write upon the wall. Belshazzar, now in mortal fear, called for the wise men of Babylon to tell him what it meant, but they could not. Finally the queen came in and told the frightened king that there was someone in the realm who could give the interpretation: the Hebrew prophet Daniel. Summoned, Daniel denounced Belshazzar for being a spineless ruler and then proceeded to give him the bad news: God had weighed Belshazzar in the balances and found him wanting. His kingdom would now come to an end and be divided between the Medes and Persians.

That night the prophecy came true. The Medo-Persian army conquered Babylon and killed Belshazzar. The Medo-Persian leadership had found the Achilles' heel in the Babylonian defense system and used it to conquer the city.

> The Persians, after laying siege to Babylon, saw they could in no way storm the massive walls or break down their gates. They had two Babylonian deserters, Gobryas and Gadatas, enter their camp. At this time, Chrysantas, a counselor to Cyrus, made the observation that the Euphrates river ran underneath these gigantic walls and was deep enough and wide enough to march an army under. Cyrus ordered his troops to dig huge ditches and the two deserters to lay plans for attacking Babylon from within her walls. While the Persians were building canals to divert the course of the river, the Babylonians were laughing and mocking their seemingly helpless enemy outside their walls. The Babylonians were carousing at an annual feast to their gods and celebrating victory over the Persians (as recorded in Daniel 5) without realizing that Cyrus had diverted the Euphrates River from underneath the walls of Babylon and was at that very time entering the city with his troops.[1]

JEWISH RETURN AND REESTABLISHMENT

The Babylonian captivity began in approximately 605 B.C., when the first group of Jews under King Jehoiakim was deported to

---

[1] Josh McDowell, *Evidence That Demands a Verdict*, rev. ed. (San Bernardino, Calif.: Here's Life, 1979), pp. 76-78.

Babylon. In 538 B.C., approximately seventy years later, the Babylonian captivity came to an end when the Persian king, Cyrus, issued a decree that the Jews could return to their land. Not only were they allowed to return, they were also permitted to take with them the remainder of the holy vessels from the destroyed temple.

Their return from captivity fulfilled many prophecies. The prophet Jeremiah had predicted the Jews' going into captivity and then returning after seventy years. The return by the command of Cyrus also fulfilled an amazing prophecy by Isaiah (Isaiah 44:28) spoken some 160 years earlier, in approximately 700 B.C. What makes this prophecy so amazing is that the Jews were not even in captivity at the time. The city of Jerusalem was intact, and the temple was still standing. Isaiah foresaw the destruction of the city and the temple some one hundred years before their occurrence. What is even more incredible is that Cyrus is named as the man who would give this commandment, yet the prophecy was given some one hundred years before Cyrus was born.

The return from captivity was led by Zerubbabel, a descendant of King David, along with the high priest Joshua. Among the group returning were many Levites and temple servants. One of the first things that the people did was to rebuild the altar on the temple court. After that, the Feast of Tabernacles was celebrated. The temple foundations were then restored. In a touching comment, we read that the older people, who had known the glory of Solomon's temple, cried when the new, less elegant temple was instituted.

As the Jews began rebuilding they were offered help by the idolatrous Samaritans, which they wisely refused. The Samaritans then became an irritant to the Jews in their rebuilding process. Things proceeded slowly and eventually came to a halt. The Samaritans had sent a letter to King Artaxerxes, who then ordered an immediate halt of all building activities in Jerusalem.

About eighteen years later, the prophets Haggai and Zechariah began challenging the people to resume rebuilding. They were helped by a letter from King Darius, who sent word to the local governor, commanding him to give all available support to the Jews to help them with their task. Within five years the second temple was completely rebuilt. It was dedicated with a great feast, after which the Feast of the Passover was again celebrated.

Sixty years passed. Since Zerubbabel there had been a number of governors of Judea (as the southern part of Palestine was then called), and the land was still a province of Persia. The new leader of the Jews was Ezra, a man well versed in the law of Moses. The Persian king ordered Ezra to investigate the state of affairs in Judea. He was to take a large gift with him and, if he found it necessary, to appoint governors. The people who returned to Palestine with Ezra also included Levites and temple servants. Ezra's desire was to teach the law of God to those who had returned to the promised land.

Upon arrival in Jerusalem, Ezra presented the king's gift and then delivered the royal decree to the Persian rulers. He met stiff opposition, however, from a large number of inhabitants who had violated God's law by engaging in mixed marriages of Jews and Gentiles. That kind of disobedience saddened Ezra, and, along with many others, he humbled himself before God and prayed. The people then met and made a decision to set up judges in different locations to see that foreign women would be sent away.

Twelve years later, Nehemiah, the cupbearer to the Persian king, heard that the walls of Jerusalem were still in ruins. That news distressed Nehemiah, and he prayed a long prayer to the Lord. Then, at the risk of his own life, he asked the king to rescind the order that had halted construction on the city walls. Nehemiah also asked permission to go and supervise the rebuilding personally. The king granted all his requests.

Arriving in Jerusalem, Nehemiah inspected the walls and gates and immediately recruited a large number of men to help him rebuild them. However he also encountered opposition from the Samaritans, who were led by three men, Sanballat, Tobiah, and Geshem. When Nehemiah discovered their plot to disrupt the rebuilding effort, he armed his builders to repulse any attack. The Samaritans, meanwhile, continued to threaten him and also set a trap for him. But all their efforts failed, and the rebuilding of the walls was completed in just fifty-two days.

After the city was made secure, Nehemiah instituted certain reforms. He wanted to see the population of the city increase, but only with full-blooded Jews, and therefore he registered all those who returned. Then Ezra read the law of Moses to the people, and the Feast of Tabernacles was once again celebrated. Soon after that, a day of repentance and prayer was held; all the people participated by humbling themselves before God and praising him for his goodness. The walls of Jerusalem were dedicated to the Lord, and temple worship was regulated. Mixed marriages were condemned. The tithe was restored, and the sacredness of the Sabbath was upheld. After twelve years, with his work completed, Nehemiah returned to Persia.

THE JEWS WHO DID NOT RETURN
Some Jews did not return from the Babylonian captivity. They were out of God's will, but certainly not out of his providential care—as the book of Esther clearly reveals. In the third year of his reign, the Persian king Ahasuerus (Xerxes 486-465 B.C.) staged a magnificent banquet during which Vashti, his queen, refused to parade her beauty at his request so he rejected her as queen. A successor thus needed to be chosen, and the choice was Esther, a descendant of the captives of Judah. It was providential that Esther became queen, because one of the king's counselors, an evil man named Haman, attempted to exterminate all the Jews. Because Esther was able to intercede for her people, Haman ended up being hanged on the gallows he had built to hang the Jew Mordecai, the man who had raised Esther when her parents died. The story of Esther and the Jews' salvation from annihilation by the Persians is still celebrated each year by the Feast of Purim.

THE INTERTESTAMENTAL PERIOD

We have now arrived at the end of the Old Testament period. Our journey has taken us through the birth, rise, and growth of God's people, the nation Israel. We have seen that their history contained great moments of glory and times of shame. But through it all they continued to exist and increase, just as God promised they would.

Now we come to four hundred silent years—a period of time when divine revelation ceased. The heavens were silent until an angel of the Lord named Gabriel visited an old priest named Zacharias and announced to him that he and his wife would have a son who would be the forerunner of the promised Messiah.

However, during the time between the Testaments, there were

many significant people and events. Much of this history was recorded in a collection of ancient documents now known as the Apocrypha of the Old Testament, particularly the books of Maccabees.

The Old Testament itself closes with the Persians in power; the New Testament begins with Rome ruling. During the intervening years, world leadership changed from Persia to Greece and then Rome.

GREEK RULE

The Persian Empire that had conquered the Babylonian kingdom held world domination for some two hundred years. In 334 B.C., however, it was invaded by the king of Macedonia, Alexander the Great. Alexander's father, Philip, had unified the Greek world by diplomatic and military action. With Greece united, Alexander's invading army conquered the entire Persian Empire (which extended to Egypt) in just three years. The next year Alexander conquered the territory that is present-day Pakistan and Afghanistan.

Alexander died in 323 B.C., and his mighty empire became divided into four parts, each part ruled by one of his leading generals. After a brief struggle for power the territory of the most powerful general was divided with Syria being given to Seleucus. Among them was the Ptolemaic dynasty, which ruled in Egypt, and the Seleucid dynasty, which reigned in Syria. Judea was under the domination of the Ptolemies until 198 B.C., when it came under Seleucid control. The Jews had considerable freedom during both the Persian and Ptolemaic periods. The Ptolemaic rulers even sponsored the writing of a Greek translation of the Old Testament. Now the whole world could read God's law and see the prophecies of the Messiah (ca. 250 B.C.). Although the country was controlled by an imperial governor, Judea was able to rule itself and follow the law under the high priest in Jerusalem of the Zadokite family, the family that had served in Solomon's temple.

In 190 B.C. the Seleucid Empire was defeated at the battle of Magnesia by the newly expanding Roman Empire. The peace that ensued forced the Seleucids to pay large sums of money to Rome, exacting a heavy toll on the Seleucid Empire. That taxation had a direct effect on Judea. Jason, the brother of Onias III, the high priest in Jerusalem, offered a bribe to Antiochus IV, the Seleucid king. Jason wanted to be the high priest in his brother's place, and Antiochus, who desperately needed the money to pay Rome, took the bribe. That set a bad precedent. A few years later Menelaus, a man not in the Zadokite family line, was made high priest when he offered a larger bribe than Jason. Now a high priest was functioning who came from a different family. To make matters worse, Menelaus, like Antiochus, cared little for Judaism and used his position as an opportunity to plunder the temple. A rebellion ensued that attempted to oust Menelaus for the Zadokite Jason. Antiochus, who saw this as insurrection, demolished Jerusalem's walls and banned the practice of Judaism under penalty of death. The temple was profaned by both Menelaus and Antiochus for some three years.

THE MACCABEAN REVOLT

The Jews would not sit still and let such profanity go unchallenged. Mattathias, a priest, along with his five sons led by Judas Maccabeus, revolted. Judas Maccabeus led an army that fought by guerrilla warfare. They defeated larger and better equipped armies. Antiochus, seeing his forces depleted, came to terms with the Jews and allowed them once again to practice Judaism. The Maccabean cleansing of the temple resulted in the celebration of the feast of Hanukkah (John 10:22).

The Jews' struggle for national independence continued, and in 142 B.C. it became a reality under the leadership of Simon, the last surviving son of Mattathias. The grateful people made Simon their leader and also designated him high priest. It was decreed that from henceforth the high priest would be taken from his family. Simon's son, John Hyrcanus, took the mantle from his father and expanded the borders of his rulership. His two sons, Aristobulus I and Alexander Janneus, continued in this expansionist tradition, further extending their realm. That expansion, however, was done not for the glory of God but for their own selfish ends. The rogue Janneus died in 76 B.C. and was succeeded by his wife Salome Alexandra. After her death, a civil war broke out between the followers of her two sons, Hyrcanus II and Aristobulus II.

ROMAN POWER

At that time Rome was continuing to expand its power and influence. In 63 B.C. it occupied Judea under the leadership of General Pompey. The alleged reason for this occupation was the civil war between the two Jewish brothers. Each brother desired the support of Rome, but Aristobulus and his partisans soon opposed Pompey. The Roman general occupied Jerusalem in the spring of 63 B.C. After a three-month siege, Judea lost its independence and became a vassal state of Rome, with Hyrcanus II ruling as a figurehead. By 47 B.C. Judea had been reduced to a Roman province ruled by an Idumean Roman governor named Antipater, who answered directly to Caesar. In that same year, Antipater's son Herod became governor of Galilee. Later, in 37 B.C., Herod became king of Judea.

The power, extent, and influence of the Roman Empire had an impact on the then-known world that changed the face of history forever.

The "grandeur of Rome" is a phrase familiar from textbooks and anthologies. Rome's achievement and her legacy continue to be celebrated. The images (or the stereotypes) conjured up by the word "Roman" are imposing: law and ordered government, disciplined legions, roads, aqueducts, monumental arches, engineering feats—the noble and dedicated Roman. It is not the modern world which created those images. Roman writers, thinkers, and propagandists perpetrated and fostered them.[2]

Through its phenomenal advances in communication, travel, intercultural exchanges, and other fields conducive to the spread of the gospel, the Roman Empire thus prepared the Western world for the coming of Jesus the Messiah, who came into the world to found and build his kingdom, the church.

THE MESSIAH

Up to this point, we have centered our attention on the people of God—the Jews, the ones whom God chose to testify to him. We

---

[2]Erich S. Gruen, *The Image of Rome* (Englewood Cliffs, N.J.: Prentice-Hall, 1969), p. 1.

now move from the people to the Person—the One to whom the law and the prophets looked forward.

The most widely used term with regard to the coming deliverer was *Messiah*. This word comes from a Hebrew word meaning "to anoint." The term *Christ*, from a Greek word, also signifies "the anointed one." It is this title, *Christ*, that Jesus accepted as properly his (for example, see Matthew 16:13-17). Also, at Antioch the believers in Jesus were dubbed "Christians," or "the people of Christ" (Acts 11:26). It thus becomes clear that Jesus, and the early church, believed that he was the Messiah.

In the first century A.D., Jesus of Nazareth claimed that the Old Testament Scriptures had predicted his coming. "You search the Scriptures, because you think that in them you have eternal life; and it is these that bear witness of Me; and you are unwilling to come to Me, that you may have life. . . . For if you believed Moses, you would believe Me; for he wrote of Me. But if you do not believe his writings, how will you believe My words?" (John 5:39-40, 46-47). After his resurrection, Jesus said to two of his followers, "'O foolish men, and slow of heart to believe in all that the prophets have spoken! Was it not necessary for the Christ to suffer these things and to enter into His glory?' And beginning with Moses and with all the prophets, He explained to them the things concerning Himself in all the Scriptures" (Luke 24:25-27).

According to those passages and many others, Jesus contended that his coming had been foretold by God through the prophets. Of course, the claims of Jesus to be the "predicted one" raise many questions. What predictions were made? How did the people understand those predictions? How did Jesus fit the prevailing concept of a coming deliverer? In this section, we will try to answer these and related questions.

JEWISH EXPECTATIONS
The Old Testament predicted that God would bring about the messianic age, a time when the kingdom of God would rule on the earth. As time progressed, it became clearer that this age would be brought by God's deliverer, or Messiah. Donald Guthrie comments:

> In the Old Testament much is said, especially in the proph-
> ets, about the coming messianic age which offered bright

prospects to the people of God (Isaiah 26–29; 40ff.; Ezekiel 40–48; Daniel 12; Joel 2:28–3:21). Numerous passages fanned the flame of Jewish hope and expectation that a deliverer would come (Isaiah 9:6ff.; 11:1ff.). But although the absolute use of the term "Messiah" does not occur, there are various uses of the word in a qualified way, such as the Lord's Messiah (that is, anointed one). The idea of anointing a person for a special mission appears in a variety of applications, but mainly of kings and priests (Leviticus 4:3ff.), also of prophets (1 Kings 19:16) and patriarchs (Psalm 105:15; see also 1 Samuel 24:6ff.; 26:9ff.), and even of a heathen king, Cyrus (Isaiah 45:1). This use of anointing to indicate a specific office became later applied in a more technical sense of one who, par excellence, would be God's chosen instrument in the deliverance of his people. The Old Testament without doubt prepares the way for the Messiah and many Old Testament messianic passages are cited in the New Testament.

During the intertestamental period, the meaning of the term underwent some modifications, in which the technical sense of the Lord's anointed one becomes more dominant (see also Psalms 17–18). The hope of the coming Messiah took many different forms, but the predominant one was the idea of the Davidic king, who would establish an earthly kingdom for the people of Israel and would banish Israel's enemies. The Messiah was to be a political agent, but with a religious bias. The concept was a curious mixture of nationalistic and spiritual hopes.[3]

The kingdom that Jesus proclaimed was in sharp contrast to the expectations of those who advocated a political or military takeover by the Messiah, as F. F. Bruce has commented:

> There were many voices in Israel at that time proclaiming the coming kingdom in terms of militant nationalism. Judas the Galilean, who had led a rising against the Roman

---

[3]Donald Guthrie, *New Testament Theology* (Downers Grove, Ill.: InterVarsity, 1981), pp. 237-238.

administration of Judea when Jesus was a boy, had come to grief, but his soul went marching on. His followers still maintained that it was wrong for the Jewish people to pay taxes to the Roman emperor, and asserted that, if only they would rise with a will against the Romans, God would help their enterprise and enable them to drive the hated imperialists out.

The way of Jesus was quite different. It was not the self-assertive who could inherit the kingdom, he said, but the humble, the meek, the merciful, the pure in heart and the peacemakers. Sorrow and suffering might be their lot at present, but they would receive a great reward. Meanwhile, the right policy was not forceful resistance but submission—turning the other cheek and going the second mile.

When was a kingdom ever established by such means as these? And when did a subject nation ever gain its freedom from oppressors by meek submission? Jesus was turning the accepted principles of political action upside down, strictly speaking. He was being much more revolutionary than the militant nationalists. They tried to overthrow their oppressors by using their oppressors' weapons and methods—and they failed. Jesus followed in practice the way he recommended in preaching—and he won. His disciples followed the same throughout two and one-half centuries of persecution—and they also won.[4]

THE MESSIAH IN PROPHECY

One of the aspects prophesied about the ministry of the Messiah was the performing of signs and wonders. The miracles of Jesus were something he frequently referred to as a sign that he was the Messiah. He challenged his disciples, "Believe Me that I am in the Father, and the Father in Me; otherwise believe on account of the works themselves" (John 14:11).

At one point, John the Baptist was in prison and was wondering whether Jesus indeed was the One who was to come. John's disciples brought this question to Jesus. In answer, Jesus healed

---

[4]F. F. Bruce, *What the Bible Teaches about What Jesus Did* (Wheaton, Ill.: Tyndale House, 1979), p. 19.

many from various diseases and evil spirits and then said to John's disciples, "Go and report to John what you have seen and heard: the blind receive sight, the lame walk, the lepers are cleansed, and the deaf hear, the dead are raised up, the poor have the gospel preached to them" (Luke 7:22). John perhaps could call to mind a prophecy such as Isaiah 35:5-6, which prophesied just such events in God's new age.

Consider briefly several other details of the Savior-King. The hint of such a deliverer was first given in Genesis 3:15, after the fall of Adam and Eve, that from the seed of the woman one would come that would crush the head of the serpent. This deliverer was later revealed to be from the seed of Abraham, the father of the Jews (Genesis 12:1-3). Although Abraham had two sons, Ishmael (from Hagar) and Isaac (from Sarah), God determined that the Messiah would come from Isaac's descendants (Genesis 17:21). Isaac had two sons also, Jacob and Esau, and God chose Jacob (Genesis 25:23ff.). Jacob had twelve sons, and God decreed that the scepter would come through the line of Judah (Genesis 49:10).

A descendant of this Judah, King David, the favorite king of Israel and a faithful servant of God, lived in the tenth century B.C. God promised David that his throne and his house would be established forever (2 Samuel 7:8-16; 1 Chronicles 17:7-14).

The kingly line of Israel deteriorated through the years, but the prophets of God spoke more and more clearly of the coming Messiah, the great future "son" of David. Amos spoke of the glorious time when Israel would be restored to its glory and the "booth of David" that was fallen would again be raised up (Amos 9:11-15). The prophet Hosea predicted that one day the children of Israel would return, seeking the Lord and David, their king (Hosea 3:5). The evil king Ahaz, a descendant of David, was given a sign by God that Immanuel (God with us) would be born of a virgin: "Therefore the Lord himself will give you a sign: Behold, a virgin will be with child and bear a son, and she will call His name Immanuel" (Isaiah 7:14).

Other specific predictions were given in the Old Testament concerning the coming Messiah (some scholars name up to 250 separate messianic prophecies), including the following: Micah 5:2 predicts the Messiah will be born in Bethlehem. Malachi 3:1 predicts the Messiah will come before the temple is destroyed. Daniel

9:26, Psalm 118:26, Zechariah 11:13, and Haggai 2:7-9 also note his coming before the temple destruction.

The prophecy in Genesis 49:10 is interesting. The verse reads, "The scepter will not depart from Judah, nor the ruler's staff from between his feet, until he comes to whom it belongs and the obedience of the nations is his" (NIV). The Jewish interpretation stated that the Jews would not lose their national identity or governmental system until the Messiah, an offspring of Judah, had come. We find that even during the Babylonian captivity, the Jews still had their own system of princes and judges (Ezra 1:5, 8). However, in A.D. 6, Archelaus was dismissed by the Romans, and Judah became a Roman province under the government of a Roman procurator. The Jews were upset that their land had fallen into the hand of Gentiles and was taken out of their control. Many Jews believed the promise of this passage had failed. But had the prophecies failed, or had Messiah come in the person of Jesus Christ, who was born as a man about eight to twelve years before?

Jesus Christ, in his birth in Bethlehem (Matthew 2:1), of a virgin (Matthew 1:25), and in the line of Abraham, Isaac, Jacob, Judah, and David (see Matthew 1:1; Luke 3:23, 31-34), in fact fulfilled all the prophecies mentioned here.

GOD'S PATTERN

Ever since the human fall in the Garden of Eden, God has instituted a way to bridge the wall of separation that resulted between him and human beings. He did it by means of sacrifice. An animal had to be put on the altar and sacrificed to God for the forgiveness of sin. The killing of an innocent animal and the blood that was shed reminded everyone of the horrible nature of sin.

We see this pattern recurring time and time again. Abel offered up the firstborn of his flocks. Noah offered up clean animals in sacrifice after the flood. When the children of Israel were in Egyptian bondage, it was the blood on the doorposts that made the Lord pass over the house. Those who did not comply with God's commandment lost their firstborn sons. All of those sacrifices looked forward to the supreme sacrifice, the sacrifice of God's Son on the cross for the sins of the world. The writer to the Hebrews makes it clear that the Old Testament sacrifices spoke of the One who was to come.

The law is only a shadow of the good things that are coming—not the realities themselves. For this reason it can never, by the same sacrifices repeated endlessly year after year, make perfect those who draw near to worship. If it could, would they not have stopped being offered? For the worshipers would have been cleansed once for all, and would no longer have felt guilty for their sins. But those sacrifices are an annual reminder of sins, because it is impossible for the blood of bulls and goats to take away sins. . . . Day after day every priest stands and performs his religious duties; again and again he offers the same sacrifices, which can never take away sins. But when this priest had offered for all time one sacrifice for sins, he sat down at the right hand of God. Since that time he waits for his enemies to be made his footstool because by one sacrifice he has made perfect forever those who are being made holy. (Hebrews 10:1-4, 11-14, NIV)

The coming of Jesus fulfilled the pattern God had established with his people, as recorded in the Old Testament. As Jesus himself said, "Do not think that I came to abolish the Law or the Prophets; I did not come to abolish, but to fulfill" (Matthew 5:17).

The Old Testament prepares us for the Incarnation, when the Son of God, the Second Person of the Holy Trinity, became man to accomplish our atonement. We have seen the preparation for the Messiah and the predictions of the Messiah. In the next part, we will see the coming of the Messiah, Jesus Christ, and the growth of his church, a testimony of his power and lordship in the lives of redeemed men and women.

PART FOUR
The Church of Jesus Christ

INTRODUCTION

For almost two thousand years the Christian church has preserved and spread the gospel, the good news of salvation in Jesus Christ. Beginning with a small group of disciples in an upstairs prayer room, the church expanded rapidly over the Roman-ruled world, becoming the state religion in just three hundred years. By the time of the Reformation, the 1500s, the church represented almost all people in the Western world and had established colonies in the New World, the bulk of the African continent, and throughout Asia. Today, through mass communication, extensive publication, and missionary activities, there are few groups of people who have not heard of the Christian gospel. Even though many "enlightened" Westerners feel they no longer need religion, including Christianity, the influence of the Christian church pervades most Western culture.

What is the power and attraction of Christianity? What is this thing we call the church? How did the church start, grow, and change over the centuries since Jesus Christ ascended into heaven, promising his disciples power to preach the good news all over the world? Is the church necessary today? This part of the book explores the answers to these questions.

Part 4, *The Church*, looks into the life, death, and resurrection of Jesus Christ, the founder of the Christian church, and then surveys the history of the church through the last two thousand years. The core of this study is Jesus' promise that he would build his church on the firm foundation of his life and mission. Christ's great commission became the fuel that began and sustains even today the spread of Christianity around the world: "Go therefore and make disciples of all the nations, baptizing them in the name of the Father and the Son and the Holy Spirit, teaching them to observe all that I commanded you; and lo, I am with you always, even to the end of the age" (Matthew 28:19-20).

SO MANY CHURCHES

Often people see the thousands of different Christian churches around the world and assume that each one represents a different faith, a different religion. They ask, "How can Christianity be true, when everybody disagrees and starts so many different churches?" Or, people assume that Christianity is but one expression of some universal faith, so that it does not matter what one believes—all faith is said to lead to God eventually. Both assumptions are wrong.

Yes, there are many different kinds of churches, but all truly Christian churches hold the same essential truths concerning Jesus Christ. It is not our intention to arbitrate among the many Christian churches or to render our own verdicts over the validity of differences among Christians. When a church denomination or movement holds to the essentials of biblical faith regarding God, Jesus Christ, humankind, sin, salvation, and the Bible, then that group is considered Christian. Peripheral issues (the type of worship, the style of music, the use or restriction of alcoholic beverages, etc.) do not determine one's Christianity or the Christianity of one's church. There is room for diversity in the church, which is called the body of Christ.

However, the assumption that all faith ultimately leads to God is not right, and we take a strong stand on the exclusive and valid claims of Jesus Christ as the God-man and the only way to salvation and peace with God. Where false religion has attacked the church throughout history, we will note the attack and show clearly the difference between Christianity and false religion.

WHAT IS THE CHURCH?

Let's begin with a working definition of the church. Contrary to popular opinion, the church is not a building; rather, it is the people who are followers of Jesus Christ. The word we translate as "church" is, in the New Testament, the Greek word *ekklesia*, which has the idea of "called-out ones." Christians are called out from among the world's people to be in a special relationship with God. Properly speaking, the church is a group of believers in Jesus Christ who are called out to worship and serve him.

We will use the term *church* in several different ways, each of which should be distinguishable by the context in which it is used. Sometimes it refers to all Christian believers throughout all time, whether living or dead. Sometimes its use is more restricted, referring to living Christians. Sometimes the context of a passage will indicate that we label the church as the religious structure under consideration (e.g., "the church of the fourth century"). Still other times *church* refers to a particular ecclesiastical body (e.g., Methodist church, Roman Catholic church).

APPRECIATING OUR HERITAGE

Studying church history is important for every Christian. Understanding the background, birth, rise, and growth of the church will help one appreciate his or her religious heritage. All believers ought to have an understanding of the contributions to their faith made by such giants of church history as Athanasius, Thomas Aquinas, Martin Luther, John Calvin, and John Wesley. We should appreciate what men and women who have called on the name of Christ have suffered over the years of persecution visited upon the church. One cannot read the history of the church without being thankful for the contributions, suffering, and heroic acts of past believers, or "holy ones" (a New Testament term for all Christians; see, for example, Ephesians 1:1, 15, 18).

Rather than merely chronicling the events that have brought the church to its present state, we place a special emphasis on those individuals who made contributions, both good and bad, to the formation of Christ's representation on earth, the church. We will learn from the triumphs of past saints and learn to avoid the errors of those who attempted to thwart the work of the Holy Spirit in building the church. In this way the reader may grow spiritually as an individual Christian and intellectually in his or her understanding of Christianity.

Before we can investigate the church and its history, we must concentrate upon the one on whom the church is built: Jesus Christ, God's Son. The church is Christ's ambassador in the world, his representative on earth today. The church brings the good news of the death, burial, and resurrection of Jesus Christ to the world. The Old Testament prophesied Jesus Christ. The New Testament revealed Jesus Christ. The church proclaims Jesus Christ to the world. We begin, then, with a consideration of Jesus Christ, the divine founder and cornerstone of our faith.

CHAPTER 1
In the Fullness of Time

The apostle Paul, perhaps the greatest early Christian missionary, as well as being a founding apostle of the church, wrote to the Galatian churches, "But when the fulness of the time came, God sent forth His Son, born of a woman, born under the Law, in order that He might redeem those who were under the Law, that we might receive the adoption as sons" (Galatians 4:4-5). It was not chance that brought Jesus Christ, Son of God and Son of Man, into human history to live as a man and die for the sins of the world about A.D. 30. This passage tells us that God's plan was fulfilled perfectly, according to his purposes and his timetable.

When Jesus Christ was born in Bethlehem, the Romans were in firm control of Israel, as we have seen. Judaism was coping as best it could under Roman rule and had developed various traditions of worship and application of the Old Testament laws. All of these formed the background for the earthly life and ministry of Jesus Christ.

JUDAISM AT THE TIME OF CHRIST

Since Jesus Christ was born a Jew (Romans 1:3), it is important to understand the Jewish religious climate of his world. The Old Testament canon was completed about four hundred years before Christ was born. During that period, Jewish religion changed and matured. We consider here four important aspects of Jewish religious life that served as background to the coming of the Messiah.

THE SECOND TEMPLE

The first Jewish temple, built by King Solomon, was destroyed in 586 B.C., when the Jews were taken into captivity by the Babylonians. When Jews were allowed to come back to Israel some seventy years later, they built a second, much smaller temple, roughly on the site of the first one. This second temple was remodeled (or replaced) by a magnificent temple structure erected by the Jewish king Herod the Great, who ruled over Judea from 37 to 4 B.C. This enlarged temple was begun in 19 B.C. and still was not completed at Jesus' death (c. A.D. 30). It was finally finished in the year 64, only to be destroyed six years later by the Romans.

This Herodian temple was awesome in its proportions, as indicated in Mark 13:1. At the temple, the rituals and ceremonies that had been commanded by God in the first five books of the Old Testament were practiced, along with elaborately embellished rituals and regulations developed by the Pharisees and other Jewish leaders. Temple worship and sacrifice were carried out by an elaborate array of priests and temple servants. The business of the temple was conducted under the watchful eye of the Roman government, represented by a governor and by a Roman garrison at the nearby Antonia fortress overlooking the courts (see Acts 21:30-32).

In the temple complex stood the court of the Gentiles, where non-Jewish people who were interested in Judaism observed the Jewish practices and where the sacrificial animals were sold to prospective penitents. This court became the setting for Jesus' display of wrath against the hypocrisy displayed by temple authorities, who placed the burden of the law on the trusting Jewish commoners and reaped the material wealth generated thereby. Twice Jesus overturned the tables of the money changers in the court of the Gentiles. (Gentiles were not allowed into the sanctified portions of the temple—see Acts 21:28-29; Ephesians 2:14.)

THE SYNAGOGUE

For the Jews this one temple in Jerusalem was the hub of their worship. It was the only place ordered by God in which sacrifice could be made for the individual and collective sins of the people. However, not all Jews could travel regularly to the temple. Therefore, during the intertestamental period, synagogues, or local places of teaching and worship (but not sacrifice), became common in every Jewish community. The synagogue was a center for worship and the study of the law. Each Sabbath day (corresponding to our Saturday) the people would gather to listen to the designated reading of the Old Testament. The synagogue also served as the local community center, the site of local government, and the schoolhouse where Jewish children were instructed in their faith. The elders of the synagogue were the civil authorities in the communities in which the Jews were the largest part of the local population.

Synagogue services and weekly family worship followed a definite pattern. When the Sabbath began on Friday evening at sundown, all business ceased. Food for the Sabbath had been prepared that day, before the setting of the sun. When the sun set, the family gathered together for prayer, and the children were told stories from the Old Testament. The next morning was the Sabbath service in the synagogue.

On the Sabbath morning the entire family went to the synagogue service. The synagogue was the most imposing building in the community. No structure was permitted to "look down" on the synagogue. The father washed his hands in the court in preparation for the service, and then entered the center door with the rest of the men of the congregation.

The women and the boys under twelve years of age had to go around to the side where they found some stone steps which led up to a second story. Here they entered a gallery that ran around three sides of the building. In front of the gallery was a wooden grill so the women and boys could see and hear the reader, while they themselves would be barely discernible. This was the women's gallery.

In the middle of the synagogue floor was a structure about twice the height of man. It was called "ark." On top of this ark were the Scrolls, or their copy of the Old Testament. When the service began, the ruler of the synagogue climbed the ladder-like stairs and took his seat near the community. He was not a teacher but was held in high honor in the community. It was his duty to keep the sacred

Scrolls in good condition. He appointed the reader and the speaker for the day.

If there were not ten men present, they could not hold a service. If there were more than ten men the service began by the appointment of the reader. The reader stepped up to the desk to lead the congregation in the reciting of the "Shema" (Deuteronomy 6:4-9), which was their confession of faith or creed. . . .

After the law was read the speaker gave the sermon or explanation of the law. This was usually based on the Tradition of the Elders, a set of interpretations or commentaries on passages of the law, handed down from past generations of scholars. These often went into great detail on what was or was not allowable according to the law.[1]

THE LAW AND THE TRADITIONS

Since the time of Moses (c. 1400–1200 B.C.), the people of Israel had a developed law, first given to them by Moses, who received the law by revelation from God (see especially Exodus 20–23). But from the fifth century B.C., during the time of Ezra, the study of the law had become intensified. Men dedicated their whole lives to understanding and developing the Jewish law into an intricate system governing every aspect of Jewish life.

The Jews were punished by God with captivity in Babylon because they had disobeyed his law, and later Jews hoped that by their study such apostasy would never occur again. Traditions arose out of this serious study, and in time the tradition and human interpretation became as binding on the people as the original divine law. Many of these new rules and regulations that were added detracted from the intent of the original law, obscured the real meaning of the law, and placed an unbearable burden on the Jewish people. Jesus often spoke out against this embellished law: "Woe to you, scribes and Pharisees, hypocrites! For you tithe mint and dill and cummin, and have neglected the weightier provisions of the law: justice and mercy and faithfulness; but these are the things you should have done without neglecting the others" (Matthew 23:23).

---

[1]Merrill Gilbertson, *The Way It Was in Bible Times* (Minneapolis: Augsburg, 1959), pp. 76-78.

MOVEMENTS IN JUDAISM

Within Judaism there were various movements, sects, and parties. Some were almost exclusively religious, others almost exclusively political, but all claimed to have the only true interpretation of God's revelation.

A group not mentioned in the Old Testament but who held a place of prominence in New Testament times was the **Pharisees.** The Pharisees were a strict religious sect who sought to adhere meticulously to the traditions and customs of Judaism. They were separate from the common people in the ways in which they observed the ceremonies and rituals of Judaism. Because they adhered so carefully to Jewish law and custom, they had little patience with anything or anyone non-Jewish, and that kind of fervor often led to pride. Jesus attacked both their arrogance and their external demonstration of piety. He knew that most of them were hypocrites and told them so: "Woe to you, scribes and Pharisees, hypocrites! For you clean the outside of the cup and of the dish, but inside they are full of robbery and self-indulgence. You blind Pharisee, first clean the inside of the cup and of the dish, so that the outside of it may become clean also" (Matthew 23:25-26). Ironically, some of the greatest enemies of God and of the gospel of Christ were these Pharisees, who were supposedly following God's commandment to the letter. They are a prime example of what can occur when external religion replaces spiritual reality.

The **Sadducees** were the other main religious party with which Jesus contended. Their influence had begun to decline by the time of Jesus, but they had once possessed great power, largely because of their wealth in property and goods. The Sadducees accepted only the five books of Moses as revelation from God. They rejected many of the beliefs of the Pharisees, including the belief in angels, demons, the resurrection of the body, and immortality (see Matthew 22:23; Acts 23:8). The Sadducees shared with the Pharisees the hypocrisy that so angered Jesus Christ and that was so at variance with the true way of salvation he revealed.

The **Essenes** were a Jewish sect we know about through the Dead Sea Scrolls. They lived along the shores of the Dead Sea. Founded by an unknown teacher of righteousness who lived c. 165 B.C., this community considered itself the true remnant of God's chosen people. All others, including other Jews, were considered enemies. They called themselves the Sons of Light. Their enemies, the Sons of Darkness, were prophesied as being destroyed in the last days. This ascetic group had no direct confrontations with Jesus Christ or his disciples as far as the New Testament records, although their teachings were diametrically opposed to the truth revealed in Jesus Christ.[2]

The **Zealots** were a largely political Jewish group that attempted to gain deliverance from Roman oppression through violent revolution (see Acts 5:36-37). They were looking for a conquering King-Messiah who would crush the Roman oppressors. These freedom fighters eventually instituted the rebellion that led to the Roman destruction of the temple and Jerusalem in A.D. 70. Barabbas, the prisoner released by Pilate instead of Jesus Christ at his crucifixion, was probably a Zealot. These radical patriots believed that submission to Rome was tantamount to idol worship.

THE FOUR GOSPELS

Having considered some of the political and religious environment into which Jesus came, we now survey the written records concerning his birth, life, death, burial and glorious resurrection, and establishment of the Christian church. Virtually everything we know about the earthly life of Jesus of Nazareth is found in the four Gospels. Although the impact of Jesus Christ has forever changed human history, we must remember that, from a secular perspective, he was only an obscure teacher in a remote corner of the Roman Empire. It would be highly unlikely that contemporary writers who were not in the immediate vicinity of Palestine would have even heard of him, much less written of him.

F. F. Bruce comments regarding the contents and role of the Gospels.

> The four Gospels—or rather the four records of the one and only Gospel, which is the good news of God's salvation brought near in Jesus Christ—are not, as is sometimes imag-

---

[2] For a discussion of the Essenes and Christianity, see William Sanford LaSor, *The Dead Sea Scrolls and the New Testament* (Grand Rapids: Eerdmans, 1972).

ined, biographies of Christ, not in the proper sense of the word at any rate. They are rather the written deposit of the early apostolic preaching and teaching, the burden of which was the works and words of Christ. The first three Gospels are commonly called the "Synoptic" Gospels, because the amount of material common to all three or to two of them makes it convenient to view them synoptically.... The fourth Gospel was probably written after the first three. The testimony of this Gospel is that it preserves the witness of John the Apostle, and this finds corroboration in our earliest external evidence bearing on the subject, according to which it was written at the dictation of John, the last survivor of the apostles, shortly before his death at the end of the first century A.D. Each of the four Gospels, with its distinctive picture of Christ, seems to have circulated at first in the churches of a particular area, but shortly after the appearance of the fourth the four appear to have been bound up together and acknowledged by the churches at large as the authoritative fourfold Gospel of Christ.[3]

The purpose of each of the Gospels is to preach the good news about Jesus Christ. The writers' desire was to convert unbelievers and to build the faith of the believers. For example, John says, "Many other signs therefore Jesus also performed in the presence of the disciples, which are not written in this book; but these have been written that you may believe that Jesus is the Christ, the Son of God; and that believing you may have life in His name" (John 20:30-31).

Some aspects of the life of Jesus Christ therefore receive scant attention by the Gospel writers. For example, we know considerable detail about Christ's birth and his flight with his family to Egypt, but only one other incident in his entire childhood is recorded in the New Testament (his trip to the temple at age twelve). Sometimes the Gospel writers are not strictly chronological in their narratives, which does not mean that they are not interested in history. Quite the contrary, they are concerned about giving an

---

[3]F. F. Bruce, *The Books and the Parchments* (Westwood, N.J.: Revell, 1963), pp. 92-93.

accurate account of what has transpired. Luke begins his Gospel by stressing his use of eyewitness testimony (Luke 1:1-4).

We must remember that New Testament history is amazingly selective. Its Old Testament basis follows the story of a small people. In the New Testament it concentrates upon one central figure and the relatively few individuals who were closely connected with him. These leading individuals did not possess high social standing or general esteem. The founder was condemned as a criminal or rebel, and the early church leaders repeatedly incurred public displeasure. In social, cultural, political, and economic position, both the chief characters and the general membership of the Christian group were so weak that its later expansion appears to offer a curious puzzle.

Yet the gospel asserts that in the story of its founder, these apostles, and this small and apparently discredited movement in this insignificant area is contained the hope of the world as well as of each individual. The message declares that this outwardly unimpressive and apparently pitiful history is the most important series of happenings in the entire sweep of world events.[4]

It is important to understand why there are four Gospels, and the special reasons for each Gospel. Each writer portrays Jesus in a special light, emphasizing a different but not contradictory side to his multifaceted character.

Matthew presents Jesus as the Messiah, the King of the Jews, emphasizing the rich Jewish heritage that led to the coming of the Messiah to bring salvation to God's people. Matthew quotes the Old Testament more than does any other Gospel writer. He shows that Jesus Christ came to fulfill the Old Testament and that the Jews are going to be judged for their hypocrisy and unfaithfulness to God's truth. The Pharisees are sharply denounced in Matthew as having an outward show of faith but not possessing any inner life. Matthew's Gospel ends with Jesus' great commission to take the gospel of Jesus the Messiah to the ends of the earth, for all people of all time.

While Matthew was written mainly to the religious person (typically Jewish) who is familiar with the Old Testament, **Mark**

---

[4]Floyd V. Filson, *The New Testament against Its Environment* (London: SCM, 1950), p. 45.

was written to a Roman audience (because Mark used the preachings and teachings of Peter to the Roman church to formulate his gospel narrative). Mark presents Jesus' teachings and emphasizes action on the basis of those teachings. The Romans did not want to know about Old Testament prophecies; they wanted to know if Jesus Christ could perform what he promised. Jesus is presented as the "arm of the Lord," God's representative on earth to reveal God's will and salvation to all who are lost. The Jesus of Mark is the man of power, more than equal to any Roman hero or god.

Luke challenges the Greek mind, that of the philosopher and intellectual. Luke stresses Jesus' perfect manhood, his dazzling intellect, and his solution to the deepest human needs. Luke's account can stand the most rigorous logical testing by the sophisticated Greeks, and his accounts of Jesus' teachings reveal Jesus' power as the revealer of all truth.

The fourth Gospel, **John,** is for the man or woman of despair and faith. In John's Gospel we find God manifest in the flesh, the one with divine power and eternal life for all who believe in him. John's Christ is the way to God, the truth of all existence, and the eternal life.

The four Gospels are thus different, and yet they all proclaim one Savior: Jesus Christ the Righteous. He is the prophet-priest of Matthew, the warrior-king of Mark, the philosopher-revealer of Luke, and the God-man of John. He is the Savior of the world. John sums up the significance of Christ in the world: "For God so loved the world, that He gave his only begotten Son, that whoever believes in Him should not perish, but have eternal life. For God did not send the Son into the world to judge the world, but that the world should be saved through Him" (John 3:16-17).

We turn now to this person who is the focus of God's Word, the shaper of history, the cornerstone of the church.

CHAPTER 2
The Greatest Story Ever Told

BORN OF A VIRGIN

In the small Palestinian village of Nazareth lived a young woman named Mary who was engaged to a man named Joseph, a carpenter and descendant of the royal line of the family of David. Nazareth, located in a remote part of Galilee in northern Israel, was occupied by the Romans and ruled by Herod.

One day a miraculous visitation took place. The angel Gabriel came to Mary to announce that she was chosen by God to bear his Messiah, the Savior of the world. A virgin, Mary would conceive a child by the miraculous power of the Holy Spirit. The child born to her would rule over the house of David forever, and he would save his people from their sins.

When Mary informed Joseph of the miraculous visitation and conception, he was confused. He assumed the worst and determined to divorce Mary privately to preserve both their reputations. (Engagement in Jewish culture could be dissolved only by formal divorce.) However, an angel appeared to Joseph, confirming Mary's story and ordering Joseph not to divorce her. Joseph became the legal father of the child, transferring the royal rights of kingship through his royal lineage to his legal son, to be named Jesus because "it is He who will save His people from their sins" (Matthew 1:21).

Mary and Joseph were natives of Nazareth. But the Old Testament prophesied that the Messiah would be born in Bethlehem (Micah 5:2). God guided the decision of the Roman emperor,

Augustus Caesar, who decreed that all Roman subjects should take part in a census, with enrollment to take place in one's ancestral home. Joseph's family claimed Bethlehem as its ancestral home, and so it was that Joseph and Mary, close to the time for delivery of her son, traveled to Bethlehem.

When they arrived in the city, it was so clogged with census participants that they were unable to find lodging. They were forced to take shelter in a stable, where Jesus Christ was born. The God of all creation, now become flesh with the nature of a man, humbled himself so much that he entered our world in a lowly stable. In startling contrast, an angel of the Lord appeared to shepherds in nearby fields and announced the birth of the Messiah. The shepherds hurried to the stable to offer worship to the small king.

In obedience to Jewish law, Jesus was circumcised when he was eight days old. His family's poverty was evidenced in the sacrifice they offered in Jesus' honor; it was the one the law allowed for those who could not afford anything more. In the temple, God the Holy Spirit moved Simeon and Anna to declare openly the baby's identity as the Messiah. Simeon, an old man who longed for death, declared, "Now Lord, Thou dost let Thy bondservant depart in peace, according to Thy word; for mine eyes have seen Thy salvation, which Thou hast prepared in the presence of all peoples, a light of revelation to the Gentiles, and the glory of Thy people Israel" (Luke 2:29-32).

Afterward, Joseph and Mary found accommodations in a house in Bethlehem. It was there that they received the wise men (magi) from the East. The origin of these wise men is unknown, as is the method by which they determined astrologically or astronomically that the King of the Jews was born and was due homage. From whatever source, the wise men learned of the miraculous birth of the King of the Jews and traveled to Jerusalem to see him and bring him gifts.

Imagine the surprise of King Herod when the wise men entered his court, asking for the new king! Herod saw an opportunity to eliminate any competition and asked the wise men to find the child and then reveal the location to him. He said he would worship the child—actually, he intended to kill him.

After the wise men found the Christ and gave him gifts and

homage, they were warned in a dream not to return to Herod's court. They departed for their home secretly. The Lord protected Jesus Christ further by instructing Joseph in a dream to take his foster son and wife and flee to Egypt to escape the coming wrath of Herod. When Herod realized he had been tricked, he panicked and ordered all male children in Bethlehem under three years of age to be murdered. He wanted to be sure this usurper was not spared. By the time of the massacre (which had been prophesied in the Old Testament), Joseph, Mary, and Jesus were long gone.

After Herod's death, Joseph had a dream telling him to return to Nazareth. Back in Nazareth the family lived quietly, and Jesus probably worked with his carpenter father, learning his trade, as the Scriptures tell us that Jesus "continued to grow and become strong, increasing in wisdom; and the grace of God was upon Him" (Luke 2:40).

Nothing more is known of the childhood of Jesus Christ until his trip to the Jerusalem temple at age twelve. Age twelve for a Jewish boy means passage from childhood to adulthood and is the time for showing one's mastery of the Torah before the people of his synagogue (or temple in Jerusalem). Jesus traveled to Jerusalem to celebrate the Feast of the Passover and while there gave the teachers of the law a glimpse of his lordship through his complete and full understanding of the Scriptures. Everyone commented that he had more wisdom concerning the Torah than the teachers in the temple! We can be confident that even the boy Jesus knew who he was and why he had been born. When Mary and Joseph admonished him for remaining in the temple after they and their friends had left Jerusalem for home, Jesus replied, "Why is it that you were looking for Me? Did you not know that I had to be in My Father's house?" (Luke 2:49). This short glimpse of Jesus as a boy serves to remind us that he was a boy unique in all of human existence.

JOHN THE BAPTIST

In the Gospel records, the greatest story ever told actually begins with the announcement of the birth of Jesus' cousin, John the Baptist. Zacharias was a priest who was righteous before the Lord. He and his wife, Elizabeth, were elderly and childless. While

Zacharias was serving in the temple one day, the angel Gabriel appeared to him with the news that he would have a son who would go forth in the spirit and power of the prophet Elijah. This son would be the forerunner of the promised Messiah. The child was subsequently born and named John. He grew strong in spirit and as an adult spent time meditating and praying in the wilderness until he assumed his ministry to Israel of announcing the coming of the Lord.

John preached baptism accompanied by repentance in the wilderness, charging the people to prepare the way of the Lord. The long-promised Messiah would soon come, and the people were to be ready spiritually by repenting of their sins and being baptized. The religious rulers from Jerusalem came out to the Jordan where John was preaching and questioned him concerning his mission and identity.

> "Who are you?" And he confessed, and did not deny, and he confessed, "I am not the Christ." And they asked him, "What then? Are you Elijah?" And he said, "I am not." "Are you the Prophet?" And he answered, "No." They said then to him, "Who are you, so that we may give an answer to those who sent us? What do you say about yourself?" He said, "I am a voice of one crying in the wilderness, 'Make straight the way of the Lord,' as Isaiah the prophet said." (John 1:19-23)

Note that John identified himself as the one prophesied by Isaiah as the forerunner or announcer of the Messiah, the coming King of the Jews, sent to bring salvation to all persons. Throughout his ministry, John the Baptist always directed attention toward the Messiah.

JESUS' BAPTISM AND TEMPTATION

Jesus' public ministry began when he was thirty. We can assume that he was probably earning a living as a carpenter, as Joseph had done before him. However, when it was the divinely appointed time for him to begin his public ministry, Jesus began to live as an itinerant preacher, traveling in various parts of Palestine, gathering around himself followers.

The day after John the Baptist had been questioned by the Jewish leaders about his identity and had said that God's Anointed would come shortly, Jesus fulfilled John's prediction by coming and being baptized.

> The next day he saw Jesus coming to him, and said, "Behold, the Lamb of God who takes away the sin of the world! This is He on behalf of whom I said, 'After me comes a man who has a higher rank than I, for He existed before me.' And I did not recognize Him, but in order that He might be manifested to Israel, I came baptizing in water." And John bore witness saying, "I have beheld the Spirit descending as a dove out of heaven; and he remained upon Him. And I did not recognize Him, but He who sent me to baptize in water said to me, 'He upon whom you see the Spirit descending and remaining upon Him, this is the one who baptizes in the Holy Spirit.' And I have seen, and have borne witness that this is the Son of God." (John 1:29-34)

We can see several interesting points from this short account. First, John knew immediately that Jesus was the Son of God. Second, John knew that the Son of God was not merely man, for he states that Jesus existed before he did, although John knew that Jesus, his cousin, was born about six months after John. Third, God the Father clearly distinguished Jesus from everyone else who was baptized. The Holy Spirit rested in the form of a dove on Jesus, signifying his divine commission from the Father. Fourth, John was absolutely obedient to the command of God to testify publicly that Jesus was the Christ, the Lamb of God sent to take away the sins of the world.

The next important event in the life of Christ was his temptation by Satan in the wilderness. For forty days and forty nights Jesus ate nothing. At the end of that time, when he was hungry, Satan came to him and tempted him to relinquish his mission and submit to Satan's power. In three different ways Satan tempted him: with material provision, promises of earthly power, and protection from all harm. In each case Satan tempted Jesus to abuse his position as the Son of God. Satan tempted Jesus to turn stones into bread to assuage his hunger. He also tempted Jesus to worship him in exchange for power over all of the kingdoms of the earth. And Satan tempted Jesus to prove his messiahship by leaping from the top of the temple and calling his angels to protect him.

In each case, Jesus replied firmly to Satan with a denial of his lies and an affirmation from the Word of God. Jesus pointed out that living by God's Word was more important than bread, that worshiping the true God was the only way to spiritual power, and that trust in God should not be flaunted. This episode in the life of Christ illustrates to us the absolute obedience to God's will that was present from the earliest moment of Jesus' ministry.

Having failed to dissuade Jesus from his mission, Satan left him in the wilderness, and angels came to Jesus, ministering to him. Jesus returned to civilization and moved to Capernaum in Galilee, which became a center of his ministry activities.

MINISTRY IN GALILEE

Each Gospel writer gives a portrait of the life of Christ from his own particular point of view, with the unique needs of different audiences in mind. This makes it difficult at some points to trace an exact chronology of the life of Jesus. In the rest of this chaper, therefore, we will not attempt to deal with Jesus' ministry in a chronological manner, but we will focus on selected miracles and teachings in the greatest life ever lived—first in Jesus' activities in Galilee, and then in his time in or near Jerusalem.

MIRACLES

We consider here three of the miracles recorded from Jesus' ministry in Galilee.

Water turned into wine. Jesus' first public miracle was in Cana of Galilee. John records that after his baptism Jesus attended a wedding with his disciples. His mother was also at the wedding, and probably she had some part in helping with the wedding feast, since she approached Jesus for help when the steward ran out of wine. Jesus turned fresh water into wine so fine that the steward marveled, wondering why the groom would save the best wine for last. This miracle of Jesus confirmed his disciples' faith in him as the Son of God; John 2:11 tells us that they "believed in Him."

Healing of a nobleman's son. A nobleman who had a son sick in Capernaum met Jesus in Cana and asked him to come to Capernaum to heal the sick child. Jesus told the man to go home alone, because his son would live. The nobleman believed Jesus' word and began the trip back to Capernaum. On the way he met one of his servants, who had been sent to tell him his son was well. The servant confirmed that the child had been healed at the exact time Jesus had declared his healing in Cana. This miracle converted the nobleman's whole household to faith in the Messiah, Jesus. This was the second recorded miracle in Cana of Galilee.

Feeding of the five thousand. This is one of the miracles that is recorded in all four Gospels. A great multitude came out to hear Jesus in a rural area. There was no food to give them except for five small barley loaves and two small fish, donated by a young boy in the crowd. Jesus commanded his disciples to have the people sit down. After blessing the fish and bread, Jesus told the disciples to distribute the food among the people. Miraculously, the fish and loaves were multiplied, all of the people were fed until they were full, and twelve baskets full of leftovers were gathered after the meal. This miracle showed his true disciples that he was the holy one of God.

TEACHING

The Gospels record many of Jesus' teachings and interactions with people—some public, some with only the disciples, and some with individuals. We have selected here six of such exchanges from Jesus' time in Galilee.

Rejection at Nazareth. When Jesus traveled to Nazareth in the power of the Holy Spirit, he accomplished many miracles of healing, and his fame spread throughout the region. One Sabbath day, as was his custom, Jesus joined the faithful Jews as they gathered in the synagogue to hear the Scriptures read and expounded. William Menzies notes the structure of synagogue Sabbath services and the startling revelation Jesus made that day in Nazareth.

The form of service generally included, in addition to various prayers, a regular reading from the Old Testament, in such fashion that the Scriptures were read through in about three and a half years. The Scripture passages were read in

Hebrew, but following each reading a translation into Aramaic, the language of the promised people, was given. This Aramaic paraphrase was called a "Targum." When a scribe was present, an exposition on the Scripture for the day was invited from him. Jesus participated in this fashion in the synagogue at Nazareth, startling the people by announcing that the passage from Isaiah that had been read was being fulfilled in Him (Luke 4:21).[1]

Jesus had read from Isaiah, saying, "The Spirit of the Lord is upon Me, because He anointed Me to preach the gospel to the poor. He has sent Me to proclaim release to the captives, and recovery of sight to the blind, to set free those who are downtrodden, to proclaim the favorable year of the Lord" (Luke 4:18-19). Then he closed the book and declared, "Today this Scripture has been fulfilled in your hearing" (v. 21). Unfortunately, the people of Nazareth rejected Jesus' claim to be the Messiah and tried to hurl him off a hillside, to kill him for committing blasphemy. Jesus, however, supernaturally passed through their midst, and they were unable to capture him.

The choosing of the Twelve. Jesus went away to a secluded place and spent the night in prayer. When it was day, he chose twelve trusted disciples from among all those who were following him. These twelve, the apostles, formed the small group Jesus instructed privately and who later were the leaders of the Christian church. The disciples who became apostles were Simon (also named Peter), Andrew, James, John, Philip, Bartholomew (also called Nathanael), Matthew, Thomas, James (the son of Alphaeus), Simon (the Zealot), Judas (brother of James; also known as Thaddeus), and Judas Iscariot. Donald Guthrie comments,

> The naming of twelve specially chosen disciples and the description of their first mission is of such importance that all the synoptic Gospels mention them. In both Matthew and Mark (Matthew 10:1; Mark 3:13-19) the commissioning is linked with authority over unclean spirits. In addition to

[1]William W. Menzies, *Understanding the Times of Christ* (Springfield, Mo.: Gospel Publishing House, 1969), pp. 69-70.

this, Matthew mentions the power to heal, and Mark the command to preach. Luke separates the story of the choosing of the Twelve from the special purpose of the office of apostle (see Luke 6:12-16; 9:1-2). The men whom Jesus chose were a representative group. They were not all drawn from the poorer classes, for the father of James and John possessed his own boat and employed servants (Mark 1:20). Matthew is a tax-collector and would be well-to-do, although hated by his compatriots. Simon may have been an erstwhile revolutionary.[2]

The Sermon on the Mount. The most famous of all the discourses of Jesus is his Sermon on the Mount. It was delivered to Jesus' disciples and crowds of followers on a mountainside in Galilee. Jesus begins by pronouncing blessings on certain classes of people (the "poor in spirit," the "mourners," the "meek," and others). He then gives his thoughts about the law, teaching the eternal nature of the law and his coming as its fulfillment. The sermon also deals with matters of personal piety, including giving, prayer, judging, and anxiety. The Lord's Prayer is found in the Sermon on the Mount. The message concludes with the two foundations upon which people can build their faith: one compared to sand, which shifts, slides, and is completely unstable; the other compared to rock, which is a firm and stable foundation. Those who build their faith on the "rock" of God's Word need never fear anything. When Jesus concluded his sermon, "the multitudes were amazed at His teaching; for He was teaching them as one having authority, and not as their scribes" (Matthew 7:28-29).

"I will build my church." At Caesarea Philippi, Jesus confronted his disciples regarding his identity. He first asked them the question, "Who do people say that the Son of Man is?" Various answers were given. He then challenged them directly: "But who do you say that I am?" The apostle Peter replied promptly, "Thou art the Christ, the Son of the living God" (Matthew 16:13-16). Jesus approved Peter's confession of faith and declared that his church would be built on the foundation of that confession.

---

[2]Donald Guthrie, *A Shorter Life of Christ* (Grand Rapids: Zondervan, 1970), pp. 88-89.

We shall see in subsequent pages that even though Peter denied Christ before his death and was discouraged before the Resurrection, he grew in faith and commitment to Jesus Christ and became one of the pillars of the church, a strong missionary and pastor who proudly proclaimed this same confession throughout his ministry and up to his martyrdom. As we shall observe in later chapters, the prophecy of Christ has come true. The church founded upon Jesus Christ still exists, and the message of salvation remains the best news anyone can hear and accept.

Jesus' refusal to be made king. The people saw the power Jesus had and remembered some of the Scripture prophesying that the Messiah would destroy Israel's enemies and establish an everlasting King after the manner of King David, the greatest king in Jewish history. They prodded Jesus to assume the title of King of the Jews and to assert his right to rule Israel and banish the hated Roman oppressors. They did not understand that God's righteous rule could not be established until salvation was obtained on behalf of all persons through the sacrifice of the King, who was also the Lamb of sacrifice.

Jesus refused the people's pleas and retreated to a mountain place by himself. At dusk the disciples set sail on the Sea of Galilee without Jesus. When Jesus later met them at their boat by walking on the water, the disciples were at first afraid, thinking he was a ghost. His voice stilled their fears, however, and Peter even stepped out of the boat and walked on the water to meet his Lord, through the miraculous power of Christ.

Jesus, the Bread of Life. In Capernaum Jesus scolded his disciples for their materialistic desires. He admonished them rather to desire "spiritual food," which results in everlasting life. Jesus pointed out the futility of trying to work one's way to righteousness: the way to God was to believe on him whom God had sent, Jesus Christ. Jesus illustrated his life-giving power by describing himself as the Bread of Life. Those who came to him would never hunger. He was also the source of "living water," and those who came to drink of that living water would never thirst again. But such life demanded commitment even in the face of adversity, and some among his followers left him at this time, not willing to make an ultimate commitment to him. When Jesus asked his apostles if they, too, would leave him, Peter answered for them, saying,

"Lord, to whom shall we go? You have words of eternal life. And we have believed and have come to know that You are the Holy One of God" (John 6:68-69).

MINISTRY IN JERUSALEM

We turn now to some of the mighty deeds and words of Christ in and around Jerusalem.

MIRACLES

Three healings highlight our review of Jesus' Judean miracles.

Healing at the Pool of Bethesda. Jesus traveled to Jerusalem at one of the Jewish feasts. He came to the pool of Bethesda, where those who were sick or lame waited, hoping for a healing miracle. One man had been waiting to be healed for thirty-eight years. Jesus approached him: "'Arise, take up your pallet, and walk.' And immediately the man became well, and took up his pallet and began to walk" (John 5:8-9).

Although everyone should have rejoiced that the man was healed through the power of Jesus' word, the hard-hearted Jews objected. They knew that it was the Sabbath, and no one should do work on the Sabbath. The Sabbath was a day of rest, not for work like healing or picking up beds! When the Jews accused the healed man of breaking the Sabbath by carrying his bed, he pointed out that he was merely following the orders of the man who had healed him. If Jesus really was the Son of God, with the power to heal, did he not also have the power over the Sabbath?

The Jews' wrath turned on Jesus, who had dared to heal on the Sabbath. Totally ignoring the spiritual significance of Jesus' ability to heal, the Jews accused him of breaking God's law by such healing. Jesus answered by saying that since he was the unique Son of God, that made him equal to God, and God certainly had the right to do what he wished on the Sabbath! (John 5:17-18).

The immediate reaction of the Jews to Jesus' claim was to accuse him of blasphemy and to attempt to kill him. However, Jesus argued ably in his defense, establishing his claim to messiahship and calling the Jews to account for their faithlessness. Jesus concluded his argument with a stern testimony of judgment: "Do not think that I will accuse you before the Father; the one who accuses you is Moses, in whom you have set your hope. For if you believed Moses, you would believe Me; for he wrote of Me. But if you do not believe his writings, how will you believe My words?" (John 5:45-47).

Healing of a blind man. Jesus healed several people of their blindness, but for one man who was born without sight, Jesus did so in an unusual manner. After spitting on the ground, Jesus made clay out of the wet earth and put it on the man's eyes. Then he told him to wash his eyes in the Pool of Siloam. The blind man did as he was ordered, and he was healed.

When his friends saw the miracle, they brought the man before the Pharisees. They concluded that Jesus was not from God, since God sanctioned no work on the Sabbath and therefore would be against healing on that day. Others, however, wondered how someone could heal as Jesus did without the power of God. Arguments ensued, with some believing he was a fraud and others accepting the evidence as proof that he was blessed by God.

Healing of Lazarus. One family very close to Jesus included two sisters, Mary and Martha, and one brother, Lazarus. When Lazarus became critically ill, the sisters sent for Jesus to come and heal him. Jesus acknowledged their need, but refused to come immediately. He then declared to his disciples that Lazarus had died, and only then did the group travel to the home of Mary, Martha, and Lazarus in Bethany, near Jerusalem.

Martha met Jesus on the outskirts of the village and immediately accused him, saying that if he had only come right away, her brother would not have died. As it was, he had been dead four days and was now decaying. All hope was lost. However, Jesus assured her that Lazarus would live. He asked Martha if she believed in the resurrection. Martha replied that she did, but that the resurrection would not occur until the last day. Jesus then replied, "I am the resurrection, and the life; he who believes in Me shall live even if he dies, and everyone who lives and believes in Me shall never die. Do you believe this?" (John 11:25-26). Martha affirmed her faith in Jesus as the Christ.

When Jesus arrived at the grave site, he called out to Lazarus, commanding him to come forth. Lazarus did just that! This miracle caused many to believe, but others went to the Pharisees, telling them of the strange powers of the Galilean. The high priest

Caiaphas decided that Jesus must be put to death, saying that it was better for Jesus to die than for the Romans to use his exploits as an excuse to destroy the nation of Israel. Plans were made secretly to capture Jesus and have him killed, and they decided to kill Lazarus too.

TEACHING

We consider finally several glimpses from Jesus' teaching ministry in Jerusalem, many of them involving sharp conflict with the Pharisees and other religious leaders of the Jews.

The cleansing of the temple. Remember that when Jesus visited the temple at age twelve, he called it his Father's house. No ordinary Jew could claim such a father-son relationship with Jehovah, and Jesus' assertion in his youth indicated that he knew that he was the Messiah, the unique Son of God. When Jesus Christ returned to the temple as an adult, he was incensed at the hypocrisy rampantly displayed at the tables of the money changers. They were more interested in making enormous wealth than in promoting true worship and sacrifice. With a handmade whip, Jesus drove the money changers out of the temple, his Father's house, and overturned their tables.

Although the people in the temple did not recognize the significance of Jesus' action in cleansing the temple, his action actually revealed his identity as the Son of the living God, the God of the temple. With this action Jesus took a stand against the false religiosity of the Pharisees, Sadducees, and scribes and for the pure worship due to the Lord.

The sign of the temple. After telling of the cleansing of the temple, John's Gospel recounts a closely related event. The Jews wanted a sign that Jesus was really the Messiah, the one who was prophesied of old. Jesus replied, "Destroy this temple, and in three days I will raise it up" (John 2:19). The Jews were amazed at his challenge: it had taken forty-six years to build Herod's magnificent temple. How could this one Galilean raise it up again in just three days? The Jews did not understand that Jesus was speaking of the temple of his body and thus was predicting his resurrection from the dead, the sure sign of his divine power and eternal existence. Jesus did provide a sign that he was really the Christ: he rose from the dead.

Jesus and Nicodemus. Only John records the meeting between Jesus and Nicodemus, a Pharisee and ruler of the Jews. To avoid being seen, Nicodemus came to see Jesus at night. He was curious about this rabbi who claimed to offer eternal life; perhaps he had heard rumors that this man might even be the Messiah. Rather unexpectedly, Jesus told Nicodemus that he must be "born again." Here Jesus was talking about a spiritual rebirth. It is impossible even for a great religious leader to enter God's kingdom unless he is born again.

Jesus, the Light of the World. After Jesus had fed the five thousand, he had claimed to be the Bread of Life. Later, in Jerusalem, he also said he was the Light of the World. Those who followed him, he said, would never walk in darkness. The Pharisees did not accept Jesus' claims, accusing him of "blowing his own horn," so to speak. Jesus countered their accusations by reasserting his claims before God, adding that God the Father also testified of him. Although the Jews wanted at that time to seize Christ and kill him, God's foreordained time had not yet come, and they were prevented from capturing him.

Jesus, the great I AM. While arguing with the religious leaders, Jesus was asked to identify himself. He made it clear that he was more than an ordinary human being. He was God manifest in the flesh, the "I AM" who had spoken to Moses out of the burning bush (see Exodus 3:14). Consider Christ's claim: "You are from below, I am from above; you are of this world, I am not of this world. I said therefore to you, that you shall die in your sins; for unless you believe that I am He, you shall die in your sins. . . . Truly, truly, I say to you, before Abraham was born, I am" (John 8:23-24, 58). The Jewish response was immediate: they took up stones to stone him for blasphemy, because he dared to identify himself with Jehovah, the only true God, the eternally existing one, the great I AM. Jesus protected himself and left the temple.

Jesus, the Good Shepherd. In another statement asserting his identity as the Messiah, Jesus claimed to be the Good Shepherd (cf. Psalm 23). John describes this illustration in great detail in chapter 10 of his Gospel, in one of the strongest identifications of Jesus Christ with God. The Good Shepherd gives his life for his sheep. The Good Shepherd knows his sheep, and the sheep know him. The Good Shepherd gives his sheep eternal life and will protect them successfully at all costs. Paralleling his own shepherdlike ministry with that of the Father, Jesus concludes his discussion by declaring, "I and the Father are one" (John 10:30). This plain assertion of his absolute deity caused the Jews again to seek his death; once again they were held back, since it was not yet God's time for Christ to die.

Judgment to come. After Jesus had been rejected by the religious people of Palestine and the religious leaders were plotting to take his life, Jesus began to speak only to his disciples of his coming crucifixion. He told his disciples that his coming death was according to God's plan and would secure salvation for the world. He asserted that he would also come again in judgment at the last day and predicted that the great temple of Herod would be destroyed, with not one stone left upon another. This was fulfilled by the Romans in A.D. 70. Jesus Christ also predicted the scattering of the Jews into all lands but promised that someday he would return and through judgment would restore righteousness throughout the earth. But that would take place at his second coming, not during his earthly life. The time was almost ready for his arrest, trial, execution, and resurrection from the dead.

CHAPTER 3
Jesus Christ Died and Rose Again

LAST HOURS WITH THE DISCIPLES

The story of the last night of Jesus' life presents us with a dynamic picture of divine power and humility. In the upper room, Jesus knew that his hour had come. He also knew that Satan had put it in the heart of Judas Iscariot to betray him. Having this knowledge, he rose from supper, took a towel, and began to wash his disciples' feet. When he came to Simon Peter, Peter refused to have his feet washed. He loved and respected Jesus so much that he did not want Jesus to humble himself in this way. However, Jesus told Peter that if he refused to be served by his master, then Jesus would cut him off. Peter's enthusiastic acceptance of Jesus' ultimatum is marked with a touch of humor, as he told Jesus to go ahead and wash his whole body! Jesus explained his humble act, pointing out that he and his disciples were chosen to serve others, not to rule others.

BETRAYAL PREDICTED

Jesus told his disciples that one of them would betray him. The disciples looked at one another, trying to determine who it could be. Pointing to Judas Iscariot, Jesus said to him, "What you do, do quickly." The other disciples did not realize that Jesus was indicating that Judas was the betrayer. Judas left, going into the night to betray his master. Afterward Jesus said it was time for the Son of Man to be glorified. He then gave the remaining faithful disciples a new commandment: "love one another, even as I have loved you. . . . By this all men will know that you are My disciples, if you have love for one another" (John 13:34-35).

When Jesus told the disciples that he was going to leave them, Peter asked Jesus why he could not follow and asserted that he would lay down his life for Jesus' sake. Jesus then made another prediction: before the rooster crowed, Peter would deny his Lord three times. Peter and the others could not believe they would ever do such a thing.

Jesus encouraged the disciples. Even though he was going away, he still loved them. He was going to prepare the way for them to be able to go to the Father. Then Jesus promised that the Holy Spirit would come as the Comforter. He would reveal to the disciples everything concerning Jesus Christ and would bring back to their memories all the things that Jesus had taught them. Jesus again emphasized that he was telling them all that would come to pass so that, when it did, the disciples would believe. At the end of Jesus' discourse, they all left the upper room.

TO GETHSEMANE

On the way to the Garden of Gethsemane, where Jesus often went to pray, Jesus made further claims about himself. He claimed to be the true vine, giving spiritual nourishment to all who came to him. Those who abide in him will bear fruit, while those who leave will be barren. Jesus commanded his disciples to love one another in the same manner in which he loved them. Christ's love has no more eloquent expression than in his laying down his life for their sake.

Jesus told the disciples that the world would hate them, but that should be no cause of alarm to them: the world also hated their Lord, Jesus Christ. Those who are not of the world, said Jesus, are hated by those who are of the world. Those who point out sin and the need for repentance are hated by those who willingly and repeatedly sin. However, through the power of the Holy Spirit, the disciples would continue to testify of salvation in Jesus Christ.

Jesus also told his disciples these things ahead of time to prepare them for the persecution that would plague them because of their testimony. As a matter of fact, all of the disciples except John eventually suffered martyrdom for their faith. However, the Holy Spirit, the Comforter, the third person of the Holy Trinity, would be with them and give them strength to endure whatever lay ahead.

After comforting the disciples, Jesus prayed to his Father. He asked the Father to glorify him with the glory they had shared before the worlds began. Jesus had fulfilled the mission given him by his Father. He had kept in the faith those disciples the Father had given him—except for Judas, who willingly betrayed him according to God's plan. Jesus prayed for his disciples that the power of God would preserve their faith in the midst of trials and against the temptations of the evil one. He prayed not only for his inner circle of disciples but also for those who afterward would believe because of the disciples' testimony. He prayed that the believers' faith would be so unified that all believers would be as one.

After this prayer, Jesus and his disciples arrived at Gethsemane. It was a familiar place to which Jesus often retreated for quiet contemplation and prayer. The traitor Judas, who had already left, would know that Jesus could be found here. While waiting for Judas to arrive with his captors, Jesus' own spiritual burden reached almost unbearable proportions. The disciples separated into two groups. Eight stayed in one part of the garden while Peter, James, and John went on with Jesus. Jesus told them, "My soul is deeply grieved, to the point of death" (Matthew 26:38). He exhorted them to stay with him and pray for God's protection against temptation.

Needing to pray alone, Jesus separated himself from the three disciples. They could see him agonizing in spiritual distress, praying, "My Father, if it is possible, let this cup pass from Me; yet not as I will, but as Thou wilt" (Matthew 26:39). The weary disciples soon fell asleep, despite their promises to stay awake and pray. Luke tells us that the Father sent an angel from heaven to give him support and spiritual strength during this agony.

ARREST AND TRIAL

Knowing that Jesus would be in the garden, Judas informed the priests that they could arrest him there. Judas had made a pact with them to betray Jesus for thirty pieces of silver, thereby unwittingly fulfilling an Old Testament prophecy (Zechariah 11:12).

Judas arrived at Gethsemane with the chief priests and a large band of men. To make sure they apprehended the right person, Judas had agreed to kiss Jesus on the cheek (a common form of greeting). When Jesus told the crowd that he was the one they were seeking, they all fell to the ground, overcome by his presence. He told the crowd to let his disciples go; they were after him, not his disciples.

After Judas's kiss of betrayal, the crowd surged toward Jesus. Peter impulsively took his small sword and cut off the ear of one of the servants of the high priest. Jesus immediately rebuked Peter and then healed his enemy's ear. Jesus pointed out that as Messiah, he could call a dozen legions of angels to protect him, if he wanted. No, it was the will of the Father that the Christ should suffer for the people.

Then Jesus turned to the crowd. He rebuked them for their almost hysterical mob actions. Why did they need to come with swords and clubs? Why did they not arrest him quietly any one of the times when he was sitting in the temple teaching? Having pointed out their inconsistencies, Jesus, in command of the situation, let them arrest him because he needed to fulfill his Father's will as revealed in the Scriptures. He was seized and led away. His disciples forsook him.

BEFORE THE JEWS

The captors bound Jesus with ropes, although Jesus could have freed himself with a word. Jesus was willingly laying down his life as the Good Shepherd of his sheep.

Jesus was taken first to the house of Annas, the former high priest and father-in-law to the present high priest, Caiaphas. Annas tried to find some legitimate way to condemn Jesus. He asked about Jesus' teaching but received no direct reply. Jesus told Annas to ask those who daily listened to him in the temple—they knew what he taught. Frustrated, Annas sent Jesus to Caiaphas. Caiaphas had previously said that it was expedient that Jesus should die "for the people." His words actually point to Christ's sacrificial death on the cross, although he meant only that Jesus should be silenced so that Caiaphas could maintain control over the people and give the Romans no excuse to oppress the Jews further.

Since the arrest and trial of Jesus was arranged so hastily, it was difficult to present a strong case against him. The temple servants tried to find false witnesses who would testify that Jesus had committed some capital offense. Finally, two people testified that Jesus said he would destroy the temple. Maybe that statement (although made concerning his own bodily resurrection, and not the Jerusalem temple) could be misconstrued to provide evidence of insurrection. However, the witnesses would not keep their testimony consistent, and it had to be rejected. Furthermore, Jesus had never said, "I will destroy the temple"; rather he had said, "Destroy this temple and I will raise it up in three days."

Finally, Caiaphas challenged Jesus but received no reply. The flustered high priest charged Jesus, under oath, to answer whether he was the Messiah, the Son of God. Jesus said that he was, and that he would come again in power and judgment. This was just what the priest was looking for. Jesus, so they thought, was guilty of blasphemy for claiming to be God. He was worthy of death.

Once judgment was declared upon Jesus, the treacherous mockery of the crowd began. He was spit upon, blindfolded, and hit repeatedly. While they were hitting him, they taunted him to identify his punishers. And yet Jesus' coming crucifixion was on their behalf, as an atonement for their sins, including the very sins of beating the Lord of heaven!

When morning came, the Jewish council met, and Jesus was brought before them. The accusers again asked him if he was the Christ. They asked not to find the truth but to find something by which they could condemn him and get him out of the way. He was becoming too popular and too powerful with the common people. Jesus finally affirmed that he indeed was the Son of the Most High God. The council confirmed the verdict of Caiaphas.

PETER AND JUDAS

Jesus was now alone, facing human and sinful judgment. One of the twelve had betrayed him. The others had scattered at his arrest. Peter, however, had followed the arrest party and was observing, from a distance, the events of the night and early morning. After Peter and another unnamed disciple (possibly John) gained access to the house of the high priest, Peter warmed himself by a fire in the courtyard.

Some of the others there thought they recognized him as a follower of the Galilean prisoner. Peter staunchly denied it, although only a few hours earlier he had declared himself ready to die for Jesus' sake. A woman noticed Peter next and said she was sure he had been with Jesus. Again Peter denied the charge, even stating that he did not know Jesus at all. An hour later, Peter denied Jesus a third time. As Peter was cursing and swearing an oath that he did not know Jesus, Jesus turned and eyed Peter from a distance. Peter's soul was pierced by that look, and at the same time a rooster crowed. Realizing his failure, he ran from the place crying bitterly.

Peter's denial, along with his subsequent restoration to fellowship with God, is in marked contrast to the story of Judas. After betraying Jesus, Judas felt remorse. He did not want any part of the "blood money," the thirty pieces of silver paid him out of the temple treasury. Although Judas was sorry for what he had done, he did not avail himself of the saving grace of God. He committed suicide.

BEFORE PILATE AND HEROD

After the Jewish council had concluded that Jesus deserved death, they sent him on to the Roman governor, Pontius Pilate, whose house was close to the house of Caiaphas. Although the Jews had convicted Jesus of a capital offense, they needed Roman approval before they could carry out the sentence.

Pilate asked what charge had been brought against Jesus. When no serious accusation was forthcoming, Pilate suggested that the matter be left to the Jews, inferring that no capital offense was involved. However, the Jews were not satisfied. They wanted Jesus dead and out of the way forever. They then tried to prove a charge of sedition against Jesus by saying that Jesus claimed to be the King of the Jews. When Pilate asked Jesus if the charge was true, Jesus replied that his kingdom was not of this world. After a private interview, the Roman governor announced that he could find no wrongdoing in Jesus.

Pilate then sent Jesus to Herod, the Jewish ruler over Galilee, Jesus' home region. Herod was in Jerusalem for the Feast of the Passover and gladly received Jesus. He had heard of Jesus' miracles and wanted to see some for himself. However, Jesus neither performed any miracles nor said one word to Herod. After attempting to ridicule Jesus, Herod sent him back to Pilate. The two former political enemies, Herod and Pilate, became friends that day because of their common problem, Jesus.

Pilate felt boxed in. He saw no reason to condemn Jesus to death, and yet the Jewish rulers gave him little alternative. His only way out was to use his custom of releasing prisoners on important occasions such as the Passover and to offer to free Jesus. However, he did not want to make his actions obvious, so he gave the Jews a choice: they could have Jesus or a common criminal, Barabbas. The choice was overwhelming: the Jews wanted Barabbas freed and Jesus killed.

Sensing that the situation was getting out of hand, Pilate handed Jesus over for crucifixion. However, he wanted to make it clear that he was doing the will of the people, not his own will. He called for a bowl of water and washed his hands in it, signifying that he was refusing to take responsibility for the crucifixion of an innocent man. Jesus would now die, not only in place of Barabbas, but as a substitute for all men and women throughout history who deserved to die because of sin but who could claim redemption through the death of the sinless Messiah.

EXECUTION AND BURIAL

Jesus was scourged by a Roman soldier before being delivered up for crucifixion. This practice consisted of whipping the prisoner with leather straps that had been embedded with chunks of metal. To further his indignity, they placed on his head a crown made out of thorns, thus mocking his claim to be King of the Jews. The soldiers also placed a purple robe around him and mockingly worshiped him.

Jesus was so weak from the beating and scourging that he could not carry his own crossbar to the hill, Calvary, where the crucifixion was to be. The Romans compelled a member of the crowd, Simon from Cyrene, to carry the cross. As the procession made its way to Calvary, the women who had been among Jesus' disciples followed along, their grief evidenced by their wailing and tears. Jesus told them, however, that they should not weep for him, but for themselves and their children.

Calvary was known as Golgotha, or the place of the skull. This is where criminals were commonly crucified. The difference between Jesus and the criminals who had preceded him there was that Jesus was innocent of all sin and lawbreaking.

Jesus was offered bitter wine as an anesthetic to the terrible pain of the nails ripping the flesh of his feet and hands, but he refused it. He wanted to be in full control of his body throughout his suffering. On the cross he asked his Father to forgive those who treated him so mercilessly. Above his cross was placed a sign, written in Hebrew, Latin, and Greek, declaring, "Jesus of Nazareth, King of the Jews." Although Pilate had ordered the sign, he did not understand its significance.

The reactions of those around are related in the four Gospels. The thieves crucified on either side of him cursed the "King of the Jews." However, one of them later repented, saying that he himself deserved death but that Jesus had committed no sin. The thief asked for and received forgiveness from the Lord. The soldiers at the crucifixion cast lots, gambling for possession of Jesus' clothes. Passersby ridiculed him. His disciples had seemingly deserted him. The religious leaders taunted him, daring him to call down angels to rescue him.

DEATH

There on the cross, the most important event since the creation took place—the death of Jesus Christ for the sins of the world. In Paul's words, "God was in Christ reconciling the world to Himself" (2 Corinthians 5:19).

At noon, after Jesus had been three hours on the cross, the sun was miraculously darkened. Three hours later, Christ's last words affirmed his absolute trust in the Father as he declared, "Father, into Your hands I commit My spirit," and then died.

In the temple hung a curtain separating the Holy Place from the Holy of Holies, the place where God's presence was manifested during the days of Israel's glory. The curtain symbolized the barrier between man and God that was caused by sin. At the moment of Christ's death, however, the curtain tore violently from top to bottom: sin had been taken care of on the cross, and now people had direct access to the Father through Jesus Christ. As Jesus declared on the cross, "It is finished," the task of redemption had been accomplished. God's plan was executed.

BURIAL

Once Jesus had died, the next step was the disposition of his body. Joseph of Arimathea, a secret disciple of Jesus, came to Pilate and asked for Jesus' body so it could be buried. Joseph was a wealthy member of the Jewish Sanhedrin and planned to use the expensive tomb nearby he had already purchased and fixed for himself. He believed Jesus was the Messiah and wanted to provide him with a grave befitting his noble station. Joseph's actions also fulfilled Isaiah 53:9.

Pilate was amazed that Jesus had already died, but when the centurion confirmed his death, Pilate gave permission to Joseph to take the body. Joseph and Nicodemus brought spices, removed the body of Jesus from the cross, and wrapped it in linen and spices. The Sabbath was to begin at sundown, and the two had little time to prepare the body before Jewish law prohibiting work on the Sabbath restricted them. After they placed the body in the tomb, they rolled a large stone in front of the entrance.

The religious leaders, remembering the prophecies by Jesus concerning his resurrection from the dead, came to Pilate and asked him to provide a guard for the tomb. They did not want anyone to steal the body and then claim that Jesus had risen from the dead. Some Roman soldiers consequently sealed the tomb and camped in front of it. Now no one could tamper with the grave.

RESURRECTION AND COMMISSION

One can imagine the feelings of disillusionment and disappointment that the disciples felt after the death of Jesus. The one in whom they had placed their hope now lay dead. The three years spent with him seemed a waste. On the other hand, the religious rulers felt vindicated. Some King of the Jews he turned out to be! He could not even protect himself! After plotting against him for most of his ministry, they had finally triumphed.

Shortly before dawn some women who were disciples of Jesus made their way to the tomb of Jesus to anoint his body. The pre-Sabbath preparations had been hasty, and they wanted their beloved Lord's body properly anointed in death. Imagine their shock as they approached the tomb site and saw the stone rolled back and the grave empty. An angel appeared and gave them the good news that Jesus was alive, risen from the dead! The women left hurriedly, running to tell the disciples that the Lord was alive. Hearing this, Peter and John ran to the tomb and found it empty. The grave clothes were still there, but the body was gone.

SEVERAL APPEARANCES

Mary Magdalene was first to see the risen Christ. When the women came to the tomb and saw the stone rolled away, Mary immediately ran back to Peter and John. She did not hear the angelic announcement. When she returned to the tomb, she was in tears, thinking someone had stolen the body. There she met the risen Christ, whom she first mistook for the gardener. However, when he said her name, she immediately recognized him and worshiped him.

Another appearance was to two other disciples on the road to Emmaus. As these two were walking along, discussing recent events, they were joined by Jesus Christ, who miraculously kept them from recognizing him. When Jesus asked them what they were talking about, they seemed surprised that their companion had not heard of the ministry and death of Jesus. They had thought he was a prophet and had looked to him to redeem Israel, but instead he had been put to death. Reports of the resurrection had reached them, but they were not convinced.

Jesus rebuked them for their faithlessness, explaining and proving from the Scriptures that it was necessary for the Messiah to suffer and die and then rise again. The two were impressed with his knowledge and asked him to eat supper with them. As Jesus broke bread with them, their eyes were opened, and they recognized him as their risen Lord. He vanished from their presence, and they rushed back to Jerusalem to tell the other disciples.

That night ten disciples of Jesus were holding a secret meeting, probably in the same room in which they had celebrated the Last Supper with Jesus. Thomas was absent, and Judas was dead. While they met, Jesus appeared in their midst. At first they thought he was a spirit or ghost, but he declared, "Touch Me and see, for a spirit does not have flesh and bones as you see that I have" (Luke 24:39). He pointed out his wounds and asked for food to eat, thus calming their fears. Jesus spoke to them of their future mission to spread the good news of the gospel and then breathed into them the Holy Spirit.

About one week later, the disciples, including Thomas, were again in the upper room. Thomas did not believe Jesus had risen from the dead and had declared that he would not believe unless he himself could examine the wounds in his body. Jesus appeared again and encouraged Thomas to put his hands into the holes in Jesus' hands and to touch the wound in his side. Thomas instantly exclaimed, "My Lord and my God!" (John 20:28). Jesus responded by stating that Thomas was blessed for seeing and believing—but even more blessed were those who did not see and yet believed.

A FINAL COMMISSION

Jesus now gave his disciples final instructions before his ascension into heaven. He would not return again until his second coming in judgment. In the meantime, his disciples and those believers after them were to spread the good news of salvation. Jesus assured his disciples that all authority in heaven and earth had been given to him. Their job as his representative was to use that authority to make more disciples. They were to teach all nations, baptizing them in the name of the Father, and of the Son, and of the Holy Spirit (Matthew 28:19-20). Jesus promised that he would be with them always, even until the end of the age. However, before they could be missionaries, they had to be empowered by the Holy Spirit for this special work. Jesus commanded them to wait in Jerusalem for the outpouring of the Holy Spirit. Then they would testify of the risen Christ.

It may be difficult to believe that the grip of death was broken and that a dead man actually came back to life. Instances have been recorded, of course, of people in modern days who have come back to life after lying dead for a few minutes—thirty at the most. And the Gospels record a few miracles of raising the dead after a longer period. All these cases, however, were not fully resurrections but resuscitations. The life that was resumed was of the same mortal order as before and was terminable again by death. Only in a limited sense could such resuscitations be represented as triumphs over death. But the resurrection of Christ was not the resuscitation of a corpse; it was a decisive conquest of death: "Christ, having been raised from the dead, is never to die again; death no longer is master over Him" (Romans 6:9). This fact is fundamental to understanding the growth of the church, both in Acts and throughout the centuries.

CHAPTER 4

The Roots of the Church

After Jesus rose from the dead, he showed himself alive for forty days by many convincing signs (Acts 1:3). During this period he gave his disciples instructions on their mission. Jesus commanded them not to depart from Jerusalem but to wait for the promise of the Father. The disciples wondered if the kingdom would soon be restored, but Jesus told them that they were not to concern themselves about such things. Rather, they should focus on being witnesses of Christ's resurrection. "You shall receive power when the Holy Spirit has come upon you; and you shall be My witnesses both in Jerusalem and in all Judea and Samaria, and even to the remotest part of the earth" (Acts 1:8).

After giving his disciples that charge, Jesus ascended into heaven. Even while they were watching Jesus' departure, God sent two heavenly messengers who told them, "Men of Galilee, why do you stand looking into the sky? This Jesus, who has been taken up from you into heaven, will come in just the same way as you have watched Him go into heaven" (Acts 1:11).

Several things about the ascension should be noted. First, this marked the end of Jesus' ministry in his first coming. He finished his job of reconciliation, and his ascension was victorious. Second, the disciples were told by the angels that they had their own job to do, now that Jesus was no longer with them. They were not just to wait around for his return; they were to work. Third, we see the promise that Jesus will come back in the same manner in which he left: visibly, physically, and on the Mount of Olives.

During the ten-day period between the ascension and Pentecost (already a Jewish holiday), the disciples were together in prayer and unity in the upper room. They also determined to find a replacement for Judas the traitor. The qualifications for an apostle included the following: the replacement had to have been part of Jesus' followers since the beginning of his public ministry and had to have been a direct witness of the resurrected Christ. The choice was narrowed down to either Joseph or Matthias, with Matthias being chosen by lots to become the twelfth apostle. Later on, God himself chose Saul of Tarsus to join the ranks of the apostles.

THE BIRTHDAY OF THE CHURCH

The day arrived for the promise of the Father to be fulfilled. It was the Jewish festival of Pentecost, coming fifty days after the Passover. Some 120 of Jesus' disciples were praying together. Suddenly, a sound like the rushing of a mighty wind filled the house where they were. The Holy Spirit came upon them all, and they were filled with his power, praising God and his mighty works in the many different languages of the various nationalities assembled in Jerusalem for the feast of Pentecost. Acts tells us that a great crowd quickly gathered, so we can assume that the meeting place was near the Jerusalem temple, where Jews from many lands had gathered for the holiday. The crowd wondered at what they were hearing, thinking perhaps the group was drunk, but then also marveling that each of them could hear the disciples praising God in his own native language.

The apostle Peter stood up and declared that none of them were drunk—it was too early in the morning. On the contrary, the crowd was witnessing the fulfillment of Joel's prophecy: "And it will come about after this that I will pour out My Spirit on all mankind; and your sons and daughters will prophesy, your old men will dream dreams, your young men will see visions. And even on the male and female servants I will pour out My Spirit in those days" (Joel 2:28-29).

With the crowd now silent, Peter began preaching the gospel. The first sermon of the newly born church is a masterpiece of spiritual strength and challenge, confirming the facts of the ministry, death, and resurrection of Jesus Christ as the fulfillment of Old Testament prophecy. In Acts 2:22 Peter makes a claim about Jesus that many people miss, as he says, "Men of Israel, listen to these words: Jesus the Nazarene, a man attested to you by God with miracles and wonders and signs which God performed through Him in your midst, just as you yourselves know. . . ." Peter called Jesus a miracle worker and appealed to the knowledge of the hearers ("just as you yourselves know"). The mere fact that he was not immediately shouted down shows that they did indeed know that Jesus was a miracle worker. But they had crucified him who was their Messiah. Nevertheless, God had raised him from the dead, and he had appeared to his disciples.

The people were convicted by Peter's sermon and asked how they could be saved. Peter replied that forgiveness of sins was available to them if they would repent and believe. Three thousand people turned to Christ that one day and were baptized and added to the church!

EARLY GROWTH

After this glorious birth of the church, the disciples maintained the truth of the gospel, defended right doctrine, had regular fellowship, prayed together, and celebrated communion, or the Lord's Supper, in remembrance of the sacrifice of Christ on the cross. Great awe fell upon the people with whom the disciples came in contact because of the miracles they performed. Many believers lived in such close fellowship that they pooled their resources and lived in Christian community. The Bible testifies that the Lord daily added new members to the congregation.

A LAME MAN HEALED

Shortly after all these events, Peter and John went to the temple for prayer. There they met a beggar, lame from birth, who asked them for a donation. Peter told the man that he had no money, but that he would give him what he did have: "In the name of Jesus Christ the Nazarene—walk!" (Acts 3:6). Peter lifted the man up by the hand, and he was fully healed. For the first time in his life, he walked. He started leaping about, praising God.

The people entering the temple recognized this beggar and wondered how he had been healed. Peter took the opportunity to preach the need for repentance to them, telling them of the great sacrifice Jesus had made on the cross for them and then of his miraculous resurrection from the dead. Peter attributed his healing power to the power of God: faith in the risen Christ had healed the lame man. Peter appealed to Scripture, showing how the Old Testament predicted Jesus Christ and his mission.

As Peter and John spoke, the Sadducees arrived with the captain of the temple guard. They were upset at Peter's talk of the resurrection and had decided to arrest the apostles. However, many in the crowd believed Peter and John, and the number of believers rose to five thousand.

The next day Peter and John were summoned before the high priest, rulers, and scribes. These leaders demanded to know by what authority Peter and John performed this deed. Peter, filled with the power of the Holy Spirit, told them it had been accomplished by the power of Jesus of Nazareth, whom they had crucified and whom God had raised from the dead. It was this power that accomplished the man's healing.

Peter took things further than that. He declared that salvation is through Jesus alone (Acts 4:12). This response unsettled the religious leaders, who realized that Peter and John were not trained in rabbinical studies or the studies of the Scripture. They spoke so clearly and forcefully, however, that the leaders were at a loss as to how to answer them. They sent Peter and John outside and held a conference together. Their discussion is instructive: "What shall we do with these men? For the fact that a noteworthy miracle has taken place through them is apparent to all who live in Jerusalem, and we cannot deny it. But in order that it may not spread any further among the people, let us warn them to speak no more to any man in this name" (Acts 4:16-17).

Peter and John, so instructed, refused to agree. They said that their responsibility was to spread the gospel, whether that pleased the religious leaders or not. The officials had no real reason to imprison them, and so had to let them go. Returning to their friends, Peter and John repeated what had happened. The Christians were encouraged by their report and prayed to God for boldness to speak his Word. They also asked God to grant them further miracles, as a sign that they were following his will. God answered their prayer and granted them greater power to witness. Again, the Scripture emphasizes that the people freely donated all they had to the cause of the church. They gave their goods to the apostles, who then distributed them as needs arose.

ANANIAS AND SAPPHIRA

In the midst of this sharing and giving, deceit arose. Ananias and his wife, Sapphira, willingly sold some of their land, promising to turn over the proceeds of the sale to the use of the church. However, they decided between themselves to keep some of the money for themselves and to lie about the actual price of the land. In judgment, both of them were struck dead by the power of God.

Despite this sad episode, the church continued to grow. Many signs and wonders were accomplished through the hands of the apostles, and many more believers were added to the church.

PERSECUTION

People from all around Jerusalem were coming to the apostles to be healed of their illnesses. This angered the Sadducees. They imprisoned the apostles, hoping to stop the moving of the Holy Spirit. However, God sent an angel to open the prison doors and to encourage the disciples to continue preaching the gospel.

The religious leaders, not knowing the apostles had been set free, called a council to put them on trial. They were surprised to find the prisoners preaching freely in the temple but summoned them to the council anyway. The chief priest wanted to know why their commandment against preaching had been disobeyed. Peter and the other apostles answered boldly, "We must obey God rather than men. The God of our fathers raised up Jesus, whom you had put to death by hanging Him on a cross. He is the one whom God exalted to His right hand as a Prince and a Savior, to grant repentance to Israel, and forgiveness of sins. And we are witnesses of these things; and so is the Holy Spirit, whom God has given to those who obey Him" (Acts 5:29-32).

This response enraged the religious leaders, and they decided to kill the apostles. Then Gamaliel, a respected man among them, stood and warned the council not to be too hasty. He mentioned other men who had started movements that had collapsed and then pointed out that if God was behind the apostles, it would be foolish to oppose them. The best policy, he said, was just to let them alone. The leaders were persuaded by Gamaliel's argument and agreed to do nothing. But they again ordered the apostles to stop preaching about Jesus. The apostles rejoiced that they were counted worthy to suffer for the sake of Christ and worked all the harder at preaching the gospel.

THE STONING OF STEPHEN

Stephen, one of seven men chosen to administer the business of the church, is the first Christian recorded in the New Testament to give his life for his faith. Religious Jews accused Stephen of blasphemy and lying. Brought before the Jewish council, Stephen defended his actions and gave a brilliant defense of the Christian faith. He proved through Old Testament history that God's people were notorious for resisting the Spirit of God—and that, now, by resisting Jesus, they were again trying to thwart God's action on earth. Stephen concluded by bluntly charging his audience with being "stiff-necked and uncircumcised in heart and ears" and "always resisting the Holy Spirit" (Acts 7:51).

The outraged religious leaders cried out, rushed Stephen, and prepared to stone him to death. Faithful to the end, Stephen called out, declaring that he saw Jesus Christ at the right hand of the Father. And so Stephen died, his Lord's name on his lips, and became the first church martyr.

While Stephen was being stoned, the Jews laid their cloaks at the feet of a young man who agreed with their actions. This zealous young Jew, Saul by name, later became Paul, one of the apostles of the church.

GROWTH THROUGH PERSECUTION

Because of great persecution, the church at Jerusalem was scattered throughout Judea and Samaria, with only the apostles staying in Jerusalem. As the people traveled, they spread the good news of the gospel wherever they went.

The deacon Philip went to Samaria, preaching the word, as miracles were accomplished at his hand in testimony to the truth of his witness. He showed great courage to preach the gospel to the Samaritans, who were only half Jewish, and who were ridiculed by strict Jews. A Samaritan sorcerer there named Simon had bewitched the Samaritans into believing that he was "the power of God." This Simon was amazed at the miracles that accompanied Philip's preaching, and he repented of his occult practices and was baptized with the rest of the converts.

When the apostles learned that the Samaritans received the gospel, they sent Peter and John there to follow up Philip's work. These two apostles prayed that the Samaritan converts would receive the power of the Holy Spirit just as they had in Jerusalem. When Simon, who had supposedly abandoned his sorcery, saw that the Holy Spirit came on those the apostles laid hands on, he offered Peter and John money for the secret to their power. Peter rebuked him, telling him that the Holy Spirit was a gift from God and could not be bought with money.

With the Samaritan revival, the second part of the prophecy of Acts 1:8 was being fulfilled. The apostles were witnesses in Jerusalem and Samaria. Soon their message would spread throughout the known world.

SAUL OF TARSUS

None of the original apostles was given the special ministry to the Gentiles, the third group alluded to in Acts 1:8 ("the ends of the earth"). Instead, God raised up another apostle, born out of due time, so to speak, and given the mission to bring the gospel to the Gentiles. This special apostle was first known as Saul and was from Tarsus. We have already seen him as the willing accomplice of those who stoned Stephen to death.

Saul hated the church and took it as his own responsibility to persecute the church wherever he found it. Saul went to the high priest to obtain letters authorizing him to imprison Christians in Damascus and return them for trial to Jerusalem. Letter in hand, Saul started through the desert for Damascus.

As he neared Damascus, a light from heaven shone around him. He fell to the ground and heard a voice calling, "Saul, Saul, why are you persecuting Me?" Saul did not know who was speaking but answered, "Who art Thou, Lord?" The voice replied, "I am Jesus the Nazarene, whom you are persecuting" (Acts 22:7-8).

What a shock to Saul! He thought Jesus was a rabble-rousing criminal who had been rightly put to death. How could this same Jesus be talking to him? The power of the Holy Spirit convicted Saul, and trembling, he asked, "What shall I do, Lord?" (v. 10).

The Lord commanded Saul to go to Damascus and await instructions. The rest of the company with Saul heard the voice but did not understand any of the words. The bright light had blinded Saul, and he was led blind to the city. Three days in Damascus he waited in darkness, neither eating nor drinking.

The Lord brought to Saul a Christian of Damascus named Ananias, who declared that God had sent him to lay hands on Saul, bringing him healing for his blindness and the infilling of the Holy Spirit. As Ananias laid hands on Saul, he immediately received his sight. He was baptized and joined the ranks of those who worshiped Jesus Christ as Lord.

Saul stayed for several days with the Christians in Damascus. The former persecutor of the Christians now preached Christ and his resurrection in the synagogues of Damascus. The crowds were amazed because they knew he was the one who was formerly the destroyer of Christians. Saul grew in his knowledge of the Lord and confounded the Jews, showing them that Jesus was the Christ. The Jews were enraged by Saul's defection and sought to imprison him. However, his new Christian friends protected him and secretly got him out of the city one night by lowering him from the city walls in a basket.

Saul returned to Jerusalem and, once accepted as a true Christian brother, continued preaching the gospel clearly and forcefully. To avoid imprisonment, Saul was sent from Jerusalem to Caesarea and then on to Tarsus. Dozens of new converts were added to the church daily, and the faith of those who were already Christians was strengthened by the miracles they saw in their midst.

SIMON PETER

The focus of the book of Acts now shifts to Simon Peter. Although Saul of Tarsus was set apart by God as the special missionary to the Gentiles, it was Simon Peter who was used by God to proclaim the gospel first to the Gentiles. Jesus had told Peter that to him would be given the keys of the kingdom, and so it was fitting that Peter was instrumental in bringing the gospel first to the Jews (Acts 2), then to the Samaritans (Acts 8), and finally to the Gentiles (Acts 10).

First, Peter traveled to Lydda, where a man named Aeneas was paralyzed and confined to his bed. Peter healed him through the name of Jesus. This miracle caused many people to convert to

Christianity. Near Lydda was the city of Joppa, the home of Dorcas, a strong Christian believer. She died, and when the other believers heard that Peter was in Lydda, they sent for him, imploring him to pray for Dorcas to be restored to life. The apostle quickly traveled to Joppa, prayed for Dorcas, and she was raised up. This miracle, too, caused many to believe in Jesus Christ as their Lord. While Peter was in Joppa, he stayed in the home of Simon the tanner.

PETER AND CORNELIUS

In Caesarea lived Cornelius, a Roman centurion who feared God. F. F. Bruce describes the meaning of "God-fearer" in Palestine at this time.

Gentiles who wished to become proselytes must be circumcised (if they were men) and undergo a purificatory baptism and offer a prescribed sacrifice. By these means they undertook the full observance of the Jewish law and became participators in all the religious and social privileges of the community of Israel.

The real test was circumcision, and this helps to explain why full proselytization to the Jewish religion was more common among Gentile women than men. Men who were attracted to the monotheism and morality of the Jewish faith and way of life were largely content with a looser attachment to the synagogue. They attended divine worship there, and observed with more or less strictness some distinctive Jewish practices, such as refraining from work on the sabbath day or avoiding certain kinds of food. In particular, they would be expected to conform to certain ethical requirements which the Jewish rabbis regarded as binding on the whole human race, since God had imposed them on Noah and his sons—abstinence from idolatry, murder and fornication. Those Gentiles who attached themselves in this loose way to the synagogue, without going so far as to become true proselytes, were called "God-fearers."[1]

---

[1] F. F. Bruce, *The Spreading Flame* (Grand Rapids: Eerdmans, 1958), pp. 14-15.

Cornelius had a vision from God in which an angel told him that his prayers and faith had been noted by God. Cornelius was to send men to Joppa to summon Peter from the house of Simon the tanner. While the servants were on the way to Peter, God prepared Peter's heart for their summons. In a trance, Peter saw heaven open and a white sheet descending, on which were all manner of animals designated by Mosaic law as unclean. God commanded Peter to kill and eat the animals. Peter objected, noting that he had never eaten anything unclean according to the law. God's response was, "What God has cleansed, no longer consider unholy" (Acts 10:15). The vision was repeated three times.

Not until the servants from Cornelius appeared did Peter understand the meaning of the vision. He returned willingly to Caesarea, where Cornelius greeted him by falling at his feet in worship. Peter objected, reminding Cornelius that he was a man and that only God was worthy of worship. Then Peter declared the meaning of his vision: although his strict Jewish practice forbade his keeping company with a Gentile, God had shown him not to call any person common or unclean.

Cornelius told Peter about his dream, and Peter shared the gospel of Jesus Christ with him. Peter knew now that God was no respecter of persons, that anyone—Jew or Gentile—could come to salvation in Christ. Peter preached the gospel, and the Holy Spirit fell on those who were listening. They all received the Holy Spirit and began to praise God in different languages (literally, "tongues"). Noting that God had sent the Spirit as a sign that he accepted the Gentiles just as he had the Jews, Peter led the new believers in baptism. He remained with the new converts for several days of fellowship.

PETER IN JERUSALEM

It became common knowledge in Judea that the Gentiles had received the word of God just as the Jews had. However, when Peter returned to Jerusalem, the Jewish believers accused him of eating with uncircumcised (unclean) men. Peter repeated everything that happened to him, including his vision and the dream of Cornelius. God spoke through Peter's words, and the Jerusalem church accepted God's work among the Gentiles, rejoicing at the increase to the church.

Shortly thereafter, the gospel came to other Gentiles in Antioch. Many believed, and the church began to grow in numbers. Barnabas taught the believers in Antioch for awhile and then brought Saul to Antioch, where Saul taught for one year. The Christians in Antioch were the first to be called Christians (Acts 11:26).

Herod the king started new persecution against the church, killing James, the brother of John. Seeing the delight of the Jews at this murder, he took Peter captive and imprisoned him. Herod surrounded Peter with guards, intending to bring him before the people at the Passover. The Christians, however, were praying earnestly for Peter's release from prison.

While Peter slept in prison, chained between two soldiers, the angel of the Lord came and woke him up. The chains fell off his wrists. Peter dressed himself and left the prison, wondering if he was dreaming. When his escape was complete, he rejoiced and praised God for miraculously delivering him from bondage. He immediately went to the house where the other believers were praying for his release.

PAUL'S FIRST MISSIONARY JOURNEY

The word of God continued to multiply, despite persecution. Barnabas, Paul, and John Mark returned to Antioch from Jerusalem. At Antioch the Holy Spirit separated Barnabas and Saul, henceforth known as Paul (the common Greek form of Saul), for special missionary ministry. Their first tour began at Cyprus, where they preached the word in the local synagogues.

At Paphos they encountered a sorcerer and false prophet named Bar-Jesus. This false prophet had considerable influence over the deputy of the country, Sergius Paulus. Sergius Paulus wanted to hear the gospel, although the false prophet tried to dissuade him. Paul rebuked the sorcerer, causing him to go blind. After such a miracle, the deputy was converted.

Paul then went to Perga in Pamphylia, but John Mark returned to Jerusalem. Next Paul and Barnabas went to Antioch in Pisidia, where Paul preached to the Jews in the synagogue on the Sabbath. Paul's common practice on arriving in a new city was to preach the gospel in the synagogues and then in the marketplace with anyone who would listen.

The Jewish leaders were concerned about the great numbers of conversions to Christ and the miracles that were done in Christ's name. Because of bitter Jewish opposition, the disciples were expelled from that region and went to Iconium.

When they reached Iconium, Paul and Barnabas went into the synagogue and boldly proclaimed the death and resurrection of Jesus Christ. The unbelieving Jews stirred up the people, dividing them into two equal groups: half with the Jews, and half with Paul and Barnabas. Persecution again pushed them on, and they journeyed to Lystra.

In Lystra, Paul healed a lame man. This miracle caused the people to exalt Paul and Barnabas as the Roman gods Jupiter and Mercury. Paul and Barnabas refused their worship, reminding them that they were only men, not gods. However, the popularity of the gospel soon stung the local Jewish leaders. They urged the people to stone Paul. They dragged him outside the city and did just that, leaving him for dead.

However, Paul rose and left Lystra with Barnabas. The two came to Derbe and then returned to Lystra, Iconium, and Antioch, strengthening the churches that they had established earlier and preaching the word of God. They journeyed throughout Pamphylia, Perga, and Attalia, spreading the gospel and increasing the church everywhere they went.

Finally Paul and Barnabas returned to Antioch and recounted their journeys. They pointed out the great number of Gentiles who had entered the church and noted the hardness of the Jewish leaders who instigated all types of persecution against God's people.

THE COUNCIL AT JERUSALEM

Certain Jewish Christians stirred up trouble in the Jerusalem church, saying that unless a convert was circumcised, he could not be saved or be a part of the church. Paul and Barnabas were sent to Jerusalem to testify before the other apostles in council concerning the Gentile position in the church.

After much discussion, Simon Peter reviewed his role in bringing the gospel to the Gentiles and stressed the role of God's grace, not works, in being saved. Paul and Barnabas then testified of the miracles God had performed among the Gentiles during their missionary journey. James, in charge of the meeting, stood and addressed the group, stating that the Gentiles had no need of circumcision or observance of the particulars of the law. They were only to refrain from idols and fornication.

The council agreed and wrote the affected churches with the news of their decision. It had been ten years since the conversion of Cornelius, and Jewish Christian opposition to the Gentile believers had been growing. The decision of the council was needed to unify the body of Christ, both Jewish and Gentile.

OTHER JOURNEYS BY PAUL

Paul and Barnabas separated before Paul's second missionary journey because they had an argument over whether or not they should take Mark with them. Paul chose Silas as his companion, and Barnabas took John Mark.

MISSIONARY TRAVELS

In Derbe again, Paul and Silas met Timothy, a young convert with a good reputation. Paul took Timothy with him as he established new churches and ordained elders in the older congregations. When they came to Galatia, the Holy Spirit forbade them to preach in Asia.

While in Troas, Paul had a vision of a Macedonian asking for help, which the missionary band interpreted as God's call to go to the Macedonians. They journeyed therefore to Philippi, the chief city of Macedonia. There they met with a prominent businesswoman, Lydia, at a Sabbath meeting near the river. She and her family listened to Paul, believed the gospel, and were baptized. Lydia invited Paul and his associates to stay with her.

As Paul and the disciples were preaching in Philippi, they met a young girl who was possessed by a divining spirit. Her masters used her condition to make money, casting fortunes and proclaiming secrets for those who paid them. This demonized girl followed Paul, calling out that he served the true God. Not wanting the endorsement of a demon, Paul cast the demon out of the girl, freeing her from its bondage.

The girl's masters were enraged that Paul would ruin their

source of income and incited a crowd against Paul and Silas. The city magistrates beat them and imprisoned them. At midnight in the prison, Paul and Silas prayed and sang praises to the Lord in front of all the prisoners. Immediately, a great earthquake shook the foundations of the prison and opened all of the doors. Everyone's bonds were broken.

The warden wanted to kill himself when he saw the destruction. He would surely be blamed for setting all of the prisoners free. However, Paul showed him that no one had left. The jailer was so impressed by the power of God that he asked Paul and Silas what he had to do to obtain salvation. Paul preached the gospel, calling on him and his family to believe on the Lord Jesus Christ and they would be saved. He and his household believed Paul's word and were baptized, joining the growing Christian community.

The missionary group then traveled to Thessalonica, where Paul preached in a Jewish synagogue, reasoning with them from the Scriptures that Christ must suffer and die, and then rise from the dead. Many Thessalonians were added to the church.

Other cities visited on this and a third missionary journey included Berea, Athens, Corinth, Ephesus, Caesarea, and Antioch. Paul was faithful to God in giving his all to preach the gospel, often to hostile audiences. Jesus Christ, for his part, was faithful to his promise to build his church.

TRIP TO ROME

Paul increasingly had a great desire to preach the gospel to the Romans in Rome itself. He knew that there was a Roman church, and he wanted to have fellowship with the believers there as he preached the gospel to those who did not know about Jesus Christ. God used a strange set of circumstances to provide Paul with a free trip to Rome.

On his way back to Jerusalem at the end of his third missionary journey, Paul stopped in Caesarea. There he received a prophetic warning that he would be bound or imprisoned if he went to Jerusalem. The entire church tried to dissuade Paul from going to Jerusalem, but his mind was made up.

In Jerusalem Paul shared reports with the elders of the Jerusalem church about God's glorious work among the nations. He was encouraged too by the activities of the Jerusalem believers.

The Jewish temple leaders, however, were waiting for Paul. At one point they thought he had brought Greeks into the temple, polluting God's holy place, and so they stirred up a mob against him. The chief captain of the Roman guard rescued Paul from the angry crowd and allowed him to speak from the steps of the palace. The next day, Paul was called before the temple council. Recognizing that the council was divided by the bickering Sadducees and Pharisees, Paul got them arguing among themselves about the nature and existence of the resurrection (Acts 23:6-8). In the midst of the turmoil, the captain removed Paul from the room. That night, God assured Paul directly that he was to go to Rome.

Informed of a plot against his life, Paul told the captain, who sent him to the Roman governor Felix in Caesarea. Felix kept Paul in custody but allowed him any visitors he wished. Paul took every advantage of the opportunity, preaching the gospel every chance he got.

Two years later Porcius Festus arrived in Caesarea, heard the Jewish arguments again, and recommended that Paul return to Jerusalem and be tried by the Jews. But Paul knew that the Jews in Jerusalem would kill him, so he appealed to Caesar—an appeal he had the right to make because he was a Roman citizen. Festus agreed, and Paul soon began his long journey to Rome.

Paul suffered many hardships along the way, including a harrowing shipwreck and the bite of a poisonous snake. In the end, however, he arrived safely in Rome, just as God has promised. There he was under house arrest but was able to preach the gospel and enjoy the company of the Roman Christians.

Paul lived in his own house, albeit under arrest, for two years. Of his fate after this time we have no sure word. However, it seems fairly certain—from evidence gathered from the Pastoral Epistles—that Paul was released from his Roman imprisonment and then traveled to various countries (one of which may have been Spain), strengthening existing churches and bringing the gospel to new frontiers. Unfortunately, Paul was again imprisoned in Rome and then executed (under Nero's rule) around A.D. 66–67.

Early Christian history tells us that Peter was also executed in Rome shortly thereafter during the persecutions instigated by Nero. The apostle John lived longer than any of the other apostles. He served as an elder in Ephesus and was later exiled to Patmos, where he wrote the book of Revelation. Either before or after his exile, John wrote his Gospel and the three short epistles. An early tradition says that he wrote his Gospel at the request of the elders in Ephesus shortly before his death. This, then, would be the last written word from one of the original twelve apostles of Jesus Christ.

CHAPTER 5
Early Christians

THE APOSTOLIC FATHERS

At the death of the last of the apostles, a new generation of Christian leaders was in place in the fledgling church. These men are known as the Apostolic Fathers. They stand in connection between the apostles of Christ in Acts and the generation of the second century. They are witnesses to the content and character of the message of the original apostles, for they learned their faith from them personally. We consider here three of these early Fathers and their writings.

CLEMENT OF ROME (c. 30–101)

Clement was the third bishop of Rome, holding that office from A.D. 92 to 101. He is thought to be the author of a letter that was written around 96 to the church of Corinth from the church of Rome. Very little is known of Clement's life except what we can glean from this letter and from comments of later writers. He is possibly the same Clement mentioned by the apostle Paul in Philippians 4:3.

From the letter we can ascertain that the writer was knowledgeable in the classics and that he was personally acquainted with the apostles. The occasion for his letter was a conflict within the Corinthian church. False leaders had set themselves over the God-ordained authorities, and Clement appeals to the Old Testament and the apostles in support of the established leadership. He also encourages them in Christian living.

IGNATIUS (d. 110)

Ignatius was the second or third bishop of Antioch, a prominent Gentile church. He was taken prisoner for being a Christian and journeyed under guard from Antioch to Rome. Along the way, he wrote letters to six churches and to Polycarp. They were, in effect, his last will and testament as he faced his own death. He exhorted his readers to unify behind their proper leaders and to resist false doctrine and unholy living; he was eager for his own martyrdom, asking the Roman church not to attempt a rescue. He tells them:

> May I have joy of the beasts that have been prepared for me; and I pray that I may find them prompt; nay I will entice them that they may devour me promptly, not as they have done to some, refusing to touch them through fear. Yea though of themselves they should not be willing while I am ready, I myself will force them to it. Come fire and cross and grapplings with wild beasts, wrenching of bones, hacking of limbs, crushings of my whole body, come cruel tortures of the devil to assail me. Only be it mine to attain to Jesus Christ.[1]

POLYCARP (c. 70–155)

Bishop of Smyrna for many years, Polycarp was a disciple of John and acquainted with the apostles. Polycarp stands in a living line from the apostles to Ireneaus and other Christian writers of the second and third centuries. He sent a letter to the church of Philippi (c. 110–117), in reply to their request that he address them and that he send along letters from Ignatius that he possessed.[2] He encouraged the Philippians in the Christian life to live uprightly and to serve God with endurance, faith, and love. He set forth the doctrine of Christ and exhorted the elders.

As an old man, Polycarp was arrested by Roman authorities in Smyrna for being a Christian. He refused to renounce his faith and, just before the end, challenged his executioner: "Thou threatenest

---

[1] Ignatius, *Letter to the Romans*, 5.
[2] Polycarp, *Letter to the Philippians* 3, 13.

that fire which burneth for a season and after a little while is quenched: for thou art ignorant of the fire of the future judgment and eternal punishment, which is reserved for the ungodly. But why delayest thou? Come, do what thou wilt."[3]

PERSECUTION

Christianity, until 313, was generally an outlawed religion. Persecutions varied from sporadic, local antagonism to empire-wide attempts to exterminate the followers of Christ. There were several reasons for such a response from the Romans. Christianity was a universal religion, intolerant of competing religions authorized by the Roman state. Christians refused to honor the emperor as divine. They separated themselves from public functions and met together secretly and often. Misunderstanding of their activities in meetings led to charges of incest and cannibalism.[4] Priests of state religions found that they lost revenue because of the competition of Christianity.

Nero, in the first century, was the first Roman emperor to initiate local attacks on Christians. Widespread persecution erupted in 249 under Decius. In order to restore to Rome its former prestige, Decius attempted to lead a return to the state religion and state deities. In this "reformation," Christianity was officially outlawed, and incredible tortures and punishments were inflicted upon the Christians. The next major persecution was in 303 under Diocletian, who ruled that the churches of Christians should be destroyed, Bibles burned, and Christians stripped of their civil rights and public offices. Moreover, they should be ordered to swear to the gods and, failing to do so, should be sentenced to death by sword or wild beasts or to working in the mines.

The spectacle of Christians being martyred, of their courage and even joy, inspired other Christians to endure. The fourth-century church historian Eusebius wrote of martyrs "with joy and laughter and gladness receiving the final sentence of death; so that they sang and sent up hymns and thanksgivings to the God of the

---

[3]*Martyrdom of Polycarp* 11.
[4]Justin Martyr, *Dialogue with Trypho,* 10.

universe even to the very last breath."[5] Some nonbelievers also were deeply moved by the way Christians faced death. Tertullian rightly observed, "The blood of the martyrs is seed [of the church]."[6]

OTHER CHURCH FATHERS

Besides the Apostolic Fathers mentioned above, several other Christian writers and leaders in the early centuries of the church exerted considerable influence upon their contemporaries. Their writings reveal many interesting details of the early years of the church, and their lives often illustrate the highest level of commitment in Christian devotion.

JUSTIN MARTYR (100–166)

Justin was a Samaritan with pagan upbringing and Greek education. He searched for truth through Stoic philosophy, Aristotle, Pythagoras, and Plato. He was dissatisfied with the Stoics, for he found no knowledge of God; with the Aristotelian philosophers, because of their demand for money; with the Pythagoreans, because of the elaborate training in music, astronomy, and geometry needed as preparation for philosophical study. Even Plato, who inspired him, left him unsatisfied. On a walk by the seashore he met an old man who explained the Hebrew prophets to him and told him about Jesus. His investigations, coupled with his admiration of Christians (especially the death of the martyrs), won him to Christ.[7] He spent his life as a Christian philosopher, wearing his philosopher's cloak, traveling and preaching the gospel. He contested Marcion the heretic in Rome. In 166 he was beheaded in Rome through the instigation of the cynic Crescens.

He wrote an *Apology* to the emperor Antoninus Pius, containing a plea to examine the charges against Christians and to free them if innocent, a refutation of the charge of atheism and idolatry, an exposition of Christ and the Old Testament, and an explanation of Christian worship. In a second apology he compares Christ and

---

[5]Eusebius, *Ecclesiastical History* 8.9.5.
[6]Tertullian, *Apology*, 50.
[7]Justin Martyr, *Dialogue*, 2–8; *Apology*, 2.12.13.

Socrates. In his *Dialogue with Trypho,* written c. 150, he presents arguments from the Old Testament to a leading Jew of the day to show that Jesus Christ and the Old Testament are compatible. He addresses the issues of his conversion, the relation of law and gospel (how can Christians love God and break his laws?), Christ as a human/divine Savior who suffered and died, and the calling of the Gentiles.

IRENAEUS (c. 120–202)

Irenaeus was born in Smyrna and was a pupil of Polycarp. He was a missionary to Gaul (France) and became bishop of Lyons in 180. He is considered to be the most orthodox and least speculative of the early Christian writers. He was concerned with preserving the genuine apostolic teachings, which were handed down in a public way to the churches, against the "secret teaching" doctrines of sects that challenged Christians in the mid-second century. He possibly died a martyr in 202. His chief writing is *Against Heresies,* written 180–190 to combat Gnosticism. Its five books deal with (1) teachings of the gnostics, (2) arguments showing the unreasonableness of their doctrines, especially the doctrine of the Demiurge, (3) arguments showing that the Scriptures are apostolic teaching and contain true doctrine, (4) refutation of the leading gnostic, Marcion, by Christ's words, and (5) arguments to support the doctrine of the resurrection.

TERTULLIAN (c. 150–220)

Born in Carthage, Africa, the son of a captain of a Roman legion, Tertullian was educated in Greek, Latin, law, debate, and politics and was probably a lawyer. Tertullian was converted to Christianity as an adult (c. 190). His character was passionate, extreme, and ascetic. In c. 202 he joined the Montanist party because he was attracted by its ascetic and morally earnest quality, its emphasis on the end of the world, and its general spiritual emphasis, contrasted with the worldliness of the established church.

Tertullian wrote an *Apology* (c. 200), defending Christianity to a Roman governor. In it he argues as a lawyer before judges, not as a philosopher with philosophers. He refutes the charges against Christianity and argues that the persecutions are ineffective because they only increase Christianity. *Against Praexus* (c. 215), an apology for Christians, is important partially because of Tertullian's use of the term *Trinity* to describe the Godhead, and the distinction between *person* and *essence* that later played an important role in that doctrine. Tertullian also produced many other writings.

ATHANASIUS (c. 296–373)

Athanasius is known through his defense of the doctrine of the deity of Christ and the Trinity. Athanasius against the World was the motto that well describes his long struggle against the Arian heresy; he is living proof that one man in the truth can overturn the order of things.

Athanasius was acquainted with Anthony the hermit and grew to be an advocate of the monastic life. In 325 he came on the scene as presbyter of Alexandria; in 328 he succeeded Alexander as the bishop. He was physically a small man, utterly single-minded concerning the deity of Christ, for which he was exiled five times. His most well-known writings are *On the Incarnation of the Word, Apology against the Arians,* and *Life of St. Anthony.*

JEROME (c. 345–420)

Jerome was brought up in a wealthy Christian home. At age eighteen he went to Rome to study to become a lawyer and was a student of Cicero's writings and of philosophy. By character, Jerome was intense and argumentative. In 370 he was baptized in Rome and then went to the desert east of Antioch to live as a hermit for five years, where he practiced extreme asceticism. In 382 he attended a council in Rome, where he became secretary and adviser to Damasus, bishop of Rome. As a scholar, Jerome was unparalleled; he knew Latin and Greek classics and Hebrew, and had mastered biblical literature and the Fathers in the original languages. He was commissioned by Damasus to revise the Latin Bible. In his Old Testament work, he translated directly from the Hebrew in order to recover the original text and meaning of Scripture. (The current Latin versions tried to follow the Septuagint but were all different.) His version was called the Vulgate, meaning "common," and became the standard translation of the Latin church. In his work on the New Testament, he used the Greek text to revise the Latin translation.

In 384 he moved to Bethlehem to study, where he built a

monastery and hospital. He wrote voluminous letters and commentaries, especially praising monasticism. His method of interpretation was less allegorical than was the custom. He distinguished two meanings in Scripture, the literal and the spiritual.

AUGUSTINE (354–430)

Augustine is perhaps the most famous church leader and theologian; his writings provided the foundation for most of the theology of the Middle Ages and of the Latin church. He was born in North Africa; his mother, Monica, was a devout Christian. He studied to be a lawyer at Carthage, went to Rome to be a teacher, and settled in Milan. He was interested in Manichaean teachings and studied Neoplatonic philosophy and Cicero. He went to hear Ambrose because of his rhetorical ability; impressed with Ambrose and with the stories that he had heard concerning Anthony and other hermits, in 386 he had a conversion experience. Sitting in his garden, he heard a child's voice saying, "Take and read." He opened the Bible to Romans 13:11-14, read, and believed. He and his son were baptized by Ambrose, and after putting away his concubine, Augustine began to live the Christian life. In 391 he was ordained presbyter, against his will, and in 395 was made bishop of Hippo, North Africa. He established a monastery and lived there, preaching, teaching, and writing.

Augustine's writings include *Confessions,* a spiritual autobiography unlike anything of the age and considered a Christian classic. His *City of God,* another classic, was occasioned by the sack of Rome. It compares the earthly city to the heavenly, eternal citizenship of the Christian in God's kingdom. *On the Trinity* is an orthodox exposition, introducing the notion of the love of the Father and the Son being embodied in the Holy Spirit. *Against the Donatists* and *Against the Pelagians* refute their views.

CHAPTER 6
The Contest of Ideas

The first centuries of the church were often ones of intense debate and theological controversy. As the message of salvation through Jesus the Messiah spread throughout the Roman world, certain heretics appeared on the scene who in different ways denied the faith "once and for all delivered unto the saints." Furthermore, controversies arose concerning certain doctrines central to the Christian faith, especially involving the person and nature of Jesus Christ. We consider here only five of the more important issues that occupied the church during its first five centuries.

GNOSTICISM

Gnosticism was an important philosophical and religious movement in the second century. Its name comes from the Greek word meaning "knowledge" *(gnosis)* and refers in particular to secret knowledge that the adherents of this heresy claimed to possess. Gnostics combined various ideas from Oriental religions, Greek philosophy, and mystical Judaism with Christian language. Each gnostic sect followed its own leader, and there were almost as many systems of Gnosticism as there were leaders.

Gnostics held that the universe consists of matter and spirit: matter is evil, and spirit is good. The ultimate spirit (the ultimate God) has nothing directly to do with matter. It emanates spirit from itself which, as the spirit is farther away, turns into matter/spirit and then, by the agency of an intermediary god (the "Demiurge"), becomes the created world of matter. This middle god is Jehovah of the Old Testament. Some gnostic groups considered Jesus to be a supernatural being who only appeared to be a man who suffered and died but who did not actually become a physical human being.

Gnostics did not believe in a bodily resurrection but rather in reincarnation in cycles until pure spirituality was attained and, finally, absorption in the ultimate spirit. People are divided into "spiritual," "psychical," and "carnal," depending upon the degree to which they possess the divine and secret knowledge. Gnostics rejected the Old Testament, and Marcion and others used a corrupted version of Luke/Acts and Paul. They either composed their own "Scriptures" or allegorized existing ones to suit their doctrines. Secret knowledge was considered to be the highest attainment; the public knowledge of Jesus' teachings found in the Gospels and Epistles and transmitted publicly by the apostles was considered to be inferior to the secret knowledge allegedly transmitted by Jesus and his followers through separate channels. In ethics the spirit/matter contrast led either to a very ascetic life (have nothing to do with matter) or to a libertine life (indulging in material pleasures because the flesh has no value anyway). The original gnostic as such is considered to be Simon the Magician, spoken of in Acts 8:9-10.

TRINITARIAN HERESIES

In dealing with the relation of Jesus and the Father, and the resulting Trinitarian concept, various attempts were made to reconcile Jesus' deity with the principle that there is only one God. Two attempts at this formulation were found to be unsound.

Unitarianism, also called "dynamic monarchianism," was an attempt to give Jesus a secondary sort of deity, and thus to preserve the unity of God by attributing true deity only to the Father. In 260, Paul of Samosata, bishop of Antioch, was the most famous teacher of this doctrine. Cloaking his views in orthodox language, he taught that Jesus was indwelt by the Logos more than others and, because of his moral development, achieved divine status. He denied personality to the Logos of God and to the Holy Spirit, which he thought to be attributes of God, not separate persons. His teachings were uncovered by Malchion; his views were condemned, and he was deposed about 268.

Modalism was the doctrine that Jesus and the Holy Spirit were not separate persons but were "modes" of God's self-revelation. Sabellius, c. 200, was the most famous proponent of this view. He taught that there is one God, who manifests himself in three forms or faces: in the Old Testament as Father, in the New Testament as Son, and since Jesus' resurrection as the Holy Spirit. These manifestations are relations of function within God's nature and have no existence separately. In his view, Jesus is Deity because he is the Father. Although it recognized the deity of Christ and led to the unity of God, this doctrine did not do justice to the relations between the Father, Jesus, and Holy Spirit that are set forth in Scripture. It was declared to be false.

ARIANISM

Around the year 318, Alexander, bishop of Alexandria, gave a sermon entitled "On the Unity of the Trinity," which his presbyter, Arius, took exception to. Arius had received his teaching from Lucian of Antioch, and Lucian in turn from Paul of Samosata. Arius was to reintroduce the substance of Paul's views into the church scene. He began to teach that the Son (the Logos) was created by the Father from nothing. Jesus had a human body but not a human soul; rather, the Logos inhabited the body. In Arius's view, therefore, Jesus was neither God nor man. Alexander contested this teaching and had him deposed, yet Arius continued to gather followers and propagate this doctrine.

When Emperor Constantine heard of this fight, he was scandalized that the one true religion should be in such a state and resolved to solve the problem through negotiation with the contending parties; this attempt failed. In 325, then, he invited three hundred bishops with their presbyters (mostly from the East) to attend a council at Nicaea, with expenses paid from the royal treasury. This was the first ecumenical, or universal, council.

At this council, three views emerged: the Arian view that the Son was a creature of different essence from the Father, the Athanasian view that Jesus was an eternal being of the same essence with the Father, and an intermediate view, held by Eusebius of Caesarea, that the Son was an eternal being of a similar but not the same nature with the Father.

Arius held that God could create the world directly and that he created the Logos in order to create. The Logos, then, is a creature. It was not created from God's nature, but from his will, and "there was a time when he was not." The Son does not have perfect knowledge of the Father, because he is a creature and cannot perfectly reveal him. Scriptures that were used were generally of three sorts: those that seem to say that the Son was created (for example, Proverbs 8:22; John 1:14; Acts 2:36; Hebrews 1:4), those that display the humanity of Jesus (e.g., his suffering, thought to be incompatible with true deity), and those that seem to imply a subordination in nature of the Son to the Father (for example, John 14:28).

Athanasius held that the Arian view produced two gods, a greater and a lesser, that the fatherhood of the Father is an eternal relation, that the Logos (being the wisdom and power of God) must have always existed, and that salvation is a work of God and could not be accomplished unless God himself performed it (i.e., it could not be delegated). He employed Scriptures that ascribed the nature and attributes of deity to Jesus, God's Son, such as worship, forgiving sins, and divine names and functions. He made the distinction of persons and essence to show that the Son is of the same nature as the Father, yet a different person; God was shown to be a three-personal being.

The Semi-Arian position, advocated as a compromise measure, was accepted by neither of the other parties. The Athanasian party pointed out that attributes or relations might be similar, but natures are either the same or different. The Arian party admitted no middle ground between deity and creature.

At first, the majority of the participants were undecided and strove to hold some middle position. The council began with the proposal of the Arian view in the form of a creed, which was promptly torn up and rejected. Eusebius proposed a creed taken from general biblical terms, avoiding the issue of "essence" or "nature"; the Arians were ready to accept it as compatible with their position, and therefore the Athanasians insisted on a clarification of the issues by suggesting that the words "same essence" be specifically included to rule out the creaturehood of the Son. Eventually nearly all the bishops in attendance agreed to this formula and signed a creed statement, and Arius was proclaimed a heretic and banned.

This decision did not end the dispute. The issue raged for over fifty years, with the Arians at first gaining ground. In the East, Arianism grew until the emperors themselves came to embrace it. Athanasius was banished into exile no less than five times. With the rise of Julian the Apostate came a contempt for all Christianity, and Julian removed the ban on Athanasius at that time, probably expecting the rival parties to exterminate each other. Instead, Athanasius grew in popularity, and his views with him. With the reign of Theodosius I, the Nicene formula was ratified permanently at the Council of Constantinople, in 381.

THE TWO NATURES OF JESUS

Once the deity of Christ had been established in a doctrinal form, the implications of that doctrine became a source of controversy. In exactly what sense is Jesus both man and God? Does he possess two natures, or one? Does he count as one person or two?

At least four views were presented, three of which were ultimately condemned. Apollinarius, bishop of Laodicaea (near Antioch), c. 360, taught that Jesus, like all men, was composed of body, soul, and spirit. He held that Jesus' body and soul were human and that his spirit was the Logos and fully divine; Jesus thus did not have a human spirit. This view was considered and condemned at the Council of Constantinople because it did not allow for Jesus to be completely human.

Nestorius, bishop of Constantinople about 428 and a powerful Christian leader, held that Jesus possessed two natures, human and divine, and that these natures were distinct and separate to the degree that he actually constituted two separate persons. The occasion for this doctrine was his objection to the word *theotokos* (God-bearer, or Mother of God), which was attributed to Mary. According to Nestorius, Mary was the mother of only the human side of Jesus. His views were condemned at the Council of Ephesus in 431. His followers continued as a separate group from the orthodox church.

Eutyches, a monk at Constantinople, argued that Jesus had only a divine nature. In him the human nature had been "taken up" into the divine nature so much as to be infinitely small. His view was condemned at the Council of Chalcedon in 451.

The formula that the church ultimately adopted was most clearly expressed by Leo, bishop of Rome, who stated that Jesus had two natures, human and divine, and that they made up one person. The natures were not mixed or mingled, but connected in one consciousness. The Logos, already divine by nature, took upon himself an additional nature; the personality of Jesus is due to the Logos, not to the human nature.

PELAGIANISM

The controversies noted earlier centered on difficult philosophical issues regarding Jesus' nature, the Trinity, and the problem of the incarnation; these issues were taken up largely by the Eastern church. In the West, the topics of discussion tended to be more practical problems, especially the problem of salvation. The precise relation between faith (or grace) and works was never really settled by the first thinkers on the subject and inevitably came up when strong doctrinal positions on this topic were put forth.

Pelagius, born in 350, was a British monk who was known for his austere and learned life. In 409 he traveled to Rome, and in 414 to Palestine, where he taught concerning free will, human moral ability, and the necessity to live a pure life. He caught the attention of the scholar Jerome, who contested many of his views. Augustine wrote refutations of Pelagius's views, and councils (especially the Council of Carthage in 418) were held to consider the charges. Pelagianism was condemned at the Council of Ephesus, 431, although no positive position was taken on the issue until the Council of Orange, 529.

Pelagianism emphasizes the ability of man to choose, and do, what is right at each particular time of decision. Pelagius taught that man's moral situation after the fall is the same as before the fall. At each point, a person has the free will to choose either good or evil, just as Adam did. Every soul is created by God and therefore is created as a good entity; God holds individuals responsible only for their own actions and therefore does not blame Adam's posterity for Adam's sin. There is therefore no "original sin," or hereditary guilt.

Pelagius pointed to Scriptures that purport to describe sinless men and women, such as Abel, Enoch, Abraham, Melchizedek, and Mary. The prevalence of sin is explained by the influence of bad living being transmitted from one generation to the next. Grace has been provided to all men and women equally. God has provided helps toward godliness in our existence: the law, the gospel, and Jesus' example and instruction. Each action results from three components: the power to choose and act (given as grace from God), the exercise of the will (one's own responsibility), and the action itself (conduct). Each person has been provided with all he or she needs to live a righteous life. People do not need rescuing; they need to make a decision to do what is right.

Augustine took violent exception to the notion that man does not stand in need of a Savior. He taught that Adam's fall has dramatic consequences for his posterity. Because of the fall, human beings are lost and cannot choose good, and need to be rescued. God takes the initiative and rescues those who are saved solely through his own efforts and because of nothing on their part. Man simply responds to the salvation that is already given.

In Augustine's view, Adam's state was one of freedom of choice, in which his spirit ruled over his body. He fell through disobedience, which had pride at its root; his sin was that of setting himself up as God. The fall affected not only Adam himself but all of human nature as such, and therefore his posterity. In some sense, everyone personally sinned when Adam sinned (see Romans 5:12).

The consequences of the fall were loss of freedom of choice, clouding of the mind, loss of paradise, loss of control over the flesh (leading to lust), physical death, and original sin and guilt. Salvation means a rescue of individuals from this condition through Jesus (the second Adam), which results in regeneration, that is, a transforming of one's nature.

Grace is that which God does on his own initiative; as such it is a gift and cannot be deserved. Grace is irresistible, that is, those to whom grace is given are automatically changed. God chooses in his sovereignty those who are saved and those who are not, through no action or will on their part; Jesus died only for the elect. (Augustine, however, did not develop the implication that God actually picks out persons for damnation.)

Many thinkers sought some intermediary position between the

views of Augustine and Pelagius. It was generally recognized that the Pelagian view overstated man's ability to choose freely, as though he did not need a Savior. Augustine's position, however, seemed to lead in practice to a fatalistic view of life and a harsh view of God's love for humankind. At the Council of Orange, 529, a "semi-Augustinian" view was accepted that became relatively authoritarian in the church.

Augustine became the foremost theologian of the Western church until Thomas Aquinas, almost nine hundred years later. Augustine's predestinarian views, however, were never fully taken up into the church's theological structure. A middle position was taken, and the difficulty in defining exactly what that position asserted remained for theologians of later generations.

CHAPTER 7
The Rise of the Roman Church

A central theme in the story of the Middle Ages is the power of Rome—first in its emperors, and then increasingly in its popes. In this chapter we consider only a few highlights of this period, which might be called the golden age of the Roman church.

CONSTANTINE

In 305 the empire was divided into eastern and western portions, the West ruled by Constantius (Constantine's father), and the east by Galerius. Maximian and Diocletian, the former rulers, had retired in 305. Maxentius, however, the son of Maximian, proclaimed himself emperor of the West; Constantius had died in 306, and the soldiers proclaimed Constantine Western emperor. Constantine and Maxentius fought a crucial battle at the Milvian Bridge (312); the day before the battle, Constantine saw a vision of a cross in the sky with the words "in this sign conquer." He vowed to become a Christian if he won the battle; he did gain a victory and became the first Christian emperor.

In 313 Constantine issued the Edict of Milan, which legalized Christianity throughout the empire. It guaranteed freedom of worship, ordered that property should be restored to the churches, exempted the clergy from public service, and instituted the "Day of the Sun" as a day of worship (Christians had already been observing Sunday as the Lord's Day). Emperors after Constantine were generally Christian, with the exception of Julian the Apostate.

The acceptance of Christianity as a recognized religious expression had both positive and negative consequences for Christianity.

Positively, with the end of persecution, Christians had a freer hand in spreading the gospel. Women's rights and slaves' conditions were improved. There was a general improvement in the justice of the state.

Negatively, there was a forced unity in dealing with issues of doctrines and practice. At certain times, religious issues were used for political gain, making it easier to be a Christian. A nominal Christianity was thereby allowed, if not encouraged. Many pagan customs were included within Christian practice. Persecution by the Christian emperors of other beliefs and of the Christians among themselves were often as severe as the former persecutions. The church became more wealthy and showed more of a tendency to worldliness and a love of luxury.

THE PAPACY

The issue of the papacy is one of the main points of division between Roman Catholic, Orthodox, and Protestant bodies. Roman Catholics hold that the bishop of Rome is the ruler of all the church, which the Orthodox church and Protestants deny.

Historically, until the year 313 each bishop was in charge of his own city or area. From 313 to 590 the Roman bishop was considered "first among equals," holding a leading role among the bishops of Alexandria, Antioch, and Constantinople. Beginning about 590, the bishop of Rome asserted his authority over all the bishops and claimed to be the sole ruler of the Christian body.

The growth in influence of the Roman bishop has various explanations. The largest and most influential cities naturally had the most influence over the Christian body as a whole. These were Rome, Constantinople, Antioch, Alexandria, and Jerusalem. The fall of the Western half of the empire and the removal of the empire's capital to Constantinople left the Roman bishop in virtual command of the secular as well as religious areas of life. As the only major bishopric of the West, it gained in power and prestige. Also, in their disputes with one another, bishops of Antioch, Alexandria, and Constantinople tended to appeal to Rome's opinions.

Furthermore, the other leading cities were eventually conquered by the Muslims and therefore lost power. Missionary efforts were undertaken mainly in the West because the East was busy fighting the Muslims, thereby allowing the Western bishop to gain power over the new converts. Finally, the orthodoxy of Rome was constant through the years; the Roman bishops generally led in promoting a stable and acceptable theology.

MISSIONARY ACTIVITY

The medieval period saw a great deal of missionary outreach throughout Europe.

England. It is possible that Paul traveled as far as England in his missionary journeys. By 208, Tertullian was able to note that England had already been evangelized, and, in 303, Alban became England's first famous martyr. Constantine and Pelagius were born in England, and there were three British bishops at the Council of Arles in 314. In 410 the Roman troops protecting England from invaders were withdrawn, and the island became virtually separated from the rest of the Christian world. In 595 Pope Gregory I sent Augustine (not Augustine of Hippo) to conduct a missionary tour of England with a band of thirty monks. He found Christian churches already there that had no real allegiance to Rome. Out of this contact, much conflict developed over the old and new customs and over the issue of the autonomy of the local body.

Ireland, Scotland. Patrick was born in Britain and taken to Ireland as a slave when he was sixteen. After returning to England, he decided to go back to Ireland to preach the gospel (c. 432). Columbanus was a missionary from Ireland to Scotland (c. 590) who traveled with twelve companions, evangelized Scotland, and started many monasteries.

France. As we saw in chapter 5, Irenaeus was an early missionary to France. The Germanic peoples who later moved southward into France and other countries were new targets of evangelism. One of the leading missionaries to them was named Ulfilas, who was an Arian Christian. Ulfilas developed an alphabet for writing the gospel message, and thousands were converted to Arianism. A major turning point for the Franks was the conversion of Clovis, who was their king from 481 to 511. Clovis married a Nicene Christian woman in 493 and before a major battle prayed to Jesus, promising to become a Christian if he won. The victory came to pass, and he and over three thousand warriors were baptized en masse. This event led to the rise of a Christian emperor in Constantinople and greatly aided the evangelization of the West.

Germany. Boniface (680–755) was the most famous apostle to the Germans. In 715 he left England for Holland and failed in his attempt to set up Christian churches there. Three years later, he visited Gregory II and was commissioned by the pope to evangelize the general area of Germany. With papal support and the encouragement from Charles Martel of France, Boniface was successful in setting up many monastic colonies and converting thousands. He was martyred by pagans.

Scandinavia. Ansgar from Flanders (801–865) answered the call of the king of Denmark for missionaries to Scandinavia; in 826, he embarked on a thirty-six-year mission to the northern countries.

Moravia. To the east, two brothers, Cyril and Methodius, went as missionaries to Moravia (in modern Czechoslovakia). They translated the Scriptures into Slavic, inventing an alphabet in order to do so. They preached in the common language, rather than in Latin, and made many converts. Because of these two brothers, the Slavic churches became connected with the Roman church rather than the Greek church in the East.

Russia. Also to the east, Vladimir, grand duke of Russia, accepted missionaries from the Greek and Roman churches, as well as representatives from Islam and Judaism. He appointed trusted men to assist him in deciding which religious group to join. They eventually chose Eastern Orthodoxy, partly because of the impression that St. Sophia's cathedral in Constantinople made on them. In 988 the people of Kiev received baptism en masse.

ISLAM

Here we need to mention the rise and spread of Islam, a competitor of Christianity that began in the early seventh century and quickly presented a serious challenge to the Roman Empire and the church. Its founder, Muhammad, was born in 570 in Mecca, southern Arabia. His early years were relatively uneventful as a manager of camel caravans and a keeper of his wife's estate. However, one evening in a cave on Mount Hira, where he often went to pray, he is said to have heard a loud voice telling him,

"Read!" Protesting that he could not read, he heard the voice command him again. He was then shown a scroll on which words were emblazoned with fire. Although he had never previously read a word, Muhammad miraculously read the scroll.

He left the cave fearing he had gone mad, but he heard the voice again. Looking up, Muhammad saw the angel Gabriel, who said to him, "O Muhammad! You are Allah's messenger, and I am Gabriel." That did not yet convince him, the story goes. Later he received another call, which he obeyed. His mission as an apostle of God was to proclaim to his idolatrous people a pure monotheism.

At the outset, his message met with great resistance, which included persecution and exile. He claimed to receive further revelations from Allah, identifying him as successor of the prophets, including Noah, Abraham, Moses, and Jesus. Muhammad eventually viewed himself as the final messenger whom Allah would send to the world.

In the year 622, a group of 150 Muslims left Mecca secretly for the town of Yathrib, or Medina. Muhammad journeyed to Medina later that year, on September 20, the date that begins the Muslim calendar. Then in 630, at sixty years of age, Muhammad and his army marched on Mecca in an attempt to claim this as the holy city of Islam, eventually conquering it against overwhelming odds. Two years later the prophet of Allah died.

The pattern had been set for the followers of Muhammad, who eagerly took up the sword against the enemies of Allah. Islam ("submission [to the will of God]") quickly spread beyond the Arabian borders, capturing Jerusalem by 638. By 715, the empire had spread from the Chinese frontier westward to the Atlantic Ocean. Islam was stopped in the West by Charles Martel of France in 732 in the battle of Tours. Today approximately one billion people, or one-sixth of the world's population, are Muslims.

Muslims speak of the five pillars of their faith: (1) the creed "There is no God but Allah, and Muhammad is his prophet"; (2) ritual prayers, performed five times a day facing Mecca; (3) almsgiving, offering one-fortieth of one's income for the needy; (4) observance of Ramadan, a month of fasting during daylight hours; and (5) a pilgrimage to Mecca, required of all Muslims who are physically and financially able. An unofficial sixth pillar is *jihad*, or holy war, used to spread Islam.

Muslims view God as an absolute deity whose will is law. God is unknowable in the personal sense; thus the goal of Islam is to obey Allah, not to know him. Jesus is considered a prophet of God who was misunderstood or misrepresented by later followers. He was not the Son of God, because God cannot have sons. Jesus, according to Muhammad, never claimed deity; he was not crucified, someone else was crucified in his place; he was assumed into heaven.

EAST-WEST SPLIT

The controversies between the Eastern and Western realms of Christianity began in the second century over the date of Easter and grew into an irreparable breach by 1054, when Michael Cerularius, bishop of Constantinople, condemned the Western church for using unleavened bread in the Eucharist (which had been a growing practice since the ninth century). Pope Leo IX sent three legates to the East, and in 1054 they excommunicated the bishop of Constantinople and his followers. The bishop of Constantinople returned the favor.

Besides the celebration of Easter, the two churches disagreed on celibacy. The East permitted priests (but not bishops) to marry; the West did not. Also, Rome added the word *filioque* ("and the Son") to the Nicene Creed, expressing their view that the Holy Spirit proceeds from both the Father and the Son; Constantinople never did add this word, teaching that the Holy Spirit proceeds from the Father alone.

East and West disagreed also about the authority of the bishop of Rome. The West held that the bishop of Rome was the ruler of all other bishops; the East did not. In communion the East used bread and wine, whereas the West used bread alone. Overall, the Eastern church tended to be relatively static in their theology, and the Western church tended toward change.

Besides such theological issues, geographical and temperamental differences also played a role. For example, the political separation of the Eastern and Western halves of the Roman Empire led to a lack of unity in their life-styles and allegiances. The bishop of Rome grew in power, and the competition that existed between the bishops did not allow them to accept the pope's primacy, nor him to accept their equality. Personal competition between leaders led to hard feelings. With such antagonism and misunderstanding, smaller differences became major issues.

THE CRUSADES

The rise and advance of Islam led to a problem in Christendom that aroused the passions of millions of people. The Holy Land had been taken by the Muslims, and places regarded as sacred were controlled by the "infidels" of Islam. Conditions were tolerable for the Christian pilgrims until 1076, when the Seljuk Turks took Jerusalem and put the Christians into prison or slavery. The Crusades were armed pilgrimages to Jerusalem for the cause of winning it back from the Muslims. The major successes occurred in 1099 and 1187, and the major defeats happened in 1229 and 1244, and so the Crusades were ultimately unsuccessful in this primary objective.

The reasons for the Crusades can be listed as follows: (1) piety for the Holy Land, including an awe of relics; (2) hatred for the Muslims, who were viewed as antichrist, the destroyers of Christianity; (3) stories of the Muslims' ill-treatment of pilgrims who were attempting to visit the gospel lands; and (4) an appeal from the Greek emperor to support him in his stand against the Muslim armies. Virtually everyone was involved in the Crusades. The kings not only planned Crusades but personally went to battle. Even the clerics and monks fought. Heavy taxes were imposed upon the people in order to finance these expeditions. There were seven major Crusades in all.

The results of the Crusades were a mixture of good and bad. On the positive side, Christianity found a new unity in pursuing a common goal, the feudal system was replaced by the modern system of nations, the benefits of trade with the East added a new perspective to the culture, and Arabian learning (especially a new appreciation for Aristotle) was transmitted to the West.

On the negative side, the main purpose of the Crusades was not achieved. Christians failed to control the Holy Land, the advance of Islam was not halted, and the East/West split was worse than ever. Also, the Crusaders did not live up to the Christian standards for which they were fighting: their lives were often immoral and cruel, which led to a hardening of the Muslims against Christianity rather than an opening for evangelism. The system of indulgences—extravagant promises of eternal reward and forgiveness of sins for those who accompanied the Crusaders—was enhanced. Finally, the reputation of Christianity for succeeding generations was tarnished by the "evangelize by the sword" tactic.

CHAPTER 8
Christians of the Roman Church

Throughout the centuries of the Roman church in the Middle Ages, countless individuals served the Lord with earnestness and often at great personal sacrifice. In this chapter we consider a few of these believers, in their different roles as monastics, popes, scholars, or dissenters.

MONASTICS
Early monasticism was tied up in large part with the spirit of asceticism, that is, the attempt to master the "passions of the flesh" by refusing to indulge them. This effort ordinarily took the form of a flight from the world, a self-imposed isolation from other people, and a strict personal discipline regarding food and drink, bodily comforts, sleep, and prayer. This attitude of extreme self-denial is held in common with the Hindus, Buddhists, and Stoics, who themselves hold a view about the world that emphasizes the spirit and devalues the body.

The ascetic movement was often motivated by religious serious-ness and a recognition of the comparative emptiness of the world. The monk or hermit strove to master his desires in order to be trained in obedience to God and saw Elijah, other Old Testament prophets, and John the Baptist as examples of those who lived the "holy" life.

Negatively, this attitude tended towards isolation and therefore lack of practical love, preoccupation with the self, and inability to change the world because of lack of involvement with it. It strength-ened the will but did not necessarily subject this strong will to the

Creator. It tended to regard sin as connected with the material life, which is a doctrine inconsistent with the gospel message.

After Constantine legalized Christianity, the life of the hermit or monk gave Christians the opportunity for spiritual heroism previously provided by martyrdom. It appealed strongly both to those who desired solitude and prayer and to those who wanted to be "spiritual athletes" and to achieve the highest possible spiritual life. The concept of monasticism went through four basic stages: personal discipline exercised within the community, the life of solitude as a hermit, the communal life of the cloister, and the fully developed, self-contained monastery.

Monasteries provided havens for travelers and immunity for soldiers. They preserved knowledge and books, especially the Bible at a time of confusion and war. They stood against the worldliness of the day and called for repentance of the populace. They ministered to the sick and poor. They organized farming, improving techniques and other practical facets of life. They sent out missionaries to the pagans, and preachers to the nominally Christian. The emphasis on celibacy, however, hindered family life. Also, the monasteries took the Christian out of contact with the non-Christian world and often promoted simply outward standards and the false idea of spiritual levels.

Benedict of Nursia (480–550) was the major figure in the growth of the monastic life. He developed the Benedictine rule, which became the basis for the majority of later monastic organizations. At the age of fifteen Benedict lived three years in seclusion in a grotto in Rome, and then in the mountains, where he started many cloisters, preached the gospel, and converted many pagans. Miracles were reported of him. In 529 he built the lasting Monte Cassino on the ruins of a temple of Apollo.

Benedict of Aniane (750–821) reformed the Benedictine monastic system. Disgusted with the world after serving in the emperor's court, he entered a cloister and eventually founded new ones based on the Benedictine rule. He was subsequently in charge of all the cloisters in western France. The monasteries became schools that emphasized education and books, architecture, trades, and practical methods of farming and raising of livestock. They became places of refuge from a dangerous world. Personally, the monks were known for acts of heroism during famine and plagues.

Bernard of Clairvaux (1090–1153) is considered to be a spiritual giant of the Middle Ages. He was many sided, being a monk, spiritual adviser and mystic, hymn writer and musician, theologian, preacher, and leader. In 1113 he joined the Cistercians and lived such an ascetic life that he later regretted his excesses. He founded the cloister of Clairvaux two years later. Many well-attested reports of miracles surround Bernard, especially healings and exorcisms. As a preacher, he was perhaps without parallel in his time, being simple to the simple, and erudite to the scholarly.

Dominic of Spain (1170–1221) was aggressive, hard, and devoted to truth. He excelled in philosophy and theology during his education, and in 1195 he became a canon. His contact with the Cathari, a dissenting "puritan" body (see "Dissenters" later in this chapter), started him on a tour of preaching. Miracles were attributed to him. In 1217 he sent out monks to start colonies, and his order spread through their evangelism. His monasteries were among the first to have definite rules of study, requiring four years of philosophy and theology before being licensed to preach, followed by three more years of theology. After his death, his monks became the main instruments of suppressing heretics.

Francis of Assisi (1186–1226) is perhaps the most popular Christian saint, known for his humility, joy, and simplicity of life in his imitation of Christ. He was born in Italy, the son of a wealthy textile merchant. In his early manhood, he was taken prisoner as a soldier and later felt God's call during an illness. In 1208 he left his father's home, gave away all his possessions, and embarked on a life of simplicity. He washed lepers, rebuilt churches, and preached the gospel; others joined him, and they preached together in the streets, worked, and begged. They ministered to the poor, slept where they could, and encouraged each other. Various miracles are reported of Francis, including the healing of lepers, the taming of animals, and the so-called stigmata, which are claimed to imitate the wounds in Christ's hands, feet, and side.

POPES

Among the popes of the earlier Middle Ages, two men stand out as strong leaders.

Leo I (c. 400–461) was archdeacon of the Roman church when elected pope in 440. He exemplified strong leadership, and promoted his own authority. He became involved in disputes and problems arising in remote areas and felt that he was Peter's successor in holding the "keys of the kingdom" and in being the primary leader of the entire church. His prestige was enhanced in particular by his efforts to save the city of Rome from the invasion of Attila the Hun. He personally visited the battle camps of Attila in order to convince him to spare Rome. His formula concerning Jesus' nature was accepted as the standard doctrine during the heated controversies of the time.

Gregory I (540–604) was born into a senatorial Roman family. He was educated for government and was appointed imperial prefect. He renounced the world, however, turned his father's palace into a cloister, and became a monk. In 590, when elected pope by the clergy, senate, and people, he reluctantly accepted but continued to live an ascetic life. He is known especially as a theologian and pastor, and as a defender of the primacy of the Roman bishop. Although constantly in poor health, he preached, wrote, administered, and started missionary works. He introduced the "Gregorian" chants and made enormous contributions to later medieval theology. Both Protestants and Catholics describe him in favorable terms.

The later Middle Ages was the time of greatest power and authority of the pope, to the extent that he became the virtual ruler of the Western world. The popes were generally stronger than the emperors because of the claim that they were God's personal representatives on earth. They led the Crusades, owned lands and armies, exercised temporal control over their subjects, supported or excommunicated emperors, and ruled the universities and monasteries. Two of the popes of this period stand out for their strength and influence.

Hildebrand, who became Gregory VII (c. 1020–1085), was a Benedictine monk. He worked for the pope as the "power behind the throne" from about 1050 to 1073; he was in charge of finances for the popes Leo IX and Nicholas II. In 1059 he headed the change in the method of selecting the pope from the popular vote to a vote of the College of Cardinals, composed of Roman clergy (partly in order to keep emperors from influencing elections). He was elected pope in 1073 and dedicated himself to church reform. He probably claimed papal authority over the other bishops and advocated the theory of the perpetual inerrancy of the Roman church.[1] He exercised his authority over the emperor Henry IV by making him stand outside barefoot in the snow for three days before allowing him full standing in the church. (Henry got his revenge later, as he drove Gregory into exile.)

Innocent III (1161–1216), elected pope in 1198, was probably the strongest pope of all time. He considered his rule a theocracy (or government by God), with himself as the "vicar of God." He was an educated man, having studied theology in Paris and law in Bologna. He successfully opposed Philip of France and John of England, gave Frederick the emperor's crown in 1212, initiated the Fourth Crusade, and ratified the Franciscan and Dominican orders.

SCHOLARS

The beginnings of the modern university system began during the early medieval period. Two scholars stand out for our consideration.

Bede (673–735) was born in England and lived in monasteries from the age of seven. He learned to live the life of a monk, emphasizing education as well as the ascetic life. He knew Latin, Greek, and Hebrew and is considered to be the most learned man of his day. He is further noted for his gentle and humble nature, and so is called the Venerable Bede. His writings include philosophical works, commentaries on the Bible, sermons, poetry, letters, and biography. His major accomplishment is probably his *Ecclesiastical History of England*, which remains the major source of English history to 800.

Alcuin (c. 732–804), also from England, was known for his scholarship and was master of the school in York. In 781 Charlemagne invited him to be in charge of the palace school. Alcuin accepted and became the emperor's theological adviser and a leader in the educational and cultural renaissance that took place under Charlemagne. He revised the Vulgate translation

---

[1]Earle E. Cairns, *Christianity through the Centuries*, rev. ed. (Grand Rapids: Zondervan, 1967), p. 229.

in 802. His writings include commentaries, books on doctrine, biographies of saints, and works regarding grammar, rhetoric, and dialectic.

The later Middle Ages saw the broadest systematic theology ever attempted. Scholarship was tied to an effort to understand thoroughly the teachings of the Bible within the categories of the day. The "scholastics" took the Scriptures and usually the Fathers (especially Augustine) and, using Aristotle's philosophical categories, attempted to draw out consistent statements in order to form a systematic whole. The medieval universities (e.g., Paris, Oxford, Cambridge) grew from the training of teachers and clerics in theology. Because printing had not yet been invented, books were extremely expensive and had to be copied by hand; the monasteries and universities were places where this task was undertaken. We may note two scholars from this period.

Anselm of Canterbury (1033–1109) is perhaps the father of scholasticism. He became archbishop of Canterbury in 1093 and is known for an argument for the existence of God and for his theory of the atonement. The so-called ontological argument attempts to deduce God's existence from the idea of a perfect being, claiming that there is a connection between this concept and the reality expressed by it. Most scholars consider this argument to be ingenuous but invalid; others have attempted to restate it in more acceptable terms. Anselm's theory of the atonement attempts to explain why Christ had to be sacrificed for us—namely, by affirming together God's justice (which demands payment) and God's love (which provides payment). Anselm is famous for his statement "I believe that I may understand," holding that, in order to know certain things, a certain belief or trust must already be present.

Thomas Aquinas (1225–1274) was the leading theologian of the Western church prior to the Reformation, and his works generally remain the standard of Roman Catholic doctrine. He was born in Italy, spent five years in the monastery Monte Cassino, and then entered the University of Naples. He joined the Dominican order in 1243, although his family was so opposed to it that his brothers kept him under guard for a year. He studied under Albertus Magnus, who predicted that this "silent ox" would become famous throughout the world for his ability in theology. He taught in Paris and other universities.

Thomas's writings include philosophical works (especially commentaries on Aristotle), Bible commentaries, apologetic works (especially to combat Islam), and systematic theology. His major work was *Summa Theologiae,* which is an attempt to present Christian theology as he found it in the Fathers and Scriptures in a clear and orderly form. His method was to state over two thousand articles, giving the positive and negative sides of each proposition with a resolution and reasons for that resolution. Insofar as possible, he concerned himself with answerable questions and refrained from being overly speculative.

DISSENTERS

During the strongest phase of the Roman rule, various bodies were formed that diverged from the standards of Roman authority. Two of the most prominent groups that dissented from the established church were the Cathari and the Waldenses. Various inquisitions were set up to stop the spread of heresy, and the Dominicans were prominent in discovering and punishing those who held to heretical views.

The Cathari (the "pure") numbered possibly four million, distributed between over seventy sects. One of the largest was the Albigenses, named for their location, in Albi (southern France). Their doctrine was decidedly gnostic (see chapter 6) in its contrast of matter and spirit. Satan was considered to be the creator of the world and of matter. Being convinced that matter is evil, they opposed having children, the doctrine of the resurrection, eating meat, and sacraments of the Eucharist and baptism; they taught that the "saved" were the elite among them and that the established church was the church of the antichrist. They were persecuted by the Roman church.

The Waldenses were more evangelical in nature and held to a more biblical view. They were named for Peter Waldo, who began a group in 1176 and encouraged lay preaching, translation of the Bible in the vernacular, the view of the Bible as the final authority in all questions of faith, and a life of simplicity. The Waldenses were called the Poor Men of Lyons, the Poor of Christ, or simply Brethren. They chose their own clergy and separated themselves from the established church, yet did not oppose the church as vigorously as did the Cathari. They made some attempts to reform the existing order, yet also kept largely to themselves. Considered illiterate and ignorant by the scholastics, the Waldenses were influential in the sixteenth century in the Reformation. Descendants of this group still exist in Italy.

CHAPTER 9
The Reformation

As events from the early fourteenth century continued to develop, a growing sense that the Roman church needed purging was strongly felt. Attempts were made to reform the church from within, but as these failed, separatist movements evolved that eventually led to the Protestant Reformation.

EARLY REFORMERS

Existing groups, such as the Waldenses in Italy, had continued underground resistance to the church authority and promoted popular support for Reformation views. John Wycliffe (c. 1330–1384) was perhaps the first reformer of this period. He studied and taught at Oxford. In 1376 he wrote *Of Civil Dominion*, in which he protested the church's abuse of property ownership, advocating that the property be taken away from the church. In 1382 in his preaching and writing he developed the views of the priesthood of believers, that Christ—not the pope—is the head of the church, that the Bible is the final authority of all believers. He was the first to translate the New Testament into English (from the Latin text). His views caused his censure, and he was forced to retire to his rectory. He founded the Lollards, a group that continued his preaching and reforming work.

Wycliffe's ideas reached Bohemia, and Jan Hus (c. 1372–1415), rector of the University of Prague, began preaching reform along similar lines. Hus was called to the Council of Constance, with the emperor's guarantee of safety, in order to examine his views. He was condemned and burned at the stake. The Moravian church grew out of his following. Hus influenced both Martin Luther (who, when

405

accused of being a follower of Hus, replied that Hus's views were pretty good!) and John Wesley (through the Moravian brethren).

REFORM ACCOMPLISHED

At least four major issues fueled the Reformation and were held jointly by each Protestant group. First, the Reformers rejected the sacerdotal system. The Roman Catholic church was a hierarchical organization, headed by the bishop of Rome, the pope. The system asserted that only duly-authorized members could dispense God's grace or withhold it, through the sacraments. They were the mediators between God and man. The Reformers protested that the church is not an organization and that all members are authorized to relate directly to God through faith. Grace was not to be dispensed or withheld by men.

Second, the Reformers disputed the authority for truth. The church asserted that since it is God's organization, then the head of the church is God's representative on earth and, as such, cannot be wrong in matters of Christian truth. The Bible is interpreted by the tradition of the church, which includes the ruling pope. The Reformers taught instead that the Bible *judges* tradition, church, and the pope, and that it should be interpreted by each believer according to objective standards and the guidance of the Holy Spirit.

Third, the spiritual life of the Roman clergy drew criticism. Leaders in the church were greedy, immoral, and unbelieving. The Reformers protested their immoral actions and called for a personal reformation.

Finally, the Reformers rejected various specific practices. In their view, the errors included the celibacy of the clergy, prayers to saints and to Mary, indulgences, the confessional, the doctrine of purgatory, and the doctrine and practice of the Eucharist.

In reviewing the Reformation, we may conveniently start with Martin Luther, whose act of posting ninety-five theses on the church door of the University of Wittenberg in 1517 is usually considered the beginning of the whole movement.

MARTIN LUTHER (1483–1546)

After attending a Brethren of the Common Life school as a teenager, Luther studied Aristotle and the scholastics at the University of Erfurt, receiving his master's degree in 1505. The next year, following a vow he made during a violent thunderstorm, Luther joined an Augustinian monastery. He received his doctorate in 1511 and taught at the University of Wittenberg, lecturing in German on various books of the Bible. In anguish of soul over his sins, Luther learned of the principle of justification by faith from Romans 1:17. He subsequently made justification by faith, along with Scripture, the ultimate authorities throughout his life.

In 1517 Pope Leo and Archbishop Albert of Mainz made a deal to raise money by selling indulgences, half to go to Albert, and half to the pope, who would use it to rebuild St. Peter's and pay off debts. These spiritual favors included forgiveness of sins, changing of vows, and less time in purgatory. Luther was horrified at this hawking of blessings and resolved to debate the issue in public. Following the custom of the day, he posted his debating points on the door at the church of the university. He wanted to defend the position that the pope had no power to forgive sins and remarked that the logical conclusion of the doctrine of papal control over purgatory was that the pope would do for money what he refused to do for love.

Luther was questioned the following year by Cardinal Cajetan in Augsburg but refused to recant until shown that he was in error by Scripture. He continued the issue by writing pamphlets opposing the doctrine that the pope is the final interpreter of Scripture and opposing the sacerdotal principle that priests can dispense or withhold grace. In 1520 Leo issued the decree resulting in Luther's excommunication, which Luther publicly burned. He was summoned by the emperor Charles V to Worms, where he was again questioned. He again refused to recant unless shown in error by Scripture.

Luther was then taken captive by his friends and transported to Wartburg Castle to protect his life. He lived there until 1522 disguised as a knight. In exile, Luther was able to translate the New Testament into German, using Erasmus's Greek text. He finished the entire Bible in 1534. He also published tracts and pamphlets.

Philip Melanchthon (1497–1560) had studied in Heidelberg and Tubingen and taught Greek at the University of Wittenburg. During Luther's exile, he published *Loci Communes*, the first treatise on Reformation theology. He became the Reformation's scholar and Luther's major support.

In Augsburg, in 1530, Melanchthon drew up a statement of faith, designed to give a clear exposition of the reformers' position, while minimizing the differences with the Roman church insofar as possible. In 1555, nine years after Luther's death, the Peace of Augsburg gave each territorial ruler or prince the right to decide the religious position of his territory.

HULDRYCH ZWINGLI (1484–1531)

During the Reformation in Germany, a similar movement was emerging in Switzerland. There, Huldrych Zwingli became engaged in opposing indulgences and other abuses at about the time Luther was posting his ninety-five theses. Zwingli had been trained for the priesthood at the University of Basel, where he studied humanism, and was an admirer of Erasmus. While a pastor at Einsiedeln in 1516, he began writing and preaching reformation. His preaching took the form of commentaries on Scripture, which became very popular. In 1523 Zwingli was called to public debate against all comers by the Zurich city rulers. In preparation for this debate, Zwingli drew up sixty-seven articles, which defended the right to preach without authorization, taught that the church is all true believers, defined the Eucharist not as a sacrifice but as a memorial, rejected the mediation of priests and saints, and upheld the right of clergy to marry. Zwingli won this debate, and by 1525 Zurich had become officially Protestant.

In 1527 the Swiss evangelical churches organized with Zwingli as their leader. He translated the Bible into the vernacular. In 1529 war between Protestants and Catholics began, and the sides were so evenly divided that it was impossible for anyone to gain a decisive advantage. Zwingli was killed in battle as he led the troops. Eventually, an agreement was reached in which each territory could choose for itself whether it would be Catholic or Protestant.

JOHN CALVIN (1509–1564)

As Zwingli was the leader of the German Swiss, Calvin became the leader and theologian for the French Swiss. Calvin was born in France and attended the University of Paris. He studied humanism, and later law, classics, and theology. In 1532–1533 he was converted to Protestant Christianity and left France for Basel, Switzerland. At the age of twenty-six he wrote *The Institutes of the Christian Religion*, which became his most famous work. Its immediate purpose was to defend Protestants in France, but it lasted as the foremost theological work of the Calvinist movement. In it, the doctrines of salvation are put forth in classic Calvinist terms: it asserts unconditional election (i.e., those who are saved are not saved because of any condition they have fulfilled), limited atonement (Christ died only for those who are saved and not for those who are not saved), and irresistible grace (God's choosing of someone for salvation cannot be rejected).

In Geneva in 1535, a general assembly had adopted Protestant ideas. Calvin came into contact with Farel, a leader of the Reformation movement there, and in 1536 agreed to join the cause. He helped Farel draw up city statutes favoring Protestant views and began setting up a virtual theocracy. He was exiled from 1538 to 1541 by the liberal party but returned when this party failed in its objectives and was overturned. From then on, Calvin was the leader of a church-state system, wherein the secular authorities were employed to enforce reformed practices and to carry out punishments of exile and even death.

ANABAPTISTS

Elements of the Reformation that leaned to more radical views were generally classified together as Anabaptists, though they were more loosely organized than the Lutherans and Reformed. They were the spiritual forerunners of the Baptists. The founder of the Anabaptists was Konrad Grebel (1498–1526), who worked for a time with Zwingli and then in 1525 left to teach on his own. Grebel's followers were virtually eliminated from Switzerland by 1535.

Thomas Munster (d. 1525) in Germany, who led the semi-organized peasants in fighting, and Menno Simons (1496–1561), of the Holland "brethren" and founder of the Mennonites, were other prominent Anabaptists.

The Anabaptists encompassed a wide variety of religious opinion and practice. They generally agreed, however, in seeking to return to basic Christianity, disdaining the growth of the institutionalized church. They repudiated any distinction between the clergy and the laity, along with the traditional methods of worship. The Anabaptists insisted that the true church were those who believed in Jesus Christ, not any building or institution; therefore they detested the idea of a state church. They derived their name from their view that infant baptism was unscriptural and that only believers were to be baptized. Some adults, having been baptized as infants, were baptized *again* when they became believers (hence the name "Anabaptist"—those baptized again). The Anabaptists were persecuted almost universally by the state church.

ENGLAND
The break with the Roman Catholic church in England was more of a break with the authority of Rome than an immediate change in doctrine or practice. Three important influences led the way to this break: *intellectual*—the universities stressed humanism and independence of thought; *religious*—Luther and other Reformers were widely read at Oxford and other universities, and the Lollards and other groups were already supporting reform; and *political*—the king of England, Henry VIII (reigned 1509–1547), desired to transfer power over English affairs from the papacy to himself.

Henry VIII was denied a divorce from his wife, Catherine, by Rome but was accommodated by the English clergy. Parliament supported his claim to religious authority by banning appeals to Rome from English courts and declaring Henry head of the church in the Act of Supremacy in 1534. Monasteries were closed, and the lands divided between the king and the nobles. Many of the Roman Catholic doctrines were in fact kept at this time, including transubstantiation, celibacy of clergy, communion in one kind, and confession.

From this time, England swung from Protestant to Catholic and back again, according to the allegiances of the rulers. Edward VI continued in Reformation doctrine as well as authority and instituted a Protestant realm. Mary, his successor, reestablished Roman Catholic rule and practice. Following her, Elizabeth took a moderate Protestant course.

A reforming party founded within the Anglican church in 1568 was called the Puritans because of their interest in purifying the church. They protested the "rags of popery" found within the established church and emphasized a return to the Bible and simple living. Thomas Cartwright (1535–1603) was an early leader of the Presbyterian groups, as was Henry Jacob (1563–1624) of the Congregationalists. Both groups advocated a state church along Reformation lines. In an English civil war, 1641–1649, the king was overthrown and executed, and Oliver Cromwell, a Puritan leader, became the virtual dictator of the English "Commonwealth." By 1660 the nation returned to the Anglican form again.

COUNTER-REFORMATION

The Roman Catholic church responded to these reform movements by actions known generally as the Counter-Reformation. Catholic leaders essentially reaffirmed the authority of the pope and solidified the sacerdotal system, while attempting to correct abuses within it. Pope Paul III (reigned 1534–1549) was the most influential pope for internal reform, being largely responsible for the creation of the Jesuit order, the Council of Trent (organized to correct abuses and define doctrine), and the renewal of the inquisition methods of the Middle Ages.

The most famous religious order created at this time was the Society of Jesus, or Jesuits, initiated by a Spanish soldier, Ignatius Loyola (1491–1556). Loyola was severely wounded in battle and during his convalescence occupied himself with reading religious literature, especially the life of Christ and the lives of saints. He was so moved that he resolved to dedicate his life to God and the Roman Catholic church. First he visited Israel in 1523 and then returned to Spain. In order to prepare himself for his envisioned ministry, he studied at the University of Paris. He wrote a book entitled *Spiritual Exercises,* which included meditations on sin, the life of Christ, and other themes intended to deepen the spiritual life. He introduced these exercises to others and gathered a group of six friends together for the purposes of starting an order. Pope Paul III approved this order in 1540. Along with the usual vows of poverty, chastity, and obedience, the Jesuits took a vow of total allegiance to the pope as head. The purpose of the order was to train men thoroughly for teaching, evangelism, and refuting heresy.

The Council of Trent met from 1545 to 1563 in three long sessions under various popes. Paul III appointed a commission to investigate and report on abuses. Immorality of various forms was discovered throughout the clergy, and many of the troubles were found to be the faults of former popes. The council decreed that the canon included the Old Testament, the New Testament, and the Apocrypha, and it placed church tradition roughly on a par with Scripture. The council established justification by faith and works and condemned predestination. It reaffirmed the seven sacraments as well as various doctrines objectionable to the Reformers, such as transubstantiation and purgatory. Finally, it established various rules designed to eliminate abuses.

In 1542 Paul III began an official inquisition, especially in Spain, to pursue and eliminate heresy. The accused were presumed guilty until their innocence was firmly established. Torture was used to extract confessions, and death was often the penalty for serious heresy. A list of books that were prohibited (the Index) was established in 1559 in order to suppress Protestant and Reformed ideas.

PIETISM

A movement that developed in Germany in the seventeenth century as a reaction to the somewhat rigid orthodoxy of Lutheranism was known as Pietism. Though based on the Scriptures, scholastic Lutheranism assumed the form of a fixed dogmatic interpretation—rigid, exact, and demanding intellectual conformity. Emphasis was laid on pure doctrine and the sacraments as constituting the sufficient elements of the Christian life. Some evidences of deeper piety existed, of which the hymns of the age are ample proof, and doubtless many individual examples of real and inward religious life were to be found, but the general tendency was a religious life that was external and dogmatic.

In reaction against this rigid doctrinal approach, Pietism stressed Christian experience, the need for the common person to take a role in his or her Christian life, and the value of an ascetic life-style. The man most responsible for the spread of Pietism was Philipp Spener (1635–1705). Spener, a Lutheran pastor in Germany, organized home meetings for Bible study and prayer. His desire for a deeper, more meaningful Christian life was put forth in his book *Pia Desideria* (Pious Desires, 1675), which had great influence upon reform movements on the Continent.

One of the fruits of the Pietistic movement was the revitalization of a group known as the Moravian Brethren. The leader of the Moravians was Count von Zinzendorf (1700–1760). Even through his early life Zinzendorf felt a deep heartfelt devotion to the Lord. While studying law at Wittenberg, he allowed his property to be used as a refuge for Bohemians who had fled their homes during persecution. They named the place Herrnhut ("the Lord's house"). Zinzendorf eventually became the leader of this group, causing the rebirth of the Moravian church, a group known for their missionary zeal. Zinzendorf traveled to America and other places to conduct preaching tours. His followers were instrumental in the conversion of John Wesley. It is interesting to see this chain of influence: Wycliffe (through the Lollards) influenced Hus (Bohemian Brethren), who inspired Zinzendorf (Moravians), whose followers aided Wesley's conversion (Methodism).

CHAPTER 10
The Expansion of the Church

The era of the Reformation contains some of the high points in the history of the church. The greed, corruption, and antibiblical practices of the time were met by opposition of the people of God who demanded consistency and purity in the church. The Reformation and its emphasis on Scripture as the sole authority, the doctrine of justification by faith, and the teaching that all believers are priests gave impetus to the modern era of evangelism and missionary expansion.

In this chapter we look at the modern period in church history, dating from approximately 1700 to the present. This period has seen a rise in the diversity of the church as well as an unparalleled development and growth of Christian missions.

PROTESTANT DENOMINATIONS

The Protestant Reformation caused a portion of the church to split from the Roman Catholic church. However, those who rejected the Catholic system were not in total agreement among themselves concerning various matters of belief and church government. While agreeing on the essential doctrines of faith (the Trinity, the deity of Christ, etc.), their differences interfered with their unity, and denominations arose. We consider now three denominations that have had a major effect on church history, especially in America.

LUTHERANISM

After the Reformation the national churches in Germany and the Scandinavian countries took the name "Lutheran," after the great

Martin Luther. Lutheranism came to America in the early seventeenth century. At first the Lutherans met with opposition from the Dutch Reformed church, which sent the first Lutheran minister back to Holland. The Lutherans continued in America but kept a low profile, mostly servicing the German and Scandinavians with Lutheran backgrounds.

The first Lutheran church in America was built in 1638 by Swedes. The Lutheran church began to grow, congregations multiplied, and by 1748 the first Lutheran synod, or collection of local congregations, was organized.

METHODISM

Methodists take their name from a study group that John and Charles Wesley and a few others founded in Oxford in 1729. They were derisively called Methodists because of the methodical way in which they conducted Bible study, prayer, and ministry to the poor. In 1738, John Wesley, while listening to the reading of Luther's preface to his commentary on Romans, had his heart "strangely warmed." He marked this point in his life as the moment of his conversion. He went to Hernnhut in quest of a more mature spiritual life, since he had been favorably influenced by Moravian preachers (especially Peter Bohler).

Invited by George Whitefield to conduct preaching tours in the colonies, John came to America and preached over forty-two thousand sermons and traveled over 250,000 miles. Wesley organized societies for the care of his converts, but did not want to break with the Anglican church. These societies organized into the Methodist church after John's death. One of the major doctrinal differences of Methodism under Wesley was the denial of predestination and the doctrine of limited atonement. Wesley emphasized Christian perfectionism, which he defined as the Holy Spirit sanctifying the willing and obedient believer into a state of sinless motives (although he did not think a believer would never commit an act of sin).

Under John Wesley the religious life of England was transformed. Among his achievements were stopping the gin traffic, establishing the first free medical dispensary, and calling for the abolition of slavery.

Unfortunately, Methodism today has loosened its structure to the point that many Methodist congregations and individuals are far more liberal in belief and practice than either John or Charles Wesley would have considered permissible.

PRESBYTERIANISM

The beginnings of the Presbyterian church go back to England and Scotland during the sixteenth century. Those who became known as Presbyterians arose as Calvinist groups that favored church rule by presbyters (i.e., elders) and representative church courts rather than an episcopate form of church government.

Presbyterianism rose quickly in popularity and by 1800 had become the most influential denomination in New York and New Jersey. The Presbyterian church remained strict in its application of conservative doctrine and practice throughout the nineteenth century, even holding ecclesiastical courts in the 1890s against such liberals as Charles Briggs. However, in the twentieth century the Presbyterians experienced internal rifts and turmoil over liberal issues, and some Presbyterians formed churches independent of the Presbyterian church as a whole. A representative conservative split from Presbyterianism is the Orthodox Presbyterian church, developed from the great Bible scholar J. Gresham Machen and his followers. Presbyterianism today is tolerant enough that it allows within its ranks conservative as well as liberal congregations and individuals.

ROMAN CATHOLICISM

The rise of the Reformation and the establishment of Protestantism as a permanent church force in the Western world did not stop the growth and spread of Roman Catholicism throughout the world. The first expeditions to the New World for conquest and colonization were from Roman Catholic countries such as Spain, Portugal, and France. The first church in America was Roman Catholic.

By 1750 the French controlled the territories of the great Northwest, while Spain ruled the Southwest. The Catholic church was at its height of power in America. Only a small number of English and northern European Protestants populated the East Coast. The balance of power switched to the Protestants, however, with the British conquest of Canada and the statehood of Texas and Louisiana.

417

Although since that time Roman Catholicism has not wielded as great a power in the United States, its influence is still great. The Roman Catholic church owns considerable property throughout the country, and there are many local communities with large Catholic populations. In Mexico, Central America, and South America, Roman Catholicism is in almost complete control, except for small challenges by atheistic Marxists and some indigenous Indian religions.

The Second Vatican Council, convened by Pope John XXIII to reevaluate church policy in every area, met from 1962 to 1965. Vatican II opened new dialogue between Catholics and Protestants, allowing for greater understanding and mutual aid. Catholic worship was revamped in an effort to make it more relevant and meaningful to modern congregations. Encouragement of Bible reading and Bible study were two positive recommendations of Vatican II.

Another force relaxing tensions between Catholics and Protestants in America has been the recent Catholic charismatic movement. When it first gained attention in 1967, the Catholic leadership in America largely condemned it, fearing a wholesale abandonment of the church by "holy-roller" Catholics. However, the Catholic charismatics, so designated by their interest in and use of the *charismata*, or supernatural gifts of the Holy Spirit, by and large stayed loyal to their church, integrating their experiences with Catholic belief. However, sharing common spiritual experiences with Protestant charismatics helped both groups appreciate each other.

Today Roman Catholicism enjoys the best image it has had in centuries, under the leadership of John Paul II, the popular Polish pope. John Paul II, who was a popular and faithful priest in Communist-ruled Poland for years before his election as pope, has traveled more miles around the world than any pope in history. He has spoken out in support of Christians who are persecuted under harsh regimes all over the world and provided spiritual leadership to his countrymen in their long struggle against Communism.

From the perspective of thirteen or fourteen hundred years of Roman Catholicism, the changes of the twentieth century are slight. Vatican II did breathe fresh air into the stale halls of Catholic theology, worship, and ecclesiology, but the basic structure, hierarchy, and dogma of the church remain the same. In Romanism, as in Eastern Orthodoxy, tradition is the vehicle for truth. In such an environment, tradition cannot be separated from the Scriptures, which were, after all, preserved through tradition. Evangelicals can rejoice at the evangelical movement within the Catholic church and still can pray for a mass movement of Catholicism toward purer biblical faith.

MISSIONARIES

This era in church history has seen a tremendous increase in missionary work. As new areas of settlement were opened up and new cultures were discovered, Christian missionaries brought the good news of the gospel to new settlers and natives alike. Around the world, men and women have given their lives to evangelize the whole earth. We mention only six of them here.

David Brainerd (1718–1747) was a missionary to North American Indians. In his short life he accomplished more than most people do in seventy years. Expelled from Yale for accusing one of his teachers of having "no more grace than a chair," Brainerd was appointed as a missionary to American Indians by the Scottish Society for the Propagation of Christian Knowledge. From 1743 to 1746 he worked with Indians in New York, Pennsylvania, and New Jersey, making many hundreds of converts. He died from complications of tuberculosis. Brainerd kept a diary of his work that Jonathan Edwards published. Brainerd's own missionary work, combined with the missionary work accomplished by those who were inspired by his journal, made a deep impact on American missions that is felt even today.

William Carey (1761–1834) was born to a poor English family. Self-educated, he was able to read the Bible in six different languages while still a teenager. This early diligence characterized his entire life. Carey joined a Baptist church and began preaching while still an apprentice. Inspired by such missionaries as David Brainerd, Carey helped organize the English Baptist Missionary Society in 1792. During his first years on the mission field, Carey suffered many hardships, all made worthwhile by the baptism of his first converts. Carey eventually translated the Bible into some twenty-six dialects and held the post of professor of Oriental languages at the University of Calcutta for thirty years. His diligent work and commitment to lost souls characterized his work and prepared India for further missionary work. Carey became known as the Father of Modern Missions.

Robert Morrison (1782–1834), born in England, was the first Protestant missionary to China. Morrison studied medicine, astronomy, and Chinese in London before making his first journey. He was sent to China in 1807 by the London Missionary Society. Upon arrival in China, Morrison was rarely seen publicly. He spent most of his time either studying or praying alone in his cellar apartment, or evangelizing the Chinese individually. In 1809 the British East India Company hired him as an interpreter. His contributions to the people of China then became mostly literary ones. He wrote a Chinese grammar, gospel tracts, and hymnbooks. Morrison's work laid the foundation for later Chinese missionary work. He gave twenty-seven years of his life to China, and although his converts numbered only four, later missionary work would have been next to impossible without his carefully laid literary foundation.

Robert Moffat (1795–1883), a Scotsman, had little formal education but made a lasting impact as a pioneering missionary. He arrived in Capetown, South Africa, in 1817, from where he preached the gospel to several cannibalistic tribes. He and his wife established a mission at Kuruman in Bechuanaland and later a mission station at Inyati. From 1839 to 1843 the Moffats crusaded in England, preaching to recruit new missionaries and to raise new missionary funds to bring the gospel to the lost of Africa. Aside from their own direct contributions to African evangelism and their inspiration to later missionaries, they were also noted for being the inspiration to Africa's most important missionary, David Livingstone.

David Livingstone (1813–1873), also Scottish, was converted at an early age and felt a call to the mission field. He prepared by studying theology and medicine. Serving with the London Missionary Society, Livingstone began his missionary work among the natives of South Africa. However, he soon ventured northward into uncharted territory, preaching wherever there were people to listen. From 1851 to 1856 he made a taxing walk east to west all the way across the continent of Africa, a prime motive for which was to protest the slave trade. He died in 1877, having preached the gospel in more uncharted areas in Africa than anyone else. His ground-breaking work inspired others to mission work in Africa.

Hudson Taylor (1832–1905) first traveled to China under the direction of the China Evangelization Society. Later he worked independently and then formed his own China Inland Mission. During a five-year hiatus in England, Taylor translated the New Testament into the Ningpo dialect. Taylor returned to China in 1866 with his wife and sixteen other missionaries. At his death, some 205 mission stations had been established, 849 Christian missionaries worked for CIM, and 125,000 Chinese had become Christians. Taylor's work revolutionized Chinese religious life.

PREACHERS

The contemporary Christian church has witnessed a number of strong believers who have been used by God in their leadership positions to affect the church and the world positively for Jesus Christ. We look briefly at six of the men who have shaped American Christianity into what it is today.

Jonathan Edwards (1703–1758) was one of America's greatest theologians. Born in Connecticut, Edwards entered Yale at the age of thirteen. He graduated four years later but stayed for two more years to study theology. He attacked the liberal idea popular at the time that sin was just ignorance. His fiery preaching, which stressed the necessity of repentance and conversion, contributed to the great American revival during the 1730s and 1740s known as the Great Awakening. Colonial religious life was deeply affected by this revival, which left its permanent mark on American churches. Edwards' writing was at its best in his still-classic "A Treatise concerning Religious Affections."

George Whitefield (1714–1770) was one of the founding members of the Bible study and prayer groups founded by the Wesley brothers that later developed into the Methodist movement. He was also the most prominent voice in the Great Awakening. Whitefield came to America in 1739 and began a traveling-preaching series that forever marked the communities he visited. Some of the crowds that greeted Whitefield at his evangelistic service numbered up to twenty-five thousand. Those who heard Whitefield preach, including Benjamin Franklin, testified that those at the farthest ends of the crowd could hear his voice clearly and distinctly. His message was never more than the simple gospel.

Charles Haddon Spurgeon (1834–1892) was one of the greatest preachers of the nineteenth century. Converted in 1850, Spurgeon began studying the Bible and became convinced that baptism must be by immersion only. He preached his first sermon at age sixteen and quickly gained a reputation as the "boy preacher." At age twenty he assumed the pastorate of the New Park Street Church, Southwark, London. Spurgeon was the most popular preacher of his day, ministering to crowds of up to ten thousand people. He remained a Baptist and a Calvinist throughout his life and wrote voluminously. Spurgeon was an Englishman, and his work served as an inspiration to evangelists and preachers throughout England. Many of them later emigrated to America, carrying Spurgeon's method and style with them.

Dwight L. Moody (1837–1899), during the latter part of the nineteenth century, became the most prominent evangelist in America, perhaps the entire Western world. Moody first came to national attention when he and his singing companion, Ira Sankey, left Chicago for a preaching tour of Great Britain (1873–1875). The tour became an enormous success, and on their return to America, the evangelist discovered that news of the crusades had preceded them. Moody then organized evangelistic crusades throughout America, emphasizing the same simple message of salvation by grace based upon the sacrifice of Jesus Christ. Moody once said, "God has given me a lifeboat and said to me, 'Moody, save all you can.'" Moody understood the importance of lay training in evangelism, and he built a foundation organization, the Moody Bible Institute, that remains today the foremost lay and clerical training center in the United States.

Billy Sunday (1862–1935), a flamboyant former major league baseball player, was the most successful evangelist at the turn of the century. Sunday was saved at a Chicago mission in 1886, and by 1895 he was a full-time preacher at revival services in small Iowa towns. He later sponsored major crusades in the largest cities of America. Sunday's message stressed conversion to Christ, morality, and patriotism.

Billy Graham (b. 1918) has preached the gospel live to more people around the world than anyone else in history—so far, to over one hundred million people. In 1946 Graham joined the newly formed Youth for Christ as an evangelist. He came to national attention that year while conducting a tent revival in Los Angeles. Newspaperman William Randolph Hearst, then owner of the *Los Angeles Times*, publicized Graham's ministry and he soon became a nationally known figure. Graham's message has always been the essentials of the gospel: man is a sinner and needs to repent of his sins and trust Christ as Savior. In his long and distinguished career, Billy Graham has influenced presidents, kings, other leaders, and vast numbers of people in favor of the simple gospel message. His crusades are planned years in advance and cover almost every section of the globe. Billy Graham has been used by God to bring more people to a saving knowledge of Jesus Christ than anyone outside of the New Testament.

CONCLUSION: A FINAL WORD

We have now come to the end of a long journey over almost two thousand years of church history. We began our journey by recounting the life, death, burial, and resurrection of Jesus Christ, the Head of the church. We concluded our journey with the testimony of a man, Billy Graham, who is used by God today to bring the message of salvation all over the world. Over two thousand years, the good news has never changed. What saved people then saves them now.

We have observed and appreciated the roots of the church, its growth, its problems and schisms, and its triumph over worldly persecution and trials. Through all the centuries, those things that glorify our Lord and Savior Jesus Christ have strengthened the church. Those things that instead reflect worldly concerns and selfish preoccupations have harmed the church. Through it all, Christ's promise concerning the church has remained true and firm: "Upon this rock I will build My church; and the gates of Hades shall not overpower it" (Matthew 16:18).

We do not know all that the future holds for the church. However, we do know that as Christians we are members of Christ's body, brothers and sisters in the Lord, fellow travelers on our way to eternal glory. Our daily prayer should include our desire to enjoy and maintain the unity of the Christian church as an expression of our love and devotion to Jesus Christ.

PART FIVE
The End Times

INTRODUCTION

We are living in a day when people switch back and forth from optimism to pessimism about the future. The feeling of hopelessness regarding the future has begun to intensify. With the advent of tactical nuclear weapons and chemical warfare falling into the hands of smaller nations, fear has engulfed the planet.

Dr. Harold Urey, a Nobel Prize-winning scientist, said, "I write this to frighten you. I am a frightened man myself. All the scientists I know are frightened. Frightened for their lives and frightened for your life." World leaders are sensing that we are living in extraordinary times and that world events and change are developing at an accelerated pace. The disintegration of the Communist empire, the swift political and economical change in the Eastern bloc of Europe, the deterioration of our planet's ecosystem, the Gulf War, etc.

Dr. George Wald, another Nobel Prize-winning scientist and former professor at Harvard University, said, "I think human life is threatened as never before in the history of this planet. Not just by one peril, but by many. They are all working together coming to a head about the same time. And the times lie very close to the year 2000. I am one of those scientists who find it hard to see how the human race is to bring itself much past the year 2000."

Dr. Jacques Monod, the molecular biologist from Paris, France, the author of *Chance and Necessity,* said: "In my opinion the future of mankind is going to be decided within the next two generations. There are absolutely two requisites that must be met to save humanity. We must aim at a stable state society and the destruction of nuclear stockpiles. Otherwise, I don't see how we can survive much later than 2050."

After studying the economic, political, military and population trends, former President Valery Giscard of France observed:

"The present world crisis . . . is not just a passing perturbation but in reality represents a permanent change. If we examine the major graphic curves that are drawn for the future by the phenomena of our times, you see that all of these curves lead to catastrophe."

One of the phenomena that is causing concern is the population explosion. In a Washington, D.C., office building, the Environmental Fund has placed a "population clock." It is a digital clock that records the growth of the world's population. The last digit moves endlessly at a speed recording almost three individuals being added to the world growth every second, 172 a minute, and 10,300 every hour.

If you are willing to watch for just a day, you will see that there are approximately one-quarter of a million more people on the face of the earth (equalling the population of Dayton, Ohio). This will add up to 90 million a year (the size of West Germany is only 73 million). At the present rate of growth, 2 billion more people will inhabit the earth within nineteen years.

Political scientist Charles E. Lindblom in his book *Politics and Markets* reflects the fears of many today when he writes, "Relentlessly accumulating evidence suggests that human life on the planet is headed for a catastrophe."

I was lecturing to the faculty of law at the University of Mexico in Mexico City. A professor said to me, "You call yourself a Christian?"

"Yes," I said.

"Are you trying to tell me that Christianity and the Scriptures are relevant today?"

"More than you will probably ever believe," I replied.

"Then you tell me, Christian, what do the Jewish and Christian prophets have to say about the Middle East situation? What do they have to say about the possibility of a nuclear confrontation and the future course of humanity?"

After some persuasion by him, I accepted his challenge and examined it. I spent more than a thousand hours in research and study. Three areas uncovered by my research amazed me.

The first was the attack by biblical critics upon biblical prophecy. The book of Daniel, as a major prophetic book of the Old Testament, has become the focal point of the critics! The prophecies in Daniel are detailed and extend even to the end of time of Hebrew history and the destiny of other nations of the world. The accuracy with which these prophecies have been fulfilled demonstrates their divine inspiration. If any credence is given to prophecy, then a God exists who knows the future, and the Bible is inspired by that God.

Another area uncovered by my research into prophecy was the optimism portrayed by the prophets. The Bible clearly tells us that God is in control. There is hope. The world is racing toward a climax. But instead of a disastrous catastrophe, there are those who believe it will be Christ's dynamic return to earth to set up a thousand-year reign of peace.

Looking at the world situation and knowing that God is in control, I am thankful to be alive today. What an opportunity—in a time of frustration, pessimism, and fear—to trust God to use his children in other people's lives—to be a ray of hope, a source of optimism, an instrument of the Holy Spirit to share Christ's love and forgiveness with others.

A third research result that amazed me was the abundance of material written on the subject of prophecy. It is overwhelming. Several thousand books cover the timing of Christ's second coming, the Rapture, the Tribulation, the Millennium, and related subjects. Many of these writings are very reliable and well researched about the "signs of the times" and the chronology of God's prophetic schedule. So much today is focusing on Israel and the Middle East. Israel and old Jerusalem are the central pillars of biblical prophecy. It seems that Daniel depicts Jerusalem as the key to prophecy when in Daniel 9:24 he speaks of the time "decreed for your *people* and your *holy city.*"

What does the Bible say about future events? Are we living in the End Times? Is there a definitive word from God about what is going to happen to cause the future history? I can answer with an emphatic *yes!*

The Bible gives us quite a detailed blueprint of the future. Dr. Paul R. Fink of Liberty University has researched and written a very easy-to-understand outline of God's program for the world, with an emphasis on what will happen to Christian believers as these events unfold.

Although Dr. Fink holds, as I do, to the premillennial view of prophecy, it is vital to have in the forefront of your mind two factors as you read:

First, there are three major views of prophecy held by Christians (see chapter 4, "Other Views about the End Times"). When studying prophecy, it is wise to consider the perspective of Justin Martyr, who observed long ago that many Christians do not agree on prophetic issues: "As I mentioned before, I and many others are of this opinion, and believe that such prophecies will take place in this manner. But, on the other hand, I told you that many who belong to the pure and righteous faith—and are true Christians—think otherwise." Let's not let our diversity regarding our views of prophecy affect our Christian unity.

Second, prophecy was not given to satisfy our curiosity but rather to instill in us godly living. I believe the book of Revelation gives the purpose of biblical prophecy: to know Jesus Christ. The book of Revelation is a revelation of God himself through Christ. If we, as believers, keep our hearts and eyes on Christ as we study biblical prophecy, then we shall come to know him even better.

May the following explanation of Christ's return help all of us to fall more in love with him.

CHAPTER 1
What Does the Future Hold for Believers?

Christians are those who have placed their faith in Jesus Christ as their personal Savior from sin and have come to know him as Lord of their lives. Salvation in Christ is commonly stated in terms of three tenses: salvation past—deliverance from the guilt of sin; salvation present—deliverance from the power of sin; salvation future—deliverance from the presence of sin. But in considering the future, as wonderful as it will be to be delivered from the presence of sin, one might respectfully wonder, "Is that all?" The answer is a resounding "No!" There is much more that lies ahead for believers in Jesus Christ.

Those who believe in the premillenial pretribulation rapture of the church, the view stated here, say that the next event in God's program for believers is the coming of Christ to take them to be forever with himself. Some theologians call this event the Rapture. Paul describes Christ's coming to take his believers to be with himself in two passages: 1 Thessalonians 4:13-18 and 1 Corinthians 15:51-52. John refers to it in 1 John 3:2-3. From these three passages of Scripture, let us ask and seek to answer four questions that will help us to understand the next event in God's program for believers.

WHERE WILL BELIEVERS BE WHEN CHRIST COMES?

For this we say to you by the word of the Lord, that we who are alive, and remain until the coming of the Lord, shall not precede those who have fallen asleep. (1 Thessalonians 4:15)

With these words Paul points out that believers who have died will not miss out on Christ's coming but will precede the believers who are living at the time of Christ's return. The authority for Paul's instruction is "the word of the Lord," which lets us know that what he is telling us is important and not to be treated lightly and that the revelation he has been given was one that was given directly to him. There is no explicit statement in the Gospels that spells out in detail about Christ's coming to take believers to be with himself. His statement in 1 Corinthians 15:51 bears this out as he says, "Behold, I tell you a mystery." In the New Testament, a mystery is not something mysterious. It is the revelation of some truth that had been previously given. Prior to the revelation of a mystery, no one could have had any knowledge or understanding concerning it.

From the verse before us, two facts become clear concerning the next event in God's calendar for believers: (1) Believers will be living when Christ comes to take them to be with himself and (2) believers who have died physically will not miss out on Christ's coming; in fact, they will already have entered the presence of Christ. We know this because the words Paul used that have been translated in the King James Version as "shall not prevent them" are more accurately translated, "we shall by no means precede them."

Clearly Paul believed that he and his Thessalonian readers might well be alive when the Lord returned. He believed that Christ's coming was imminent, that it could take place at any moment. Many times he used statements such as "the time is short" (1 Corinthians 7:20), "the Lord is near" (Philippians 4:5). The truth of the imminency of Christ's return was to bring comfort to their hearts (see 1 Thessalonians 4:18).

WHAT WILL HAPPEN WHEN CHRIST COMES?

> For the Lord Himself will descend from heaven with a shout, with the voice of the archangel, and with the trumpet of God; and the dead in Christ shall rise first. (1 Thessalonians 4:16)

With these words Paul now tells why we know that the living believers will not precede the believers who have already died. Two events will transpire when Christ comes to take believers to be with himself.

432

The first event to transpire when Christ come to take believers will be that Jesus himself will descend from heaven. Looking at the verse more closely, three truths become apparent: (1) It will be Jesus and no one else who will descend from heaven. Later when Jesus returns to the earth to set up his kingdom, he will send his angels out to do the job of separating his elect (Matthew 24:31), but when he comes for the believers of this age, he comes personally. (2) Jesus will be coming from heaven into which he was last seen going. The last time Jesus was seen by the human eye is recorded for us in Acts 1:9-11 as the disciples watched Jesus ascend into heaven. The angel predicted that "this Jesus, who has been taken up from you into heaven, will come in just the same way as you have watched Him go into heaven." (3) Jesus' coming will be accompanied with an appropriate signal. Paul describes the signal that will accompany Christ's return as being "with a shout, with the voice of the archangel, and with the trumpet of God." Paul is not identifying three different signals. We can understand Paul's thought when we realize that this is a triad in which the last two things describe the first. Paul is saying that Christ's return will be accompanied with a shout and that shout will be like the voice of an archangel and like the trumpet of God. The only sound that will be heard will be the shout and when it is heard some will think that an archangel has spoken or sounded God's trumpet. This "shout" is a military term that is used of the signal that was sounded to gather the troops together. That's exactly what Jesus will do—he will gather all believers of this age whether living or dead together to take them to heaven.

The second event to transpire when Christ returns will be the resurrection of the bodies of the believing dead to be reunited with their spirits. Paul says that "the dead in Christ shall rise first." The word *first* is the most important word in the statement because as Paul wrote it he put it first. We know that we will not precede the believers who have died prior to Christ's return because the dead in Christ will rise first.

WHAT WILL HAPPEN TO LIVING BELIEVERS WHEN CHRIST RETURNS?

Paul does not answer this question in 1 Thessalonians 4 because his emphasis there is to point out what will happen to those "in Christ" who died physically prior to Christ's return since that was the specific concern of the Thessalonian believers. Believers who have died will not miss out on anything; indeed they will have a part in those events transpiring when Christ returns. Between 1 Thessalonians 4:16 and 17 one should put a notation in the margin of his Bible to see 1 Corinthians 15:50-52. It is there Paul tells us what will happen to believers who are living when Christ returns. From this passage we see four things that will happen to the raptured.

First, they will be immediately glorified. Paul tells us:

> Now I say this, brethren, that flesh and blood cannot inherit the kingdom of God; nor does the perishable inherit the imperishable. Behold, I tell you a mystery; we shall not all sleep, but we shall all be changed, in a moment, in the twinkling of an eye, at the last trumpet; for the trumpet will sound, and the dead will be raised imperishable, and we shall be changed. (1 Corinthians 15:50-52)

Believers need to be glorified when Christ returns because unglorified humanity cannot go into God's presence. A change must take place before mortal physical beings can be equipped for the eternal state.

That change is glorification, by which everything that makes them mortal is removed and they are made immortal. All living believers will be transformed. This fact is proclaimed in the words "but we shall be changed." This verse summarizes the process that will equip the living saints for an eternal existence. Their bodies will be changed so that they will not wear out or decay. They will truly "inherit the kingdom of God." This process is described in three dimensions: (1) As relates to time, it will be "in a moment" (v. 52a). The word Paul uses (atomoi) describes the smallest indivisible unit known in Paul's day. In this context Paul is referring to time and thus refers to the smallest indivisible unit of time. That is how long it will take for God to effect the change in the body of every living believer when Christ returns. (2) As relates to sight, it will be "in the twinkling of an eye" (v. 52b). Paul's expression is used to describe any rapid movement such as the flapping of wings or the twinkling of lights. Again, the emphasis is upon speed. God will change the believers' bodies in the same amount of time it takes the eye to twinkle when it is struck by light. (3) As relates to sound, "at the last trumpet; for the trumpet will sound," (v. 52c). This "last trumpet" is the same trumpet mentioned in 1 Thessalonians 4:16. It is the same time at which God will raise the bodies of all the believing dead. With these three figures, Paul is showing that a lot will happen in a very short period of time. At the same time that every body of the believing dead is raised, every body of living believers will be changed. Only the great God could accomplish such a feat!

Concerning those believing saints who died before Christ's second coming, Paul says, "Behold, I tell you a mystery." Prior to this revelation it had not been revealed what happened to believers who are living at the time the dead were resurrected. From this time on the previously unknown is known. The revelation that Paul was given and declared to the Corinthians points out two things: (1) Some believers will not die physically ("we shall not all sleep"—15:51b). Paul uses the word *sleep* to describe the physical death of believers both in 1 Corinthians 15 and 1 Thessalonians 4. The figure is a beautiful one because when one "sleeps" he does so to take a rest in the full expectancy of being awakened to continue meaningful activity. It is important to note that it is *not* the soul that sleeps; it is the body. When a believer dies, his body is asleep. That's why it has to be buried in a cemetery. Our word *cemetery* comes from two Greek words, *koime* (sleep) and *tere* (a keeping place). Thus a cemetery is a place where the sleeping bodies of believers are kept until the time that Christ returns to awaken those sleeping bodies, glorify them, and reunite them with their souls that upon death went immediately into his presence. The bodies of believers who have died sleep because they will be awakened and God will glorify them and equip them to be perfect for all eternity. The important thing that Paul is revealing to the Corinthians is that at the time that Christ returns there will be some believers living but who will have to undergo a change in order to be able to enter God's presence.

These words describe the two events that will transpire when Christ descends into the heavens at the time of the Rapture. God has two programs: one for believers who have died and one for believers who are living. These are two separate "programs" that

God will "run" when Christ returns. They will be run successively, but together they will be accomplished so quickly that it will appear as if they are done simultaneously. In the smallest possible moment of time, every body of every believer who has believed in Christ from the day of Pentecost until the day that Christ returns will be raised from the graves in which they have been resting. The bodies of those believers who died such violent deaths that they were not able to be buried in the traditional way will also be raised. These resurrected bodies will be immediately glorified. Both of these programs of God will be completed in less time that it takes for an eye to twinkle when it is struck by light! How great our God is! What a glorious future lies ahead for those who have believed in him!

The second experience that living believers will undergo when Christ returns for them is that the living, glorified believers will be reunited with the resurrected believers who have preceded them in being glorified. To learn about this we must return to 1 Thessalonians 4.

Then we who are alive and remain shall be caught up together with them. (1 Thessalonians 4:17a)

In the Latin version of the New Testament this word is translated by the word *rapiemur* from which we get the English word *rapture* to describe the event. In this event believers will be removed from this earth and reunited with the resurrected believers. What a meeting that will be!

The third experience that living believers will undergo when Christ returns for them is that they will meet Jesus personally in the air.

. . . in the clouds to meet the Lord in the air.(1 Thessalonians 4:17b)

This is the second meeting of the universal body of believers known as the church, the body of Christ. The first meeting of this body of believers took place on the day of Pentecost when the church was begun. Since that time the universal church has not met. This will be its second meeting and once it is in session, it will last for all eternity! From the text we learn that this meeting will take place "in the clouds," which is Paul's way of describing our atmospheric heavens. Paul uses a picturesque word to describe this meeting. It is a word used of greeting a newly arrived magistrate. Such meetings usually took place outside of the city walls and then they all returned to the regular abode to continue the formalities. This, then, is a picture of how we will meet the Lord and then later will return to reign with him when he comes to set up his kingdom, but we'll see more about that later.

The fourth experience that living believers will undergo when Christ returns for them is that they will be with Jesus forever.

> . . . and thus we shall always be with the Lord. (1 Thessalonians 4:17c)

With this statement Paul lets us know that this meeting with the Lord will never end. It will be a personal association with resurrected believers and with Christ. This will be the final fulfillment of our Lord's promise in John 14:3, "I will come again, and receive you to Myself; that where I am, there you may be also."

WHAT EFFECT SHOULD CHRIST'S RETURN HAVE ON US TODAY?

Christ's return should comfort our hearts.

> Therefore comfort one another with these words.
> (1 Thessalonians 4:18)

It is to be our habitual practice to comfort one another whenever there is the loss of a loved one. It is true that the death of a loved one brings sadness to us, but we "do not grieve, as do the rest who have no hope" (cf. 4:13b) for we have comfort. Comfort— because we know that our loved ones will not miss out on Christ's coming—they will have precedence and prominence in it. Comfort—because we know that if we should be living when Jesus returns, we will be immediately glorified, caught up into the atmospheric heavens to be reunited with them to meet the

Lord and be forever with him! It is "these words" that Paul has given us that provide the means for this comfort.

Further, Christ's coming causes us to purify our lives.

> Beloved, now we are children of God, and it has not appeared as yet what we shall be. We know that, when He appears, we shall be like Him, because we shall see Him just as He is. And everyone who has this hope fixed on Him purifies himself, just as He is pure. (1 John 3:2-3)

We should purify our lives because of our present position. We are "children of God," and we should bear the image of our heavenly Father, which is absolute purity.

The soon coming event in God's program for believers of this age is to take us from this world and so to be forever with the Lord. Paul says that we know that this is true and certain because of our belief in the death, burial, and resurrection of a Person, Jesus Christ (see 1 Thessalonians 4:14).

CHAPTER 2
What Will Happen to Believers during the Judgment?

We now turn to consider three events in which the believers will participate after Christ comes to take them to be with himself and while judgment is being poured out upon the earth.

The judgment seat of Christ is one subject about which there is much confusion among believers. Most believers know that there is such a thing as the judgment seat of Christ and picture it as some dreadful scene at which all of the sins that they have successfully hidden during life will be revealed. Others view it as a time when unconfessed sins done in life are paid for and punishment meted out. Two passages of Scripture are particularly pertinent for our study.

> For it is written, "As I live, says the Lord, every knee shall bow to Me, and every tongue shall give praise to God." So then each one of us shall give account of himself to God. (Romans 14:11-12)

> For we must all appear before the judgment seat of Christ, that every one may be recompensed for his deeds in the body, according to what he has done, whether good or bad. (2 Corinthians 5:10)

THE TIME OF THE JUDGMENT SEAT OF CHRIST

It is apparent that the judgment seat of Christ must take place after the time that believers are taken to be with Christ because reward follows resurrection. This principle is made clear in Luke 14:14 when Jesus in conflict with the Pharisees encouraged his host to invite the poor, maimed, lame, and blind to his feast. These poor people could not in any way remunerate the host for his expense. Jesus said, "You will be repaid at the resurrection of the righteous." In other words, there is coming a time when all righteous deeds must be recompensed. This time of reward would take place when the just (righteous) are resurrected. That time of reward is the judgment seat of Christ.

When we use the word *judgment* it is generally in a punitive context in which someone who has done something wrong is called to account for his wrong deeds. However, such is not the case at the judgment seat of Christ. Its purpose is not punitive, that is, to punish believers for any sins that they have not previously taken care of. In the Romans 5 and 2 Corinthians 5 passages when Paul uses the terms *we, us, every one,* etc., he is referring to believers. At the judgment seat of Christ there will be only believers present. Unbelievers will appear at the great white throne judgment, which will occur one thousand years later. The subjects of the judgment seat of Christ, then, are only those who have believed in Jesus Christ as their own personal Savior. This is a time when they will appear before their Savior "that each one may be recompensed for his deeds in the body, according to what he has done, whether good or bad" (2 Corinthians 5:10). But more of this later.

THE JUDGE OF THE JUDGMENT—JESUS CHRIST

For we must all appear before the judgment seat of Christ.
... For we shall all stand before the judgment seat of God.
(2 Corinthians 5:10; Romans 14:10)

From these portions of these two verses it is obvious that this judgment will take place before Jesus, the Son of God, into whose hands God the Father has committed this judgment. His presiding at this judgment is a part of his exaltation and to him has been committed the right to manifest divine authority in judgment. The fact that the judge is none other than Jesus Christ assures that the judgment will be objective, thorough, and completely righteous. It is Jesus Christ who will render judgment upon those for whom he has died and belong to him.

There are four bases—two negative and two positive—upon which judgment will be rendered at the judgment seat of Christ. The negative bases of the judgment are: (1) It is not to determine salvation because only believers will be there. Since only believers are there, the basis of this judgment cannot be to determine the salvation of the subjects. That was already determined while the subjects were still living upon earth and received Jesus Christ as their Savior from sin. (2) It is not a judgment or punishment of sin or sins because believers' sins have already been judged. The most common misconception concerning the judgment seat of Christ is that it will be a judgment at which believers will be called into account for sins committed after they were saved, especially for any sins that they failed to confess, whether willfully or out of ignorance. This cannot be the case because Christ's payment for sins was once for all and complete. It must be remembered that every believer's sin was future with reference to the time when Christ died. The penalty for every believer's sin past, present, and future was completely paid for by the once-for-all sacrifice of Christ. That means that there is no sin for which the believer must pay anything. Jesus paid it ALL! The judgment seat of Christ will not be an investigation at which believers' "dirty linen" is discovered and laid out to open view.

The positive bases for the judgment seat of Christ are: (1) It is to reveal the essential righteous character of the believers. Rather than to display the secret sins of believers, the judgment seat of Christ will display their righteousness and demonstrate that they rightly belong in heaven to be with Jesus forever.

(2) It is for the purpose of receiving rewards for Christian stewardship. This is Paul's emphasis as he said:

> For we must all appear before the judgment seat of Christ,
> that each one may be recompensed for his deeds in the
> body, according to what he has done, whether good or bad.
> (2 Corinthians 5:10)

The emphasis that is usually drawn from this verse is that the believer will stand before the judgment seat of Christ in great fear as all of his shortcomings and failures in life are rehearsed before everyone in heaven. Then there will be tears of regret as the believer weeps for his failure to share the gospel or do some good work. The judgment seat of Christ, however, is not punitive. Some will receive more rewards than others but there will be no jealousy or envy or regrets over rewards not received. Just to be in heaven forever with Jesus will in itself be reward enough!

THE PURPOSES OF THE JUDGMENT

There are two purposes for the judgment seat of Christ—one for the present and one for the future. Paul reveals to us the purpose of the judgment seat of Christ for the present:

> Therefore knowing the fear of the Lord, we persuade men.
> (2 Corinthians 5:11)

The "fear of the Lord" is not something that is fearful or dreadful. It is the "awe" or "awesomeness" of the Lord. It is a reference to his majesty and omnipotence. Since Jesus Christ is the Judge at the judgment of believers, the only sensible thing for them to do in the present is to seek to persuade all mankind to receive him as their personal Savior. The purpose of the judgment seat of Christ for the present, then, is to motivate us to be faithful in our witness for him.

The purposes of the judgment seat of Christ are twofold. The first purpose is to examine the character and motivations of believers' works. Paul states:

> Each man's work will become evident; for the day will show it, because it is to be revealed with fire; and the fire itself will test the quality of each man's work. If any man's work which he has built upon it remains, he shall receive a reward. If any man's work is burned up, he shall suffer loss; but he himself shall be saved; yet so as through fire.
> (1 Corinthians 3:13-15)

In the immediately preceding verses, Paul points out that there are two categories of material that the believer can use to build upon the foundation "which is laid, which is Jesus Christ:" (cf. 1 Corinthians 3:11). They are perishable materials—"wood, hay, straw"—and imperishable materials—"gold, silver, precious stones." The judgment seat of Christ will determine "of what sort" the believer's works were. It is possible for one to give himself to "hay works," which may seem impressive to some people in this life, but at the judgment seat of Christ they will all disappear. Another may give himself to small "gold nugget" works, which may not be at all impressive to man but will endure for all eternity and bring God's eternal reward.

The second purpose of the judgment seat of Christ is to render one of two decisions: (1) the loss of rewards or (2) to give rewards. Paul describes the loss of rewards as he writes:

> But I buffet my body and make it my slave, lest possibly, after I have preached to others, I myself should be disqualified. (1 Corinthians 9:27)

In this statement Paul is not expressing fear that he might lose his salvation. Rather, he is expressing the possibility of standing before the judgment seat of Christ and being "disapproved." In the whole context of Paul's statement he is talking about receiving rewards and he does not want to come before the Judge and be disapproved for receiving a reward.

There are five rewards or crowns that will be given to believers at the judgment seat of Christ. They are (1) an incorruptible crown (1 Corinthians 9:25), which will be given to those who mastered their fleshly desires, (2) a crown of rejoicing (1 Thessalonians 2:10) for those who were soul winners, (3) a crown of life (James 1:12) for those who endured trials, (4) a crown of righteousness (2 Timothy 4:8) for those who loved his appearing, and (5) a crown of glory (1 Peter 5:4) for those who were willing to feed the flock of God. These crowns (or, diadems, from *diadema*) are rewards associated with honor and dignity and are bestowed upon the victors who overcame the world, the flesh, and the devil. These crowns are not for the eternal glory of the recipient but for the glory of God who gave them. In all likelihood those who receive the crowns, like the twenty-four elders (Revelation 4:4), will throw their crowns at Jesus' feet in an act of worship and adoration.

Husbands, love your wives, just as Christ also loved the church and gave Himself up for her; that He might sanctify her, having cleansed her by the washing of water with the word, that He might present to Himself the church in all her glory, having no spot or wrinkle or any such thing; but that she should be holy and blameless. (Ephesians 5:25-27)

Having demonstrated the righteousness of the believers and given them rewards for faithfulness, believers (the church) will be presented by God the Father as a gift to the Son to be his bride for all eternity. Then the holy, spotless bride will be presented to the Groom who has so recently presided as her Judge. Then comes the next momentous event, believers will participate in the marriage of the lamb.

And I heard, as it were, the voice of a great multitude and as the sound of many waters and as the sound mighty peals of thunder, saying, "Hallelujah! For the Lord our God, the Almighty, reigns. Let us rejoice and be glad and give the glory to Him, for the marriage of the Lamb has come and His bride has made herself ready." And it was given to her to clothe herself in fine linen, bright and clean; for the fine linen is the righteous acts of the saints. And he said to me, "Write, 'Blessed are those who are invited to the marriage supper of the Lamb.'" (Revelation 19:6-9a; see also Matthew 25:1-13; 22:1-14; Luke 12:35-41)

It is necessary to distinguish between two events: (1) the marriage of the Lamb and (2) the marriage supper of the Lamb. The marriage of the Lamb is an event that takes place in heaven following the judgment seat of Christ in which the body of believers (the church) is eternally united to Christ. The marriage supper of the Lamb takes place on earth when Christ returns with his bride to set up his kingdom. The marriage supper of the Lamb is a parabolic symbol of the entire millennial age to which Israel will be invited during the tribulation period. Most of Israel will reject the invitation so they will be cast out. Many, however, will accept the invitation and will be received into the kingdom to participate in the marriage supper of the Lamb. Because of Israel's rejection of the invitation, the invitation will likewise go out to the Gentiles of the tribulation period. The Gentiles who accept the invitation will be included in the millennial kingdom and will participate in the marriage supper of the Lamb. Let us now consider the marriage of the Lamb.

THE TIME OF THE MARRIAGE OF THE LAMB

From the passage quoted above (particularly Revelation 19:7) it is apparent that the marriage of the Lamb takes place between the time that the believers are taken to be with Jesus (the Rapture) and the time that he returns to the earth with his believers (the church) to set up his kingdom. It occurs in heaven during the period of judgment that will be poured out upon the earth. In our present study we have seen that the marriage of the Lamb is preceded by the judgment seat of Christ (Revelation 19:8) and the presentation of the believers to Christ as his pure and holy bride. It occurs before Christ returns to earth to set up his kingdom (the second advent).

THE PLACE OF THE MARRIAGE OF THE LAMB

And the armies which are in heaven, clothed in fine linen, white and clean, were following Him on white horses. (Revelation 19:14)

The marriage of the Lamb must take place in heaven because it follows the judgment seat of Christ. It is from heaven (the air) that Christ comes with his believers (the church) when he returns to earth to set up his kingdom. No other place would be fit for a heavenly people (see Philippians 3:20).

CHAPTER 3
The Millennial Kingdom and Beyond

Now we must ask, What will happen to believers when Jesus Christ comes to the earth to set up his kingdom? In this portion of our study we will examine three events that believers will experience when Jesus Christ returns to the earth to set up his kingdom.

BELIEVERS WILL ACCOMPANY JESUS ON HIS RETURN TO THE EARTH

And I saw heaven opened; and behold, a white horse, and He who sat upon it is called Faithful and True; and in righteousness He judges and wages war. And His eyes are a flame of fire, and upon his head are many diadems; and he has a name written upon Him which no one knows except Himself. And He is clothed with a robe dipped in blood; and His name is called The Word of God. And the armies which are in heaven, clothed in fine linen, white and clean, were following Him on white horses. And from His mouth comes a sharp sword, so that with it He may smite the nations; and He will rule them with a rod of iron; and He treads the wine press of the fierce wrath of God, the Almighty. (Revelation 19:11-15)

When Christ comes to the earth to set up his kingdom he will come as a victorious conqueror. He will be mounted on a white horse (Revelation 19:11) and his true nature—faithful and true—will be recognized (Revelation 19:11). There will be no doubt as to his identity—it is Jesus Christ, the Son of God, coming as a conquering King! He is the only one who is completely faithful: he is the only one who is completely true.

THE DESCRIPTION OF CHRIST

From John's description of Christ as he returns to the earth to set up his kingdom we can learn at least five things. First, "His eyes are a flame of fire" (Revelation 19:12a)—he will see things clearly; nothing will escape his notice. There will be no danger that judgment will be meted out unjustly because he will see things as they truly are. Nor will there be any danger that anything or anyone deserving his judgment will be overlooked, for nothing will escape his notice. For those deserving it, there will be no possibility of their escaping his judgment. Second, "Upon his head are many diadems" (Revelation 19:12b). There will be no question as to his authority to judge, for the crowns upon his head indicate that he is indeed the King of kings and has the authority to execute judgment. His authority will be unquestioned and unchallenged. Third, "He has a name written upon Him which no one knows except Himself" (Revelation 19:12c). John's language indicates that though they know who he is and do not question his authority to judge, still he is indescribable to unbelieving man. Though they recognize their judgment is just, there is no attempt on their part to repent and to become rightly related to him. They do not *know* him. Fourth, "He is clothed with a robe dipped in blood" (Revelation 19:13a). This is John's way of letting us know that when he returns to the earth to set up his kingdom, Jesus will be dressed for judgment. This is his immediate purpose and he is adequately and appropriately dressed for the task that he will conduct with swift efficiency. Fifth, "His name is called The Word of God" (Revelation 19:13b). Though mankind does not recognize him because they are spiritually separated from him, believers know who he is and John identifies him as he had done in his Gospel (cf. John 1:1)—the Word of God. He is the same one who was "in the beginning" and was eternally in fellowship with God the Father and has the essential character of being God himself. He embodies all that God wants to say to man and embodies all there is of God in himself.

448

He is the eternal Son of God who became flesh, died on Calvary's cross for the sins of the world, was received back into heaven, and now is returning to the earth to set up his kingdom.

THE ARMY ACCOMPANYING CHRIST

When Christ returns to the earth to set up his kingdom, he does not come by himself; there is a great army with him. John's description tells us three things about this army. First, these are the "armies which are in heaven" (Revelation 19:14a). These are the ones who were with Christ in heaven during the immediately preceding seven years. In other words, these are the believers who seven years earlier were caught up into heaven to be forever with the Lord. These are the believers of this age who comprise the body of Christ, the church. The word translated as *armies*, while legitimate, gives somewhat of a distorted picture to our minds. It would be better to use the word *hosts*, for John's purpose in using the plural is to emphasize the vast numbers of believers that will comprise this group. They are not a combat army, for Jesus will not need any help to accomplish his purpose of pouring out judgment upon all unbelievers and setting up his kingdom. He is more than equal to the task!

Second, "the armies . . . were following him on white horses" (Revelation 19:14b). The white horse is symbolic of a victorious conqueror. Christ has conquered all and is fittingly portrayed as riding upon a white horse (Revelation 19:11). Believers of this age who comprise this vast host returning with him have likewise been victorious over all because of their relationship to Christ. Their righteousness was established and at last they were completely victorious over Satan and all of his schemes. As they return with Christ to the earth to set up his kingdom, they are properly portrayed as riding upon white horses as victorious conquerors.

Third, they are "clothed in fine linen, white and clean" (Revelation 19:14c). John's language tells us that the righteousness of believers that had been forever established at the judgment seat of Christ is given recognition by the garments that they wear—fine linen, white and clean. Their sins have been paid for by the once-for-all sacrifice of their Savior. They accompany him in this victorious procession as the King comes to claim his kingdom.

Initially, Christ will use "the sharp sword" that John portrays as going "from his mouth" to "smite the nations." He will indeed execute judgment against and defeat the nations of the world that will be drawn up in array against him (more of this later). John's primary emphasis in talking about "the nations" is not to describe political entities but rather individuals collectively comprising the body of unbelievers. Every single unbeliever will be the recipient of God's judgment and will be summarily judged when Christ returns to the earth. When that judgment is executed and his kingdom is set up, Christ will "rule them with a rod of iron." Suffice it to say at this point that when Christ returns to the earth to set up his kingdom every last unbeliever will be put to death. The only ones who will survive that judgment will be those who have embraced Christ in response to the witness of the 144,000 during the tribulation. The believers who survive the tribulation will be the subjects of Christ's millennial reign over his kingdom on this earth. They will produce offspring just as human beings do today. Over these human beings Christ will rule with a rod of iron. To rebel against him will mean instant judgment.

John describes Christ's immediate mission with the words, "He treads the wine press of the fierce wrath of God, the Almighty." This language describes the Battle of Armageddon. It will be so fierce that the battle is described as a winepress. The winepress was a common sight in John's day and can still be seen in many places in Israel even today. The winepress is about the size of a bathtub and is hollowed out of rock. The ripe grapes are dumped into the winepress and then the treaders trample on them to cause the juice to run out of the winepress and into the collection vat underneath. What the treaders do to the grapes is a graphic picture of what Jesus will do to the unbelievers drawn up in array against him. He will trample them in the execution of God's righteous judgment and he will be thorough in his work!

BELIEVERS WILL WITNESS THE BATTLE OF ARMAGEDDON

And then that lawless one will be revealed whom the Lord will slay with the breath of His mouth and bring to an end by the appearance of His coming; that is, the one whose coming is in accord with the activity of Satan, with all power and signs and false wonders. (2 Thessalonians 2:8-9)

"Behold, I am coming like a thief. Blessed is the one who stays awake and keeps his garments, lest he walk about naked and men see his shame." And they gathered them together to the place which in Hebrew is called Har-Magedon. (Revelation 16:15-16)

And from His mouth comes a sharp sword, so that with it He may smite the nations; and He will rule them with a rod of iron; and He treads the wine press of the fierce wrath of God, the Almighty. (Revelation 19:15)

The Battle of Armageddon is commonly mistaken as being a culminative battle ushering in the end of the world. Such, however, is not the case. The Battle of Armageddon does bring the Great Tribulation to an end, but the world will continue at least a thousand years longer while Christ sets up his kingdom and rules and reigns over it. From the passages of Scripture cited, there are at least five facts that we can learn about the Battle of Armageddon.

THE TIME OF THE BATTLE OF ARMAGEDDON
While the Battle of Armageddon culminates at the end of the tribulation period on earth it is set in motion before Christ returns to earth to set up his kingdom. In the middle of the tribulation, having failed in his attempt to bring a successful charge against believers in heaven at the judgment seat of Christ, Satan is cast out of heaven to the earth (Revelation 12:9). He will manifest great wrath upon the earth "knowing he has only a short time" (Revelation 12:12b).

The Battle of Armageddon will transpire at "a place which in Hebrew is called Har-Magedon" (Revelation 16:16). The name literally means "Hill of Megiddo." This is the location of the well-known Plain of Esdraelon, which extends eastward from Mount Carmel to the Jordan Valley and southward down the Jordan valley past Jerusalem to Edom: a distance of more than two hundred miles. This will be the scene where the armies—the greatest military machines ever known to man—will assemble to engage in battle.

THE PARTICIPANTS IN THE BATTLE OF ARMAGEDDON

And they worshiped the dragon, because he gave his authority to the beast; and they worshipped the beast, saying, "Who is like the beast, and who is able to wage war with him?" (Revelation 13:4)

And I saw the beast and the kings of the earth and their armies, assembled to make war against Him who sat upon the horse, and against His army. And the beast was seized, and with him the false prophet who performed the signs in his presence, by which he deceived those who had received the mark of the beast and those who worshiped his image; these two were thrown alive into the lake of fire which burns with brimstone. (Revelation 19:19-20)

The first participant in the Battle of Armageddon is Satan. While he may not take part overtly in the battle, he is there as the motivating power behind the beast. He is the real power behind the throne.

The second participant is the beast. He is generally known as the antichrist (1 John 2:18, 22), but is also known as the king of the west. Dr. J. Dwight Pentecost gives an extensive list of aliases by which the beast is known as he writes:

Many names and titles are given to this individual in the Scriptures. Arthur W. Pink gives a list of names that are applicable to him: The Bloody and Deceitful Man (Psa. 5:6), the Wicked One (Psa. 10:2-4), the Man of the Earth (Psa. 10:18), the Mighty Man (Psa. 52:1), the enemy (Psa. 55:3), the Adversary (Psa. 74:8-10), the Head of Many Countries (Psa. 111:6), the Violent Man (Psa. 140:1), the Assyrian (Isa. 10:5-12), the King of Babylon (Isa. 14:2), the Sun of the Morning (Isa. 14:12), the Spoiler (Isa. 16:4-5; Jer. 6:26), the Nail (Isa. 22:25), the Branch of the Terrible Ones (Isa. 25:5), the Profane Wicked Prince of Israel (Ezek. 21:25-27), the Little Horn (Dan. 7:8), the Prince that shall come (Dan. 9:26), the Vile Person (Dan. 11:21), the Wilful King (Dan 11:36), the Idle Shepherd (Zech. 11:16-17), the Man of Sin

(2 Thess 2:30), the Son of Perdition (2 Thess. 2:3), the Lawless one (2 Thess. 2:8), the Antichrist (1 John 2:22), the Angels of the Bottomless Pit (Rev. 9:11), the Beast (Rev. 11:7; 13:1). To these could be added: the One Coming in His Own Name (John 5:43), the King of Fierce Countenance (Dan. 8:23), the Abomination of Desolation (Matt. 24:15), the Desolator (Dan. 9:27).[1]

This long list of names lets us know that this individual is much more prominent in Scripture than is often thought. He will be participating in the Battle of Armageddon as the king of the west, but his name, the beast, portrays him as God sees him. He is Satan's man. He is Satan's king.

The third participant is the false prophet (Revelation 16:13; 19:20; 20:10). This individual comes on the scene out of the land of Palestine (Revelation 13:11) and thus in all probability is a Jew. He as well as the beast is motivated by Satan (Revelation 13:11) and functions primarily as a spokesman for the beast. This person will compel men to worship him under penalty of death (Revelation 13:15). His religious leadership will receive authentication by his working of signs and miracles, thus "proving" to his people that he is Elijah (Revelation 13:13-14). He together with the beast and Satan constitute an unholy trinity functioning as counterparts of God the Father (Satan), Son (the beast), and Holy Spirit (false prophet).

The fourth participant in the Battle of Armageddon is really a very large group comprised of all the kings of the earth and their armies (Revelation 19:19b).

The fifth participant in the Battle of Armageddon is comprised of Jesus and his armies from heaven (Revelation 19:19b). Jesus is the one who "sat upon the horse," and the believers of the present age constitute "his army" (Revelation 19:19), which has accompanied him on his return from heaven "on white horses" (Revelation 19:14). The army, as such, does not participate in the Battle of Armageddon. Jesus is the only one who enters into the conflict. He does not need the help of his army of believers. They merely witness the mortal combat: Jesus against Satan, the beast,

---

[1]J. Dwight Pentecost, *Things to Come* (Findlay, Ohio: Dunham Publishing Company, 1958), p. 334.

the false prophet, the king of the west, the king of the east, and their armies.

PORTENTS OF THE BATTLE OF ARMAGEDDON

And then the sign of the Son of Man will apppear in the sky, and then all the tribes of the earth will mourn, and they will see the Son of Man coming on the clouds of the sky with power and great glory. (Matthew 24:30)

As the tribulation draws to its climax the armies are drawn up for battle on the Plain of Esdraelon. Before they can do battle with one another "the sign of the Son of Man" appears "in the sky." Exactly what this sign is, is not known. Whatever it is, it is a sign that means that Jesus is about to return to the earth to set up his kingdom. He is about to show that the kingdom is God's and that no one else deserves to reign over the world for even a moment. Instead of entering into battle with each other, the kings of the earth become confederates in the vain attempt to keep Jesus from returning to the earth to set up his kingdom.

THE OUTCOME OF THE BATTLE OF ARMAGEDDON

The first outcome of the Battle of Armageddon will be the destruction of all the armies in that region arrayed first against each other and later against the Lord himself.

And the angel swung his sickle to the earth, and gathered the clusters from the vine of the earth, and threw them into the great wine press of the wrath of God. And the wine press was trodden outside the city, and blood came out from the wine press up to the horse bridles, for a distance of two hundred miles. . . . And the rest were killed with the sword which came from the mouth of Him who sat upon the horse, and all the birds were filled with their flesh. (Revelation 14:19-20; 19:21)

The attempts to keep Jesus from returning to the earth to set up his kingdom will be futile. Jesus will slay them with the "breath of His mouth" (2 Thessalonians 2:8). The mightiest military machines that man can muster are no match for the victorious returning Jesus! The carnage will be so great that the blood will run up to bridles of the horses' mouths for the entire two hundred-mile length of the Plain of Esdraelon—from Mount Carmel down to the city of Petra.

The second outcome of the Battle of Armageddon is that the beast and the false prophet will be cast into the lake of fire.

> And the beast was seized, and with him the false prophet who performed the signs in his presence, by which he deceived those who had received the mark of the beast and those who worshiped his image; these two were thrown alive into the lake of fire which burns with brimstone. (Revelation 19:20)

The beast and the false prophet will not realize their goals to be recognized as God and God's prophet, respectively. Though they have enjoyed a fairly complete success, they will be demonstrated to be the counterfeits that they are and will be cast alive into the lake of fire where later they will be joined by none other than Satan himself for all eternity.

The third outcome of the Battle of Armageddon is that the unbelieving Jews will be purged out of Israel.

> "And it will come about in all the land," declares the Lord, "that two parts in it will be cut off and perish; but the third will be left in it." (Zechariah 13:8)

The words "it will come about" indicate that there is a long period of time between the events of Zechariah 13:7 and 13:8. The events of 13:7 and 13:8 are separated by two thousand (or more) years. The events of 13:7 took place at the time of the death of Jesus while the events of 13:8 will take place in the tribulation period. During the tribulation period two-thirds of the nation Israel's people will die. A good portion of them will be put to death as the beast vents his wrath against them, but the unbelieving Israelites who have embraced the beast as their messiah will be put to death upon the return of Jesus to the earth. Unbelieving Jews will be purged out of the nation Israel.

The fourth outcome of the Battle of Armageddon will be that

believing Jews will be cleansed as a result of the events of the last half of the tribulation and will become subjects of the millennial kingdom.

"And I will bring the third part through the fire, refine them as silver is refined, and test them as gold is tested. They will call on My name, and I will answer; I will say, 'They are My people,' and they will say, 'The Lord is my God.'" (Zechariah 13:9)

This verse tells us that the tribulation period has two purposes from God's viewpoint. The tribulation will destroy the unbelieving two-thirds of Israel and will purify the remaining third. God will bring them to saving faith, keep them safe from the beast's attempts to slay them, and will bring them safely into the kingdom that Jesus will set up when he returns to the earth. This will be the ultimate fulfillment of Jeremiah's New Covenant (Jeremiah 31:31-34).

The fifth outcome of the Battle of Armageddon is that Satan will be bound.

And I saw an angel coming down from heaven, having the key of the abyss and a great chain in his hand. And he laid hold of the dragon, the serpent of old, who is the devil and Satan, and bound him a thousand years, and threw him into the abyss, and shut it and sealed it over him, so that he should not deceive the nations any longer, until the thousand years were completed; after these things he must be released for a short time. (Revelation 20:1-3)

Since his fall Satan has been futilely attempting to show that he is God by frustrating God's eternal plan. His career has enjoyed only partial success. He failed in his attempt to show that the believers of this age do not belong in heaven and was cast out upon the earth. He failed in his attempt to have his man, the beast, recognized as God, and he failed in his attempt to keep Christ from returning to the earth. That Satan is not God and that Jesus is God is amply demonstrated by the fact that God's angel comes with a great chain and binds Satan and casts him into the bottomless pit.

Satan is helpless before God and all of his demons cannot help him. The bottomless pit is not the same as the lake of fire into which the beast and false prophet have been cast and into which Satan will ultimately be cast at the end of Christ's earthly reign. The bottomless pit is a temporary holding place where Satan is isolated so that he cannot corrupt Christ's kingdom. He will be kept there until the very end when he will be released to gather together those who have given only outward obedience to Christ in one final rebellion. That rebellion will be met summarily by Jesus, and Satan will be cast into the lake of fire where the beast and false prophet are (Revelation 20:7-10).

THE NEW EARTH

The establishment of Christ's reign upon the earth is the beginning of a new order, and a number of events will transpire in order to institute that reign. To the human eye these events will transpire simultaneously, but for purposes of our consideration we will consider them logically. The first event that will transpire to institute Christ's reign upon this earth is that believers will take up residence in the heavenly city, New Jerusalem.

> And I saw the holy city, new Jerusalem, coming down out of heaven from God, made ready as a bride adorned for her husband. And I heard a loud voice from the throne, saying, "Behold, the tabernacle of God is among men, and He shall dwell among them, and they shall be His people, and God Himself shall be among them, and He shall wipe away every tear from their eyes; and there shall no longer be any death; there shall no longer be any mourning. or crying, or pain; the first things have passed away." (Revelation 21:2-4)

While there is much diversity in thought among Bible students concerning the order and interpretation of events as they are presented in the book of Revelation, most are agreed that the key to the book is found in Revelation 1:19: "Write therefore the things which you have seen [1:4-18], and the things which are [1:20–3:22], and the things which shall take place after these things [4:1–22:21]."

Following this general layout of the book, it is clear that chapters

457

4–22 deal with things that are future with relation to John's time. John's time and ours are essentially the same; thus the things dealt with in chapters 4–22 are future to us as well. In other words, chapters 4–22 of Revelation deal with God's future program, which will transpire when his present program is finished. To relate it to our study, Revelation 4–22 deals with God's future program which, so far as believers are concerned, will commence when Jesus comes again. If one views chapters 4–22 of Revelation consecutively as one continuous unbroken event, the result is confusion and misunderstanding. However, one must realize that in chapters 4–22 John is transported to heaven and views things from God's perspective (chapters 4–5). In chapters 6–19, John traces and retraces the period of the tribulation from a number of different perspectives. Then in chapters 20–22 John traces and retraces the events following the tribulation from a number of perspectives.

With that as a background, Revelation 21 can be viewed as follows: 21:1 is a quick survey of the ending of the millennium and eternity future. In 21:2–22:5 John focuses on the millennium and his thought is developed as follows: 21:2-8 gives an overview of the millennium and 22:9–22:5 retraces the millennium giving details concerning that period. The first detail that John reveals about the millennium, which is the thousand-year period that Christ will reign upon this earth, is the descent of the heavenly city, New Jerusalem. This will be the abode of the believers of this age during the time of Christ's reign upon this earth. John describes it as follows:

> And one of the seven angels who had the seven bowls full of the seven last plagues, came and spoke with me, saying, "Come here, I shall show you the bride, the wife of the Lamb." And he carried me away in the Spirit to a great and high mountain, and showed me the holy city, Jerusalem, coming down out of heaven from God, having the glory of God. Her brilliance was like a very costly stone, as a stone of crystal-clear jasper. It had a great and high wall, with twelve gates, and at the gates twelve angels; and names were written on them, which are those of the twelve tribes of the sons of Israel. There were three gates on the east and

three gates on the north and three gates on the south and three gates on the west. And the wall of the city had twelve foundation stones, and on them were the twelve names of the twelve apostles of the Lamb. And the one who spoke with me had a gold measuring rod to measure the city, and its gates and its wall. And the city is laid out as a square, and its length is as great as the width; and he measured the city with the rod, fifteen hundred miles; its length and width and height are equal. (Revelation 21:9-16)

During this time believers will witness the removal of the curse from the world.

And the wolf will dwell with the lamb, and the leopard will lie down with the kid, and the calf and the young lion and the fatling together; and a little boy will lead them. Also the cow and the bear will graze; their young will lie down together; and the lion will eat straw like the ox. And the nursing child will play by the hole of the cobra, and the weaned child will put his hand on the viper's den. They will not hurt or destroy in all My holy mountain, for the earth will be full of the knowledge of the Lord as the waters cover the sea. Then it will come about in that day that the nations will resort to the root of Jesse, who will stand as a signal for the peoples; and his resting place will be glorious. (Isaiah 11:6-10)

For I consider that the sufferings of this present time are not worthy to be compared with the glory that is to be revealed to us. For the anxious longing of the creation waits eagerly for the revealing of the sons of God. For the creation was subjected to futility, not of its own will, but because of Him who subjected it, in hope that the creation itself also will be set free from its slavery to corruption into the freedom of the glory of the children of God. (Romans 8:18-21)

When Christ sets up his kingdom on the earth all of the curse that was instituted because of Adam's sin will be removed. Then the words of the familiar Christmas carol will be a reality:

Joy to the world! the Lord is come;
Let earth receive her King;
Let every heart prepare him room,
And heaven and nature sing.

Joy to the earth; the Savior reigns;
Let men their songs employ;
While fields and floods, rocks, hills and plains
Repeat the sounding joy.

No more let sins and sorrows grow,
Nor thorns infest the ground;
He comes to make his blessings flow
Far as the curse is found.

He rules the world with truth and grace,
And makes the nations prove
The glories of his righteousness,
And wonders of his love.

All of the curse inflicted in Genesis 3 will be reversed. Numerically, survivors of the great tribulation will be a relatively small number. These human beings will begin to populate the earth. The birth rate will be prolific and all of the births will be "natural" and without pain. The curse will be lifted from the ground. There will be no more weeds, no more thorns, and no more natural catastrophes to interfere with the earth's vegetation. Death will be the exception rather than the rule. The only ones who will die during the period of Christ's reign upon the earth are those unbelievers who disobey. If they are a hundred years of age at that time they will be mourned because they were only children (Isaiah 65:20). As the result of the curse man was made to perspire. When Christ reigns upon the earth the anatomical changes that unglorified man's body will undergo will not only involve a lengthened life but will also involve no perspiration! The earth will be restored to Edenic conditions so that the entire earth will be like a greenhouse. There will still be seasons, but the whole earth will be semitropical. Animals will lose their ferocity. The lion and the lamb will lie down together—side by side. All of God's animal kingdom will lose its fierceness and even deadly snakes will be harmless.

Then believers will witness the resurrection of those who have believed during Old Testament times and during the tribulation.

> And many of those who sleep in the dust of the ground will awake, these to everlasting life, but the others to disgrace and everlasting contempt. (Daniel 12:2)

> Do not marvel at this; for an hour is coming, in which all who are in the tombs shall hear His voice, and shall come forth; those who did the good deeds to a resurrection of life, those who committed the evil deeds to a resurrection of judgment. (John 5:28-29)

> After these things I looked, and behold, a great multitude, which no one could count, from every nation and all tribes and peoples and tongues, standing before the throne and before the Lamb, clothed in white robes, and palm branches were in their hands. . . . "These are the ones who come out of the great tribulation and they have washed their robes and made them white in the blood of the Lamb." (Revelation 7:9, 14b)

Both Daniel and Jesus mention two resurrections, one to life and one to death. These are separated by the thousand-year reign of Christ upon this earth; the resurrection to life takes place at the beginning of his reign and the resurrection to death takes place at the end of his reign. It is at the resurrection to life that two groups of believers will be resurrected. The first group to be resurrected are all of the believers. Adam will be resurrected and those living in Christ's earthly kingdom will be able to talk with him and ask him all about the details of how it was in the Garden of Eden. Noah will be resurrected and we will be able to ask him questions about how it was when he stood alone against 1.5 billion people of the world of his day. Abraham will be resurrected and will at last realize the nation that he was promised in Genesis 12:2-3 but never received. David will be resurrected and will realize the promises made to him in 2 Samuel and will be declared king of Israel forever! Jeremiah will be resurrected and will witness the national conversion of Israel when every single Israelite will believe in their Messiah as he prophesied (31:31-34). It will be a wonderful day as all of the promises God made to the Old Testament saints are realized. In God's time they and their inheritance will get together (see 1 Peter 1:4-5). They will be an eternal testimony to God's truth.

The second group to be resurrected will be the tribulation saints—those who during the tribulation have believed the gospel of the kingdom (Matthew 24:14) preached by the 144,000 and their converts. For them to believe in that day will be tantamount to signing their death warrants and nearly all of them will be put to death for their faith. When Christ sets up his kingdom, they will be raised from the dead. Their number will be so great that no man will be able to count them (Revelation 7:9). These resurrected tribulation believers will enjoy life as glorified subjects of Christ's kingdom together with the Old Testament believers. They too will be eternal testimonies to God and his great faithfulness.

At this time believers will witness the renovation of our earth and heavens. Because of the devastating judgments of God that were poured out upon the earth and atmospheric heavens, they will need to be restored to Edenic conditions. During the tribulation period, one-third of the sun will be darkened, one-third of the stars will lose their light, wars will have wreaked devastation with the earth, earthquakes will have rearranged the earth's surface. In short, the heavens and earth will have suffered unparalleled devastation. All of this will be undone as the earth and atmospheric heavens are renovated and restored to Edenic conditions.

Using the difference in the time measurement in Daniel 12:7 and 12 it is apparent that it will take seventy-five days from the time that Christ returns to the earth until his kingdom is actually set up officially. From that time through the end of the thousand-year period, things will continue to be the same. Four events will characterize the activities of believers during this age.

First, believers will reign with Christ (Revelation 20:6). Christ as God's King will rule and reign over all the earth. Believers of this age who, prior to their return with Christ to set up his kingdom were married to him, will rule and reign with him as his co-regents. This is what Paul was talking about when he asked the Corinthians, "Do you not know that the saints will judge the world?" (1 Corinthians 6:2a). Paul continued and asked the Corinthians a second question,

"Do you not know that we shall judge angels?" (1 Corinthians 6:3). As a part of our reigning with Christ the angels will also be made subject to us and we will judge them. Paul only states the fact without developing the ramifications of his statements.

Second, believers will reside in the heavenly city, New Jerusalem. This beautiful city is described in Revelation 21:10-27. In addition to the beautiful gold and precious stones of which the city is built, it will not need sun, moon, or stars because its illumination will be provided by the glory of God. Jesus, the Lamb of God, will also make his home in it. The unglorified earthly believers will also be able to visit this beautiful eternal residence of believers of this age. There will be nothing sinful or corrupt there. It will be a perfect environment for a glorified people!

Third, the doors to the heavenly city New Jerusalem will never be shut (Revelation 21:25), which indicates that there will be unlimited access to the city. Believers of this age will travel unrestricted, perhaps even at the speed of light. As beautiful as some places in our earth might be now, they will be even more beautiful then because all the traces of the curse will be removed from the scene. There will be no dead trees or scarred land. No putrid rivers, no pollution of any kind. What a beautiful place this world will be.

Fourth, all believers will be a living testimony for Christ. Believers of this age will be on display all during the time Christ is reigning upon the earth. They will be visible testimony of what God can do for a human sinner who he has saved by his grace and glorified.

The earthly reign of Christ will be such a wonderful time that one might wish that it would last forever. The fact is that it will last forever, but a transition must take place to shift from the medium of time as we know it to timeless eternity. Four events will lower the curtain on Christ's thousand-year reign upon the earth.

First, believers will witness Satan's release from his prison. During the thousand-year reign of Christ upon the earth Satan will be bound in the bottomless pit so that he cannot in anyway interfere with the reign of Christ.

Second, believers will witness Satan's final attempt to defeat God. The believers who survive the great tribulation and enter Christ's kingdom in an unglorified state will have children. Those children will have Adamic natures and will need to believe on Jesus Christ as their personal Savior from sin. Most of them will be regenerated and embrace Jesus Christ, who will visibly be ruling with a rod of iron. Many, however, will only give an outward show of obedience, and some will disobey overtly and summarily be put to death.

Third, believers will witness Satan's final defeat. At the end of Christ's thousand-year reign there will be a great number of unbelievers who must be removed from the scene in order to prepare for eternity future. Satan will be loosed from his prison so that he can come and gather these together for one final assault against God's King in the vain attempt to overthrow him (Revelation 20:7-9a).

Fourth, believers will witness Satan's eternal judgment. Satan and his army will be dealt with summarily. His army will be put to death and he will be taken and cast into the lake of fire into which the beast and false prophet were cast a thousand years earlier (Revelation 20:9b-10). This is his eternal destiny. Never again will he be permitted to challenge God or his program.

The end of the glorious thousand-year reign of Christ on the earth does not exhaust God's plan and program for believers of this age. It goes on for all eternity. Believers will witness the great white throne judgment.

> And I saw a great white throne and Him who sat upon it, from whose presence earth and heaven fled away, and no place was found for them. And I saw the dead, the great and the small, standing before the throne, and books were opened; and another book was opened, which is the book of life; and the dead were judged from the things which were written in the books, according to their deeds. And the sea gave up the dead which were in it, and death and Hades gave up the dead which were in them; and they were judged, every one of them according to their deeds. And death and Hades were thrown into the lake of fire. This is the second death, the lake of fire. And if anyone's name was not found written in the book of life, he was thrown into the lake of fire. (Revelation 20:11-15)

It is at the great white throne judgment that every unbeliever who has ever lived on the face of the earth from Cain on down will be raised from the dead. This is the second resurrection. Daniel called that resurrection the resurrection to "disgrace and everlasting contempt" (Daniel 12:2b) while Jesus called it the "resurrection of judgment" (John 5:29b). All of the unbelieving dead (those who are separated spiritually from God) will stand before the Judge, Jesus Christ. All the record will be there and all the records will be checked. There will be no appeal. They will be judged according to their works in order to determine the severity of their punishment (Luke 12:46-48). There is no doubt of their destiny; it is the lake of fire where they will be in the company of Satan, the beast, and the antichrist forever. This is the second death, which is to say that this is their eternal separation from God and all of his benefits. It should be observed that the book of life is checked not to see if any of their names appear on its pages but to confirm that none of their names appear there. It will not be a pleasant scene, but believers of this age will witness it. Believers will witness Christ's delivering up the kingdom to the Father.

> Then comes the end, when He delivers up the kingdom to the God and Father, when He has abolished all rule and all authority and power. . . . And when all things are subjected to Him, then the Son Himself also will be subjected to the One who subjected all things to Him, that God may be all in all. (1 Corinthians 15:24, 28)

Having defeated Satan, the beast (antichrist), the false prophet, and all unbelievers, and having cast them all into the lake of fire for all eternity, God and his program are finally vindicated. His plan for this world is accomplished. He has demonstrated his ability to rule and reign and keep all things in absolute control for thousand years—there is nothing left to accomplish. At this time, Jesus will deliver the kingdom up to the Father that he might be "all in all." Though Christ has demonstrated his superiority over every being and everything that is not God, the economic differences between the members of the Godhead will continue for eternity. God the Father will be "all in all"—absolutely sovereign. God the Son will be subject to God the Father and God the Holy Spirit will be subject to God the Son and to God the Father. Believers of this age will witness this "change of command" ceremony! Believers will witness the destruction of the present heavens and earth.

But the day of the Lord will come like a thief, in which the heavens will pass away with a roar and the elements will be destroyed with intense heat, and the earth and its works will be burned up. . . . The heavens will be destroyed by burning, and the elements will melt with intense heat! (2 Peter 3:10, 12)

With the defeat of every enemy and with the kingdom's having been delivered over to the Father, God's use for the stage upon which his plan of redemption has been acted out has served its purpose. In itself it is useless and worthy only of destruction. Thus God destroys it. The language that Peter uses to describe this destruction sounds like the language of atomic fission. Since the detonation of the first atomic bomb, man has feared that he would destroy the earth in some atomic war or atomic mishap. Such an accident will never occur. God reserves the right and privilege of destroying the heavens and the earth for himself. He made it and he will destroy it, but believers of this age will have the privilege of witnessing its destruction. One might wonder what will happen to those who have come to believe on Christ during his reign upon the earth and what will happen to the glorified Old Testament and tribulation believers who have inhabited the earth during Christ's reign when this destruction takes place. God does not tell us specifically, but this offers an additional reason for believing that the heavenly city, New Jerusalem, descends out of heaven at the beginning of Christ's reign upon the earth and is the residence of the believers of this age throughout Christ's reign upon the earth. We observed earlier that this is a 1500-mile cube with twelve "floors" 120 miles apart. There is more than enough room for every human being who has ever been born or ever will be born to have ample room. Of course, there will be no unbelievers there, so they will not need to have space reserved for them. During the time that God destroys the present heavens and earth it is probable that all the Old Testament believers, tribulation believers, and millennial believers take up temporary residence in the heavenly city, New Jerusalem, until the new heavens and the new earth appear. Believers of this age will witness all of these momentous events. Believers will witness the coming of the new heavens and earth.

And I saw a new heaven and a new earth; for the first
heaven and the first earth passed away, and there is no
longer any sea. (Revelation 21:1)

But according to His promise we are looking for new
heavens and a new earth, in which righteousness dwells.
(2 Peter 3:13)

The new heavens and the new earth will be the eternal abode of
all of those who have believed God's revelation and become
rightly related to him with the exception of those who believe on
him during the present age. Believers of this age will abide eternally in the New Jerusalem. Believers of this age will witness the
coming of the new heavens and earth. The new heavens and new
earth will never be corrupted by sin because righteousness dwells
in them.

[God] raised us up with Him, and seated us with Him in
the heavenly places, in Christ Jesus, in order that in the ages
to come He might show the surpassing riches of His grace
in kindness toward us in Christ Jesus. (Ephesians 2:6-7)

First graders come to the end of the school year thinking that
they know all there is to know—only to find out that there's a
second grade. After elementary school there's junior high, then
high school, then college, then graduate school, then post-gradu-
ate school, and so it goes. One literally could go to school all of the
days of his life on this earth. So it is with God's truth. We never can
or will be able to learn all there is to know about his truth in this
life. Whatever else we might do throughout all eternity, we will
learn more of "the surpassing riches of his grace in kindness
toward us in Christ Jesus." For all eternity believers of this age will
learn what God accomplished in obtaining and achieving our
salvation. Eternity will never exhaust the subject! Believers of this
age are not all of those who have ever believed God's revelation
and received his righteousness. There are five groups of believers:
(1) Old Testament believers prior to Israel (from Adam to Abraham), (2) Old Testament Israelite believers (from Abraham to the
Day of Pentecost), (3) Believers of the present age (from the found-

ing of the church on the Day of Pentecost to the coming of Christ into the air for those who have believed in him), (4) Believers in the tribulation period, and (5) Believers during the thousand-year reign of Christ on the earth. All of these have the common feature of having believed God's revelation (though the content of that revelation was not always the same) and having been given God's righteousness. They all comprise the "family" of God, but they are like five different children in that family. All have God's righteousness, and all will be with him forever and enjoy fellowship with all other believers. However, the differences between them will never be dissolved. The believers of this age will be distinct in that they will reside in the heavenly city, New Jerusalem, forever. The other four groups of believers will inhabit the new earth. All will worship Jesus Christ forever and together with him will worship God the Father forever. All will exhibit in their own peculiar way how God can bring to glory human beings in whatever circumstance. We have been dealing with the future God has planned for believers of this age. We have seen that the best is yet to come! We will have eternal fellowship with God and the other glorified believers of all time. The only question that remains is, What will your relationship be to the future program God has for those who believe in Jesus Christ? Will you be a part of it or will you miss out on it and instead experience God's judgment and be eternally separated from him and from all of his benefits? You can know now! If you will receive Jesus Christ as your personal Savior from sin, the glorious future of believers will be yours.

CHAPTER 4
Other Views about the End Times

When it comes to understanding God's program for the world, what is the most important passage of Scripture? Or to put it another way, if you were told that you had to give up all of your Bible but one passage, which passage would you choose? What passage is the basis for all of the others? The answer might surprise you!

The basic passage that reveals God's program—what he intends to do, what he continues to do in the present, and ultimately, what he will accomplish—is found in Genesis 12:2-3:

> And I will make you a great nation, and I will bless you, and make your name great; and so you shall be a blessing; and I will bless those who bless you, and the one who curses you I will curse. And in you all the families of the earth shall be blessed.

In these words which God spoke to Abraham, God promised Abraham three things: (1) national blessings—"I will make you a great nation," (2) personal blessings—"I will bless you," and (3) universal blessings—"in you all the families of the earth shall be blessed."

In dealing with these words one has three options: (1) God meant them and they are unconditional; hence if they have never yet been completely fulfilled there must yet be a future time when they will be completely fulfilled. (2) God meant them, but Abraham's descendants disobeyed and God changed his mind—they will be fulfilled spiritually. (3) God meant them, but Abraham's descendants disobeyed and hence the promise was withdrawn—they will never be fulfilled. The views presented in the preceding pages stem from the conviction that the first option is the correct one.

GOD WILL FULFILL HIS PROMISES
TO ABRAHAM LITERALLY

Those holding to this conviction are known theologically as premillennialists. They believe that Christ's coming to the earth will put an end to the tribulation period and result in his establishing his kingdom over all the world and reigning over it for a thousand years. Within premillennialism there are three schools of thought; each one places the rapture—Christ's second coming in the air to take his church to be with himself—at a different point with respect to the tribulation period.

(1) Premillennial pretribulational—the church, the body of Christ, will not go through the tribulation at all because the rapture will occur before the tribulation judgment is poured out upon the earth. Jesus will come again to the earth seven years later to end the tribulation and establish his kingdom on the earth.

(2) Premillennial midtribulational—the church will go through the first half of the tribulation because the rapture will occur at the middle of the tribulation, with Jesus coming to the earth three and a half years later to set up his kingdom.

(3) Premillennial posttribulational—the church will go through the seven-year tribulation period, at the end of which Christ will come and take his church to be with himself while judgment is poured out upon the earth. When that is completed, Jesus will return to the earth with his church to set up his kingdom.

All of these agree that the words given to Abraham are to be understood literally—there will be an earthly, Davidic, millennial kingdom over which Jesus Christ will personally reign. Their differences concern the relationship of the church to the tribulation. The view presented in the preceding pages is premillennial pretribulational.

GOD WILL FULFILL HIS PROMISE
TO ABRAHAM SPIRITUALLY

Those who do not believe that God will literally fulfill his promise to Abraham to make a literal nation out of him are known theologically as amillennialists. Believers holding this position are divided on the matter of whether God withdrew his promise completely as the result of Israel's disobedience or whether as a result of Israel's disobedience he simply changed his mind and has opted to fulfill his promises spiritually in a spiritual Israel, the church. For all practical purposes, the end result is the same.

Amillennialism stems from making an essential identification between Israel and the church—Israel being the Old Testament people of God and the church being the New Testament people of God. The promises given to Abraham were literal, but because of Israel's disobedience will not be fulfilled literally but will be fulfilled spiritually in the church. Growing out of this identification, the second coming of Christ is not a literal coming either into the air for his church or to the earth to set up his kingdom but rather is his coming in the heart of the New Testament people of God at the point of salvation. There never will be a time when Christ will visibly return either in the air to take his church to be with him eternally or come to the earth to set up his kingdom and reign over it. Amillennialists are indefinite with reference to the future events that will ultimately merge into the eternal state in which God will reign supreme.

GOD'S PROMISE TO ABRAHAM IS INSIGNIFICANT

Those who hold this position are known theologically as post-millennialists. They note God's promise to Abraham but concentrate on the fact that the Old Testament prophecies reveal a Messiah who is to be prophet, priest, and king. These prophecies are ultimately fulfilled in Christ, who presently is reigning in heaven as the king of the eternal kingdom of God. Like the amillennialists, postmillennialists identify Christ's coming for believers with his coming into their hearts at the moment of salvation. If there is a tribulation, it is past. Things will continue to get better and better until finally the situation on earth will become good enough that Christ will be able to bring his heavenly kingdom to earth and reign forever.

CONCLUSION

Looking at the three major schools of thought from the perspective of history, the most commonly held view is the view of premillennialism. This seems to be the view of the New Testament writers, who expected the return of Christ in their day.

The next most commonly held view is the view of amillennialism, which had its beginning with Augustine in the fourth century. Numerically speaking, it is the view that is most popularly held among Christendom, for it is the view of reformed theology and Roman Catholic theology alike. It is also the view of most mainline Protestant denominations.

Until recent days, postmillennialism was largely forsaken; World War I, the Great Depression of the thirties, and World War II proved to be inconsistent with the concept of a present millennium. In recent days, however, an offshoot of postmillennialism has become popular in some small circles.

While divergent views about the end times stem from divergent practices in the interpretation of the Scriptures, each person holds his view for reasons sufficient for himself. Each holds to the fundamental doctrines of the inspiration of Scripture, the virgin birth of Jesus Christ, and the absolute necessity of the death of Christ for salvation of mankind. Differences of opinion concerning future events are not worth severing fellowship between believers.